Lecture Notes
in Business Information Processing   106

Series Editors

Wil van der Aalst
   Eindhoven Technical University, The Netherlands
John Mylopoulos
   University of Trento, Italy
Michael Rosemann
   Queensland University of Technology, Brisbane, Qld, Australia
Michael J. Shaw
   University of Illinois, Urbana-Champaign, IL, USA
Clemens Szyperski
   Microsoft Research, Redmond, WA, USA

Laila Niedrite
Renate Strazdina
Benkt Wangler (Eds.)

Workshops on Business Informatics Research

BIR 2011 International Workshops
and Doctoral Consortium
Riga, Latvia, October 6, 2011
Revised Selected Papers

 Springer

Volume Editors

Laila Niedrite
University of Latvia
Riga, Latvia
E-mail: laila.niedrite@lu.lv

Renate Strazdina
Riga Technical University
Riga, Latvia
E-mail: renate.strazdina@cs.rtu.lv

Benkt Wangler
Stockholm University
Kista, Sweden
E-mail: benktw@gmail.com

ISSN 1865-1348   e-ISSN 1865-1356
ISBN 978-3-642-29230-9   e-ISBN 978-3-642-29231-6
DOI 10.1007/978-3-642-29231-6
Springer Heidelberg Dordrecht London New York

Library of Congress Control Number: 2012934583

ACM Computing Classification (1998): J.1, H.3.5, H.4, K.3

© Springer-Verlag Berlin Heidelberg 2012
This work is subject to copyright. All rights are reserved, whether the whole or part of the material is
concerned, specifically the rights of translation, reprinting, re-use of illustrations, recitation, broadcasting,
reproduction on microfilms or in any other way, and storage in data banks. Duplication of this publication
or parts thereof is permitted only under the provisions of the German Copyright Law of September 9, 1965,
in its current version, and permission for use must always be obtained from Springer. Violations are liable
to prosecution under the German Copyright Law.
The use of general descriptive names, registered names, trademarks, etc. in this publication does not imply,
even in the absence of a specific statement, that such names are exempt from the relevant protective laws
and regulations and therefore free for general use.

Typesetting: Camera-ready by author, data conversion by Scientific Publishing Services, Chennai, India

Printed on acid-free paper

Springer is part of Springer Science+Business Media (www.springer.com)

Foreword

The book consists of a selection of papers presented at the Workshops and Doctoral Consortium associated with the 10th International Conference on Perspectives in Business Informatics Research (BIR 2011), held in Riga, Latvia, October 6–8, 2011.

The BIR conference series was established 11 years ago with the aim of providing researchers in the field of business informatics with an international forum for exchanging their achievements.

Four one-day workshops and doctoral consortium associated with the BIR 2011 conference were organized:

- 4th International Workshop on Information Logistics and Knowledge Supply for Viable Enterprises (ILOG 2011)
- First International Workshop on Alignment of Business Process and Security Modeling (ABPSM 2011)
- Second International Workshop on Intelligent Educational Systems and Technology-Enhanced Learning (INTEL-EDU 2011)
- First International Workshop on User-Oriented Information Integration (UOII 2011)
- BIR 2011 Doctoral Consortium (BIR 2011 DC)

The 4th Workshop on Information Logistics and Knowledge Supply for Viable Enterprises (ILOG) brought together researchers and practitioners from both industry and academia that have a strong interest in viable enterprises, information logistics and knowledge supply. ILOG 2011 received 16 submissions. The Program Committee selected four submissions for publication in this volume.

The First International Workshop on Alignment of Business Process and Security Modeling (ABPSM) intended to gather researchers and practitioners in the field of business process and security modeling. The main goal of this workshop was to build a common understanding about the interplay between business processes and security. Nine papers were accepted for presentation at the workshop and three of them are included in the proceedings.

The main aim of the Intelligent Educational Systems and Technology-Enhanced Learning (INTEL-EDU) series of workshops is to provide an international platform for the presentation of research on intelligent educational systems theory, development of advanced tools and technologies, and their innovative applications. In all, 36 participants from 12 European countries took part in the Second International Workshop (INTEL-EDU 2011) and 20 presentations were made, with seven papers selected for publication in the proceedings.

The main goal of the First User-Oriented Information Integration (UOII) workshop was to provide a forum for academics and practitioners for the presentation of their research in the fields of information integration and user modeling.

The goal of the workshop was to bring together these two parties—users and information—considering the requirement for information rather than information supply as a key factor. Ten papers were accepted for presentation at the workshop. Four of the best papers were selected for publication in this volume.

The Doctoral Consortium associated with the BIR 2011 conference brought together researchers and doctoral students and provided an opportunity to the doctoral students to discuss the current state of their research. Five papers were accepted for presentation at the Doctoral Consortium and two best papers are included in these proceedings.

We would like to express our thanks to all the people that contributed to the success of the workshops and Doctoral Consortium.

We thank all the authors for their submitted papers, the members of the Program Committees and external reviewers for their time and contribution to ensuring the quality of the scientific program. We are particularly grateful to those Program Committee members of the Doctoral Consortium who also agreed to be discussants at the Doctoral Consortium sessions.

We thank all members of the conference and workshops organizing teams for their support to ensure the success of the conference. We express our thanks to the company Baltic Data, whose financial support covered the registration fees for doctoral students of accepted papers, and we thank Baltisch-Deutsches Hochschulkontor for financing the Local Proceedings of BIR 2011 Associated Workshops and Doctoral Consortium.

We would like to thank all Workshop and Doctoral Consortium Chairs and their Program Committees for their diligence in selecting the best papers and reviewing the extended versions of the papers included in this volume.

January 2012   Laila Niedrite
                                                     Renate Strazdina
                                                      Benkt Wangler

BIR 2011 Associated Workshops and Doctoral Consortium Organization

Steering Committee

Kurt Sandkuhl	University of Rostock, Germany (Chair)
Eduard Babkin	State University – HSE, Nizhny Novgorod, Russia
Per Backlund	University of Skövde, Sweden
Rimantas Butleris	Kaunas University of Technology, Lithuania
Sven Carlsson	Lund University, Sweden
Peter Forbrig	University of Rostock, Germany
Horst Günther	University of Rostock, Germany
Marite Kirikova	Riga Technical University, Latvia
Harald Kjellin	Kristianstad University College, Sweden
Lina Nemuraite	Kaunas University of Technology, Lithuania
Jyrki Nummenmaa	University of Tampere, Finland
Hans Röck	University of Rostock, Germany
Eva Söderström	University of Skövde, Sweden
Bernd Viehweger	Humboldt University, Germany
Benkt Wangler	University of Skövde, Sweden
Stanislaw Wrycza	University of Gdansk, Poland

BIR 2011 Workshops Co-chairs

Laila Niedrite	University of Latvia, Latvia
Renate Strazdina	Riga Technical University, Latvia
Benkt Wangler	University of Skövde, Sweden

BIR 2011 Organizing Committee Chair

Renate Strazdina	Riga Technical University, Latvia

BIR 2011 Doctoral Consortium Organizing Chair

Gundars Alksnis	Riga Technical University, Latvia

BIR 2011 Doctoral Consortium Organizing Deputy Chair

Ligita Businska	Riga Technical University, Latvia

Workshops Organizing Team

Darja Solodovnikova	University of Latvia, Latvia
Natalija Kozmina	University of Latvia, Latvia
Arnis Voitkans	University of Latvia, Latvia

Preface

The following preface is a collection of the prefaces of the proceedings of individual workshops and the doctoral consortium. The actual workshop and doctoral consortium papers, grouped by event, form the body of this volume.

4th Workshop on Information Logistics and Knowledge Supply for Viable Enterprises (ILOG 2011)

Organizers: Kurt Sandkuhl, Marite Kirikova, and Ulf Seigerroth

For viable enterprises, optimized information flow and efficient reuse of existing knowledge is part of the business strategy. Particularly in knowledge-intensive industry and service sectors, information is a major factor in production processes, and knowledge constitutes an important asset of the enterprise. Similarly, public organizations and governmental bodies are dependent on accurate and timely information supply for efficient and high-quality processes and services. Intelligent information supply has become an important issue that is characterized by just-in-time, demand-oriented and context-sensitive information.

Experience shows that successful solutions for intelligent information supply involve several ingredients: a sound business case with clearly defined benefits and returns for the (networked) organization, a clear understanding of the users' demands including the organizational context, and the right use of "enabling technologies" like semantic technologies, knowledge management or ubiquitous computing.

The workshop on Information Logistics and Knowledge Supply for Viable Enterprises (ILOG 2011) addressed the above subject area with a specific focus on practices, i.e., submission of case study and experiences papers were encouraged, and contributions bringing together business cases and enabling technologies were given priority. ILOG 2011 was the fourth workshop on this subject following events in 2004, 2007 and 2010. The first ILOG workshop was organized in conjunction with "Multikonferenz Wirtschaftsinformatik 2004." In November 2007, the second event in this series was located at Jönköping University. The third edition was part of the international conference on Business Information Systems (BIS) in Berlin. Each of the three workshops had roughly 25 participants.

ILOG 2011 received 16 submissions. The Program Committee selected four submissions for publication in this volume.

We thank all members of the Program Committee, the authors and local organizers for their efforts and support.

January 2012   Kurt Sandkuhl
                                                                  Marite Kirikova

Program Committee

Kurt Sandkuhl	University of Rostock, Germany (Co-chair)
Marite Kirikova	Riga Technical University, Latvia (Co-chair)
Ulf Seigerroth	Jönköping University, Sweden (Co-chair)
Clara Bassano	University of Naples, Italy
Andreas Billig	Fraunhofer ISST Berlin, Germany
Eva Blomqvist	CNR-ISTC, Italy
Tobias Bucher	PHOENIX Group, Germany
Susanne Busse	FH Brandenburg, Germany
Albertas Caplinskas	Institute of Mathematics and Informatics, Lithuania
Wolfgang Deiters	Fraunhofer ISST Dortmund, Germany
Barbara Dinter	Chemnitz University of Technology, Germany
Henrik Eriksson	Linköping University, Sweden
Janis Grabis	Riga Technical University, Latvia
Darek Haftor	Stockholm University, School of Business, Sweden
Yanbo Han	Institute of Computing Technology CAS, China
Tomasz Kaczmarek	Poznan University of Economics, Poland
Mira Kajko-Mattsson	Stockholm University, Sweden
Ramin Karim	Luleå University of Technology, Sweden
Peter Kawalek	Manchester Business School, UK
Ralf D. Kutsche	Berlin University of Technology, Germany
Tatiana Levashova	St. Petersburg Institute Informatics and Automation RAS, Russia
Anita Mirijamdotter	Linnæus University, Sweden
Paolo Piciocchi	University of Salerno, Italy
Alexander Smirnov	St. Petersburg Institute Informatics and Automation RAS, Russia
Janis Stirna	Stockholm University, Sweden
Vladimir Tarasov	Jönköping University, Sweden
Jan Willem	Nashuatec/Ricoh Group, The Netherlands

First International Workshop on Alignment of Business Process and Security Modeling (ABPSM 2011)

Organizers: Raimundas Matulevičius and Guttorm Sindre

The First International Workshop on Alignment of Business Process and Security Modeling (ABPSM 2011) served as a forum to gather researchers and practitioners working in the intersection between these two fields. Often, business process modeling, on the one hand, and IS security issues, on the other hand, stand out as quite separate research topics, seldom addressed together in the same research projects or publications. The main goal of this workshop was to create an arena where researchers in these two domains could meet and build a common understanding about the interplay between business processes and security. The workshop was of interest both for researchers who have already done research combining business process modeling and security, and for those who have primarily worked in one of these areas and wanted to learn more about the other.

The call for the workshop included the following topics:

- Security challenges in business process management
- Inclusion of security in business process modeling techniques
- Security modeling approaches
- Techniques for secure software engineering
- Security risk management
- Alignment between business process and security
- Models and methods for measuring such alignment
- Connection between business process modeling and security modeling
- Cost–benefit analysis of alignment between business process and security
- Security and SOA
- Security challenges in enterprise IS (e.g., ERP, SCM)
- Security challenges in e-commerce, e-gov, etc.

The call resulted in 14 submissions, and out of these, nine papers[1] were presented at the workshop. The extended versions of three selected papers are included in these proceedings.

---

[1] Matulevičius, R., Sindre, G., (eds): 1st International Workshop on Alignment of Business Process and Security Modelling (ABPSM 2011). In: Local Proceedings of the 10th International Conference, BIR 2011, Associated Workshops and Doctorial Consortium: JUMI Publishing House Ltd. MI, 2011, 97-170.

Paja et al. introduce a method to understand security needs through participants' objectives and interactions. [2] Security requirements are captured in terms of social commitments between the actors of the system. These security requirements are then used to annotate business processes modeled in BPMN.

Herrmann et al. propose a method for risk-based requirements prioritization (RiskREP). [3]. The security requirements are understood by considering the business goals, analyzing their potential risks, and defining security countermeasures. An important step of the approach is the prioritization activity, where effectiveness of the security counter-measures is assessed in terms of costs, dependencies, and reduced risk of the misuse case.

While the previous two studies focused on the link between security goals and security requirements, Gaaloul et al. introduce security controls that are applied in the workflow specification. [4]. More specifically, this paper presents an extended role-based access control model (RBAC) for workflow systems. Here a task delegation construct is introduced into a formal security model. Then, such a model can be applied to implement security requirements for task delegations and to define the security authorization constrains on the workflow specifications.

The organizers want to thank all reviewers, authors, and workshop participants for their contributions and hope that this workshop can contribute to a closer integration of research in security and business process modeling in the future.

January 2012   Raimundas Matulevičius
                                                        Guttorm Sindre

---

[2] Paja, E., Giorgini, P., Paul, S., Meland P. H.: Security Requirements Engineering for Secure Business Processes. In Proceedings of the Selected Papers from Workshops and Doctoral Consortium of the 10th International Conference BIR 2011, LNBIP, Springer, (2012).
[3] Herrmann, A., Morali, A., Etalle, S., Wieringa, R.: Risk and Business Goal Based Security Requirement and Countermeasure Prioritization. In Proceedings of the Selected Papers from Workshops and Doctoral Consortium of the 10th International Conference BIR 2011, LNBIP, Springer, (2012).
[4] Gaaloul, K., Proper, H.A. (Erik), Charoy, F.: An Extended RBAC Model for Task Delegation in Workflow Systems. In Proceedings of the Selected Papers from Workshops and Doctoral Consortium of the 10th International Conference BIR 2011, LNBIP, Springer, (2012).

Program Committee

Raimundas Matulevičius	University of Tartu, Estonia (Co-chair)
Guttorm Sindre	Norwegian University of Science and Technology, Norway (Co-chair)
Birger Andersson	Stockholm University and Royal Institute of Technology, Sweden
Marlon Dumas	University of Tartu, Estonia
Khaled Gaaloul	CRP Henri Tudor, Luxembourg
Dieter Gollmann	TU Harburg, Germany
Saulius Gudas	Vilnius University, Lithuania
Siv Houmb	Telenor GBD&R, Norway
Jan Jürjens	TU Dortmund and Fraunhofer ISST, Germany
Audronė Lupeikienė	Institute of Mathematics and Informatics, Lithuania
Christoph Meinel	University of Potsdam, Germany
Per Håkon Meland	SINTEF, Norway
Haralambos Mouratidis	University of East London, UK
Fleming Nielson	Technical University of Denmark
Oksana Nikiforova	Riga Technical University, Latvia
Andreas Lothe Opdahl	University of Bergen, Norway
Günther Pernul	University of Regensburg, Germany
Viara Popova	University of Tartu, Estonia
Joachim Posegga	University of Passau, Germany
Meelis Roos	University of Tartu, Estonia
Einar Arthur Snekkenes	Gjøvik University College, Norway
Uldis Sukovskis	Riga Technical University, Latvia
Darius Šilingas	No Magic Europe, Lithuania
Rose-Mharie Åhlfeldt	University of Skövde, Sweden

Additional Reviewers

Christian Broser	University of Regensburg, Germany
Oliver Gmelch	University of Regensburg, Germany
Henrich Pöhls	University of Passau, Germany

Organization Chair

Peter Karpati	Norwegian University of Science and Technology, Norway

Second International Workshop on Intelligent Educational Systems and Technology-Enhanced Learning (INTEL-EDU 2011)

Organizers: Janis Grundspenkis and Leonids Novickis

The Second International Workshop on Intelligent Educational Systems and Technology-Enhanced Learning (INTEL-EDU 2011) continued the first workshop held in Riga in 2009 in conjunction with the 13th East-European Conference on Advances in Databases and Information Systems (ADBIS 2009).

The main goal of the INTEL-EDU series of workshops is to provide an international platform for the presentation of research on intelligent educational systems theory, development of advanced tools and technologies, and their innovative applications. In all, 36 participants from 12 European countries (Austria, Belgium, Latvia, Estonia, Finland, France, Germany, Lithuania, The Netherlands, Norway, Sweden, Switzerland) took part in INTEL-EDU 2011 and 20 presentations were made.

The accepted papers cover a wide spectrum of topics on social media features added to e-learning, remote collaborative working of teachers and students, psychophysiological model-based adaptive tutoring systems, estimation of quality and exploitation effectiveness of e-learning systems, integration of intelligent tutoring and knowledge assessment systems.

The Baltic Sea Region INTERREG Programme project's BONITA RTU Showroom launch event was organized as a special session of the INTEL-EDU 2011 workshop. During this session both physical exhibits in e-learning (IKAS system), e-logistics (www.elogmar.eu), robotics devices, virtual interactive platforms and virtual showroom prototypes to promote innovative ICT solutions were demonstrated to the participants.

January 2012   Janis Grundspenkis
                                                                 Leonids Novickis

Program Committee

Janis Grundspenkis	Riga Technical University, Latvia (Co-chair)
Leonids Novickis	Riga Technical University, Latvia (Co-chair)
Krzystof Amborski	Warsaw University of Technology, Poland
Eberhard Blümel	Fraunhofer Institute IFF, Germany
Michael Boronowski	University of Bremen, Germany
Alexander Berezko	Russian Academy of Science, Russia
Agostino Bruzzone	University of Genoa, Italy
Andrzej Dzielinski	Warsaw University of Technology, Poland
Egils Ginters	Vidzeme University of Applied Science, Latvia
Alla Anohina-Naumeca	Riga Technical University, Latvia
Zhou Mingtao	Beijing HOPE Software Company, P.R. China
Antanas Mitasiunas	Vilnius University, Lithuania
Jurijs Lavendels	Riga Technical University, Latvia
Jurijs Merkurjevs	Riga Technical University, Latvia
Boriss Mishnev	Transport and Telecommunication Institute, Latvia
Tatiana Rikure	Riga Technical University, Latvia
Vjacheslav Shitikov	Riga Technical University, Latvia
Abdel-Badeeh M. Salem	Ain Shams University, Egypt
Uldis Sukovskis	Riga Technical University, Latvia

First International Workshop on User-Oriented Information Integration (UOII 2011)

Organizers: Guntis Arnicans and Laila Niedrite

The main aim of the First User-Oriented Information Integration (UOII) workshop was to provide a wide international forum for academics and practitioners for the presentation of their research. Ten papers were accepted for presentation at the workshop. Selected papers for this issue cover different aspects of data integration taking into account users' needs as much as possible. The term "user" is used in different meanings starting from several groups of users and ending with individuals or a particular device that consumes integrated data.

The paper "A Formal Quality Framework for Data Integration Incorporating User Requirements" presents a framework for the specification of data integration quality criteria and associated user requirements with quality factors and metrics relating to completeness and consistency. A description language formalization with associated reasoning capabilities is used, which enables a data integration setting to be tested to identify those elements that are inconsistent with users' requirements.

Two papers describe results of real applications. The paper "Timely Report Production from WWW Data Sources" presents a case study of data integration for reporting within the World Health Organization. In order to automate the production of the reports, the authors have introduced a method of integrating data from multiple sources by using an RDF (resource description framework) format. The model of the data is described using RDF ontology, making possible the validation of the data from multiple sources. A graphical tool is developed for the end user to hide the technical level of RDF and to reduce the complexity configuring the data sources of a given report. The paper "Toward Introducing User Preferences in OLAP Reporting Tool" presents an OLAP reporting tool and an approach for determining and processing user OLAP preferences, which are useful for generating recommendations on potentially interesting reports. The authors explain the metadata layers of the reporting tool including their proposed OLAP preferences meta-model, which supports various scenarios of formulating preferences of two different types: schema-specific and report-specific.

The paper "A Multimodal Approach for Determination of Vehicle Position" shows that consumers of integrated data can be humans but also electronic devices. One of the most important tasks during the development of hardware/software systems for assisted and automatic driving is the determination of a vehicle's position with sufficient accuracy in real time. Usually, a device alone cannot satisfy user requirements. By data integration from various external data sources, the device can correct its own measurements and reach the required precision of measurements.

During discussions at the workshop, the participants established a fact that users demand data integration satisfying the individual user rather than the user group. This means that the integration problem becomes more difficult and new research is needed.

January 2012   Guntis Arnicans
                                                         Laila Niedrite

Program Committee

Guntis Arnicans	University of Latvia, Latvia (Co-chair)
Laila Niedrite	University of Latvia, Latvia (Co-chair)
Zohra Bellahsene	LIRMM, France
Ladjel Bellatreche	Poitiers University, France
Janis Bicevskis	University of Latvia, Latvia
Rimantas Butleris	Kaunas University of Technology, Lithuania
Gerti Kappel	Vienna University of Technology, Austria
Jens Lechtenbörger	University of Münster, Germany
Daniel Lemire	Université du Québec à Montréal (UQAM), Canada
Audronė Lupeikienė	Institute of Mathematics and Informatics, Lithuania
Jaan Penjam	Institute of Cybernetics, Estonia
Karlis Podnieks	University of Latvia, Latvia
Olivier Teste	IRIT, France
Riccardo Torlone	"Roma Tre" University, Italy
Olegas Vasilecas	Vilnius Gediminas Technical University, Lithuania
Robert Wrembel	Poznan Unviersity of Technology, Poland

Additional Reviewers

Baiba Apine	PricewaterhouseCoopers, Latvia
Juris Borzovs	University of Latvia, Latvia
Kestutis Kapocius	Kaunas University of Technology, Lithuania
Philip Langer	Vienna University of Technology, Austria
Konrad Wieland	Vienna University of Technology, Austria
Janis Zuters	University of Latvia, Latvia

BIR 2011 Doctoral Consortium (BIR DC 2011)

Organizers: Gundars Alksnis

The aim of the Doctoral Consortium which was organized in association with the 10th International Conference on Perspectives in Business Informatics Research (BIR2011) held October 6–8, 2011, in Riga, Latvia, is to facilitate research contributions in business informatics from doctoral students and to give them a feedback from experienced researchers of the field. This year the Doctoral Consortium attracted submissions from three countries, namely, Lithuania, Latvia and Poland.

These proceedings include two revised Doctoral Consortium papers that were extended to include detailed ideas in the area of business informatics research. Each paper covers its own problem domain. The first paper by Askoldas Podviezko discusses the enhancements in the evaluation of the level of soundness and stability of commercial banks. By proposing to use multicriteria decision-aid methods, it is possible to observe both the strength and weaknesses of commercial banks by means of different performance criteria. The second paper by Peteris Rudzajs describes the architecture of the system for education information extraction by means of automated document analysis. Such a system is supposed to monitor educational demand and offer. Its distinction is the use of various approaches in order to extract and analyze information from unstructured or semistructured textual information sources, such as university vacancy and course descriptions.

The Organizers want to thank all members of the Doctoral Consortium Program Committee for their contributions, especially Per Backlund from the University of Skövde, Sweden, and Horst Günther from the University of Rostock, Germany, for their comments on the paper versions that where selected for these proceedings. Their reviews and feedback provided valuable information for the doctoral students.

January 2012   Gundars Alksnis

Program Committee

Gundars Alksnis	Riga Technical University, Latvia (Chair)
Andrzej Kobylinski	Warsaw School of Economics, Poland
Alla Anohina-Naumeca	Riga Technical University, Latvia
Benkt Wangler	University of Skövde, Sweden
Christian Stary	University of Linz, Austria
Dimitris Karagiannis	University of Vienna, Austria
Eduard Babkin	State University – HSE, Nizhny Novgorod, Russia
Egils Stalidzans	Latvia University of Agriculture, Latvia
Egons Lavendelis	Riga Technical University, Latvia
Enn Õunapuu	Tallinn University of Technology, Estonia
Girts Karnitis	University of Latvia, Latvia
Guntis Arnicans	University of Latvia, Latvia
Hele-Mai Haav	Tallinn University of Technology, Estonia
Horst Günther	University of Rostock, Germany
Irina Arhipova	Latvia University of Agriculture, Latvia
Janis Barzdins	University of Latvia, Latvia
Janis Grabis	Riga Technical University, Latvia
Janis Grundspenkis	Riga Technical University, Latvia
Janis Osis	Riga Technical University, Latvia
Kurt Sandkuhl	The University of Rostock, Germany
Laila Niedrite	University of Latvia, Latvia
Lina Nemuraite	Kaunas University of Technology, Lithuania
Marite Kirikova	Riga Technical University, Latvia
Michal Gregus	Comenius University of Bratislava, Slovakia
Nava Pliskin	Ben-Gurion University of the Negev, Israel
Oksana Nikiforova	Riga Technical University, Latvia
Per Backlund	University of Skövde, Sweden
Petr Sodomka	Brno University of Technology, Czech Republic
Renate Strazdina	Riga Technical University, Latvia
Rimantas Butleris	Kaunas University of Technology, Lithuania
Stanislaw Wrycza	University of Gdansk, Poland
Sven Carlsson	Lund University, Sweden
Uldis Sukovskis	Riga Technical University, Latvia

Additional Reviewer

Margit Schwab	University of Vienna, Austria

Table of Contents

4th Workshop on Information Logistics and Knowledge Supply for Viable Enterprises (ILOG 2011)

Telemedical Events: Intelligent Delivery of Telemedical Values Using CEP and HL7 1
    Sven Meister

Information Logistics in Engineering Change Management: Integrating Demand Patterns and Recommendation Systems 14
    Kurt Sandkuhl, Alexander Smirnov, and Nikolay Shilov

Selecting KMS for SME - A Need for Value-Orientation 26
    Ulrike Borchardt

Managing Change in Fractal Enterprises and IS Architectures from a Viable Systems Perspective 38
    Paolo Piciocchi, Clara Bassano, Marite Kirikova, Janis Makna, and Julija Stecjuka

1st International Workshop on Alignment of Business Process and Security Modeling (ABPSM 2011)

An Extended RBAC Model for Task Delegation in Workflow Systems ... 51
    Khaled Gaaloul, Erik Proper, and François Charoy

Risk and Business Goal Based Security Requirement and Countermeasure Prioritization 64
    Andrea Herrmann, Ayse Morali, Sandro Etalle, and Roel Wieringa

Security Requirements Engineering for Secure Business Processes 77
    Elda Paja, Paolo Giorgini, Stéphane Paul, and Per Håkon Meland

2nd International Workshop on Intelligent Educational Systems and Technology-Enhanced Learning (INTEL-EDU 2011)

Applied Knowledge Transfer to European SMEs by Expertise Networks Using Mixed Reality 90
    Eberhard Blümel, Helge Fredrich, and Andre Winge

Enterprise SPICE Based Education Capability Maturity Model 102
    Antanas Mitasiunas and Leonids Novickis

Intellectual Ability Data Obtaining and Processing for E-Learning
System Adaptation.. 117
  Vija Vagale and Laila Niedrite

Perceived Social Influence in Watching Online Theory Presentations.... 130
  Frank Goethals

The Conceptual Framework for Integration of Multiagent Based
Intelligent Tutoring and Personal Knowledge Management Systems in
Educational Settings 143
  Janis Grundspenkis

Evaluation of Engineering Course Content by Bloom's Taxonomy:
A Case Study 158
  Andrejs Romanovs, Oksana Soshko, Yuri Merkuryev, and
  Leonids Novickis

Calculate Learners' Competence Scores and Their Reliability in
Learning Networks 171
  Martin Hochmeister

1st International Workshop on User Oriented Information Integration (UOII 2011)

Timely Report Production from WWW Data Sources 184
  Marko Niinimaki, Tapio Niemi, Stephen Martin,
  Jyrki Nummenmaa, and Peter Thanisch

An Ontology-Based Quality Framework for Data Integration 196
  Jianing Wang, Nigel Martin, and Alexandra Poulovassilis

Towards Introducing User Preferences in OLAP Reporting Tool........ 209
  Natalija Kozmina and Darja Solodovnikova

A Multimodal Approach for Determination of Vehicle Position......... 223
  Artis Mednis

Doctoral Consortium Papers

Augmenting Multicriteria Decision Aid Methods by Graphical and
Analytical Reporting Tools...................................... 236
  Askoldas Podviezko

Towards Automated Education Demand-Offer Information Monitoring:
The System's Architecture 252
  Peteris Rudzajs

Author Index... 267

Telemedical Events: Intelligent Delivery of Telemedical Values Using CEP and HL7

Sven Meister

Fraunhofer Institute for Software and Systems Engineering ISST,
Emil-Figge-Straße 91, 44227 Dortmund, Germany
`sven.meister@isst.fraunhofer.de`

Abstract. Today's central issues in the healthcare supply make it imperative to develop new concepts to reduce the emerging costs and ensure high quality standards. Applying ICT and especially telemedicine – technologies that offer the chance to optimize medical data transfer – is regarded as the promising strategy, when developing cost saving concepts. As a result, physicians, as recipients of medical data, are confronted with a growing amount of information. This has to fit seamlessly into the process of information exchange and therefore has to be transported according to the principles of information logistics (ILOG). Therefore the author proposes a new approach based upon complex event processing (CEP), named Telemedical ILOG Listener (TIL). Every telemedical value, like for instance blood-pressure, has to be described as a telemedical event. For this reason in the following the author will describe how to use HL7 V3, a worldwide used standard for medical data exchange, to define a message type which is able to include the medical data, data necessary for CEP and at least data to represent the dimension of ILOG.

Keywords: ILOG, CEP, Telemedicine, HL7.

1   Introduction

Information and communication technology (ICT) like electronic health records or medical sensors are considered to be essential for solving the three main issues in today's healthcare supply:

1. The demographic change amplifies the need for new concepts of medical supply.
2. Many countries are at risk to suffer of undersupply of medical attendance in rural areas.
3. The economic structure is out of balance.

Especially telemedicine is accepted as a research area which delivers concepts and technologies to solve the problems shown above. Telemedicine allows for communication between healthcare professionals and patients over distance. Like any other ICT, telemedicine increases the amount of information which has to be processed by physicians. This situation is also known as information overload [1]. One example: The measuring of blood sugar concentration. The patient would send

L. Niedrite, R. Strazdina, B. Wangler (Eds.): BIR 2011 Workshops, LNBIP 106, pp. 1–13, 2012.
© Springer-Verlag Berlin Heidelberg 2012

his values in a predefined interval to the physician. Considering the number of patients of a physician this would amount into an unmanageable number of messages. Most of these messages won't be related to a critical situation like hypo- or hyperglycemia, which means that it is irrelevant information from the physician's point of view.

Approaches aiming to solve the problem of information overload in telemedical scenarios and furthermore in scenarios where medical data is transported have to consider three aspects. The first issue refers to the amount of data which leads to information overload and needs to be reduced. The second problem takes the hierarchy of health professionals into account. Information has to be distributed along levels of escalation, e.g. the nursing service is called before the physician. The third and last problem is related to the particularization and diversification of telemedical applications. There exist hundreds of different telemedical applications using different data formats for different telemedical value types. Existing approaches for intelligent medical data transfer and processing are highly customized to use cases, like e.g. measuring the blood sugar concentration. Different applications will describe the same vital sign in different data formats. An integration of ILOG concepts, which implies to deliver the right information at the right time to the right place, is missing [1, 2]. The result is that there is no possibility to aggregate information from different telemedical sources to more significant information. There is also a lack of modularity. Once developed concepts cannot be reused in other use cases.

Therefore we are investigating into a new approach named Telemedical ILOG Listener (TIL) using complex event processing and HL7 [3]. HL7 is a widespread international standard for data exchange in the healthcare sector, which implies that this kind of data can easily be integrated into existing healthcare systems [4]. Corresponding to the high level definition of CEP as "...anything that happens, or is contemplated as happening" also every vital sign produced in a telemedical scenario can be interpreted as an event [5], in the following named telemedical event. In order to describe a telemedical event and solve the problem of diversification as well as particularization of telemedical applications we suggest using HL7 V3. Based on it we are defining a message format, called HL7 Telemedical Event Format, which includes all parameters necessary for CEP and information logistics dimensions like time and place. Every message sent by a system is interpreted as an event, which implies that all formal operations of CEP can be used to aggregate simple telemedical events from different sources to more significant information and thus reducing the amount of unnecessary information. The rest of the paper is organized as follows: First we'll give a broad overview of the two underlying use cases for processing telemedical events. Afterwards there will be a discussion of important related work in the field of information logistics and complex event processing. In the main section we'll introduce the idea of telemedical events and its description using HL7 in more detail and we'll end up with a conclusion and outlook on further research.

2   Motivating Use Cases

We chose two use cases as a basis to define and, at a later time, evaluate the concept of Telemedical ILOG Listeners. The use cases reflect common health issues in Germany and most of them are also widespread worldwide.

The first use case is named "Telemedical Monitoring of cardiac insufficiency patients" and is related to the problem of the increasing amount of patients with cardiac insufficiency. The parameter weight and blood pressure play an important role during monitoring. Changes in weight are an important indicator for water retention in the lungs and limbs. A significantly increased blood pressure, especially in combination with weight gain can be a sign for an aggravating cardiac insufficiency.

The second use case is named "Monitoring of sports by patients having hypertension" and related to the most common chronic health condition of hypertension (high blood pressure). The choice and control of intensity of sports applied as intervention mechanism against hypertension requires intensive monitoring of the blood pressure and the pulse. The measurement and evaluation of the blood pressure value, considering its development, is the most significant vital parameter for optimizing the therapy. Observing the pulse is also vital, especially when certain heart rate modulating drugs are prescribed.

3   Related Work

The ongoing work is related to two research areas: ILOG is the central aggregator with its metaphor of transporting and filtering information in an intelligent manner. CEP is a promising technology for a fast, on-time processing of data.

3.1   ILOG

At present ILOG is viewed as detached research area to deliver the right information, in the right format at the right time to the right place [2, 6] and is partially used for information filtering or with context-models to optimize communication in the healthcare domain [1, 6]. Dinter and Winter [7] give also a definition for information logistics as "the design, control, execution and control of all data flows…and the storage and post processing". It's a more organizational/data flow driven point of view. Haftor [8] et al. give a broad overview of the state-of-the art research in information logistics by analyzing 102 scientific publications. There are four active research directions in which user-demand-based information supply is the dominating one, advanced by the Fraunhofer ISST and also focused within this paper.

Information logistics is also strongly related to the topics of information overload and information need. According to Wilson and others [9, 10], information overload expresses "that the flow of information…is greater than can be managed effectively". Wilson emphasizes that the situation is not only caused by an improvement of technology but is also related to organizational, personal and external factors. There is not only an increasing amount of information which one can query (pull), e.g. scientific publications or journals but also an increment of channels for a proactive information delivery (push) [9, 10]. An intelligent information supply requires also a clear definition of information need. Line [11] distinguishes five subcategories: Need, want, demand, user, requirement. It's important to give a clear distinction between need and demand. The former describes all pieces of information which are needed to answer a given question and the latter the amount of inquired information, which is assumed to be useful to answer a given question [12].

3.2   Complex Event Processing

The link between CEP and ILOG is given by Chandy [13] by mentioning that "Disseminating and distributing is also about getting the right information to the right consumers at the right time.". The basics of CEP were developed and defined by Luckham, Chandy and Bates [14, 15, 16] as "…an object that is a record of an activity in a system". Hripcsak et al. [17] were among the first researchers who combined the abstract concepts of HL7 with the term events which they call clinical event monitor (CEM). The CEM monitors the clinical situation of a patient and triggers the delivery of a message to a predefined recipient. The knowledge necessary for the decision for triggering the message is formalized using the Arden-Syntax, which is also part of HL7. Hazlehurst et al. [18] extended the concept in their implementation MediClass. They analyzed HL7 CDA documents to recognize clinical events. Neither Hripcsak nor Hazlehurst give a definition for a general messaging format on the basis of HL7 which could be used in CEP. Furthermore, the idea of intelligent information transfer using ILOG is missing within their concepts. Actual research in combining CEP and HL7 is covered within the development of Stride "The Stanford Translational Research Integrated Database" [19]. Stride is some kind of data warehouse with over 100 million of data entries, e.g. diagnosis or laboratory results. One can query the stored data to answer a given question or use them as a trigger to get informed when a given pattern is fulfilled. Weber [20] gives a first impression how Stride could be used together with Esper, an event processing engine, to process health data. The ongoing work of Weber and other researchers at the Stanford University aims to establish a better integration of HL7 and CEP.

The Dagstuhl Seminar on "Event Processing" in 2010 gives a detailed overview of open questions and the current state of research in CEP [13]. Within the proceedings the authors point out that there is a lack of standardization effort of event data and message formats. There is only some work done within Web Service Events (WS X) and OASIS CBE. Also the domain specific requirements aren't taken into account. Missing standardization leads to missing interoperability, reason for which we propose the HL7 Telemedical Event Format as a message format for telemedical events.

3.3   Alternative Scientific Approaches

There are two important research areas one should take into account, when talking about possible solutions for an intelligent information supply and filtering in telemedicine. At first there is the ongoing research on clinical databases and database management systems, e.g. Stride "The Stanford Translational Research Integrated Database" [19]. One extension are data streams for real-time processing of data like shown within STREAM [21]. Another research area is the field of agent-based systems, defined as "a system that perceives its environment and acts upon the information it perceives" [22]. Different kind of agents could be aggregated to a network called multi-agent system. Both databases or data streams and agent-based systems could be used to filter information but there is a lack of standardizing the structure of information, developed concepts are not that modular and they do not take ILOG into account.

4   Information-Logistical Processing of Telemedical Values Using CEP and HL7

With regard to the missing elements of the existing approaches mentioned under the section related work we are introducing the concept of TIL to be able to process telemedical values in the sense of telemedical events. Figure 1 gives a conceptual overview about the basic building blocks to process telemedical events using CEP, extending the work of Etzion [23]. Important building blocks regarding to the following work are marked with dashed lines.

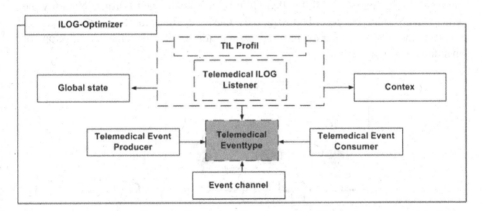

Fig. 1. Building blocks for the conceptualization of telemedical event processing using CEP

The concept of TIL will include solutions for the following problems or requirements [3]:

- A method for generic processing of telemedical values is needed. Therefore the concept has to include a general description of these, bearing in mind the ability to process CEP and ILOG.
- The monitoring of telemedical values produces a high amount of data. The importance of a particular value depends on the order and also the dependency between different types of telemedical values. According to ILOG principles,

a physician or any other healthcare provider should only be informed if a telemedical value is important so that the amount of information can be reduced.
- Telemedical applications are highly distributed in the sense that every telemedical value has its own telemedical application and client. Thus the concept has to aggregate data from different sources to facilitate monitoring for the physician or any other healthcare provider.

Within this paper we cover especially the definition of the term telemedical event and the modeling of the HL7 Telemedical Event Format using HL7.

4.1   Architectural Overview

Figure 2 gives a broad technology-independent architectural overview on how communication of telemedical values could be optimized using the concept of Telemedical ILOG Listeners. At the bottom we have different kinds of telemedical applications and sensors which generate telemedical values like blood sugar concentration or the blood pressure. Today, in the majority of cases, these values are enveloped in a proprietary data format. This implies that a recipient has to use a specific client and also inhibits the potential for a high level aggregation of different telemedical values. Even though there are some applications using HL7 there is a lack of information to use this messages for CEP and ILOG. Therefore, we are developing a message format based on HL7 called HL7 Telemedical Event Format. Not only the medical data could be described with this message but also ILOG parameters to represent the time or parameters necessary for CEP, like the description of dependencies through events.

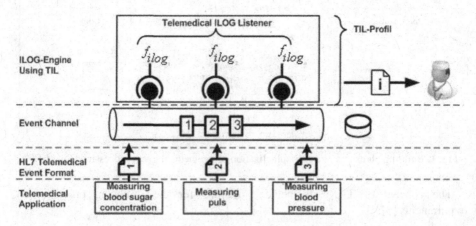

Fig. 2. Architectural overview for processing telemedical values under information logistics principles

The event channel layer in figure 2 should be some kind of intermediate, e.g. a bus, event stream or event cloud to collect the incoming telemedical events enveloped in the HL7 Telemedical Event Format. The processing of them is done at the top using some kind of engine. Related to the topic of CEP we propose the usage of a well-established event processing engine like Esper [24]. For sure some work has to be done to integrate the concepts of TIL, TIL profiles and telemedical events. A TIL is some kind of event processing agent (EPA) which analyzes a set of telemedical events to detect patterns of interest. The crosslinking of different TILs in terms of an event processing networks (EPN) for a specific patient is called TIL profile.

4.2   Telemedical Events and HL7 Telemedical Event Format

We already emphasized that there is a need to standardize the envelopment of telemedical values so that:

1. The telemedical value is included and described in a syntactical and semantic form.
2. Parameters for complex event processing could be attached.
3. Information logistics dimensions like time parameters could be included.

As starting point we introduce the term telemedical event as a *measurement of a telemedical value and an instance of a telemedical event type, formatted in the HL7 Telemedical Event Format.* So a telemedical event expresses a change of the state in a healthcare monitoring scenario in the way that, e.g. a patient measures some kind of vital sign. Like described above there are some aspects one should take into account when talking about telemedical events. Therefore there is a need to define a basic structure which allows for integrating these domain specific aspects, named telemedical event type. A telemedical event type is a *template defining basic attributes that every telemedical event of a specific vital sign has to satisfy.* To standardize the processing there will be one root telemedical event type, so a definition of attributes that every telemedical event has to fulfill.

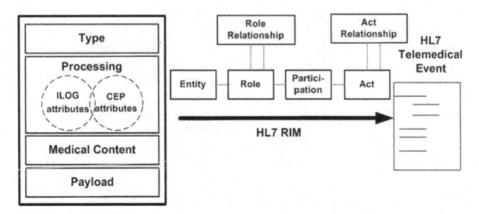

Fig. 3. Definition of the telemedical event type (left) and derivation of HL7 Telemedical Event

The specific telemedical event types for, e.g. blood pressure or pulse will be inherited from the root element. Hence in the following we show the investigated basic model of the root telemedical event type. Regarding to Etzion [23], who defined a basic segmentation of events for general purpose event processing, we added some domain specific extensions which are shown in figure 3.

Bearing the aspects mentioned at the top of this chapter in mind, we distinguish four segments:

- Type segment: First of all we cover a possibility to specify the type of a telemedical event. On the one hand this information is related to the level of inheritance and on the other hand to the measured vital sign.
- Processing segment: Most of the attributes will be related to ILOG and CEP processing. This segment allows for grouping those.
- Medical content segment: This segment contains information about the measured vital sign which caused the change of state and is the nucleus of the following event processing.
- Payload segment: Sometimes there is a need to store attributes that are not directly related to the genesis of the telemedical event but important to assure a consistent event processing. One example is the storage of runtime attributes that are specific to the event processing engine.

With respect to previous work of Luckham and Etzion [16, 25] there are some common parameters necessary to process events, e.g. time, eventID or producer. Especially time is important for ILOG processing, but one has to distinguish on a semantic level between the time of generation, time of arrival, time of processing etc. From the ILOG point of view there are also parameters like the receiving application or person. From a conceptual point of view table 1 gives an overview of the most important attributes that should be covered by a telemedical event type.

Table 1. Basic attributes which are important for a telemedical event type

Parameter	Segment	Description
eventTypeID	Type	An ID to specify the type of the event.
eventAnnotation	Type	Some kind of textual description of the event.
eventID	Type	An ID that uniquely identifies the event.
simpleEvent	Processing	Expresses whether the event is a simple or a complex event.
detectionTime	Processing	The time point of the detection of the event.
createTime	Processing	The time point of the creation of the event.
processTime	Processing	The time point of processing the event.
eventSource	Processing	A reference and description of the emitter of the event.
parentEvents	Processing	A reference to the parental events.
receivingResponsibility	Processing	The receiving party of the event.
timeEmitter	Processing	Regarding to heterogeneous event processing infrastructures it is important to specify a global clock.
Content	Medical content	The event value that is recorded as a result of the state change of the system.

These parameters and data have to be described in a standardized and well accepted format in the medical context. Now, what is the idea behind using HL7 to describe telemedical events and define a message format? HL7 is a worldwide used standard for medical data exchange [4]. Version 3 of HL7 is based upon the Reference Information Model (RIM). Using the six core classes of RIM (Entity, Role, Participation, Act, Act Relationship, Role Relationship) one can model every medical data. In contrast to other modeling languages HL7 RIM enables one to model the situation of acting in a medical process, e.g. the activity of documentation (Act) at a given point of time (Attribute) under participation (Participation) of an author (Entity, Role). In terms of HL7 the resulting model is also called R-MIM, which could be used to derive a XML schema. In figure 4 we introduce the first version of the R-MIM of the HL7 Telemedical Event Format.

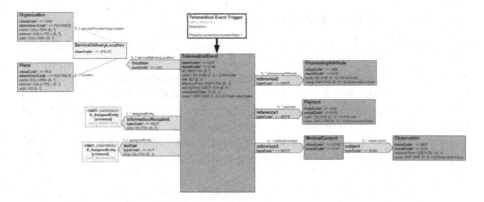

Fig. 4. R-MIM of the modeled HL7 Telemedical Event

The initial point in the model is the *Telemedical Event Trigger* which is the signal for a state change, e.g. a new measurement of a vital sign. The following *TelemedicalEvent* act is an observation (classCode=OBS) of the measurement. The value of the measurement (medical content segment) itself is included into the *TelemedicalEvent* act just as well as information about the type (type segment) using the *code* attribute. The specification of attributes, necessary for CEP and ILOG processing (processing segment), is done in the *TelemedicalEvent* act and in the referenced *ProcessingAttribute* act. The referenced *Payload* act is used to add payload attributes (payload segment). Like described above using HL7 RIM enables one to model the situation of acting so that the resulting XML HL7 message format includes not only the measured vital sign but also the context of a measurement like participating actors, locations etc. Therefore, every *TelemedicalEvent* act has to be related to some kind of *author*, expressed by using the corresponding participation relationship. This could be a device, a software application or a human being. In addition to the author there's also the possibility to add a set of recipients, e.g. physicians or nurses. The location can be defined over the participation relationship of type *location* which refers to the *ServiceDeliveryLocation* role which in turn refers to a *Place* and an *Organisation* entity. There is also a possibility to add additional medical information using a reference to the *MedicalContext* act and defining some observations.

Related to the motivating use case "Telemedical Monitoring of cardiac insufficiency patients" two different instances of the telemedical event type have to be covered. Primary both instances will differ in the usage of the medical content segment. One instance covers the blood pressure value and the other one the weight value. Also the type segment will differ in the type attribute – one instance will be referred to a weight value event and one to a blood pressure event. At a later stage when the world of telemedical events is getting more complex, we'll need a structured repository of telemedical event type, e.g. using taxonomies or ontologies.

4.3 Telemedical ILOG Listeners (TIL)

Why is CEP a probate technology for ILOG processing in telemedicine? Every value monitored by a telemedical application is some kind of event. This event is related to additional information like the time of generation or the telemedical value itself. This information normally will be transported to a receiver, e.g. a physician. As a result a lot of information has to be analyzed by the receiver. Following the metaphor of ILOG to deliver the right information, in the right format at the right time to the right place mechanisms needed to transport, aggregate and filter information. Also the consideration of the history and order of telemedical values related to an abstract time axis is important.

The concept of CEP allows for aggregating, filtering and building causal relationships of events [16]. Also time could be taken into account. To process events a piece of software called event processing engine (EPE) is needed. A lot of open source and commercial EPEs are available. They differ from the algorithms used to fulfill the operations mentioned above. Thus CEP seems to be a probate technology to integrate with the concepts of ILOG so we will build our approach on these concepts.

A Telemedical ILOG Listener (TIL*) is some kind of event processing agent that "monitors an event execution to detect certain patterns of events" which is specialized for one type of telemedical values,* e.g. blood pressure events [16, 26]. This deduces that a TIL only processes a specific type of telemedical events. Using event pattern rules and defining constraints enables a TIL to fulfill task like aggregation, filtering or observing the history of events for instance blood pressure increased over the last 10 events. Building a complex event by aggregating single blood pressure events for example, won't result in a blood sugar concentration event. Using TILs results in high modularity because one can reuse a TIL in every telemedical scenario in which a similar telemedical question arises. This reduces cost and time investigation in the development of ILOG infrastructures in telemedicine scenarios.

A typical requirement in monitoring telemedical values is the correlation of different types of telemedical events, e.g. blood pressure and weight. A TIL profile is some kind of event processing network. Thus it is a concept that aims to organize

EPAs "into networks to communicate with one another" [16]. It is optimized for a single patient respectively a given question, e.g. blood pressure > x AND weight > y related to the patients' medical situation. In the majority of cases every telemedical event is produced by its own telemedical application. Therefore HL7 Telemedical Event Format is required to harmonize or standardize the communication.

Referred to the motivating use case "Monitoring of sports by patients having hypertension" this means that two TILs have to be defined one for blood pressure and one for pulse. Probably, these two values will be measured using two different sensors or applications in general. Dependencies between the histories of events are expressed with the usage of a TIL profile defining, e.g. that a decrease of pulse and blood pressure should cause a new event to inform a physician.

5   Summary and Outlook

In summary, we can show how the concepts of ILOG and CEP could be integrated and used to optimize the transfer of telemedical values. Optimizing means that with the usage of CEP one can filter and aggregate telemedical values in a way that the overall amount of communication gets reduced. The integration of the ILOG metaphor that is to transport the right information, at the right time to the right place, enables one to optimize information supply by routing the values in a more intelligent manner. Taking CEP and ILOG together we fulfill two of the three mentioned criteria in chapter 4. To be able to also fulfill the requirement of processing telemedical values in distributed and heterogeneous scenarios we defined the term telemedical event and the according HL7 Telemedical Event Format as a bridging element. Now we have the possibility to communicate telemedical values from different telemedical event sources in a standardized format. The logic to filter and aggregate information sent in the HL7 Telemedical Event Format is encapsulated in the so termed Telemedical ILOG Listeners. In this way, we will be able to fulfill the overall requirement in healthcare to monitor telemedical values with the least amount of information overload, in accordance with the principles of ILOG.

From a generic point of view the developed concepts focus to bridge the lack of methods for an intelligent information supply in telemedical scenarios. So our approach is not only usable in telemedical scenarios but very specific to the healthcare domain, e.g. the usage of HL7. Generic contributions like the representation of events in HL7 are adaptable to all kind of medical events. While we are using CEP to process data we believe that the overall idea of combining CEP and ILOG is also adaptable to other domains. The usage of event processing gets more and more popular in other domains, e.g. in the field of logistics. The idea of formalizing the processing of information as defined by ILOG using CEP provides the opportunity to solve problems also in other domains. Our steps to generalize the approach are as follows: First we have to abstract the conceptual idea of Telemedical ILOG Listener to a generalized, domain independent type of ILOG Listener. For sure an ILOG Listener has to fulfill all requirements to process telemedical events. The second step is to build a family of XML based events, which is some kind of typology. The HL7

Telemedical Event Format has to be part of it. So, our process is based upon the idea of inheritance in software development, starting with domain specific solutions from which we can deduce overall requirements for domain independent processing.

Having a short outlook, the next step will be an evaluation of event processing engines with regard to the necessity to integrate the concepts of TIL and TIL profiles. Afterwards we'll start the basic implementation of the use cases mentioned in chapter 2. In parallel, we will discuss the evaluation of the concept, using the use case described above. Further research is needed, especially in the field of structuring telemedical events and in the field of integrating context. We believe that using ontologies or taxonomies could be appropriate concepts for structuring telemedical events. To cope with the question of using context, like it is discussed in different scientific communities, together with the concept of TIL to optimize the processing of telemedical events, one should take ongoing research of using context in the healthcare domain into account.

References

1. Koch, O., Rotaru, E.: Using Context to Improve Information Supply in the Medical Sector. In: Abramowicz, W., Tolksdorf, R., Węcel, K. (eds.) BIS 2010. LNBIP, vol. 57, pp. 192–203. Springer, Heidelberg (2010)
2. Deiters, W., Löffeler, T., Pfennigschmidt, S.: The Information Logistics Approach toward User Demand-Driven Information Supply. In: Cross-media Service Delivery: Based on Papers Presented at the Conference on Cross-Media Service Delivery, CMSD 2003. Kluwer Academic Publishers (2003)
3. Meister, S.: Usage of CEP and HL7 to Solve Information Logistics Problems in Telemedicine. In: 4th International Workshop on Information Logistics and Knowledge Supply for Viable Enterprises, pp. 4–11 (2011)
4. Hinchley, A.: Understanding Version 3: A primer on the HL7 Version 3 Healthcare Interoperability Standard, pp.1– 4. Mönch (2007)
5. Luckham, D., Schulte, R.: Event Processing Glossary. Technical Report Version 1.1, Event Processing Technical Society, http://www.ep-ts.com/component/option, com_docman/task,doc_download/gid,66/Itemid,84/ (accessed August 18, 2011)
6. Willems, A., Willems, J., Hajdasinski, A.: Information Logistics Research Report - Frameworks in Healthcare Industry, http://www.nyenrode.nl/FacultyResearch/research/Documents/ ResearchPaperSeries/2009/NRI09-04digitaleversie31jul09 (website).pdf (accessed August 18, 2011)
7. Winter, R., Schmaltz, M., Dinter, B., Bucher, T., Klesse, M., Lahrmann, G., Töpfer, J., Wegener, H.: Integrierte Informationslogistik. Business Engineering. Springer, Heidelberg (2008)
8. Haftor, D.M., Kajtazi, M.: What is Information Logistics? An Explorative Study of the Research Frontiers of Information Logistics, http://www.cil.se/data/files/Publikationer/Vetenskapliga_ artiklar/What_is_IL_v.04-06-2009.pdf (accessed August 18, 2011)
9. Hunt, R.E., Newman, R.G.: Medical Knowledge Overload: A Disturbing Trend for Physicians. Health Care Manage, 70–75 (1997)

10. Wilson, T.D.: Information Overload: Implications for Healthcare Services. Health Informatics Journal 7, 112–117 (2001)
11. Line, M.: Draft Definitions: Information and Library Needs, Wants, Demands and Uses. Aslib Proceedings 26, 87 (1974)
12. Vuori, V.: Methods of Defining Business Information Needs. In: Maula, M., Hannula, M., Seppä, M., Tommila, J. (eds.) Frontiers of e-Business Research ICEB + eBRF 2006, pp. 311–319 (2006)
13. Chandy, M.K., Etzion, O., von Ammon, R.: 10201 Executive Summary and Manifesto – Event Processing. In: Dagstuhl Seminar Proceedings (2011)
14. Bates, J., Bacon, J., Moody, K., Spiteri, M.: Using Events for the Scalable Federation of Heterogeneous Components. In: Proceedings of the 8th ACM SIGOPS European Workshop on Support for Composing Distributed Applications, pp. 58–65. ACM, New York (1998)
15. Chandy, K.M., Charpentier, M., Capponi, A.: Towards a Theory of Events. In: Proceedings of the 2007 Inaugural International Conference on Distributed Event-Based Systems, pp. 180–187. ACM, New York (2007)
16. Luckham, D.C.: Power of Events: An Introduction to Complex Event Processing in Distributed Enterprise Systems. Addison-Wesley, Boston (2002)
17. Hripcsak, G., Clayton, P.D., Jenders, R.A., Cimino, J.J., Johnson, S.B.: Design of a Clinical Event Monitor. Computers and Biomedical Research 29, 194–221 (1996)
18. Hazlehurst, B., Frost, H.R., Sittig, D.F., Stevens, V.J.: MediClass: A System for Detecting and Classifying Encounter-based Clinical Events in any Electronic Medical Record. Journal of the American Medical Informatics Association 12, 517–529 (2005)
19. Lowe, H.J., Ferris, T.A., Hernandez, P.M., Weber, S.C.: STRIDE–An Integrated Standards-based Translational Research Informatics Platform. In: AMIA, pp. 391–395 (2009)
20. Weber, S., Lowe, H.J., Malunjkar, Ş., Quinn, J.: Implementing a Real-time Complex Event Stream Processing System to Help Identify Potential Participants in Clinical and Translational Research Studies. In: AMIA 2010, pp. 472–476 (2010)
21. Arasu, A., Babcock, B., Babu, S., Cieslewicz, J., Datar, M., Ito, K., Motwani, R., Srivastava, U., Widom, J.: STREAM: The Stanford Data Stream Management System. Stanford InfoLab (2004)
22. Foster, D., Mcgregor, C., El-Masri, S.: A Survey of Agent-Based Intelligent Decision Support Systems to Support Clinical Management and Research. In: 1st Intl. Workshop on Multi-Agent Systems for Medicine, Computational Biology, and Bioinformatics (2006)
23. Etzion, O., Niblett, P.: Event Processing in Action. Manning (2010)
24. Esper: Esper (2011), http://esper.codehaus.org/ (accessed August 18, 2011)
25. Etzion, O.: Event Processing: Past, Present and Future. Proc. VLDB Endow. 3, 1651–1652 (2010)
26. Meister, S., Stahlmann, V.: Telemedical ILOG Listeners: Information Logistics Processing of Telemedical Values Using CEP and HL7. In: Wichert, R., Eberhardt, B. (eds.) Ambient Assisted Living. Advanced Technologies and Societal Change, vol. 2, pp. 245–260. Springer, Heidelberg (2012)

Information Logistics in Engineering Change Management: Integrating Demand Patterns and Recommendation Systems

Kurt Sandkuhl[1], Alexander Smirnov[2], and Nikolay Shilov[2]

[1] Rostock University, Institute of Computer Science, Rostock, Germany
Kurt.Sandkuhl@uni-rostock.de
[2] St.Petersburg Institute of Informatics and Automation
Russian Academy of Sciences, St. Petersburg, Russia
{smir,nick}@iias.spb.su

Abstract. During the last decade, manufacturing industries experienced a shift towards networked organisation structures. In such organizations, engineering change management is a complex process aiming at implementing required changes in the product timely, completely and by including all affected and involved partners. Information demand patterns have been proposed as a way of capturing organizational knowledge regarding the information flow for such change management processes. This paper aims at extending this work by investigating approaches from group recommendation systems for implementing IT-support of the pattern use. The paper presents an approach for integration information demand patterns and recommendation systems, an architecture for recommendation systems and a clustering approach.

Keywords: Information Demand Pattern, Recommendation System, Information Logistics, Engineering Change Management.

1   Introduction

During the last decade manufacturing industries experienced a shift towards networked organisation structures, which affects all enterprise functions including the product lifecycle management (PLM). In addition to the growing complexity caused by this development, increasing customer expectations and product variety cause a significantly increasing complexity in all PLM processes, which at the same time become more and more knowledge-intensive. Among the many activities to be performed in the life of products, engineering change management can be considered as in particular complex. Especially in networked organizations involving many different partners with complementing competences and distributed responsibilities for different elements of the product, it is crucial to implement changes in the product timely, completely and by including all affected and involved partners. Delayed or insufficient implementation of changes can lead to costly problems of products and affect customer relationships.

L. Niedrite, R. Strazdina, B. Wangler (Eds.): BIR 2011 Workshops, LNBIP 106, pp. 14–25, 2012.
© Springer-Verlag Berlin Heidelberg 2012

Earlier work in this area showed the importance of demand-oriented information supply for all roles involved in the engineering change management process. As a contribution to solving this problem, an information demand pattern capturing the typical information demand of the "change administrator" role was proposed [19]. The pattern captures organisational knowledge about what information is of what importance for the role, but it does not include the actual solution for providing the information. This paper aims at extending this work by investigating approaches from group recommendation systems[1] for implementing IT-support of the information demand pattern. Group recommendation systems aim at supporting information supply in such a way that the preferences from multiple users can be taken into account satisfying both the individual and the group of these users [12].

The main contributions of this paper are (1) to show that approaches from group recommendation systems and information demand patterns can be integrated, (2) to present an architecture for a recommendation system and (3) to discuss matching between demand described in a pattern and content originating from engineering change management processes.

The paper is structured as follows: Section 2 motivates the work by presenting an industrial case in engineering change management. Section 3 describes the background for the paper from the areas of information logistics including the information demand pattern for a change administrator. Section 4 presents the approach for using group recommendation systems as means to implement IT-support for the demand pattern. Section 5 summarizes the work and gives an outlook on future work.

2   Industrial Case

The work presented in this paper is motivated by experiences from the R&D project InfoFlow[2], which includes 6 industrial and academic partners. Within InfoFlow, modelling of information demand was performed in a number of industrial cases in order to collect experiences from various situations and domains. This section will briefly discuss one of these cases in order to show the process of modelling, the organisational setting, and the results. The industrial case selected is a sub-supplier to different first-tier suppliers in automotive and telecommunication industries who performs various surface treatment services of metal components. Surface treatment in this context includes different technical or decorative coatings to achieve certain functionality or appearance.

The case had the focus on engineering change management in the production process. The challenge is to handle the continuously incoming change specifications for products manufactured for many different OEMs in the automotive industry. Not implementing the changes in time would lead to products with wrong characteristics, penalties for the sub-suppliers because of these shortcomings, and long-term economic consequences. After modelling the change management process and its

---

[1] Recommendation systems also are referred to as "recommender systems" or "recommending systems". In this paper, we will use the term "recommendation system".

[2] See http://www.jth.hj.se/infoflow

relation to the production processes, an information demand analysis of a specific part of the ECM process (from quotation to production planning) was performed using the information demand method described in [11]. The models served as vehicle to develop shared knowledge among roles at the sub-supplier about different aspects of the practice in terms of information demand and information flow.

The analysis of the modeling results in the above case showed that the engineering change management processes in the organization were well-defined and implemented. Despite this favorable situation, many problems still occurred in daily practice of change management due to exceptions from the standard process or ad-hoc problem management when there was time pressure, i.e. there is a need for improving robustness and reliability of engineering change management (ECM) in practice. Delayed or insufficient implementation of changes can lead to costly problems of products and affect customer relationships. The aim of the sub-supplier is to avoid wrong decisions, delayed actions and insufficient change implementation in ECM caused by insufficient information supply.

3   Capturing Information Demand

The background for work presented in this paper is from the area of information logistics [4]. More specific, approaches for information demand modeling in general (3.1) and information demand patterns in particular (3.2) contribute to this paper. In order to illustrate the approach, an example pattern is included in 3.3.

3.1   Information Demand Modeling

A core subject of demand oriented information supply is how to capture the needs and preferences of a user in order to get a fairly complete picture of the demand in question. This section will briefly introduce three approaches for this purpose: user profiles, situation-based and context-based demand models.

User profiles have been subject to research in information systems and computer science since more than 25 years. User profiles are usually created for functionality provided by a specific application. They are based on a predefined structured set of personalization attributes and assigned default values at creation time. Adaptation of such profiles requires either an explicit adjustment of the preference values by the user (see [9] for an example), or involves deducing attribute values through logging and interpreting of user actions [20]. Experiences from projects in information logistics indicate that user profiles are suitable when the information demand is quite stable. The WIND application is an example, providing weather information on-demand based on user profiles [8].

A *situation-based* approach was proposed for implementing demand-oriented message supply. The basic idea is to divide the daily schedule of a person into situations and to determine the optimal situation for transferring a specific message based on the information value. This approach defines a situation as an activity in a specific time interval including topics and location relevant for the activity.

Information value is a relation between a message and a situation which is based on relevance of the topics of a message for the situation, utility of the message in specific situations and acceptance by the user. Details and examples from collaborative engineering are given in [13]. Situation-based description of information demand allows for a more sophisticated capturing of user demands as compared to user profiles. However, this approach is subject to the same criticisms as user profiles: the task of defining situations and topics is requiring considerable efforts and has the danger of becoming inaccurate over time.

The *context-based* approach is based on the basic idea that information demand of a person in an enterprise to a large extent depends on the work processes this person is involved in, on the co-workers or superiors of this person, and on the products, services or machines the person is responsible for. This led to the proposal to capture the context of information demand [10], i.e. a formalized representation of the setting in which information demand exists, including the organizational role of the person under consideration, work activities, resources and informal information exchange channels available. To create or derive such a context model could be done in different ways, such as interviews with different persons (roles) within an organization, work or information flow analysis, or enterprise modeling. Information demand patterns (see section 3.2) are based on this context-based viewpoint.

3.2   Information Demand Patterns

The general idea of information demand patterns (IDP) is similar to most pattern developments in computer science: to capture knowledge about proven solutions in order to facilitate reuse of this knowledge. In this paper the term information demand pattern is defined as follows: *An information demand pattern addresses a recurring information flow problem that arises for specific roles and work situations in an enterprise, and presents a conceptual solution to it.*

An information demand pattern consists of a number of essential parts used for describing the pattern: pattern name, organisational context, problems addressed, conceptual solution (consisting of information demand, quality criteria and timeline), and effects. These parts will be described in the following. An example for an actual pattern is presented in section 3.3.

- The *pattern name* usually is the name of the role the pattern addresses.
- The *organisational context* explains where the pattern is useful. This context description identifies the application domain or the specific departments or functions in an organisation forming the context for pattern definition.
- The *problems* of a role are identified. The tasks and responsibilities a certain role has are described in order to identify and discuss the challenges and problems, which this role usually faces in the defined organisational context.
- The *conceptual solution* describes how to solve the addressed problems. This includes the *information demand* of the role, which is related to the tasks and responsibilities, a *timeline* indicating the points in time when the information should be available, and *quality criteria* for the different elements of the

information demand. These criteria include the general importance of the information, the importance of receiving the information completely and with high accuracy, and the importance of timely or real-time information supply.

- The *effects* that play in using the proposed solution are described. If the needed information should arrive too late or is not available at all, this might affect the possibility of the role to complete its task and responsibilities. Information demand patterns include several kinds of effects: potential economic consequences, time/efficiency effects, effects on increasing or reducing the quality of the work results, effects on the motivation of the role responsible, learning and experience effects, and effects from a customer perspective.

3.3   Information Demand Pattern for the Role "Change Administrator"

In order to contribute to engineering change management and to illustrate the approach presented in section 3.2, the information demand pattern "change administrator" was developed and is presented in [19]. The pattern was developed in the context of the industrial case introduced in section 2, a second case from the same project infoFLOW and recommendations for engineering change management from CMII [3]. The enterprise knowledge models from the two cases and the CMII recommendations were analysed starting from the roles and their relations to processes and infrastructure resources. The tasks of "change administrator" appeared in several models, but sometimes were called "project manager" for change projects. We decided to use the term "change administrator", since the CMII standard uses this term. The information demand pattern follows the structure introduced in section 3.2.

For brevity reasons, we only include context, problem and information demand in this paper, since these are the essential parts for showing the connection to group recommendation systems in section 4.

The first element of the description is the context where the pattern is useful:

Context

The context for this pattern is configuration and change management in manufacturing industries, in particular industry sectors with complex physical products. Changes in products, product parts or installed systems are usually initiated by change reports or enhancements requests. Systematic handling of such requests requires coordination of decision making and implementation, often in a team with members from many different engineering disciplines. The role responsible for coordinating change request for a specific product, product part or system is often called change administrator. [...] The pattern describes the information demand typically experienced by the role change "administrator".

The pattern is supposed to be useful for enterprises developing and producing physical products with different variants and various released configurations. The pattern focuses on the change administrator, i.e. it does not include change implementation and change audit. In enterprises integrating change administration, implementation and audit in the same role, the pattern can be used as starting point, but needs to be extended.

The next part is the problem addressed by the pattern:

Problem

The pattern addresses the general problem of delayed decisions, redundant activities and inconsistent data in engineering change management and the resulting product or quality problems. This includes the following problems, which were observed by practitioners in engineering change projects:

- *Different problem reports or enhancement requests often are related or originate from the same product characteristic, but this is difficult to detect in the description of the change request. Thus, different change implementation processes for the same cause are initiated. [...]*
- *Test results or policy changes, possibly from other business areas of the company using components from the same supplier, indicate that the use of the component or supplier should be changed. This information is not reaching the change administrator, as this role is not part of the respective work process or organization unit where the relevant information is produced.[...]*

It follows the information demand, which is based on the tasks and responsibilities of the role under consideration:

Information Demand

The information demand is based on the tasks and responsibilities of the role. The tasks of the change administrator include

- *Responsibility: to manage all change requests directed to the product or product part in the change administrator's responsibility area (a) according to the enterprise quality standards (b) with economic resource use and (c) priority-driven change implementation*
- *To initiate up-front planning and decision making*
- *To ensure completeness and integrity of the data*
- *To coordinate decision making about feasibility and priority*
- *[...]*

The information demand of the role material responsible consists of:

- *To receive all **problem reports** or enhancement requests regarding the product or product part in the change administrator's responsibility area*
- *To get all information about **changes in company-internal policies** or in public laws and regulations [...]*
- *To receive all information about **status changes** of all on-going change projects*
- *To have access to information about the **released configurations** for all variants*
- *To have access to the documentation of all **completed change processes**

4   Integrating Recommendation Systems and Demand Patterns

Recommendation systems are widely used in the Internet for suggesting products, activities, etc. for a single user considering his/her interests and tastes [6], in various business applications [e.g., 7, 24] as well as in product development [e.g., 15, 2]. Group recommendation is complicated by the necessity to take into account not only personal interests but to compromise between the group interests and interests of the individuals of this group. In literature [e.g., 1, 14] the architecture of the group recommending system is proposed based on three components: (1) profile feature extraction from individual profiles, (2) classification engine for user clustering based on their preferences [e.g., 17], and (3) final recommendation based on the generated groups. Development of clustering algorithms capable to continuously improve group structure based on incoming information enables for self-organization of groups [5].

This section will present an approach integrating recommendation systems and information demand patterns for demand-oriented information supply with engineering change management as an example. Section 4.1 introduces the general approach, section 4.2 the architecture and section 4.3 a clustering algorithm, which is a central element of the approach.

4.1   Approach

The information demand patterns introduced in section 3.2 and 3.3 define the typical information demand of an organisational role. In the case of engineering change management, several organisational roles have to interact in order to implement efficient implementation of changes. The CMII standard [3] defines in addition to the change administrator also the roles of a change project manager (responsible for implementing a certain, specified change in the product) and the change auditor (responsible for validating the correct implementation of a change according to the specification). Thus, an IT support for engineering change management should include all three roles and their interaction.

The general task to be supported is to provide the information needed for performing a task to the role responsible for the task, i.e. whenever new information is created within the enterprise under consideration or is provided from external partners, this information should be examined in order to initiate information supply to the right role. Since the role-based information demand is defined in the information demand pattern, the IT solution for supporting the above described information provision has to include two configuration aspects:

- Configuration of the demand patterns for the enterprise under consideration. The pattern describes a typical demand. When used in a specific organisation, this typical demand has to be made concrete for the actual enterprise, e.g. by specifying for what product or product group the change administrator is responsible and what information sources to use to track status changes
- Individual information for the person fulfilling the role should be added. This personal information demand strictly seen is not needed for the role as such, but will support acceptance for the solution.

An information demand pattern configured for a certain organisation and enhanced for a specific person having the role will in the following be called user profile. In the case of engineering change management, several user profiles will exist, i.e. profiles for the three persons having the role of change administrator, change project manager, and change auditor.

4.2   Architecture

The proposed group recommendation system architecture is presented in Figure 1. It is centralized around the user clustering algorithm [21] originating from the decision mining area [16, 18, 22]. However, the development of the algorithm has made it possible to use it for building self-organizing user groups. The proposed clustering algorithm is based on the information from user profiles. The user profiles contain information about users including their information demand, preferences, interests and activity history, as described in section 4.1. In this context, the clustering algorithm's precision will benefit from the demand pattern, since it basically describes the context of the role (including current user task, product(s) she/he works with, time pressure and other parameters). The semantic integration between the different profiles and the demand pattern is supported by an ontology covering the domain-specific and enterprise-specific concepts.

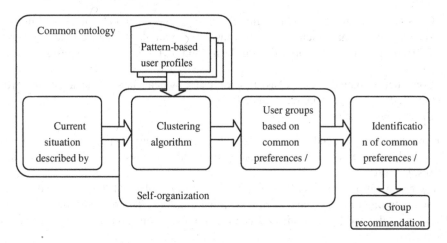

Fig. 1. Group recommendation system architecture

The personal information in the user profiles is considered as dynamic and, hence, the updated information is supplied to the algorithm from time to time. As a result the algorithm can run as updated information is received and update user groups. Hence it can be said that the groups self-organize in accordance with the changes in the user profiles and context information.

Since, in the case considered as an example, the major difference between users is the part of the engineering change management process they work with, the generated groups are expected to be process related. However, in other environments this has not necessary to be the case and groups can be product-oriented, resource-oriented or other. When groups are generated the common preferences/interests of the groups can be identified based on the results of the clustering algorithm. These preferences can be then generalized and analysed in order to produce group recommendations.

4.3   Clustering Algorithm

Due to the specifics of the tasks in the considered company (process orientation) the implemented algorithm [adapted from 21] of user clustering is based on analysing input information and has the following steps:

1. Extract words/phrases from the input information (text processing).
2. Calculate similarity between the input information and ontology elements (i.e. compare text strings extracted from the input information and names of classes and attributes). The algorithm of fuzzy string comparison similar to well-known Jaccard index [23] is used for this purpose. It calculates occurrence of substrings of one string in the other string. For example, string "motor" has 5 different substrings (m, o, t, r, mo) contained in the string "mortar". The total number of different substrings in "motor" is 13 (m, o, t, r; mo, ot, to, or; mot, oto, tor; moto, otor). The resulting similarity of the string "motor" to the string "mortar" is 5/13 or 38%.
3. Construct weighted graph consisting of ontology classes and attributes, and users. Weights of arcs are calculated on the basis of (1) similarity metrics (i.e. they are different for different input information) and (2) taxonomic relations in the ontology.
4. Construct weighted graph consisting of users (when classes and attributes are removed arcs weights are recalculated).
5. Cluster users graph.

For the clustering procedure a weighted user – ontology graph is considered. It contains three types of nodes: C – classes from the ontology, A – attributes of the classes, U – users.

The graph consists of two types of arcs. The first type of arcs I (CA, CC) is defined by the taxonomy of classes and attributes in the ontology. The second type of arcs II (CU, AU) is defined by relations between input information and classes/attributes (cf. Figure 2a).

Weights of arcs between nodes corresponding to classes and users CU_{weight} and corresponding to attributes and users AU_{weight} are defined via the similarity CU_{sim} and AU_{sim} of the class or attribute (calculated via the fuzzy string comparison algorithm described above). The similarity is a property of relations between class – user/solution or attribute – user/solution. Weights of arcs are defined as follows: $CU_{weignt} = 1 - CU_{sim}$; $AU_{weight} = 1 - AU_{sim}$.

Arcs CA and CC tying together classes and attributes via taxonomic relations (defined by ontology relations class-class, class-attribute) have CA_{weight}, $CC_{weight} \in (\varepsilon, 1)$ defined empirically. CC_{weight} means arcs' weight of linked classes in the ontology. CA_{weight} – arcs' weight of linked attributes and classes.

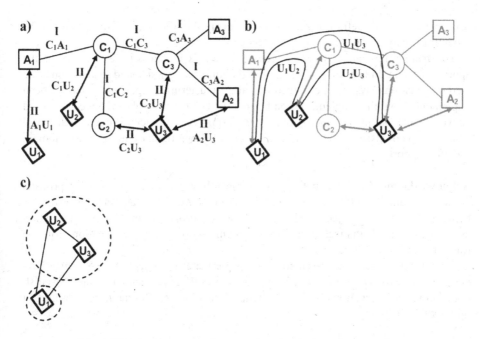

Fig. 2. Weighted user – ontology graph and user clustering procedure

Since users have to be assigned to relevant input information, based on this graph the input information and weight consequently users are clustered on the basis of the lowest weights of connecting arcs. This is performed in the following sequence. First, the shortest routes between users are calculated (cf. Figure 2b). E.g., weight of the arc U_1U_2 will be calculated as follows: U_1U_2 weight = A_1U_1 weight + C_1A_1 weight + C_1U_2 weight; weight of the arc U_2U_3 can be calculated in 3 ways, it is considered in Figure 2b that U_2U_3 weight = C_1U_2 weight + C_1C_3 weight + C_3U_3 weight is the shortest one; etc.

Based on the calculated weights a new graph consisting of the users only is built (cf. Figure 2c). The value of the parameter D_{max} is set empirically. Assuming that U_1U_2 weight > D_{max}, U_1U_3 weight > D_{max}, and U_2U_3 weight < D_{max}, two clusters can be identified: the first cluster includes users U_2 and U_3, and the second one includes customer U_1 (dashed circles in Figure 2c).

The algorithm can run when updated information is received and update user groups thus providing for self-organizations of user groups in accordance with the changes in user profiles and context information.

5   Summary and Future Work

Starting from work on information demand patterns and from an industrial case in engineering change management, the paper proposes an integration of recommendation systems and information demand pattern for the implementation of demand-oriented information supply. The approach of using information demand patterns was found useful for processes with many different roles involved and at the same time many exceptions and ad-hoc decisions.

The main limit of the research presented here is the missing evaluation of the approach in an industrial setting. Both, the information demand pattern and the recommendation system architecture and clustering algorithm, have been implemented, but this implementation has not yet been thoroughly evaluated. It would be worthwhile and interesting to both test the proposed approach in several real-world cases and to compare different industrial domains, in particular aiming at non-domain specific support for information flow.

Acknowledgements. Some parts of the research were carried out under projects funded by grants # 09-07-00436-a and # 11-07-00045-a of the Russian Foundation for Basic Research, and project # 213 of the research program "Intelligent information technologies, mathematical modelling, system analysis and automation" of the Russian Academy of Sciences.

Other parts of the work presented in this paper were supported by the Swedish KK-Foundation, project infoFLOW-2 (grant # 2009/0257), and by the Swedish Foundation for Internationalisation in Higher Education and Research, project DEON (grant # IG 2008-2011).

References

1. Baatarjav, E.-A., Phithakkitnukoon, S., Dantu, R.: Group Recommendation System for Facebook. In: Meersman, R., Tari, Z., Herrero, P. (eds.) OTM-WS 2008. LNCS, vol. 5333, pp. 211–219. Springer, Heidelberg (2008)
2. Chen, Y.-J., Chen, Y.-M., Wu, M.-S.: An expert recommendation system for product empirical knowledge consultation. In: 3rd IEEE International Conference on Computer Science and Information Technology, pp. 23–27. IEEE Press, New York (2010)
3. CMII Research Institute: CMII Standard for Product Configuration Management. Document CMII-105C, http://www.cmiiresearch.com (accessed on February 4, 2010)
4. Deiters, W., Löffeler, T., Pfenningschmidt, S.: The Information Logistical Approach Toward a User Demand-driven Information Supply. In: Cross-Media Service Delivery, pp. 37–48. Kluwer Academic Publisher (2003)
5. Flake, G.W., Lawrence, S., Giles, C.L., Coetzee, F.: Self-Organization and identification of Web Communities. IEEE Computer 35(3), 66–71 (2002)
6. Garcia, I., Sebastia, L., Onaindia, E., Guzman, C.: A Group Recommender System for Tourist Activities. In: Di Noia, T., Buccafurri, F. (eds.) EC-Web 2009. LNCS, vol. 5692, pp. 26–37. Springer, Heidelberg (2009)
7. Hornung, T., Koschmider, A., Oberweis, A.: A Recommender System for Business Process Models. In: Proceedings of the 17th Annual Workshop on Information Technologies & Systems (2009), http://ssrn.com/abstract=1328244
8. Jaksch, S., Pfennigschmidt, S., Sandkuhl, K., Thiel, C.: Information Logistic Applications for Information-on-Demand Scenarios: Concepts and Experiences from WIND Project. In: 29th Euromicro Conference, Antalya, Turkey, pp. 141–147. IEEE Press, New York (2003)

9. Kotinurmi,   P.:   User   Profiles   and   Their   Management   (2001),
    http://www.tml.tkk.fi/Studies/Tik-
    111.590/2001s/papers/paavo_kotinurmi.pdf
10. Lundqvist, M.: Context as a Key Concept in Information Demand Analysis. In: Doctoral
    Consortium Associated with the 5th Intl. and Interdisciplinary Conference on Modelling
    and Using Context, Paris, France, pp. 63–73 (2005)
11. Lundqvist, M., Sandkuhl, K., Seigerroth, U.: Modelling Information Demand in an
    Enterprise Context: Method, Notation and Lessons Learned. IJISMD 2(3), 74–96 (2011)
12. McCarthy, K., Salamo, M., Coyole, L., McGinty, L., Smyth, B., Nixon, P.: Group
    Recommender Systems: A Critiquing Based Approach. In: 11th International Conference
    on Intelligent User Interfaces, pp. 267–269. ACM Press (2006)
13. Meissen, U., Pfennigschmidt, S., Voisard, A., Wahnfried, T.: Context- and Situation-Awareness
    in Information Logistics. In: Lindner, W., Fischer, F., Türker, C., Tzitzikas, Y., Vakali, A.I.
    (eds.) EDBT 2004. LNCS, vol. 3268, pp. 335–344. Springer, Heidelberg (2004)
14. Middleton, S.E., De Roure, D., Shadbolt, N.R.: Ontology-Based Recommender Systems.
    In: Staab, S., Rudi, S. (eds.) Handbook on Ontologies, International Handbooks on
    Information Systems, pp. 477–498. Springer, Heidelberg (2003)
15. Moon, S.K., Simpson, T.W., Kumara, S.R.T.: An Agent-Based Recommender System for
    Developing Customized Families of Products. Journal of Intelligent Manufacturing 20(6),
    649–659 (2009)
16. Petrusel, R., Mican, D.: Mining Decision Activity Logs. In: Abramowicz, W., Tolksdorf,
    R., Węcel, K. (eds.) BIS 2010. LNBIP, vol. 57, pp. 67–79. Springer, Heidelberg (2010)
17. Romesburg, H.C.: Cluster Analysis for Researchers. Lulu Press, California (2004)
18. Rozinat, A., van der Aalst, W.M.P.: Decision Mining in Business Processes, BPM Center
    Report no. BPM-06-10 (2006)
19. Sandkuhl, K.: Improving Engineering Change Management with Information Demand
    Patterns. In: 8th International Conference on Product Lifecycle Management, Eindhoven,
    The Netherlands. Inderscience Enterprises (2011)
20. Setten, M., Veenstra, M., Nijholt, A.: Prediction Strategies: Combining Prediction
    Techniques to Optimize Personalization. In: 2nd Workshop on Personalization in Future
    TV, Malaga, Spain (2002)
21. Smirnov, A., Pashkin, M., Chilov, N.: Personalized Customer Service Management for
    Networked Enterprises. In: 11th International Conference on Concurrent Enterprising,
    pp. 295–302 (2005)
22. Smirnov, A., Pashkin, M., Levashova, T., Kashevnik, A., Shilov, N.: Context-Driven
    Decision Mining. In: Encyclopedia of Data Warehousing and Mining, Information Science
    Preference, 2nd edn., Hershey, New York, vol. 1, pp. 320–327 (2008)
23. Tan, P.-N., Steinbach, M., Kumar, V.: Introduction to Data Mining. Addison Wesley
    (2005)
24. Zhena, L., Huangb, G.Q., Jiang, Z.: Recommender System Based on Workflow. Decision
    Support Systems 48(1), 237–245 (2009)

Selecting KMS for SME - A Need for Value-Orientation

Ulrike Borchardt

University of Rostock, 18057 Rostock, Germany
ulrike.borchardt@uni-rostock.de

Abstract. Knowledge Management supported by IT solutions has been around for years, yet the question how these are applied in SME and if by which extend still remains. This paper presents 2 surveys conducted on the matter. The first one covers the region of Mecklenburg-Vorpommern, Germany and the second how social software applications, especially wikis are used for KM in SME. By using the result we are able to show, that the principle of KM reached the SME but the understanding of it and the still unstructured support by IT are affected by the fact that the value of individual applications, e.g. wikis, is not clarified. Accordingly, we describe the idea of a framework allowing for these decisions to be made more structured.

1 Motivation

Knowledge Management(KM) was one of the buzzwords during the last years, especially with regard to the manifold applications developed and introduced to the market aiming to support the process of KM. This is the one side of KM, but the market in the EU mostly consists of SME (small and medium enterprises - 99% of all businesses in the EU are SME [5]) and these do have specific needs, mostly due to their sparse resources. When looking through literature many articles on KM, KM practises and KMS (knowledge management systems) can be found. However, rarely any information is provided on SME and especially not on their adaption and perception of KM and KMS in the enterprises as we have already shown in [2]. To fill this gap, we conducted two questionnaires via online platforms to knowledge-intensive SME, whose results are presented in this paper. The according questionnaires were designed to capture the recent state of the art in the participating SME with regard to their use of KMS and especially their perception of the usefullness of such systems. Focusing on SME, we conducted one survey in our region only and the other one in comparison with larger enterprises all over Germany. During completion and evaluation of the first survey the question arose whether SME really are able to operate a full KMS architecture, or if they are better served with smaller solutions in the form of individual applications, therefore the second survey focused on social software as one group offering support.

L. Niedrite, R. Strazdina, B. Wangler (Eds.): BIR 2011 Workshops, LNBIP 106, pp. 26–37, 2012.
© Springer-Verlag Berlin Heidelberg 2012

Accordingly, the research questions to be answered are the following:

1. Have SME fully adapted the concepts of KM and KMS?
2. Which role does social software play in the KM for SME?
3. How do SME chose which KMS to implement?

To show how this questions were answered by the surveys this paper is structured as follows. Section 2 delivers general background on the topics of KM and KMS as well as SME. Section 3 presents the two surveys on KMS and SME and finally section 4 provides our idea on how the found issues could be addressed via a value-oriented framework.

2 Background

This chapter shortly presents theoretical backgrounds used for this paper, as there are KM and KMS, as well as some general remarks on SME.

2.1 Knowledge Management Systems

Definitions of the term KM in literature vary widely [14], [13] However, two main approaches can be identified. [11]

1. The human-oriented approach focuses on the transfer of knowledge between individuals or groups of employees and does not necessarily contain a technical component.
2. The technical-oriented approach focuses on supporting the process of KM by means of ICT.

As this paper focuses on the use of KMS and falls into the line with the technical orientation, following this idea a KMS can be defined according to Maier([11], p.86):

"A knowledge management system is an ICT system in the sense of an application system or an ICT platform that combines and integrates functions for the contextualized handling of both explicit and tacit knowledge, throughout the organization or that part of the organization, that is targeted by a KM initiative. A KMS offers integrated services to deploy KM instruments for networks of participants, i.e. active knowledge workers, in knowledge-intensive business processes along the entire knowledge life cycle. Ultimate aim of KMS is to support the dynamics of organizational learning and organizational effectiveness."

Having a closer look at the given definition it should be recognized, that Maier assumes KMS as an integral part of a KM initiative. Consequently, the implementation of such a KMS should be part of the overall implementation process of KM in an enterprise. This can be assured e.g. by aligning the KMS to the KM goals. The definition of these goals is according to [14] a prerequisite for a successful KM initiative, where deferring KM goals from business strategy is indicated the initial step in KM. Maier's ideal KMS architecture consists of six layers with the core knowledge services in the third and forth layer (see figure 1). He identifies four main knowledge services, however the architecture leaves room for more services to be named.

Fig. 1. Knowledge Management System architecture according to [11]

2.2   SME

Though having no standard definition on the term SME, EU guidelines [5] distinguish SME with the help of two characteristics. These two attributes in use are: number of employees and annual turnover. With regard to the annual turnover it is stated that the value of the balance sheet can be used instead, and consequently one or the other has to be fulfilled. However, one of the two and the amount of employees must be met, one attribute does not suffice. Accordingly, an enterprise with less than 10 employees is a micro enterprise. Moreover, the enterprise's turnover is not larger than 2 million Euro per year. This indicates that an enterprise with 10 to 49 employees and a turnover of 10 million Euro (same value holds for the balance sheet) is considered a small enterprise. Consequently, a SME with 50 to 249 employees and an annual turnover of 50 million Euro (balance sheet: 43 million Euro) is considered a medium enterprise. In Germany additionally the term "Mittelstand" exists, which also counts enterprises with less than 500 employees into the group of medium enterprises, as long as their annual turnover does not exceed 50 million Euro.[9]

Furthermore, it can be stated with regard to KM that SME apparently suffer stronger from difficulties caused by information overload than larger enterprises do. One explanation for this fact might be the fewer resources, e.g. employees responsible for certain tasks. An employee in a SME usually is not as specialized in a certain field as may be in larger enterprises. Moreover, he or she usually has no backup. Consequently, KM problems arise when the employee is no longer available due to e.g. retirement or illness. One way to address this problem may be to generate a backup for these situations without stressing the resources as far as hiring a new employee, by the electronic capture of knowledge as supported by KMS and KM applications.

3   Using KMS in SME

Here the initial considerations for the design of surveys on the field of KMS for SME are described, and details from the surveys and as well as a comparison are presented.

3.1   Design

As shown by systematic literature research in [2], publications on how SME deploy KM and KMS can hardly be found. Accordingly, we assume a gap to be filled by empirical study. To address this two surveys were designed, each one with a slightly differing purpose.

The first survey was directed at providing a general state of the art on KM and KMS and was restricted to the area of Mecklenburg-Vorpommern, a federal state of Germany. Yet the second survey aimed at a larger population, namely enterprises all over Germany, which included SME to a sufficient degree. Both surveys focused on knowledge-intensive enterprises since these should be confronted with a stronger need for KM.

In designing the surveys we directed them at SME and were confronted with the question of definition. To address this problem, we decided to use the EU definition for the first survey and the extended "Mittelstand" definition for the second survey. This also reflects the question whether KM is considered sooner if there are more employees in the SME. As no full KMS were found in the first survey, the second survey also covered issues on Social Software, especially with regard to wikis. For the design of these surveys following questions to be answered could be identified:

- By which degree has KM reached SME?
- Which KMS or KM applications are used?
- By which degree is the use of KMS/ KM applications successful and planned?
- Is social software used for the means of KM?
- Do wikis contribute to successful KM?

3.2   Knowledge Management in SME in Mecklenburg-Vorpommern

This survey on KM and its application in the form of KMS was conducted as an online questionnaire, with focus on SME according to the European definition only. Only knowledge-intensive SME in Mecklenburg-Vorpommern were asked to fill out the questionnaire to provide us with a current state of the art in KM focusing on IT support within the enterprises. The survey took place in November and December 2010. The according questionnaire was provided online and the link was sent to 596 enterprises fulfilling the criteria of being knowledge-intensive. The actual distinction on whether the enterprise was a SME was made based on the amount of employees, since an inquiry on the annual turnover was unlikely to be answered.

Of 596 enterprises 48 send answers, resulting in a response rate of 7.89% since one of the answers was given by an enterprise which could no longer counted a SME. The distribution over the enterprise sizes is: 6 answers were gained from medium, 14 from small and 27 from micro enterprises. Since these numbers do not fully resemble the official numbers for the distribution (micro: 88.84%, small: 9.02%, medium: 1.9%) for the area [7], as well as the fact that the basic population is not very big, an evaluation according to the different groups will not be presented here. Regarding the obtained general results several points were interesting:

- Only 9 out of the remaining 47 answering enterprises employ a systematic KM approach.
- Only 5 out of these 9 enterprises use a KMS to support their activities. When asking for the system itself the answers were: wiki, Sharepoint2010, One Note, SVN and MediaWiki.
- One of the enterprises answered that it uses several applications to support KM and these do not have the possibility to exchange data. The other enterprises at least have this opportunity enabled.
- Though KMS need a certain amount of administration, not all enterprises have a dedicated person for this task (4 out of 5).

With regard to these results it can be concluded that most enterprises still are not familiar with the actual meaning of the term KMS as introduced by Maier, and assume any application a KMS that supports their handling of organizational knowledge. Moreover a total of 80% of the enterprises in the survey do not practise KM at all. In the questionnaire we also asked for the goals which were pursued by the introduction of a KMS.

- The most common answers were transparency of knowledge, improving documentation, distribution of knowledge.
- When provided with a list of objectives, the participants considered almost every objective as very important, though the list contained 12 objectives.
- When asked for the individual accomplishment of these goals, half the SME answered they achieved them to a high till very high degree, whereas the other half indicated this degree was low.

Drawing conclusions it can be stated that SME are not fully aware which goals belong to KM and therewith focus on basic functionalities. And even more important, it does not seem to be clear which goal can be addressed with which IT solution. Moreover, the relation to business goals was not made or at least it was not indicated by answers provided to us. So SME want to improve, want to add to their business value and know that IT can somehow deliver to it. Yet, which solution supports precisely which goal needs further clarification.

The survey also asked how KM if practiced was integrated into the enterprise. The obtained results here were.

- None of the enterprises could name a specific strategy as suggested in literature for their implementation strategy of KM.
- Only one of the enterprises actually writes down its goal for KM, and these were not even controlled. All other enterprises rely on general oral statements on the goals for their enterprises, and control them by a regular personal estimation. Only one enterprise tries to control success by means of indicators.

- On the terms of how KM and KMS were introduced into the enterprise 6 answers said as a project, the rest mentioned a top-down approach.
- 8 out of 9 enterprises answered that their employees have less than 10% of the time for the fulfillment of KM tasks, two stated that it were even said less than 5%. Assuming 40 office hours a week this indicates less than 2 hours.

Interpreting these results it can be seen, that KM has reached the SME in the area of Mecklenburg-Vorpommern, however only partially. Some enterprises certainly got in touch with the concept and made up their own idea about it, yet a consequent alignment of KM and KMS to the business strategy was not found. However, the results on the objectives in KM indicate that a strategy is needed, as insecurity leads to a lack of priority setting and delays decisions on the use of KM. Accordingly, the well planned use of the available applications apparently does not exist.

3.3   Social Software and Wikis for KM

The second survey focused on how social software and especially wikis can support KM. In December 2010 and January 2011 the survey was distributed online and as Excel file, and 510 enterprises were invited to answer. 141 complete answers could be retrieved resulting in a response rate of 27.65%. Out of the 141 answers 48 were given by SME (or enterprises which apply to the definition "Mittelstand"). 31 answers were given by enterprises with a total amount of employees between 500 and 1000, the remaining answers were provided by larger enterprises. Since our objective are SME we here present the results for the first group and only when comparison is useful the results gained for the group of larger enterprises.

To start with the topic of KM the questionnaire included the questions whether KM is used and if, when was it introduced:

- 40 out of 48 SME apply KM, resulting in 83.3% of SME dealing with KM
- SME started KM earliest in 2001 (3 of 40), but the majority started in 2003 (17 of 40), whereas most other enterprises implemented KM between 2001 and 2003 (46 of 62), all numbers can be find in table 2
- KM was introduced into the enterprise by: "employees initiatives" (10 of 40), "by the use within a single department" (9 of 40), "by the initiative of upper management" (14 of 40) and "do not know"(7 of 40).

Looking at the results it can be concluded, that 4 out of 5 SME have implemented KM throughout the last 10 years, mostly due to the initiative of single employees or the upper management.

Consequently, we asked which applications were in use for KM purposes, to see whether a full KMS architecture could be identified as suggested by Maier. The answers were:

Comparing this to the larger enterprises it was recognized, that the strong differences in the use of intranet solution (47 of 62 enterprises with more than

Table 1. Years of introduction of KM

Year	SME (out of 40)	Large enterprises (out of 62)
< 2000	-	3
2000	-	5
2001	3	10
2002	6	19
2003	10	17
2004	7	6
2005	5	1
2006	4	1
2007	5	-

Table 2. Groups of application in use for KM in SME

Application	Amount of answers (out of 40)
Intranet	16
DMS	33
CMS	31
Groupware	10
Workflow Management Systems	3
Data-Mining	2
Data Warehouse	8

500 employees use this application type), workflow management systems (46 of 62) and groupware (46 of 62) exists.

When going further into details on the use of social software following answers were retrieved:

- 7 of 40 SME use social software to support their KM initiative. 24 enterprises stated that they have no use for social software, 9 stated that they cannot answer.
- The main intention in its use was "Provision and structuring of contents through the user" with 47.8%, which was considered "highly relevant" or "very highly relevant" by 54.1%. In comparison large enterprises answered: "optimal usage of knowledge" (70%), "easier identification of knowledge"(68%), "better distribution of knowledge"(67%) and "better provision of information"(63%).
- Asking for perceived changes in their KM by using social software, the results on this question did not differ significantly between the enterprise groups and the basic population of SME answering this question was rather small. The overall most prominent perceptions were "a more efficient usage of knowledge" (77%) and "less effort for information procurement" (84%), yet only 40% reported "cost savings".

Concluding from its rare usage the potential of Social software for KM apparently is not highly regarded. However, the enterprises apparently see a supportive function for their KM. The questionnaire proceeded with specific questions on the use of wikis delivering following results:

- 15 SME and 46 larger enterprises have a wiki installed
- Wikis were introduced on behalf of "initiative of a single employee in a project" (3), "a single department" (3), "the upper management" (7). In 2 enterprises the way of introduction was not known.
- 76.7% of the SME having implemented a wiki use it at least once a week.
- When using a wiki securing a good quality of the contents is important, even if resources are sparse. SME mostly rely on particular persons being responsible for certain topics (45.6%). This value is the highest when compared to other enterprises where 37.5% (up to 1000 employees) or 19.6% (more than 1000 employees) answered that they use responsibles.
- The type of wiki used in the SME was in 6 cases a MediaWiki, in 5 a TWiki, 1 DokuWiki and the remaining did not know the platform.

These results show that the wikis are well integrated in the enterprise, as well as accepted. However, following barriers were named: "Management has other priorities" (74,6%), "Fear of loosing control over information" (70.7%), "competency level of employees does not suffice to deal with technology" (64.9%) and "IT infrastructure lacks compatibility" (63.9%). Moreover, more than half of the enterprises were not sure about which value such a system can deliver (55.8%), moreover 51% enterprises faced security issues.

With regard to these results we can say that SME tend to use well known technical solutions, but in general the opportunities technology offers are not realized. In addition, a control question was added asking whether wikis do support KM or not. The result was that only 4 out of 15 SME consider wikis as helpful for KM. This supports that there is lacking awareness of what value applications can deliver. Nevertheless, frequent questions on how KM can be understood at all, showed that the enterprises are of the opinion they apply the principle of KM, though the understanding of it varies widely. We did not find a full KMS as suggested by Maier. And the perception of the applications for the use in KM varies, expressing that enterprises are still uncertain which value can be expected from them.

3.4 Comparison and Conclusion

When looking at the results delivered by the two conducted surveys it can be seen, that KM has reached SME, at least by the name. The individual results however show very different understandings of the concept. Moreover, SME show a delayed implementation of KM support when compared to larger enterprises, in the region of Mecklenburg-Vorpommern even more than in general. In addition, the actual amount of employees seems to influence the adaption of KM which is derived from the second survey with a weaker KM definition and higher KM usage. A fully implemented ideal architecture of a KMS as by Maier [11] was not found, so the question remains whether such architecture is suiting for SME. Among the used applications a wide variety was found indicating the different understanding of the terms surrounding KMS.

The overall understanding of KM varies among different enterprises an observation that was confirmed by both surveys. And though literature shows the helpfulness of the implementation of KM for certain kinds of enterprises [15] - the value and the necessity of KM for SME is still not fully clarified and apprehended. None of the participating SME was able to relate the use of KM application to the overall business strategy or success. The enterprises are by now not aware of the individual potentials a solution like a wiki can deliver. It appears more like they are implementing an application because it is hyped, or one initiative is bringing it in, because individual persons are convinced of the usefulness, however cannot name the value precisely. Social software, including wikis, seems to belong into that group of hyped applications, because by control questions it became obvious that their potential is not realized.

In addition, we were able to see that a general "guideline" how to bring KMS or KM applications into the enterprise was not followed or found. Though several guidelines exist [6], [3], they are not adapted by the participating SME.

Subsequently, after this capture of the recent state of the art, a prospect into the future development is desirable. Thus a follow up survey going into details of future plans, as well as dwelling on the individual perception with the help of structured interviews is designed. However, the main focus there lies on gathering the value the KM solutions can deliver to SME, as well as the attitude towards the possibilities of KM. This is for instance interesting since only a small part of SME follow a systematic approach, why does not the rest. By such a structured interview even the shortcomings of online surveys could be compensated.

4   Prospects

Though KM still is one of the recent buzzwords, it remains vague what the individual SME can expect from the utilization of a KMS. Looking at the results of the two conducted surveys, the question arises, how KM applications can efficiently support the SME in their KM initiatives. The focus herewith lies on the "efficient". It was shown by the surveys, that by some extend KM application like a wiki support the SME, yet it remains unclear how exactly this support is given and which part of the business strategy is supported. Yet the actual potential of such a wiki still remains undefined, which got clear when asking for the KM support a wiki can deliver. While looking on the SME which are not implementing KM at all, or by the means of IT solutions, it is of interest how much uncertainty influences that decision. This problem is already addressed by the follow up survey. We assume that a lot of uncertainties as well as priority setting base on the fact, that it is not determined what a certain application can contribute to business value and accordingly no foundation for an educated decision is given.

With the help of the gained results we are able to answer the question whether SME are able to operate a full ideal KMS as suggested by [11]. They certainly are not and moreover, are not even interested in doing so. Such a full architecture stresses their sparse resources too much, and in addition SME have no need for all components of it. Nevertheless, this does not make the idea of such an architecture a bad idea, but a good basis to determine components according to the individual needs of a business. Accordingly it would be of interest to be able to change the SME's perception of KM applications and KMS towards a more value-driven way, however to do so more research work on this field is necessary.

4.1 Allowing for a Structured Decision on KMS

By using the results of the surveys presented here we are able to draw conclusions on the establishment of a framework addressing precisely this problem, namely building up a basis for a specific decision as already suggested in [2] and further explained in [1]. Using a value-driven framework it should be possible to decide on the application type by defining the own business strategy. Consequently, the three dimensional framework, including the dimension of e.g. the perceived value approach adopted from [4], the knowledge services from Maier's architecture and finally the relationships between these two, would allow to describe a wiki as a means mainly for knowledge documentation, which given a certain information quality will strongly influence the user satisfaction and therewith the use of the system. The dimensions mentioned would therewith build the frame for the decision, the individual application classes and their "possible value" are supposed to form the content of the framework.

Within the framework the main idea is to provide the people running or establishing a KMS in their enterprise to chose one based on their needs, which should be derived in the dimensions of the frame. The first step therefore would be to ask them for their knowledge need or requirements. Based on these requirements it should be possible to identify the knowledge management services to be supported by the KMS. These are to be determined based on the services suggested in Maier's architecture layer III. We therefore assume that it is not of interest to start with a complete KMS as suggested but pick the services most important to address the urgent problems of the enterprise. At this stage even the possibilities on determining the knowledge demand of the organization have to be discussed.

Once the demand is clarified the framework should be able to recommend an application class to use based on the individual benefit such a system can offer. Consequently, it is necessary to categorize the benefit, the value of individual application classes. To do so we decided to use the KMS Success model of [8] (see figure 2) to determine the benefit the applications can offer for SME.

Accordingly, the framework can be filled with new application classes, as they emerge as e.g. is social software. Moreover, updates should allow it to be adapted to the changes in organizational KM and the developing or disappearing applications. Using KMS Success from Jennex and Olfman we are aiming not on the monetary value the system might deliver, but at the perceived benefit the organization can experience from the usage of it. By using this model different categories can be evaluated, which then can be interrelated to the organizations strategy or knowledge need. Accordingly, the idea of an holistic approach of KM including a KMS is preserved.

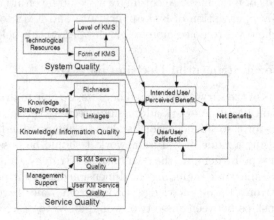

Fig. 2. KMS Success according to [8]

4.2   Further Work

The interconnections between the dimensions of the suggested framework are still to be proved and the general outline of the framework still has to be populated by attributes, from literature as well a from further empirical research with SME elaborating on their individual problems and strategies. Only after this done, the framework can follow its initial intention of serving as a guideline.

In addition it might be of interest to see how SME in other countries evolve, so see whether such a framework would apply for them as well. Therefore, it is necessary to repeat the surveys on other SME population to determine their behavior. Moreover, it might be considered whether different groups of SME might be identified having different needs with regard to KM, e.g. SME in a supply chain. These might make more specific decisions on KM and KMS as they have to combine more knowledge and have to make more structured decisions than stand alone organizations.

References

1. Borchardt, U.: Towards A Value-Oriented KMS Recommendation For SME. In: Liu, K., Filipe, J. (eds.) KMIS 2011: Proceedings of the 3rd International Conference on Knowledge Management and Information Sharing, Paris, France, October 26-29. SciTePress (2011)
2. Borchardt, U.: Towards Value-Driven Alignment of KMS for SME. In: Abramowicz, W., Maciaszek, L., Węcel, K. (eds.) BIS Workshops 2011 and BIS 2011. LNBIP, vol. 97, pp. 220–231. Springer, Heidelberg (2011)
3. CEN/ ISSS Knowledge Management Workshop: European Guide to good Practice in Knowledge Management: CWA 14924 (2004)
4. Delone, W., McLean, E.: The DeLone and McLean Model of Information Systems Success: A Ten-Year Update. J. Manage. Inf. Syst. 19, 9–30 (2003), http://portal.acm.org/citation.cfm?id=1289765.1289767

5. European Commission "Enterprise, Industry": The new SME definition: User guide and model declaration (2003), http://ec.europa.eu/enterprise/policies/sme/facts-figures-analysis/sme-definition
6. Feggeler, A., Lensing, W., Mühlbradt, T., Schieferdecker, R., Strothotte, M.: Wissensmanagement mit Bordmitteln. Wirtschaftsverlag Bachem, Köln (2007)
7. Statistics agency Germany: Enterpriseregistry (2007), www.regionalstatistik.de
8. Jennex, M.: Assessing knowledge management success/effectiveness models. In: 37th Hawaii International Conference on System Sciences, HICSS35. IEEE Computer Society (2004)
9. Lamieri, L., North, K.: Wissensmanagement in Klein- und Mittelbetrieben. Praxis Wissensmanagement (2001)
10. Legler, H., Frietsch, R.: Neuabgrenzung der Wissenswirtschaft - forschungsintensive Industrien und wissensintensive Dienstleistungen (NIWISI-Listen 2006). Fraunhofer ISI, Karlsruhe (2007)
11. Maier, R.: Knowledge Management Systems: Information and Communication Technologies for Knowledge Management, 3rd edn. Springer, Heidelberg (2007)
12. Institut für Mittelstandsforschung: The new SME definition: User guide and model declaration (2002), http://www.ifm-bonn.org/index.php?id=90
13. Nonaka, I., Takeuchi, H., Mader, F.: The Knowledge-Creating Company: How Japanese Companies Create the Dynamics of Innovation. Oxford University Press, Oxford (1995)
14. Probst, G., Raub, S., Romhardt, K.: Wissen managen: Wie Unternehmen ihre wertvollste Ressource optimal nutzen, 6th edn. Gabler Verlag, Wiesbaden (2010)
15. Salojärvi, S., Furu, P., Sveiby, K.: Knowledge management and growth in Finnish SMEs. Journal of Knowledge Management 9(2), 103–122 (2005)

Managing Change in Fractal Enterprises and IS Architectures from a Viable Systems Perspective

Paolo Piciocchi[1], Clara Bassano[2], Marite Kirikova[3],
Janis Makna[1], and Julija Stecjuka[3]

[1] Department of Political, Social and Communication Science, University of Salerno,
via Ponte don Melillo, Fisciano, Italy
p.piciocchi@unisa.it
[2] Business Studies Department, "Parthenope" University of Naples,
via Medina, 40, Naples, Italy
clara.bassano@uniparthenope.it
[3] Institute of Applied Computer Systems, Riga Technical University,
1 Kalku, Riga, LV-1658, Latvia
{marite.kirikova,julija.stecjuka}@cs.rtu.lv, promis@apollo.lv

Abstract. The paper aims to analyze the concept of viability in fractal enterprises and IS architectures from a holistic and viable systems perspective. The methodology is based on the conceptual framework of the Viable Systems Approach (VSA) whereby the monitoring of fractal enterprise viability is put in place thanks to the "abilities" of government to manage the operative structure efficiently and to govern the system strategically. In particular, by means of systems viability monitoring, fractal enterprises are governed in terms of structure (i.e. component and relational consonance) and system (interaction and performance resonance).

Keywords: Fractal enterprise, IS architectures, viable systems, systems viability monitoring, consonance & resonance.

1 Introduction

Our research, based on the concept of systems viability, examines the issue from a dual perspective: governance and stability; factors that characterize the viability of any system including fractal enterprises [1].

Our conviction is that the two key concepts of governance and stability for viability are closely related.

In particular, skilled governance ensures the survival of the system while stability derives from coordinating ability to ensure flexible (non rigid) conditions in inter-firm relationships.

Warneke [2] in "The Fractal Company: A Revolution in Corporate Culture" envisioned a new kind of flexible organizational structure for manufacturing - a fractal enterprise where each fractal is an independent corporate entity, the goals and performance of which can be delineated. A similar concept is also discussed in Hoverstad's "The Fractal Organization: Creating Sustainable Organizations with the

L. Niedrite, R. Strazdina, B. Wangler (Eds.): BIR 2011 Workshops, LNBIP 106, pp. 38–50, 2012.
© Springer-Verlag Berlin Heidelberg 2012

Viable System Model" [3]. In addition, in "The Viable Systems Approach (VSA)" in "Governing Business dynamics", Golinelli [4] introduces an innovative concept of flexibility in terms of the capacity of systems – as a result of government action - to promote and guide structural dynamics in harmony with the expectations and pressures deriving from their relevant supra systems, i.e., the ability to adjust to changing environmental needs.

Various definitions of flexibility exist; however, most of them focus on the ability to respond to external changes over an appropriate period of time, using a reasonable quantity of resources [2], [3], [5], [6]. Flexibility, however, still possesses some degree of stability seeing as whenever a part of the system is made flexible, some other part remains unchanged (stable) [5]. From the point of view of the fractal paradigm [2], [3] the stable portion is perceived as a pattern inside the system that is replicated on different scales. From the Viable Systems Approach (VSA) perspective, replication on different scales is intended in the sense of a "recurring/recursive process": in this respect, any kind of entity besides fractals can be considered a viable system i.e. self-sufficient organizations – capable of self survival – and at the same time, components of a suprasystem in consonance with systems at a higher level [7]. In other words, recursiveness means that each process activated by a system is incorporated into a wider process, originating in turn with/from interaction of other systems.

With reference to VSA in general, the paper, interprets fractal enterprises as viable and service systems that optimize information and resource flow and knowledge sharing in order to enhance efficiency and effectiveness. In particular, it examines methods and principles that underpin information systems (IS) architecture management in viable enterprises.

According to their dynamic viability processes, fractal enterprises need to be governed by means of an adequate monitoring mechanism of relational and interaction business dynamics (consonance and resonance).

Consequently, the paper develops a conceptual framework for the efficient and effective monitoring of fractal systems viability, in terms of the structure (i.e. component and relational consonance) and the system (i.e. interaction and performance resonance) by analyzing the concept of viability in fractal enterprises and IS architectures from a holistic and viable systems perspective.

According to Golinelli, in a context that favors the evolution of synergic relationships, fractal enterprises can develop and stabilize themselves over time as a viable system [4].

According to Arrow however, the failure or partial nonsuccess of systems often depends prevalently on the incapacity of government, in other words the ability of top management to share goals and to reduce the risk of opportunistic and antagonistic behavior in relationships (what Arrow calls the issue of moral hazard) [8].

Furthermore, the paper examines the effective management (or governance) of viability where the focus is on changes in the system to acquire best practices for propagating and leveraging (devising a new pattern of stability). Best practices emerge thanks to the existence of fractal structures, which succumb to different processes implemented by the various structural units to achieve the same organizational goal. The processes vie with one another until the superiority of one emerges and becomes visible. At that stage, a process common to all the structural units can be delineated and introduced to leverage the best practices in the enterprise in order to support its viability by changing its internal architecture. Specifically, the paper focuses on best practices that involve IS services and reflects on the changes in IS architecture that can commonly occur during the leveraging process in fractal businesses.

The paper is structured as follows. In Section 2 the conceptual framework of the VSA is introduced together with the concept of fractal processes, viable systems, and holistic service systems. Section 3 illustrates how fractal enterprises can achieve viability through efficacious viability monitoring and control processes. In section 4 a change in the method of management/governance is delineated in an attempt to concretize theoretical concepts. Section 5 sums up and outlines brief conclusions.

2   Methodological Approach: An Analysis of Fractal Processes, Viable Systems, and Holistic Service Systems from an Integrative Perspective

Methodologically, the term fractal has to be re-read in a viable systems perspective in terms of re-evaluation that enhances relational contexts, on the basis of their nature of complex systems. This implies the efficient monitoring of both structure (adequacy of the components and relations) and system (performance).

Through the systems concept, an organization can determine effects and performance not attributable to single businesses or to the concept of networked firms; in effect, the relational aspect is a necessary but not sufficient condition for the viability of a complex system.

In particular, fractal processes have to be analyzed as a system for "governed interaction" by means of governance enjoying a position of prominence, based on two variables [1]: power – capacity to "direct" and "transmit" relations within the network – and prestige, – legitimacy and recognition on the part of the related nodes within the system. The "star" position has to be interpreted and seen in terms of government and management of flows of resources, information and the coordination of operational processes.

The structural configuration of systems affects conditions of governance and stability throughout the network. If a viable system is accomplished, then government can and has to monitor conditions of viability and check operational efficiency.

In other words, management in fractal enterprises reflects governance that is strongly geared towards system control (system resonance) and operative control (structural consonance). In fractal processes in other words, the power of government and control is seen not as domain over components but rather as the capacity to manage complex systems as a whole.

The need to introduce control and coordination in business systems mechanisms to deal with opportunistic attitudes on the part of the contracting parties should also be taken into account.

In most business systems such as networks, organizational problems concern the qualification of coordinated measures that aim for partner equifinality. In this sense, two dimensions of the issue emerge:

- co-ordination (shared governance);
- cooperation (consonance and resonance).

Both are fundamental to achieving network synergy taking into account potential relational inefficiencies that can generate conflicts and/or ignite crises (distractions) with respect to the entire system. In particular, the coordination dimension demands adequate government to ensure that the system survives both in the context and in the network itself; the cooperation dimension relates, on the contrary, to the conditions of efficiency and effectiveness of processes and therefore to optimizing shared business.

The purpose of the paper in particular, concerns the aspects related to the coordination dimension with reference to the modalities of system interaction for viability in complex systems: government has to manage the flows of operational information – conflicts and adjustments within the context, to avoid affecting current and future system viability.

The role of coordination represents a critical element of the optimization process of business and research efficiency. In fact, collaboration and sharing – strategic and operative – enable the nodes in the network to achieve partial and individual objectives through synergies produced in the pursuit of overall system performance: in short, coordination requires the creation of an adequate and effective monitoring system and control process.

In such a logic, a system of monitoring of viability [9] in fractal enterprises is proposed that is capable of ensuring   effective and efficient system control (performance and legitimacy) and structural control (adequacy and operative means). But the question is, how can a viable system be identified in order to qualify the viability of a fractal enterprise?

System viability depends on the ability of government to map the different entities of the context to implement differentiation (degree of fulfillment of systems process) [10].

From a VSA perspective, fractal enterprises become viable systems when they satisfy five principles – postulates – the validity of which is not inferred, but posited a priori in order to explain various phenomena or theories [11]: (1) Survival: a viable fractal has the aim of surviving in a specific context; (2) Eidos: from an ontological viewpoint, a viable fractal can be considered from a structural and systemic perspective; (3) Isotropy: in terms of behavior, a viable fractal distinguishes between a decision making area and an operative area; (4) Interaction: in order to reach a goal, an objective achieved through the interaction of supra and/or subsystems from which to receive, but also to supply, indications and rules; finally, (5) Extensiveness: external entities are also viable fractals, components deriving from a higher level.

VSA studies the viability of systems in complex environments. In other words, viability is both objective survival and subjective ability to respond to environmental change, where environmental change is mostly generated by other viable systems (even those belonging to the same fractal). Viability depends first and foremost on a capacity for government; both internal self governance and external relationship governance that creates value for the stakeholders or suprasystems. Each system has to achieve consonance (a potential for value creation) and resonance (the realization of value creation) with its environment in order to be viable. The innovative concepts of consonance and resonance are fundamental to all VSA analyses of problematic issues. Consonance is the structural compatibility or adequacy involving diverse entities, while resonance is the outcome of the interaction between such consonant entities.

The axiomatic interpretation illustrated above can also be enriched by IBM's theoretical approach – Service Science Management Engineering and Design (SSME+D) – [12] if fractals are considered in terms of self-organizational services or as components of complete service systems. The SSME+D framework starts with an analysis of service systems in a real-world problematic situation. In broader terms, the SSME+D analysis approach (1) identifies all the stakeholder service system entities – including fractals – in a network being studied (a network analysis is always done in the context of the entire service system ecology), (2) examines existing relations in order to consider the problems and opportunities the stakeholders have identified, (3) improves existing value co-creation mechanisms (e.g. by freeing up and redistributing resources from existing service system entities (4) in the event of additional problems and opportunities, creates new service system fractals to address them.

SSME+D is a specialist segment of Systems Science in which fractal service entities interact and create outcomes. VSA and SSME+D perspectives interpret fractals as Holistic Service Systems (HSS) and Whole Service (WS) to better illustrate one way in which optimization on a local scale can lead to global optimization in complex human systems. The architecture of a fractal enterprise [2], [3], [13], [14], [15], [16], [17], [18] consists of self-similar, self optimizing, goal-oriented fractals (independently acting corporate entities), which perform services, are the object of constant change (dynamic restructuring) and are integrated into the goal-formation process. In specific settings it is possible to identify fractal processes [19]. Such processes reflect similar features to those of the constituents of fractal enterprises [19]:

- Self-similarity: fractal processes have similar inputs and outputs, but each fractal may have its own unique inner structure [2]. Thus, in fractal processes, system self-similarity is manifested when processes on different scales have common objectives and similar input and output. The scale in the fractal process system is represented by process destructuring. Fractal process entities simultaneously, possess two essential relational elements (1) they are both part-of a relationship and (2) a (category) of relationship; i.e. each process which is a subprocess of a specific process is at the same time, a process of the same type as the process of which it is part. In an educational institution, for instance the University (see further in the text), research administration processes are in place: research administration processes take place at University level, at Faculty level (Faculty in the sense of a large Department comprising Institutes performing research and administrative duties), at Institute level and at specific Department level. Research administration processes at University level includes research administration at Faculty level, which in turn includes research administration at Institute level, which in turn, includes research administration at Departmental level. Several of these research activities, e.g. preparation of reports could be similar at all levels.
- Self-organization: ability to adopt process behavior and interaction mechanisms with others fractals for achieving a system's common objective [2]. Fractal processes boast suitable methods for controlling workflows and for optimizing the composition/structuring of processes in the system. The self-organization

method, referred to as a dynamic restructuring process, is a method of reorganizing fractals in the system by reconfiguring fractal network connections [14].

- Goal-orientation: each fractal (process) has its own specific goal. Fractals exploit a goal-formation process to generate their own goals by coordinating processes with participating fractals and by modifying goals as necessary. A system's common objectives are achieved in an iterative way, by developing each single fractal's specific objectives, taking into account feedback.
- Dynamics and viability: coordination and cooperation processes among self-organization fractals are characterized by individual dynamics and the ability to adapt to dynamic environments. IS plays a vital role in achieving this property of fractal business processes.

Clearly, one of the essential features of fractal processes is the possibility of carrying out different processes in parallel in order to achieve one and the same goal. This could contradict with the notion of process optimization; however, such parallelism in specific situations allows for greater flexibility. Universities for instance, in situations differing in terms of local external environments (e. g. the Institute of Mechanics with an emphasis on patents and the Institute of Economics with an emphasis on indexed journal papers) demand slightly different data gathering approaches. The possibility of running similar parallel processes also encourages the emerging of process best practices as is evident in Section 4.

While viability is a desirable feature of enterprise and IS, a lack of practical approaches for applying theoretical principles in enterprises is still evident. VSA, proposed as a conceptual framework for the monitoring of viability in fractal enterprises, would ensure efficient monitoring of structure (adequacy of the components and relations) and system (performance). Additionally, specific methods, applicable from a VSA perspective, are suggested for managing change in processes and IS architecture in the event of best practices in a fractal enterprise where fractal business processes can be identified. The University as a fractal enterprise is used to illustrate the proposed methods. The University model is an appropriate example since it satisfies all five VSA principles set out above.

3 Systems Viability Monitoring in Fractal Enterprises and IS Architectures from a Viable Systems Perspective

Viability has to be expressed in terms of coordination and cooperation. In particular, *coordination* requires the adequacy (and adaptability) of the government to ensure survival conditions. *Cooperation* relates instead, to the efficiency and efficacy of the process. In other words, the management of fractal enterprises is reflected in governance that is geared towards both system control (system resonance) and operative control (structural consonance) [9].

In our conceptual framework (Fig. 1) three functions of the organization as a viable system are represented as ITO (Input, Transformation and Output).

In particular, the first function is input of resources (for example: energy, raw materials and information) (I).

The second is transformation to enhance the value of the resources (T) developing a function of input.

The third function is that of output of resources (O).

However, another fundamental function has to be considered: EQUILIBRIUM. To achieve equilibrium, a system of viability monitoring [9] is used.

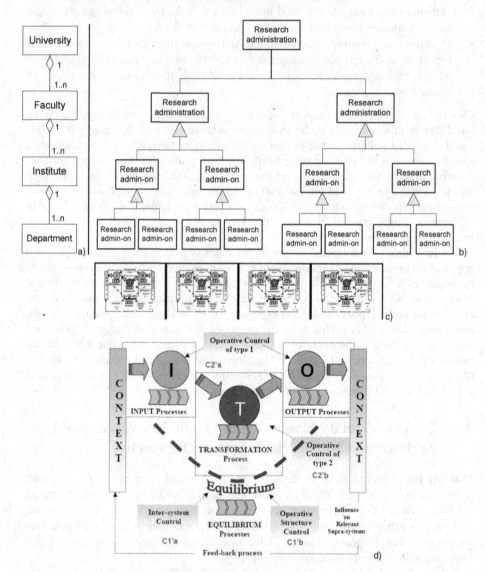

Fig. 1. Viability monitoring in fractal enterprises; a) levels of fractals; b) fractal structure – the University model; c) the viability of each fractal, d) conceptual model adapted from [9]

The system is characterized by two levels of control: system control and structure control. Each level of control is sub-divided into two levels of control:

- system control guarantees the governance of fractals in the context;
- structure control guarantees the stability of the network structure.

In particular, system control is made up of inter-system control (C1'a) and operative structure control (C1'b).

The former verifies coordination procedures for achieving consonance with the supra-systems. The latter controls the operational flows among the parties involved.

However, it should be kept in mind that structure control also includes two sub levels: operative control (type 1) as illustrated by C2'a and operative control (type 2) indicated by C2'b. The former verifies the efficacy of cooperation among the parties involved. The latter controls the technical and productive efficiency of the network structure.

When changes are made in the viable system, it should be ensured that system viability is not hindered by changes in the system and structure. To this aim, IS change management patterns [20] delineated in Table 1are adapted.

Table 1. Change patterns for viability monitoring (adapted [20])

IS and business process element	Corresponding viability issues	Pattern 1 Internal improvement	Pattern 2 Improvements based on handed over activities	Pattern 3 Improvements based of received activities
BP activities	T	Improved	Handed over	Received
Data	I, O	New or Improved	Received	Handed over
Knowledge	I, O	New	Handed over	Received
IS users		No change	New	Moved
IS activities	T	Extended	Suspended or Handed over	Received
Control	C1a, C2a	Improved	Improved	Improved
Territory	C1a, C2a	No change	Handed over	Received
Resources	C1b, C2b	Cheaper or Different	Cheaper	More expensive
Products	I, O	Improved	Improved	Improved

Pattern 1 refers to internal changes in the fractal entity not affecting other entities. Pattern 2 can be applied to situations where tasks of one fractal are delegated to other fractals. Pattern 3 refers to situations where fractals enlarge the realm of their responsibility. Correspondence between change elements (Column 1) and viability issues is shown in Column 2.

4   Changing the Business Process and IS

How business processes might be changed in the setting of fractal University business processes, i.e., when processes are self-similar, self-organized, goal-adaptive, and structurally dynamic is a relevant issue. Change procedures are illustrated in the following example.

Each year Universities prepare mandatory reports on their scientific activities. This is achieved by delegating the mandate "Prepare Report" from University level fractal via Institute fractals down to Department level fractals. Departments are free to achieve this goal in the way that suits them best. Departments send information to the higher level fractal process to compile the Institute level annual Report on scientific activities, using the template introduced at Institute level.

For instance, let's suppose that Department 1 has more staff than other Departments and the capacity to develop a business process support system for the acquisition and maintenance of information on scientific activities. The use of the system allows the Department to accomplish the process much more efficiently compared to other Departments. This attracts the interest of a second Department which considers the possibility of implementing the practices of Department 1. To achieve this, Department 2 has to manage the change from the AS IS process to the TO BE process which can be equated to the process performed by Department 1. This involves a change in the information and knowledge processing systems of Department 1 and Department 2. At this stage, it is irrelevant how the best practice was developed – whether it was the result of "Innovating" or the result of "Running" (See section 2). In any case Department 2 learns from Department 1 and transforms/copies its processes and supporting IS services. It is essential that at this point, supra fractals are not involved in decision-making processes; it is Department 2's responsibility to acquire best practices on its own initiative from Department 1. The transfer of best practices require at least four steps: (1) Best practice identification; (2) Best practice acquisition planning; (3) Best practice acquisition cost estimation; and (4) Best practice acquisition.

Best practice identification in a fractal setting where several parallel ways of process organization are tolerated, can be informal, i.e. the situation can arise where one way of performing a particular task is acknowledged as worthy of imitation by several structural units. When best practices are identified it is advisable to plan for their acquisition. This involves analysis of AS IS and TO BE business processes (Step 2). Best practice acquisition planning involves the following sub-steps: (2.1) Changing the granularity of process description; (2.2) Identifying activities to be changed; and (2.3) Changing process risk analysis.

To identify actual changes in business processes we suggest specific tables [18] used for task analysis consisting of columns of performer activities, marked for both AS IS and TO BE cases. The Change Analysis Table for Department 2 secretary's duties is represented in Table 2.

Table 2. Business Process Change Analysis Table: Department 2 secretary's duties

AS IS	Department 2 secretary: tasks description	TO BE
+	Receive the template (7)	
+	Create the list of employees to whom to send the template (7)	+
+	Send the template (7)	
+	Determine who has not sent back the filled template (9)	
+	Send filled template to Institute 1 responsible executive (12)	
+	Make sure the template is sent (12)	
+	Find out who is not available (business trip, conference, vacations) (7)	+

The sign "+" denotes a completed task, the sign "–/+" denotes a partly performed task because another part of it is performed by IS or other business processes and an empty TO BE cell means that the task is fully performed by another business process or computer system.

Business process changes may considerably influence responsibilities, knowledge/information patterns, and business process performer tasks [19], [21], [22], [23], [24]. Therefore multiple aspects have to be analyzed to assess the risks of best practice acquisition. Taking into consideration that the changes in the processes depend on the changes in IS, risk analysis is based on IS change management patterns [20] illustrated in Table 1. Risk analysis concerns each activity to be changed due to best practice acquisition. The patterns given in Table 1 are used as guidelines for risk analysis points. The pattern for changed activities is chosen depending on whether the activities are handed over (Pattern 3), acquired (Pattern 2), or changed internally (Pattern 1). Table 3 shows how Pattern 2 is used for the assessment of risks related to activities handed over by Department 2's secretary.

Table 3. Risk analysis issues for tasks handed over by Department 2's secretary (excerpt)

Change element	Mandatory considerations	Sources of risks
BP activities	Handed over	It is essential to analyze all activities the secretary is going to hand over at an appropriate level of granularity. The frequency of tasks can vary, therefore it might be cumbersome to take into account all tasks in one go. On the other hand, it is essential to ensure that all activities handed over are received by everyone and the systems to which they are handed over.. At the same time, capacity for performing said activities should be ascertained and ensured.
Data	Received	The secretary receives data on the scientific activities of staff, - therefore IS activities to represent such data should be implemented.
Knowledge	Handed over	All staff need knowledge for performing activities handed over to them by the secretary. If all activities are not handed over in one go – knowledge should also be transferred periodically. Knowledge transfer should be properly organized, because it might happen that the secretary is not able to transfer all required knowledge to a large number of employees simultaneously. It is necessary to take into consideration that additional individual smaller scale knowledge transfers will be needed over the period of time during which the new working methods are gradually adopted.
...	...	...

After risk assessment, business process change cost estimation is to be performed, taking into consideration tasks with "+" in the Business process change analysis table and the issues revealed in risk analysis. Following this sub-step final decisions on best practice acquisition can be made. To date, best business processes practices acquisition at one fractal level has been discussed. However, it is possible to leverage practices and apply them on a higher fractal levels. This is illustrated in Fig. 2.

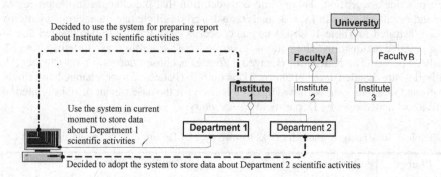

Fig. 2. Leveraging the best practices

Leveraging of best practices requires business process design on a higher level of fractal hierarchy. It concerns mainly IS services, because the difference between two similar information systems services on the lower level of hierarchy and one service on a higher level of hierarchy does not considerably change manual processes at the lower level of hierarchy. Thus the SMEE+D approach can be used to decide whether (or otherwise) to leverage Department 1 best practice at Institute level.

In this case, best business practices leveraging involves the change of responsibility for IS services. Instead of having three separate IS services it is possible to operate with only one Institute 1 level service. IS service has to be changed for the leveraged process in order to accommodate two or more Departments instead of one department. In case of fractal business processes this is mainly a matter of scale rather than complex IS change endeavor due to the similarity of activities at different levels of scale of the administrative hierarchy.

5   Conclusions

The analysis leads to the definition of a complex system in which the management of viability in fractal enterprises is based on a system of relationships needing organizational design, the development of a strong structural consonance among the components and resonance in system aims and objectives.

As regards the conceptual framework adopted, the paper aims to highlight the crucial role of systems viability monitoring for fractal enterprises capable of ensuring effective and efficient system control (performance and legitimacy) and structural control (adequacy of operative means).

In particular, in this paper we illustrate that in enterprises with fractal processes the VSA approach to business process and IS development is applicable [23] and enables incremental bottom-up changes in enterprise processes and supporting IS services. The approach reflects the systems development process that is in line with viable systems theory, where common processes are gradually delegated to higher fractal levels of the system for the sake of higher functional efficiency of the system [25]. Gradual bottom-up delegating promotes emergence of best practices, deliberate propagation of these practices at a particular level of scale that may lead naturally to the design of new processes and services at a higher level of hierarchy. This is decided at higher levels of fractal hierarchy. Fractals as holistic service systems integrated within a whole service perspective can be represented in terms of multilevel governance and component interaction.

Specifically, with reference to VSA, the paper represents our first attempt to interpret fractal enterprises as viable and holistic service systems useful for optimizing information and resource flow and for knowledge sharing to enhance efficiency and effectiveness. In addition the paper suggests specific business process analyses and risk assessment methods useful in a VSA setting. Obviously there are some limits to our study. First of all, the study is merely descriptive, not being based on empirical research. However, in future we intend to examine empirically the efficacy of the monitoring model for achieving flexibility in business processes i.e. the propagating of bottom-up business process best practices and leveraging these practices at higher organizational levels by means of appropriate information system design.

In particular, coordination and monitoring mechanisms will play a crucial role in achieving the stability and success of a modular business by reducing relational uncertainty, increasing synergies through efficiency (consonance) and effectiveness (resonance) and by defining an "area of concordance" in the fractal processes.

References

1. Piciocchi, P., Bassano, C.: Governance and Viability of Franchising Networks from a Viable Systems Approach (VSA). In: 2009 Naples Forum on Service: Service-Dominant Logic, Service Science, and Network Theory, Capri, Italy, Giannini Editore, Napoli (2009)
2. Warneke, H.J.: The Fractal Company: A Revolution in Corporate Culture. Springer, Heidelberg (1993)
3. Hoverstadt, P.: The Fractal Organization: Creating Sustainable Organizations with the Viable System Model. Wiley (2008)
4. Golinelli, G.M.: The Viable Systems Approach (VSA). In: Governing Business Dynamics. Kluwer, Padova (2010)
5. Regev G., Wegmann A.: Business Process Flexibility: Weick's Organizational Theory to the Rescue (2006),
   http://lamswww.epfl.ch/conference/bpmds06/program/
6. Daoudi, F., Nurcan, S.: A Benchmarking Framework for Methods to Design Flexible Business Processes. In: Software Process Improvement and Practice. Wiley & Sons (2006)
7. Spohrer, J., Golinelli, G.M., Picocchi, P., Bassano, C.: An Integrated SS-VSA Analysis of Changing Jobs. Service Science 2(1/2), 1–20 (2010)

8. Arrow, K.J.: Rationality of Self and Others in an Economic System. In: Hogarth, R.M., Reader, M.W. (eds.) Rational Choice. The University of Chicago Press, Chicago (1987)
9. Piciocchi, P.: Crisi d'impresa e monitoraggio di vitalità. L'approccio sistemico vitale per l'analisi dei processi di crisi, Collana del Dipartimento di Studi e Ricerche Aziendali – Università degli Studi di Salerno, Giappichelli (17) (2003)
10. Piciocchi, P., Bassano, C., Paduano, E., Galvin, M.: The Viable Systems Approach (VSA) for Re-interpreting Network Business Dynamics. In: Grabis, J., Kirikova, M. (eds.) BIR 2011. LNBIP, vol. 90, pp. 304–320. Springer, Heidelberg (2011)
11. Barile, S., Calabrese, M.: A New Frontier in Consulting: the VSA Consulcube, Contributions to Theoretical and Practical Advances in Management. In: A Viable Systems Approach, pp. 245–262 (2011)
12. Spohrer, J., Maglio, P.: The Emergence of Service Science: Toward Systematic Service Innovations to Accelerate Co-Creation of Value. Production and Operations Management 17(3), 238–246 (2008)
13. Canavesio, M. M., Martinez, E.: Enterprise Modeling of a Project-Oriented Fractal Company for SMEs Networking. Computers in Industry (2007), http://www.sciencedirect.com
14. Fryer, P., Ruis, J.: What are Fractal Systems: A Brief Description of Complex Adaptive and Emerging Systems (2006), http://www.fractal.org
15. Hongzhao, D., Dongxu, L., Yanwei, Z., Chen, Y.: A Novel Approach of Networked Manufacturing Collaboration: Fractal Web Based Enterprise. Int. J. on Advanced Manufacturing Technology 26, 1436–1442 (2005)
16. Ramanathan, Y.: Fractal Architecture for the Adaptive Complex Enterprise. Communications of ACM 48(5), 51–67 (2005)
17. Ryu, K., Jung, M.: Fractal Approach to Managing Intelligent Enterprises. In: Gupta, J.N.D., Sharma, S.K. (eds.) Creating Knowledge Based Organisations, pp. 312–348. Idea Group Publishers (2003)
18. Sihn, W.: Re-engineeringthrough Fractal Structures. In: IFIPWG5.7 Working Conference Reengineering the Enterprise, pp. 21–30 (1995)
19. Stecjuka, J., Kirikova, M.: The Process-Oriented Fractal Information System Development Method. In: 14th International Conference on Information and Software Technologies, pp. 171–181. Kaunas University of Technology (2008)
20. Makna, J., Kirikova, M.: Pattern-Based IS Change Management in SMEs. Information Systems Development. Part 1, pp. 55–56. Springer, Heidelberg (2011)
21. Schaad, A., Moffett, J.: Separation, Review and Supervision Controls in the Context of a Credit Application Process: Case Study of Organisational Control Principles. In: 2004 ACM Symposium on Applied Computing, pp. 1380–1384. ACM, New York (2004)
22. Tripathi, U.K., Hinkelmann, K.: Change Management in Semantic Business Processes Modeling. In: 8th International Symposium on Autonomous Decentralized Systems, pp. 155–162. IEEE Computer Society, Washington (2007)
23. Rinderle, S., Kreher, U., Lauer, M., Dadam, P., Reichert, M.: On Representing Instance Changes in Adaptive Process Management Systems. In: 15th IEEE International Workshops on Enabling Technologies: Infrastructure for Collaborative Enterprises, pp. 297–304. IEEE Computer Society, Washington (2006)
24. Kim, D., Kim, M., Kim, H.: Dynamic Business Process Management based on Process Change Patterns. In: International Conference on Convergence Information Technology 2007, pp. 1154–1161 (2007)
25. Cottam, R., Ranson, W., Vounckx, R.: Life and Simple Systems. Systems Research and Behavioral Science 22(5), 413–430 (2005)

An Extended RBAC Model for Task Delegation in Workflow Systems

Khaled Gaaloul[1], Erik Proper[1,2], and François Charoy[3]

[1] Public Research Centre Henri Tudor,
L-1855 Luxembourg-Kirchberg, Luxembourg
[2] Radboud University Nijmegen
P.O. BOX 9010 6500, GL Nijmegen, The Netherlands
[3] LORIA, Université de Lorraine
BP 239, F-54506 Vandœuvre-lès-Nancy Cedex, France
{khaled.gaaloul,erik.proper}@tudor.lu, charoy@loria.fr

Abstract. In role-based access control models, delegation of authority involves delegating roles that a user can assume or the set of permissions that he can acquire, to other users. Several role-based delegation models have been proposed in the literature. However, these models consider only delegation in presence of the role type, which have some inherent limitations to *task delegation* in workflow systems. In this paper, we address task delegation in a workflow and elaborate a security model supporting delegation constraints. Delegation constraints express security requirements with regards to task's resources, user's assignment and *privileges* (delegation of authority). Further, we show how, using a role-based security model, we inject formalised delegation constraints to compute principals and privileges to be specified into delegation policies within an access control framework.

Keywords: Workflow, access control, delegation, constraints, privileges, authorisation policy.

1 Introduction

With the broad adoption of workflow management systems to model and automate business processes cross organisations, security becomes a crucial and essential topic. Typically, activities that are part of a process are represented as tasks. Organisations establish a set of authorisation policies that regulate how business processes and resources should be managed within a workflow [1]. Authorisation information is given which authorises users to perform tasks. Such authorisation information may be specified using a simple access control list or more complex role-based structures [2].

In current workflow management systems, the role-based access control (RBAC) model is widely adopted, where system administrators assign roles to users. It is more convenient for administrators to manage roles than to manage users

L. Niedrite, R. Strazdina, B. Wangler (Eds.): BIR 2011 Workshops, LNBIP 106, pp. 51–63, 2012.
© Springer-Verlag Berlin Heidelberg 2012

directly [3]. One important factor that affects access control (authorisation) distribution among users is delegation. Delegation involves a user passing its authority to other users. If delegation is allowed, a delegator delegates authority (a privilege) to another active entity, called the delegatee, to carry out a task on behalf of the former. In the context of workflow systems, delegation can be very useful for real-world situations where a user who has to perform a task is either unavailable or too overloaded [4]. Hence, we define task delegation as a means for assigning a task and its access rights from a delegator to a delegatee.

The concept of delegation has been presented in [1,5]. Significant contributions to role-based delegation can be found in [6,7]. While much of the work in the area of delegation is limited to role-based access control, the goal of our paper is to consider task delegation constraints in workflow systems. Delegation constraints needs to tackle several issues with regards to workflow's invariants in terms of users, tasks and resources. In doing so, we need to come up with an access control model supporting the assignment of task delegation. Delegation assignment deals with delegation principals (delegator, delegatee) their respective rights (privileges) and their availability (no conflicts during task assignment). In this paper, we extend the RBAC model of Sandhu et al. [3] in two directions: (i) our formal security model defines a *Task-oriented Access Control (TAC)* model which is capable of supporting task assignment condition in workflows and (ii) we leverage TAC specifications to inject delegation constraints, thereby computing potential delegatees and their required privileges, thereby specifying them in terms of delegation policies.

The remainder of this article is organised as follows. Section 2 presents fundamental concepts of the organisational management in workflows. Section 3 defines workflow authorisation constraints during task execution. In section 4, we present a formal security model to reason about task assignment within a workflow. This model is used to integrate delegation constraints in order to compute delegatees with their respective privileges and to specify delegation policies in section 5. Section 6 presents related work. Finally, we conclude and discuss future work.

2 Background

In this section, we aim to give an overview of the organisational aspect to support human and material resources specifications in the context of workflow management systems. The aforementioned resources will play an important role to define task delegation constraints and its security requirements in Sect. 4.

2.1 Resource Management in Workflows

A workflow is made of tasks, where a task defines a unit of work that at each invocation performs the binding between different resources needed to complete a specific part of the workflow [8]. The resources that may be involved are different. We distinguish material and human resources for business objects and workflow's actors, respectively. Generally, the manipulation of material resources is interfaced by one or several entities called applications or services.

A resource model contains the definition of human and material resources that are involved in the execution of a workflow model. While the resource model is a structured representation of organisational entities, it should be noted that both this model as well as the elements contained therein follow a life cycle and change over time. Therefore, a workflow management system not only needs to provide a mechanism to represent the organisational elements involved in the execution of workflows, but it also needs to provide mechanisms for continuous change within these elements [9]. Our change scope in this paper deals with task delegation.

2.2 Organisational Resources Analysis

During the design time, the workflow application designer has to design both the structure of the business process to be automated, and the structure of the resources that carry out the process. Resources and workflow's tasks are linked through the construct role [10]. From a process perspective, a role is a subject to authorisations that define permissions (operations) for the execution of a task. From a resource perspective, a role represents a granted authorisation for a workflow actor (so-called user). Based on these two perspectives, the design of the resource model can follow two different directions namely the material and human resources. Material resources define business objects and the way to use them. Human resources define the actors of the workflow.

From a material resource perspective, we define permissions as functions with operations to manipulate business objects. From a human resource perspective, we define a subject as an assigned user who is member of a role to claim a task instance. The task execution is added to the subject's worklist. A worklist defines the set of task instances claimed by this subject. The access to resources will be dependent on the execution model of the task. Figure 1 shows a meta model for a task-based organisational structures, which analyses the possible ways the resources access can be defined during the task execution. Figure 1 includes a white and a blue blocks. Each block defines a set of concepts and their relationships when executing a task within a workflow. The white block represents the material resource to carry out a task, and the blue block defines how a human resource (an actor) is managed to execute a task. This distinction will help us to specify our task-oriented access control model (see Sect. 4).

In figure 1, we define a task as a set of applications or services that are accessed by subjects via specific functions. These applications consist of functions that manipulate business objects. From one task several task instances can be generated. Note that we distinguish task type element from task since we assume that a task represents an instantiation of a task type during execution, equally for business objects. A task instance corresponds to an actual execution of a task. This specific execution of the task (a task instance) is allocated to only one subject through its unique worklist, where a subject defines a user selecting a role during runtime.

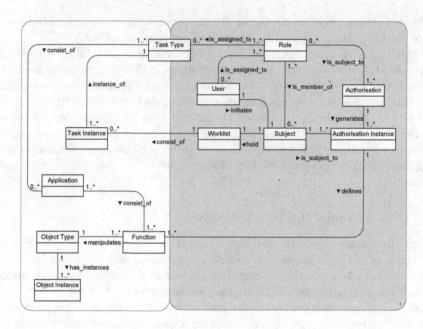

Fig. 1. A model for task-based organisational structures

We aim to address issues related to the organisational management in work-flow systems with regards to user's assignments, task's definition and resource's access. We mainly focus on both material and human resources to analyse task's requirements. We can identify from our analysis the main relationships between tasks, roles and resources.

– The set of *Tasks*, *Applications*, *Objects* and *Functions* defines the material requirements that are necessary to carry out a task.
– The set of *Roles* assigned to a task. A role inherits permissions based on the defined authorisation from an access control model.
– The set of *Authorisations* defines the condition of assignment that a role must have as permissions to execute a task, where a permission defines which action/function to perform over a business object of a task.
– The set of *Subjects*, *Worklists*, *Task Instances* and *Authorisation Instances* defines the task assignment condition.

Authorisation constraints need to be specified under access control models and expressed in terms of authorisation policies that regulate business processes and resources within a workflow [1]. In the rest of this paper, we explain how such constraints are specified and expressed in an extended role-based access control model supporting task delegation.

3   Workflow Authorisation Constraints

A workflow comprises various activities that are involved in a business process. Activities that are part of a process are represented as tasks [11]. Authorisation information is given which authorises users to perform tasks. Such authorisation information may be specified using a simple access control list or more complex role-based structures [12].

A task instance is created and then assigned to a user. The assigned user can start or delegate the task which gathers all operations and rights over the business objects related to task's resources (see Fig. 1). Seeing a task as a block that needs protection against undesired accesses, access control will depend on the specified authorisation information.

We define a permission as an authorisation allowing a user to perform a task. Authorisation makes an explicit binding between a user, a task resource (business object) and his rights over it (function/action). In our work, we define a task oriented access control model based on the RBAC model. We focus on task's requirements to analyse and specify security constraints while accessing workflow's data. Data access defines permissions on business objects related to task's resources.

4   Task-Oriented Access Control Model

We propose a *Task-oriented Access Control (TAC)* model to support authorisation requirements in workflow systems (see Fig. 2). Authorisation information will be inferred from access control data structures, such as user-role assignment (URA) and task-role assignment (TRA) relations. In addition, we model permission assignment relations for tasks and roles in order to support the task execution context. The remaining relations are generic relations based on the RBAC model [3].

Formally, we define sets U, R, OU, T, P, S and TI as a set of users, roles, organisations units, tasks, permissions, subjects and task instances, respectively. We use a subject to denote the time a user selects roles for a session. During the task instantiation assignment, we create a user's current active role set and define it as a subject (see Fig. 2). For example, the user *Alice* with the role *clerk* defines a subject to execute the instance of a task 'Check credit' in a bank loan process.

We define RH (Role Hierarchy), where RH is a partial order on R, r_i and $r_j \in R$. RH denotes that r_i is a role superior to r_j, as a result, r_i automatically inherits the permissions of r_j.

We define RM (Role Mapping), where $RM \subseteq OU_i \times OU_j$ with OU_i and OU_j two organisations units. RM defines external roles accessing distributed resources cross-organisations. It provides a decentralised access control mechanism where externally known roles are publicly available:
$r_k \in OU_i$ and $r_l \in OU_j$, RM denotes that r_l is a role mapped to r_k, as a result, r_l shares the permissions of r_k.

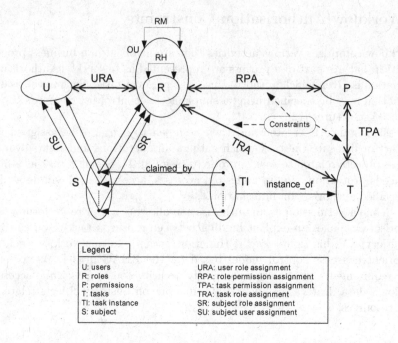

Fig. 2. Task-oriented access control (TAC) model

4.1 Definitions of Map Relations

Formally, we define a set of relations as follows:

- $URA \subseteq U \times R$, the user role assignment relation mapping users to roles they are member of.
- $RPA \subseteq R \times P$, the permission role assignment relation mapping roles to permissions they are authorised to.
- $TPA \subseteq T \times P$, the task permission assignment relation mapping tasks to permissions. This defines the set of permission required to execute a task (see Definition 2).
- $TRA \subseteq T \times R$ the task role assignment relation mapping roles to tasks they are assigned to.

4.2 Definitions of Functions

Formally, we define a set of functions as follows:

- $SU: S \to U$ a function mapping a subject to the corresponding user.
- $SR: S \to R$, a function mapping each subject to a role, where $SR(s) = r, (SU(s), r) \in URA\}$ with a subject s having a permission $p|(r, p) \in RPA\}$.
- $instance_{of}: TI \to T$, a function mapping a task instance to its task type.

– $claimed_{by}: TI \rightarrow S$, a function mapping a task instance to a subject to execute it. It defines the user-task assignment condition s = $claimed_{by}(t_{i1})$ where :
$\{t_i = instance_{of}(t_{i1}), (r, u) \in URA | (SR(s) = r \bigwedge SU(s) = u), (t_i, r) \in TRA\}$.

4.3   Definitions of Constraints

Here we discuss Separation of duty (SoD) and Binding of duty (BoD) constraints. It defines security constraints between two tasks that compose a business process [13]. Such constraints help to verify whether a user is not allowed to execute a task due to some conflicts (e.g., conflict of interest). We define an exclusive relation between tasks for SoD, and a binding relation between tasks for BoD :

$$TT_{SOD} : \{(t_i, t_j) \in T \times T \mid t_i \ is \ exclusive \ with \ t_j\}$$

$$TT_{BOD} : \{(t_i, t_j) \in T \times T \mid t_i \ is \ binding \ with \ t_j\}$$

If $(t_i, t_j) \in TT_{SOD}$, then t_i and t_j cannot be assigned to the same user. If $(t_i, t_j) \in TT_{BOD}$, then t_i and t_j must be assigned to the same user which defines a binding relation between two tasks.

4.4   Model Contributions

The main contribution of the TAC model is to specify the task assignment relation where two conditions have to be verified: (1) the first condition is related to task's resources requirements. The role's permissions defined in RPA (role-permission assignment) needs to satisfy the permissions defined in TPA (task-permission assignment). (2) the task is executed if and only if the user/role is assigned to it. Basically, having a permission to execute a task but not being assigned to it will not satisfy the outlined conditions and, therefore, will deny the access to its resources.

Definition 1 (Task Assignment). *A task instance t_i is assigned to a user u with an active subject s if and only if :*
$(t, r) \in TRA \Rightarrow \{p \in P | (t, p) \in TPA\} \subseteq \{p | (r, p) \in RPA\} \bigwedge claimed_{by}(t_i) = s$, *where $(SR(s) = r \bigwedge SU(s) = u)$.*

The user-task assignment requires the $claimed_{by}$ function. For instance, a task t_i is assigned a set of permissions based on the TPA relation in order to carry out this task. A user u_1 with a role r_j is assigned to t_i if and only if u_1 verifies the TRA and $claimed_{by}$ conditions. However, if we consider another user u_2 member of same role r_j having the same permissions based on the RPA relation but u_2 is not defined in $claimed_{by}(t_i)$, which means not assigned to this task. In this case, u_2 is not allowed to execute t_i since he does not fulfil the user-task assignment relation (see condition 2).

In the banking process example, let user *Bob* a member of role *Clerk* but not from the same bank agency. Bob is not allowed to perform the task 'Check credit' since he is not assigned by the system to execute it. Within organisations, users can share different roles but are not assigned to the same tasks. This is due to privacy and security constraints such as the separation of duty. Therefore, we leverage condition 2 as an additional constraint when claiming a task instance by a user.

5   Securing Task Delegation

In this section, we leverage the user-task assignment conditions to support task delegation assignment with regards to the delegatees and its required privileges. We use computed privileges to specify delegation policies within an existing access control framework.

5.1   Access Control over Delegation

Delegation is a mechanism that permits a user to assign a subset of his assigned authorisations (privileges) to other users who currently do not possess it.

Definition 2 (Delegation Relation). *We define a delegation relation $DR \subseteq T \times U \times U \times 2^{DC}$ where T a set of tasks, U a set of users and DC a set of delegation constraints. A task delegation relation is defined as* $DR = (t, u_1, u_2, \{DC\})$, t *is the delegated task and* $t \in T$, u_1 *the delegator and* u_2 *the delegatee* $\in U$.

For instance, delegation constraints (DC) can be related to time or evidence specifications [4]. In addition, organisational constraints regarding roles mapping cross organisations or role hierarchies within an organisation define user-to-user delegation constraints (see RM and RH relations of the TAC model in Fig. 2). For instance, a subordinate in an organisation hierarchy can act on behalf of his superior where the latter is the delegator and the former is the delegatee.

Here, a delegation relation defines the main constraints to be considered when delegating privileges with regards to users/roles, task and resources. Our focus is to integrate such constraints in a secure manner. In doing so, we leverage the TAC (task-oriented access control) model specifications to compute delegatees and privileges. The TAC model allows to compute the list of potential delegatees using the RPA (role-permission assignment) relation that may satisfy the delegated task requirements based on the TPA (task-permission assignment) relation. In doing so, we define a method for access control over task delegation using TAC. In the following, we detail our method and describe how valid delegatees are checked and whether they need delegated privileges grant.

Input: u_1, $u_2 \in U$; r_1, $r_2 \in R$; t_i, $t_j \in T$.

1. Defining the role and permission assignments for each user (URA and RPA);
2. Instantiating the task t_{i1} and assigning it to the delegator s_1 who is the current user u_1;

3. Checking security constraints before delegation (SoD and BoD);
4. Computing the delegatee s_2, who is the current user u_2, based on his permissions assignment $((t_i, p_{r2}) \in TPA)$ or;
5. Granting privileges for s_2 based on the task instance permissions assignment $(p'_{r2} \leftarrow p_{r2} \cup p_{ti})$ which is defined in the $claimed_{by}$ function;

Output: Delegation relation instance : $dr_1 = (t_{i1}, s_1, s_2, \{DC\})$;

The main contribution of this method is to specify the delegated task assignment conditions based on Definition 2. If the two conditions are satisfied, then the task t_i is delegated to the delegatee u_2. However, if u_2 does not have the permission required and there is no conflicts (BoD or SoD) to execute t_i. Then the delegated privileges are granted for u_2 based on the $claimed_{by}$ function.

The computation of the privileges is based on the TRA and $claimed_{by}$ specifications defined in our TAC model (see $claimed_{by}$ condition for permissions). Basically, we provide a method to compute the least privileges to delegate based on the current requirements of the task instances t_{i1} which is generated from the delegated task. At this stage, delegated privileges are done manually supporting a user-to-user delegation. However, the administration of new access rights has to be specified later into authorisation policies in a compliant and dynamic manner. Authorisation policies will regulate how the business process and resources should be managed during delegation.

5.2   Delegation Policies

We introduce authorisation policies based on our access control (TAC) model. We then identify the delegation constraints that have to be specified in the delegation policies. An access control has to be defined to check the authorisation of the initiating user so-called subject. An authorisation makes an explicit binding between a role (subject), a task resource (object) and his rights (action) over it. This binding is defined based on the main relations: user-role assignment (URA), task-permission assignment (TPA) and task-role assignment (TRA) in our access control model (TAC). Subsequently, an authorisation expresses a user's permissions on a task's resources, where a permission is the right to execute an action on a resource.

Definition 3. *We define a policy $P \subseteq target \times rule \times 2^C$, where* target *defines where a policy is applicable,* rule *is a set of rules that defines the policy decision result, and* C *the policy constraints set that validates the policy rule.*

A target defines the entities of an access request. It is composed of a role associated to the subject and an action on a business object of a task type. A pseudo formal expression of a target is:

```
<target>
  <Subject>[role]
  <Resource>[object]
```

```
    <Action>[operation]
    <Task>[task type]
  </target>
```

A rule effect defines an authorisation decision. It can return as a result a permit, a deny or an indeterminate request [14]. Constraints are related to the work-flow authorisation specifications. For instance, the separation of duty (SoD) is a constraint for a user-task assignment. In the aforementioned banking process, a pseudo formal expression of a policy for a subject member of role *clerk* on the task T1 'Check credit' on a business object 'bo1' is:

```
  <Policy>
    <target>[clerk,bo1,read,T1]
    <rule>[Permit]
    <C>[none]
  </Policy>
```

The policy decision returns the result "Permit" where the user Alice member of role *clerk* can access to the resource 'bo1' of task ' Check credit ' and read it.

5.3 Deployment

We use the PERMIS policy editor for creating and editing delegation policies. PERMIS is a policy based authorisation system, a Privilege Management In-frastructure [15]. Given a username, a target and an action, the PERMIS de-cision engine says whether the user is granted or denied access based on the policy for the target. The policy is role/attribute based where users are given roles/attributes and roles/attributes are given permissions to access targets.

The interface to the PERMIS decision engine has been enhanced to support dynamic delegation of authority [16]. It can be considered as a lightweight au-thorisation decision engine. In order to execute our delegation request, we use the policy tester which is a tool used to test PERMIS policies created by the policy editor. The PERMIS Policy Tester can also allow dynamic updates of policies. This offers a suitable solution to add new delegation rules that grant or revoke delegated privileges. However, this tool does not support dynamic poli-cies and any further changes in policy will be made externally from PERMIS. A prototype of this implementation can be found in [4] (cf. pp. 156-166).

6 Related Work

Barka et al. proposed a role-based delegation model based on the RBAC model. Their unit of delegation is a role. Authors focused also on role-based models supporting role hierarchies when studying delegation in the context of both RBAC0 model (flat roles) and RBAC1 model (hierarchical roles) of the RBAC96 family [6]. In this paper, we motivated additional requirements where users may want to delegate a piece of permission. This is the case when computing delegated privileges which are not covered by RBAC.

Task-based access control (TBAC) aims to provide a task context during permission assignments [17]. A workflow system consisting of tasks is assumed. Each of these tasks is then assigned a "protection state", providing information as to who gets to have which permission on a task basis. According to the current state of the workflow system moving through the process instance, different permission assignments are activated or deactivated as ordered by the protection state. The TBAC design is process oriented, however, ignoring human-centric interactions such as user-to-user delegation. Delegation involving users is discussed in the TAC model and aligned with the workflow invariants in terms of tasks, users, and resources.

Team based access control (TMAC) is an access control scheme similar to RBAC, but it provides the assignment of both users and permissions to teams [18]. Each team then is bound to the task it was created for. At runtime, more than one team can be created out of the same template, but each team will be working on a different task instance and accordingly will need access to different object instances. TMAC model is out of the scope of this paper where we consider constraints on tasks and users rather than a team.

There exists several work about delegation policies. In [16,19], authors investigated how an authorisation management system based on the XACML (eXtensible Access Control Markup Language) can be extended to use flexible delegation mechanisms. The proposed architecture offers a flexible and dynamic way to manage users credentials and administrate delegation policies. However, it is not enough to support dynamic delegation of authority. Delegating a task requires more effort and involves additional specifications related to delegation constraints. In this paper, we proposed an approach to inject delegation constraints within an access control model as a means to specify dynamic delegation policies within workflows.

7   Conclusion

In this paper, we integrated task delegation constraints into a formal security model. In doing so, we analysed task authorisation constraints to support security requirements for delegation. Based on the RBAC model, we proposed the task-oriented access control (TAC) model. This model can grant authorisations based on workflow specifications and user authorisation information. It offers a fine grained access control protocol to support delegation. Moreover, we presented a method to compute potential delegatees and their delegated privileges, thereby specifying delegation policies in existing access control framework.

The next stage of our work is the implementation of our approach within an existing workflow system supporting human interactions. Intalio Tempo is a set of runtime components that support human-centric workflow within a service-oriented architecture. The main goal is to provide a complete and extensible workflow solution with a bias towards interoperable technologies such as BPEL, BPEL4People, RBAC, and web services. In this context, we will work on extending the security framework based on RBAC with the delegation of authority constraints defined in our model.

References

1. Atluri, V., Warner, J.: Supporting conditional delegation in secure workflow management systems. In: SACMAT 2005: The Tenth ACM Symposium on Access Control Models and Technologies, New York, NY, USA, pp. 49–58 (2005)
2. Crampton, J., Khambhammettu, H.: On delegation and workflow execution models. In: SAC 2008: Proceedings of the 2008 ACM Symposium on Applied Computing, pp. 2137–2144. ACM, New York (2008)
3. Sandhu, R.S., Coyne, E.J., Feinstein, H.L., Youman, C.E.: Role-based access control models. IEEE Computer 29(2), 38–47 (1996)
4. Gaaloul, K.: A Secure Framework for Dynamic Task Delegation in Workflow Management Systems, Ph.D. thesis, The University of Henri Poincaré, Nancy, France (2010)
5. Crampton, J., Khambhammettu, H.: Delegation in Role-Based Access Control. In: Gollmann, D., Meier, J., Sabelfeld, A. (eds.) ESORICS 2006. LNCS, vol. 4189, pp. 174–191. Springer, Heidelberg (2006)
6. Barka, E., Sandhu, R.: Framework for role-based delegation models. In: Proceedings of the 16th Annual Computer Security Applications Conference, pp. 168–176. IEEE Computer Society, Washington, DC, USA (2000)
7. Zhang, X., Oh, S., Sandhu, R.: PBDM: a flexible delegation model in RBAC. In: SACMAT 2003: Proceedings of the Eighth ACM Symposium on Access Control Models and Technologies, pp. 149–157. ACM Press, New York (2003)
8. Russell, N., van der Aalst, W.M.P., ter Hofstede, A.H.M., Edmond, D.: Workflow Resource Patterns: Identification, Representation and Tool Support. In: Pastor, Ó., Falcão e Cunha, J. (eds.) CAiSE 2005. LNCS, vol. 3520, pp. 216–232. Springer, Heidelberg (2005)
9. Zur Muehlen, M.: Workflow-based Process Controlling. Foundation, Design, and Application of workflow-driven Process Information Systems. Logos Verlag, Berlin (2004)
10. Curtis, B., Kellner, M.I., Over, J.: Process modeling. Commun. ACM 35(9), 75–90 (1992)
11. WFMC, The Workflow Management Coalition: Workflow Management Coalition Terminology and Glossary (1999); Document Number WFMC-TC-1011
12. Crampton, J., Khambhammettu, H.: Delegation and satisfiability in workflow systems. In: SACMAT 2008: Proceedings of the 13th ACM Symposium on Access Control Models and Technologies, pp. 31–40. ACM, New York (2008)
13. Botha, R.A., Eloff, J.H.P.: Separation of duties for access control enforcement in workflow environments. IBM Systems Journal 40(3), 666–682 (2001)
14. Moses, T.: eXtensible Access Control Markup Language (XACML) Version 2.0, Committee specification, OASIS (2005)
15. Chadwick, D.W., Otenko, A.: The permis x.509 role based privilege management infrastructure. In: SACMAT 2002: Proceedings of the Seventh ACM Symposium on Access Control Models and Technologies, pp. 135–140. ACM, New York (2002)
16. Chadwick, D.W., Otenko, S., Nguyen, T.A.: Adding support to xacml for multi-domain user to user dynamic delegation of authority. Int. Journal Information Security 8(2), 137–152 (2009)

17. Thomas, R.K., Sandhu, R.S.: Task-based authorization controls (tbac): A family of models for active and enterprise-oriented autorization management. In: Proceedings of the IFIP TC11 WG11.3 Eleventh International Conference on Database Securty XI, pp. 166–181. Chapman & Hall, Ltd., London (1998)
18. Thomas, R.K.: Team-based access control (tmac): a primitive for applying role-based access controls in collaborative environments. In: RBAC 1997: Proceedings of the Second ACM Workshop on Role-Based Access Control, pp. 13–19. ACM, New York (1997)
19. Seitz, L., Rissanen, E., Sandholm, T., Firozabadi, B.S., Mulmo, O.: Policy administration control and delegation using xacml and delegent. In: GRID 2005: Proceedings of the 6th IEEE/ACM International Workshop on Grid Computing, pp. 49–54. IEEE Computer Society, Washington, DC, USA (2005)

Risk and Business Goal Based Security Requirement and Countermeasure Prioritization

Andrea Herrmann[1], Ayse Morali[2], Sandro Etalle[3], and Roel Wieringa[4]

[1] Independent Researcher
AndreaHerrmann3@gmx.de
[2] Ascure N.V., St. Denijs-Westrem, Belgium
Ayse.Morali@ascure.com
[3] Eindhoven Technical University, Eindhoven, The Netherlands
s.etalle@tue.nl
[4] University of Twente, Enschede, The Netherlands
roel.wieringa@utwente.nl

Abstract. Companies are under pressure to be in control of their assets but at the same time they must operate as efficiently as possible. This means that they aim to implement "good-enough security" but need to be able to justify their security investment plans. Currently companies achieve this by means of checklist-based security assessments, but these methods are a way to achieve consensus without being able to provide justifications of countermeasures in terms of business goals. But such justifications are needed to operate securely and effectively in networked businesses. In this paper, we first compare a Risk-Based Requirements Prioritization method (RiskREP) with some requirements engineering and risk assessment methods based on their requirements elicitation and prioritization properties. RiskREP extends misuse case-based requirements engineering methods with IT architecture-based risk assessment and countermeasure definition and prioritization. Then, we present how RiskREP prioritizes countermeasures by linking business goals to countermeasure specification. Prioritizing countermeasures based on business goals is especially important to provide the stakeholders with structured arguments for choosing a set of countermeasures to implement. We illustrate RiskREP and how it prioritizes the countermeasures it elicits by an application to an action case.

Keywords: Non-functional requirements, Risk assessment, Misuse Cases, IT architecture, Security, Prioritization.

1 Introduction

Today, organizations are under high pressure to prove that they are in control of their assets, which means among other things that they must prove that they sufficiently secured their IT assets. At the same time, they are increasingly cost-sensitive and hence they aim at reducing security risks in a cost-effective way. The common solution is to use checklists to identify the largest risks and mitigate them. However, checklists are based on past experience and are useful for achieving consensus among experts, but do not necessarily provide justifications that are based on business goals or technical characteristics of the system. Such ad hoc analyses are risky in the face of

L. Niedrite, R. Strazdina, B. Wangler (Eds.): BIR 2011 Workshops, LNBIP 106, pp. 64–76, 2012.
© Springer-Verlag Berlin Heidelberg 2012

current fast-changing information technology (IT) [14, 20]. Furthermore, such justifications provide a proof of common maturity level which is necessary for networks of businesses to operate securely and effectively. In a previous work we presented RiskREP [8]. RiskREP allows the justification of security investments in terms of the vulnerabilities of the business processes and the IT architecture in relation to the business goals to be achieved.

We build on current proposals for extending requirements engineering (RE) methods with security risk assessment (RA) [4, 6, 7, 13, 15, 18, 19]. In Section 2, we compare some RE methods and RA methods to necessary requirements elicitation and prioritization features. We present the metamodel of RiskREP in Section 3, present how RiskREP elicits and prioritizes countermeasures by linking business goals to countermeasure specifications in Section 4, and discuss lessons learned from an action case study in Section 5.

2   Related Work

In this section, we compare some well-known RE and RA methods based on their requirements elicitation and prioritization properties. Tables 1 and 2 present an overview of this comparison. Please note that this list cannot be complete, considering the vast amount of existing methods. Here, we present only those methods that satisfy most of the properties which we considered as success criteria when developing RiskREP. Tables 1 and 2 use these properties as criteria for comparing the methods.

We advocate that the elicitation of security requirements must follow a systematic process, because this supports the traceable justification each requirement. In order to be complete, we want to differentiate between business and quality goals, to consider both permissible use and misuse, and to explicitly include different stakeholder views in order to arrive at security requirements which reflect the multi-perspective nature of security.

When prioritizing requirements and identifying the optimal set of security requirements to implement, one needs to know the risks against which the requirement will counteract. Risk is described by impact and incident likelihood. Security requirements are compared to each other both based on their monetary costs and effectiveness against the risk, i.e. risk reduction achieved. Additionally, combined effects of requirements play a role, like the potential of security measures to replace each other or to complement each other.

To systematically elicit security requirements, Elahi and Yu [5], Stamatis [18] and Mayer et al. [12] propose to derive requirements from high level goals. . We believe that a security requirements elicitation method should also differentiate between business goals (i.e. desired properties of the business) and quality goals (i.e. desired properties of the software) – where quality goals include security goals). Despite the fact that most of the approaches that we compare, e.g. [6, 11, 15, 19] differentiate between functional and non-functional goals of software systems, none of them differentiate between business and quality goals.

To address the security concerns of system owners, recently developed RE methods, e.g. [5, 9, 17, 19], model not only permissible uses but also misuses of system components.

Eliciting information on permissible uses and misuses, on business goals as well as quality goals, requires expertise of stakeholders with different backgrounds. Only a few of the approaches that we consider in this comparison ([2, 5, 9, 11, 17]) express how different stakeholder views can be considered when eliciting information. GSRM [9], for instance, differentiates the perspectives of user, business analyst, requirements engineer, and risk manager.

Once the security requirements are identified, one has to check whether they are implementable within the available budget. Usually, this is not the case, and one has to decide which set of requirements should be implemented and which requirements can be disregarded. Making such a decision requires the estimation of the security risks the system is exposed to, considering the trade-off among the different requirements, as well as their costs and effectiveness. However, only some methods (such as FMEA [18], Tropos based approaches [1, 5], GSRM [9], Attack Graphs [16], extended KAOS [19], and the approach proposed by Mayer et al. [12]) take into consideration the risk the system is exposed to.

Table 1. Comparison of some RE methods with respect to requirements elicitation and prioritization features

	Elahi and Yu [5]	Misuse Cases [17]	extended KAOS [19]	ATAM [11]	NFR frame-work [15]
Requirements elicitation					
Systematic process	derives soft-goals from goals	yes	no	no	derives soft-goals from goals
Differentiation between business and quality goals	goals and soft-goals	no	functional and non-functional goals	yes	technical and business objective
Considering both permissible use and misuse	use and misuse	use cases & misuse cases	goal and anti-goal	no	no
Considering different stakeholder views	yes	yes	no	yes	no
Requirements prioritization					
Estimation of impact	no	no	no	no	no
Estimation of incident likelihood	level of evidence	no	for deter-mining the granularity	no	no
Prioritization based on monetary costs of requirements	yes	real cost	no	volume of change	no

Table 1. (*continued*)

Considering effectiveness of requirements	3 levels	no	no	no	no
Considering combined effects of requirements	between soft-goals	no	no	trade-off points	between soft-goals

Table 2. Comparison of widely known RA methods with respect to requirements elicitation and prioritization features

	FMEA [18]	Attack Graphs [16]	CORAS [2]	Secure Tropos [1]	GSRM [9]
			Requirements elicitation		
Systematic process	yes	no	no	yes	yes
Differentiation between business and quality goals	no	no	no	3 layers: asset, event, treatment	project goals and sub goals
Considering both permissible use and misuse	no	no	no	yes: tasks and risks	risk events and tasks
Considering different stakeholder views	no	no	yes	no	yes
			Requirements prioritization		
Estimation of impact	failure effect	no	depends on selected model	severity of impact	risk impact
Estimation of incident likelihood	occurrence of failure	probability, average time or cost/effort	depends on the model	event likelihood	risk likelihood
Prioritization based on monetary costs of requirements	no	financial loss or loss of system	no	yes	no
Considering effectiveness of requirements	detection rate	no	no	qualitatively	effectiveness
Considering combined effects of requirements	no	no	no	qualitatively	no

The methods that take into consideration effectiveness levels of requirements refer to different attributes of the IT system that is analyzed. Elahi et al. [6] differentiate among three levels according to whether the countermeasure alleviates the effects of vulnerabilities, patches them or prevents malicious tasks. Secure Tropos [1] differentiates between four categories of countermeasures (removal/avoidance, prevention, attenuation, and retention) depending on how they mitigate the risk in the event layer. Finally, FMEA [18] differentiates according to incident detection rate.

When taken together, requirements may contradict with each other or support each other. Elahi and Yu [5], NFR framework [15], Mayer et al. [12], and Secure Tropos [1] consider these combined effects and prioritize the requirements accordingly. ATAM [11] also considers how requirements affect each other "trade-off points".

Tables 1 and 2 show that the RE and RA methods we have compared do not have all the requirements elicitation and prioritization features that we think are important. Therefore, we developed RiskREP [8]. RiskREP is built on the CRAC++ [14] and MOQARE [7] methods. The following Section 3 presents RiskREP´s metamodel which explicitly considers different perspectives on security, and Section 4 illustrates RiskREP´s systematic process with extracts from an action case.

3   Metamodel of RiskREP

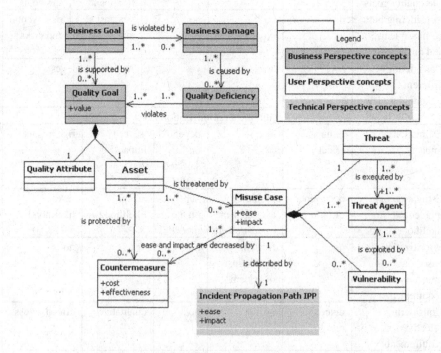

Fig. 1. Metamodel showing the concepts and their interrelations

The metamodel (Figure 1) contains concepts from three perspectives, i.e. the *business perspective*, the *user perspective* and the *technical perspective*. Before

RiskREP is applied, a model of the system´s architecture and specifications of the system´s functionality from user perspective (e.g. modeled as use cases) must exist. To these system models, RiskREP adds the security aspect.

Business Perspective. *Business goals* are desired properties of the business. Business goals justify system requirements. An example of business goal is "efficient business processes". A *business damage* is a state or activity of the business that violates a business goal. The business damage completes the business view by asking what should not happen. An example of business damage is "users don't use the system to be". A *quality goals* are desired qualities of the IT system, i.e. a desired state of the system. These goals are expressed as high-level quality requirements that consist of a quality attribute and an asset, like "confidentiality of password". A *quality deficiency* is a lack of quality attribute for an asset that violates quality goals and might causes business damage.

User Perspective. Quality attributes are attributes of the system to be protected. They describe aspects or characteristics of quality, e.g. confidentiality. We use the quality attributes of the ISO 9126 [3] and assume that these completely categorize all relevant aspects of an IT systems quality. Assets are parts of the system that are valuable for the organization, e.g. information, software, or hardware. They need to be protected from malicious activities in order to achieve business goals. Value quantifies the criticality of each quality goal with respect to the business. The value is used to prioritize the quality goals against each other. It is determined by the impact that the compromise of an asset would cause to the business.

Misuse Cases [17] describe scenarios in which a threat agent can cause a quality deficiency. The misuse case takes the perspective of the user and describes what happens at the interface between user and system. They are identified by analyzing the business process and the Use Cases of the system. The misuse cases are prioritized based on their execution ease and the impact, which they cause to the asset(s). *Threats* are actions, which cause a quality deficiency that causes the violation of a quality goal, e.g. data theft violates the confidentiality of data. *Vulnerabilities* are a property of the assets or the IT system or its environment that can be exploited by threat agents. This exploitation could violate a quality goal. Vulnerabilities can be unwanted properties like "lack of technical change management" or also wanted properties of the system such as "Single-Sign On". A *threat agent* is a person, i.e. an insider or an outsourcer or an outsider that intentionally or unintentionally executes a threat. A threat agent can be characterized in terms of his motivation, goal and attributes, e.g. disgruntled employee.

Countermeasures are mitigation, detection or prevention mechanisms. They partly or completely counteract a threat-vulnerability pair or the threat agent, and reduce the estimated impact at threat/vulnerability and/or the ease of threat execution. Countermeasures are expressed as (security) requirements on the IT system. Cost is an attribute of a countermeasure. It consists of implementation cost and the cost of ownership. Depending on the depth of the assessment we either use partially ordered scale or the real costs. In case the real costs are used then the risk expert may calculate the implementation cost based on required hours and salary per hour.

The *expected effectiveness* of a countermeasure is given by the expected risk reduction it achieves. Most countermeasures either influence the impact or the execution ease of an Incident Propagation Path.

Technical Perspective. *Incident Propagation Paths* are descriptions of misuse case from the technical perspective. In some cases, an Incident Propagation Path consists of several interconnected steps. That is a threat agent causing a quality deficiency on an asset by executing one or more threats, which exploit vulnerabilities of several assets. Such Incident Propagation Path scenarios are important for humans to imagine the flow of events including the causes and consequences of incidents. Like the misuse cases, the Incident Propagation Paths are prioritized based on their execution ease and the impact they have. There may be several Incident Propagation Paths realizing the same misuse case. The *execution ease* of a misuse case is an estimation of the effort required to carry out a misuse case. This effort is determined by the most resistant vulnerability that needs to be exploited to carry out the misuse case. In our approach, the execution ease is considered to be in correlation with the likelihood that a threat is actually executed by the "strongest" threat agent. *Impact* is the damage caused to the assets by the execution of a misuse case.

4   Steps of the RiskREP Method

The four steps of the method are:

1. *Quality goal analysis:* identify business goals, business damages, quality deficiencies and quality goals;
2. *Risk analysis:* identify misuse case (threats, threat agents, vulnerabilities) and estimate their impact on assets, and their ease of execution by means of incident propagation paths;
3. *Countermeasure definition:* specify countermeasures and estimate their cost; and
4. *Countermeasure prioritization:* assess effectiveness of countermeasures in reducing misuse case risk, their cost and dependencies.

At each of these steps, it is possible to either analyze the complete system, all business goals, and all misuse cases, respectively or to focus on the most important aspects. RiskREP is currently supported by spreadsheet tables.

The information that the RiskREP method uses is elicited from three stakeholder categories: business owner, IT manager and security officer who represent the business, IT and user perspective, respectively. The method is executed by an RE expert and a risk expert, who elicit the necessary information by semi-structured interviews with the other stakeholders. We applied the method in the TUgether project of the University Braunschweig (TU), in which a portal is developed to provide all on-line services of the TU, such as email, library access, registration for exams etc. available to students and employees. The portal must allow students to sign-on via one individually configurable interface. One major objective is that all students should eventually use the portal.

In the first phase of the project the portal framework product was selected which satisfied requirements best. Eighty functional and non-functional requirements were specified and about 70 products were considered. Our case study is restricted to the eleven security requirements of the 80 requirements.

The TUgether project was at an early development stage at the time we started applying RiskREP to it. We received from the project team the complete requirements specification. After analyzing it, we had several meetings with the project team to elicit the information RiskREP uses, such as the IT architecture of the TUgether portal. We concluded the action case by presenting the output of the method to the business owner, IT manager and security officer in a meeting and asked their opinion about the information RiskREP delivered. We now run through the steps of the method.

Step 1: Quality Goal Analysis. We could infer the security-related business perspective concepts from a project report which had been written before the case study. Figure 2 shows an extract of this analysis. Business goal "gaining user acceptance" (BG5) is threatened by one business damage, "Portal will not be used" (BD6). Three quality deficiencies may cause this, viz. User unfriendliness (QD7), lack of trust (QD8), and lack of added value (QD9). Because of the scope of our case study, we analyzed only quality goal "lack of trust" (QD8) further. QD8 can be avoided by three high level quality goals, i.e. Confidentiality of assets (QG5), Integrity of assets (QG6), and Availability of assets (QG7). Step 1 ensures that all software quality goals are justified by to business goals – including security.

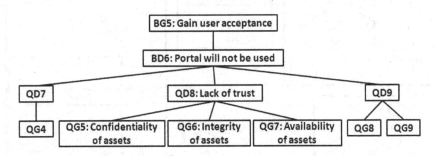

Fig. 2. Business concepts elicited with RiskREP

Step 2: Risk Analysis. The risk expert first identifies possible misuse cases that may threaten a quality goal and estimate their impact on assets and ease of execution. In addition, the security expert draws Incident Propagation Paths through the architecture that connects entry points of the system to the misuse case. This allows us the estimation of the ease of execution of the misuse case. Modeling the execution ease is also the main difference between Incident Propagation Paths and Misuse Case Maps [10].

The risk expert also assesses the value of each quality goal, for example by using value models for availability [20] or confidentiality [14] and then estimates the impact or damage caused by the misuse case to these quality goals. This way we maintain the link between business goals and impact of a misuse case.

For example, in the case study, misuse case "Manipulation of account data" (MC5) threatens quality goal "Integrity of assets" (QG6). There are five threat agents, viz. user, hacker, portal admin, portal developer and service developer. In the portal architecture (Figure 3), the critical IT assets related to misuse case "Manipulation of data" (MC5) are: TUgether portal server, LDAP server and Development server. We used a scale from 1 (low) to 3 (high) to indicate execution ease and impact. The execution ease of misuse case "Manipulation of data" (MC5) was estimated 1.5 and its impact was estimated 1. Incident Propagation Paths are described by the misuse case good enough here and therefore we did not draw them. In total, related to quality goal "Integrity of assets" (QG6), we identified ten misuse cases, one of which we show in Table 3. As this table illustrates, the risk of a misuse case is represented by a pair (ease of execution, impact on assets) where each of the two components of risk has a totally ordered scale. This defines a partial ordering of misuse cases according to their risk. Unlike in other risk assessment methods, we do not multiply ease with impact, but instead form categories of misuse cases, based on the priorities of the stakeholders. For instance, an misuse case with ease and impact equal to 3 can be called a "catastrophe", and the misuse case category "frequent, but harmless" describes misuse case where ease is high, but impact is low.

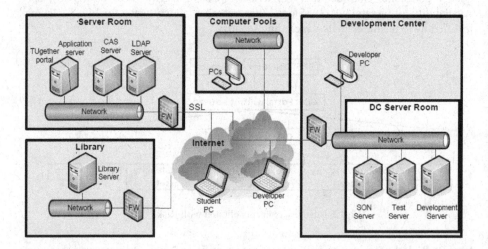

Fig. 3. TUgether portals IT architecture. (FW: Firewall, DC: Data Center, CAS: Central Authentication Service, SON: Personal Development Server).

Step 3: Countermeasure Definition. The security officer and RE expert compose a set of countermeasures by taking them from existing checklists. These checklists are part of RiskREP and contain general countermeasures for 167 threat vulnerability pairs. In this step of RiskREP, one brings these general measures to a concrete, realizable level by specifying which component each of them applies to and how.

Table 2 shows the results of this step on our case. Cost estimations are indicated by a 0 (no cost), 1 (changing the settings of applications), 2 (installing and maintaining freely available countermeasures) and 3 (purchasing, installing and maintaining countermeasures).

Table 3. Some misuse cases (MC) and their attributes

MC ID	risk (ease, impact)	Threat agent	Threat	Vulnerability
MC5: manipulation of account data	(1.5,1)	Hacker	data get lost or are manipulated during transfer	Portal does not manage data and therefore data synchronization between portal and services is necessary
MC9: no logout in computer pool	(1,3)	User	does not log out after having used the portal on a computer in the public computer pool	no access control to computer pools

Step 4: Countermeasure Prioritization. By applying countermeasures to misuse cases, one reduces risk. However, applying countermeasures usually means increased spending. Therefore, RiskREP aims at finding the ideal set of countermeasures to be applied. The best set of countermeasures is that with minimum total cost and maximum risk reduction. To find an optimum set, we must compare several sets of countermeasures. In practice, the security budget of the system is often the main delimiter for the ideal set of countermeasures. To prioritize countermeasures, their effectiveness in reducing the risk of misuse case must be quantified. We measure the effectiveness of a countermeasure with respect to a risk by the effect on decreasing both the ease of an attacker executing an attack and the impact of that attack. Ease as well as impact can be increased (+1), decreased (-1) or unaffected (0 points) by the application of a countermeasure. In this way it is easy to estimate and is less prone to mistakes. If necessary, RiskREP allows using more sophisticated scales.

Countermeasures interact with each other. For instance, some may be overlapping, or diminish each other's effectiveness. We documented the combined effect of pairs of countermeasures for TUgether in a two dimensional matrix containing 10 interactions, and discussed this with the security officer. The matrix is sparse and not symmetric; because it is possible that countermeasure c_1 influences c_2, but not vice versa. In the case study, it contains 10 interactions, whereas among the 10 countermeasures 90 different interactions would be theoretically possible.

We then prioritized countermeasures according to their cost and effectiveness. Just as for risk, no multiplications or additions can be done because the scales we use are ordinal. The security objectives of companies and their security strategies differ from each other. Therefore, RiskREP defines company-specific heuristic for the countermeasure prioritization. We classified countermeasures according to their cost and effectiveness in the following categories:

- *no effect:* both execution ease and impact of a misuse case are not modified by the countermeasure
- *contra-effective:* both execution ease and impact of a misuse case are increased, or one is increased and the other one is not modified, by the countermeasure;
- *counter-effective:* The countermeasure increases execution ease and reduces impact of the misuse case, or vice versa;
- *low hanging fruit:* cost is 0, either only execution ease or only impact of a misuse case is reduced by the countermeasure; or both execution ease and impact of a misuse case are reduced by the countermeasure;
- *cost-efficient:* cost is 1 and either only execution ease or only impact of a misuse case is reduces by the countermeasure; or both execution ease and impact of a misuse case are reduced by the countermeasure;
- *cost-effective:* cost is 2 and both execution ease and impact of a misuse case are reduced by the countermeasure;
- *expensive:* cost is 2 or above and either only execution ease of a misuse case is reduced by the countermeasure or only impact of a misuse case is reduced by the countermeasure;
- *expensive effectiveness:* cost is 3 and both execution ease and impact of a misuse case are reduced by the countermeasure.

To choose the optimal set of countermeasures, we did not use a formula which optimizes the systems added value automatically, but rather decided for a countermeasure selection strategy together with the stakeholders. In this case, the strategy is on countermeasure effectiveness and cost. Accordingly we suggested the stakeholder to implementing all "low hanging fruit" countermeasures. Furthermore, since defining the categories also influences the strategy, we asked for stakeholders' approval after defining them. This way of choosing the countermeasures to be implemented is a heuristical one which allows making decisions transparently and based on objective criteria, but still is simple and easy to execute.

5 Analysis and Discussion

RiskREP is designed to elicit security requirements following a systematic process, and considering several perspectives of security: the business perspective, user perspective and technical perspective, and both permissible use and misuse. For prioritizing countermeasures, RiskREP considers misuse cases´ impacts and incident likelihoods, countermeasures´ monetary costs and effectiveness against the risk, and combined effects of countermeasures. We have applied RiskREP to an action case in order to verify whether RiskREP supports security requirements elicitation and prioritization in a way that one can control whether the result is complete or lightweight.

Our action case study showed that RiskREP can be used and leads to a list of misuse case partially ordered by risk, and motivated in terms of system architecture as well as business goals. It also leads to a prioritized list of countermeasures agreed on by stakeholders. It took us about four hours to apply RiskREP to one quality goal. This is comparable to the time currently spent on security RE. So, we conclude that RiskREP can be used within the available budget for security RE.

But is it better than the method currently in use? Did it lead to a better understanding of security risk and/or to a better set of countermeasures, in terms of estimated cost and estimated effectiveness? Before we applied RiskREP, the university was using a collection of requirements grouped according to each attribute of the system. These requirements were elicited from different stakeholders, and eleven high-level requirements were about security. They were of different granularity levels, and it was neither possible to compare their risk level, nor to validate their completeness. By contrast, RiskREP systematically analyzes the risks both from user perspective and technical perspective under consideration of all use cases and data flows. We argue that this an improvement w.r.t. the previous way of working. While RiskREP potentially could elicit all countermeasures completely, at each step it is possible to focus on the most relevant aspects, e.g. most important quality goals, most important misuse case etc. and to document this decision. So, RiskREP supports also a light-weight analysis that is focused on the most important elements.

Comparing RiskREP to other security RE methods we note that we do not use our ordered scales of misuse cases (based on ease of execution and impact on assets), cost and effectiveness in inadmissible ways, such as by multiplying impact and ease of executing an Incident Propagation Path. This makes the results of using our method more meaningful than the results of other methods. Assuming that in this particular case study, RiskREP could be used and is an improvement, could it be used in other cases, too? Would other people be able to use it with the same effectiveness in other cases? RiskREP assumes that the information listed in the metamodel can be elicited and that stakeholders are able to reach agreement about a countermeasure prioritization in terms of their cost and effectiveness. However, for it to be used by other requirements engineers than us, we need to supply RiskREP with tool support and supporting manuals. We are planning to develop this in the near future.

References

1. Asnar, Y., Giorgini, P., Mylopoulos, J.: Goal-driven Risk Assessment in Requirements Engineering. Requirement Engineering Journal, 1–16 (2010)
2. Braber, F., Hogganvik, I., Lund, M., Stølen, K., Vraalsen, F.: Model-based Security Analysis in Seven Steps — a Guided Tour to the CORAS Method. BT Technology Journal 25(1), 101–117 (2007)
3. I.S.O. I.E. Commission. ISO/IEC 9126, Information Technology - Software Product Evaluation - Quality Characteristics and Guidelines for Their Use (1991), http://www.iso.org
4. Dubois, E., Heymans, P., Mayer, N., Matulevicius, R.: A Systematic Approach to Define the Domain of Information System Security Risk Management. In: Nurcan, S., et al. (eds.) Intentional Perspectives on Information Systems Engineering, pp. 289–306. Springer, Heidelberg (2010)

5. Elahi, G., Yu, E.: Modeling and Analysis of Security Trade-offs - A Goal Oriented Approach. Data Knowledge Engineering 68, 579–598 (2009)
6. Elahi, G., Yu, E., Zannone, N.: A Vulnerability-centric Requirements Engineering Framework: Analyzing Security Attacks, Countermeasures, and Requirements Based on Vulnerabilities. Requir. Eng. 15(1), 41–62 (2010)
7. Herrmann, A., Paech, B.: MOQARE: Misuse-oriented Quality Requirements Engineering. Requir. Eng. 13(1), 73–86 (2008)
8. Herrmann, A., Morali, A.: RiskREP: Risk-Based Security Requirements Elicitation and Prioritization (extended version). Technical Report TR-CTIT-10-28, Centre for Telematics and Information Technology. University of Twente, Enschede (2010) ISSN 1381-3625, http://eprints.eemcs.utwente.nl/18342/
9. Islam, S., Houmb, S.: Integrating Risk Management Activities into Requirements Engineering. In: Proc. of the 4th Int. Conf. on Research Challenges in Information Science. IEEE Computer Society (2010)
10. Karpati, P., Sindre, G., Opdahl, A.L.: Visualizing Cyber Attacks with Misuse Case Maps. In: Wieringa, R., Persson, A. (eds.) REFSQ 2010. LNCS, vol. 6182, pp. 262–275. Springer, Heidelberg (2010)
11. Kazman, R., Klein, M., Clements, P., Compton, N.: Atam: Method for Architecture Evaluation. Technical Report CMU/SEI-2000-TR-004, CMU (2000)
12. Mayer, N., Dubois, E., Rifaut, A.: Requirements Engineering for Improving Business/IT Alignment in Security Risk Management Methods. In: Proc. of the 3rd Int. Conf. Interoperability for Enterprise Software and Applications, I-ESA, p. 12 (2007)
13. Moore, A.P., Ellison, R.J., Linger, R.C.: Attack Modeling for Information Security and Survivability. Technical Report CMU/SEI-2001-TN-001, CMU (2001)
14. Morali, A.: IT Architecture-Based Confidentiality Risk Assessment in Networks of Organizations. PhD thesis, University of Twente, Enschede, The Netherlands (2011)
15. Mylopoulos, J., Chung, L., Liao, S., Wang, H., Yu, E.: Exploring Alternatives during Requirements Analysis. IEEE Software 18, 92–96 (2001)
16. Phillips, C., Swiler, L.: A Graph-based System for Network-Vulnerability Analysis. In: Proc. of the 1998 Workshop on New Security Paradigms, pp. 71–79. ACM (1998)
17. Sindre, G., Opdahl, A.: Eliciting Security Requirements with Misuse Cases. Requir. Eng. 10(1), 34–44 (2005)
18. Stamatis, D.: Failure Mode and Effect Analysis FMEA from Theory to Execution. American Society for Quality Press (2003)
19. van Lamsweerde, A., Brohez, S., Landtsheer, R.D., Janssens, D.: From System Goals to Intruder Anti-goals: Attack Generation and Resolution for Security Requirements Engineering. In: Proc. of RHAS Workshop, Essener Informatik Beitraege, vol. Bd 6, pp. 49–56 (2003)
20. Zambon E.: Towards Optimal IT Availability Planning: Methods and Tools. PhD-thesis, University of Twente, Enschede, The Netherlands (2011)

Security Requirements Engineering
for Secure Business Processes

Elda Paja[1], Paolo Giorgini[1], Stéphane Paul[2], and Per Håkon Meland[3]

[1] Universitá degli studi di Trento, Italy
paja@disi.unitn.it, paolo.giorgini@unitn.it
[2] Thales Research and Technology, France
stephane.paul@thalesgroup.com
[3] Sintef, Norway
Per.H.Meland@sintef.no

Abstract. Traditional approaches to business process modelling deal with security only after the business process has been defined, namely without considering security needs as input for the definition. This may require very costly corrections if new security issues are discovered. Moreover, security concerns are mainly considered at the system level without providing the rationale for their existence, that is, without taking into account the social or organizational perspective, which is essential for business processes related to considerably large organizations. In this paper, we introduce a framework for engineering secure business processes. We propose a security requirements engineering approach to model and analyze participants' objectives and interactions, and then derive from them a set of security requirements that are used to annotate business processes. We capture security requirements through the notion of social commitment, that is a promise with contractual validity between participants. We illustrate the framework by means of an Air Traffic Management scenario.

Keywords: Security requirements, business process, BPMN, social commitments.

1 Introduction

Business processes are the combination of a set of activities within an enterprise following a structure that describes their operational order and dependence, to pursue a desired objective or result. Business process modelling enables a common understanding and analysis of a business process [1]. It can be used to describe complex interactions between business partners and to indicate related business requirements on an abstract level. With the growth of businesses, business processes have experienced considerable growth, not only in size but also in complexity. The evolution in the nature of organizational information systems into cross-organizational systems has exposed an organization's assets and resources in terms of business services [2]. These business services are modelled as

L. Niedrite, R. Strazdina, B. Wangler (Eds.): BIR 2011 Workshops, LNBIP 106, pp. 77–89, 2012.
© Springer-Verlag Berlin Heidelberg 2012

business processes reflecting the control and information flow, without considering any security related issues. But, security is an important aspect that needs to be considered early during the modeling phases [3]. Information systems are inevitably subject to threats [4] that may influence organizational assets. This might increase the vulnerability of the provided business services, hence that of business processes.

Current approaches to business process modelling lack a security focus in the early phases [5]. This is often due to the fact that business analysts are not security experts and assume that this will be bolted on later. Fortunately, this trend is changing and we are seeing examples where security requirements are integrated into business processes. For instance, Wolter et al. [2], describe an approach to integrate security goals and constraints in business process modelling together with a model-driven transformation that focuses on authorisation requirements. In a similar way, Rodriguez et al. [3] introduce an extension to the *Business Process Modeling Notation* (BPMN) to allow business analysts express security needs from their perspective. However, these approaches do not facilitate the creation of security policies in compliance with the modelled security properties. Moreover, they provide no rationale on how the business analyst should decide upon security requirements in the business process. In [6], Menzel et al. employ a model-driven approach to generate security policies based on security patterns. They provide an enhancement to BPMN to enable the assessment of risks based on the evaluation of assets and the trustworthiness of participants, and to enable the annotation of security requirements such as confidentiality or integrity.

Pavlovski and Zou [7] extend BPMN to capture non-functional requirements related to business process models, among which security policies that apply. Their extension involves two notations: *operating condition*, which refer to constraints over activities, and *control case*, which describes the risks associated to the operating condition together with mechanisms to mitigate or reduce business risks. Cardoso et al. [8] start from goal modeling to elicit business process models. Goals are considered as objectives to be achieved by the execution of a business process. The authors show how the elicitation process takes place starting from a preliminary phase to a supplementary one, which refines the goal models by using NFR (Non-Functional Requirements) catalogues. However, how goal models are related to business process models is left as future work.

For high-level business process modelling in UML, the approaches by Sindre and Opdahl [9] related to misuse cases and UMLSec by Jürjens [10], are well-known. In [11], Sindre proposes another technique, which complements misuse cases, to capture security issues throughout business process diagrams. The author extends UML activity diagrams by adding malicious activities and malicious actors to identify possible threats, and then adds defensive processes to mitigate the identified risks, suggesting where in the process the mitigation activities would be placed. These approaches are complementary to ours.

In this paper we will support security requirements engineering in the context of cross-organizational business processes. We present a novel framework that elicits a set of security specifications, analyzing first the organizational objectives of different roles and analysing security from an organizational perspective. As cross-organizational business processes capture collaborations and interactions among different organizations or partners, it is important to provide a level of abstraction on which partners first agree on the business goals of their collaboration [12]. We adopt an interaction-oriented perspective to identify and express security needs. We analyse social interactions in the organization, responsibilities of relevant actors, information flow constraints, and rules actors should comply with. *Social commitments* are a powerful formalism to model actors' interactions [13] in the pursuit of achieving their objectives. A social commitment stands for a promise from a debtor (actor) to a creditor (actor) that if the antecedent is brought about, the consequent will be brought about (antecedent and consequent are propositions, promises actors exchange). Formally, a social commitment is represented as a quaternary relation C(debtor, creditor, antecedent, consequent). Commitments are created and evolve according to the messages actors exchange. These social abstractions are rooted in interaction, therefore they are very effective to capture security needs, as most of the security issues arise during interaction. They have contractual validity: their violation might lead to further commitments by the violator. The contractual validity of commitments enables the development of robust interactions, wherein violations eventually result in penalties and loss of reputation. The derived commitments serve as security specifications while modelling business processes.

In a nutshell, our approach is to *security-annotated-BPMN* [3], what BMM [1] is to BPMN: it provides the justification for the security requirements by capturing security needs. This statement is particularly true for market social structures, as defined in [14], that is, loci of interaction between participants who are peers of one another. It however remains valid for enterprise-type social structures, as demonstrated in this article's running example, where an enterprise is an organization with identifiable officers and with internally established goals that reflect the purpose of the organization.

The paper is structured as follows. Section 2 introduces our modelling framework, including the three operational views of the modelling language (SecCo) that allow one to model and express security needs and the specification of security requirements via commitments. Section 3 shows how SecCo requirements can be transferred to BPMN. Section 4 discusses the approach and future directions, whereas section 5 makes some final remarks.

2 Modelling Security via Commitments

Figure 1 outlines our modelling framework, namely *SecCo*, which stands for *Se*curity via *Co*mmitments. The figure shows how security requirements for the business processes under design are derived from the security needs expressed by the stakeholders.

Security needs are *expressed in* the *business view*. In the current version of the framework the *business view* consists of three different views: *social view*,

---

[1] Business Motivation Model Version 1.1 http://www.omg.org/spec/BMM/1.1/

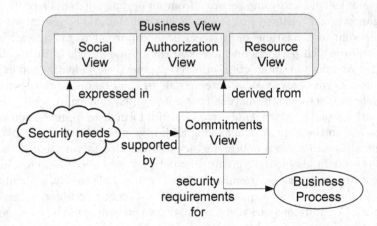

Fig. 1. Outline of our approach: from security needs to security requirements

authorization view, and *resource view* (Fig. 1). These views provide different perspectives over the considered setting. More detail about the views is provided in Section 2.2.

Together, these views give a comprehensive picture of the organization addressing at the same time both business concerns and security aspects. *Security needs* are *supported by* the *commitments view*, which consists of a set of commitments between actors. The *commitments view* is a high-level specification of the security requirements for the system-to-be. As long as the actors do not violate those commitments, the security needs in the setting are ensured. The commitments view can be automatically derived from the business view using a dedicated modelling tool.

2.1   Running Example

Air traffic management involves many critical processes between several organizations. We will illustrate the features of SecCo with the help of a running example developed from a report published by the Aniketos project [15].

Handover scenario: En-route air traffic controllers work in facilities called Area Control Centers (ACC). Each ACC is responsible for a vast airspace. As an aircraft reaches the boundary of an ACC, it is handed over to the Adjacent ACC. This transfer of responsibility involves electronic exchange of information between the ACCs and the aircraft, with the purpose of collaboratively managing the flight's Reference Business Trajectory (RBT). The sharing of RBT related information is carried out according to the Flight Object (FO) paradigm. The FO contains flight data, including RBTs. Today, handover is handled by voice (radio), sometimes supported by dedicated point-to-point electronic means (data link). During the handover, the aircraft is given a new radio frequency and the pilot begins talking to the next controller. This process continues until the aircraft is handed over to a terminal controller. In the short future, Flight Handover will be enabled by the SWIM (System Wide Information Management) infrastructure. All the information exchange will be made possible through SWIM, an internet-like network for the aviation community. Like for the internet, SWIM will enhance communications, but will also be vulnerable to new threats. In our handover case-study, SWIM will be responsible for: managing the handover request it receives from the controlling ACC, check the eligibility of the ACC to handover the flight, determine the next ACC to be contacted, notify the handover request to the identified FO server, and finally change the unit's role, making the adjacent ACC the new controlling ACC.

We have modelled the scenario using SecCo as shown in Fig. 2 and Fig. 3.

2.2   Multi-view Modelling

A distinguishing feature of SecCo is to rely on multiple views of the same model. Each view represents a specific perspective on the business view. Multi-view modelling promotes modularity and allows modellers to focus on well-defined tasks, as opposed to building a single model representing orthogonal concerns.

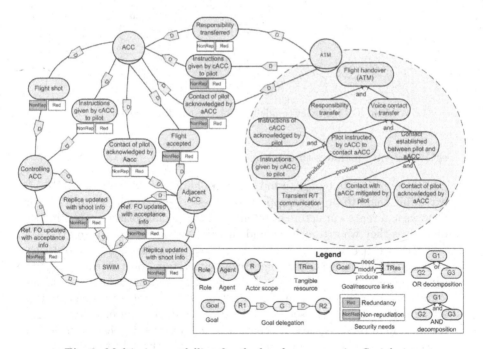

Fig. 2. Multi-view modelling for the handover scenario: *Social view*

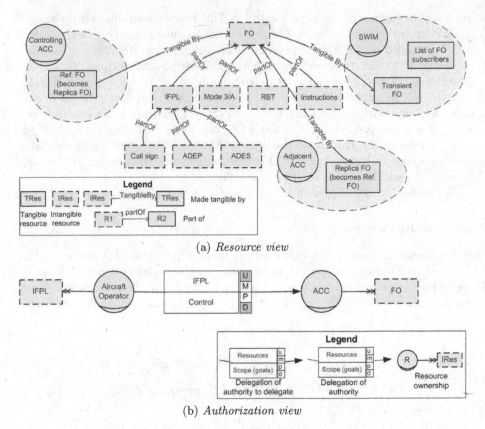

(a) *Resource view*

(b) *Authorization view*

Fig. 3. Multi-view modelling for the handover scenario

SecCo currently includes three views:

1. *Social view (Fig. 2)*: builds on top of traditional *i**-based frameworks [16,17], extending them to provide support for cross-organizational settings. In this view we can represent actors as intentional and social entities, capturing the objectives they want to achieve and their interactions respectively.

    There are two types of actors: *agent* and *role*. An agent refers to the actual participants who are going to adopt certain roles at runtime. As a consequence an agent can play multiple roles. At design-time, we do not know most actors, so they are modelled as roles, except for the agents that are already present in the setting and are known since requirements time. Actors, as intentional entities, are characterized in terms of *goals*, their desired objectives. Referring to our running example, ATM for instance, is a role, and it has the goal of handing over the flight ("Flight handed over"). Goals can be refined by *AND/OR-decompositions*. For example, the goal "flight handed over" is further AND-decomposed into "responsibility transferred" and "Voice contact transferred". The latter goal is also further refined by

AND-decompositions. Goals are linked to *tangible resources*—information represented by some support means—in various ways: a goal can *read (use)*, *produce*, *modify*, or *distribute* a resource. In our example, we show how ATM *produces* the tangible resource "Transient R/T communication" while achieving the goal "Contact established between pilot and aACC". Resource *possession* indicates that an actor has or possesses a certain resource without the need of interacting with others. In the social view there are two social relationships: *resource provision* and *goal delegation*. Resource provision captures the distribution and exchange of information, whereas goal delegation captures how an actor (delegator) transfers the responsibility of achieving a goal (delegatum) to another actor (delegatee). Goal delegation indicates that the delegator expects the delegatee to achieve the delegated goal. In the handover scenario, there are several goal delegations, such as Adjacent ACC delegates the goal "Ref. FO updated with acceptance info" to SWIM.

2. *Resource view (Fig. 3a)*: represents the resources in the given setting, providing a structure of how the various resources are interconnected. We distinguish between tangible resources, which denote the representation of information by some means (already introduced in the social view) and *intangible resources*, which denote information irrespective of its representation. For instance, "FO" (flight object) and its constituent information, such as "IFPL", "RBT", etc., are intangible as long as they are not represented by any tangible resources. Resources can be hierarchically structured via the *part-of* relation, which relates homogeneous resources (intangible to intangible, tangible to tangible). Intangible resources are *made tangible by* tangible resources. For example, "FO" is made tangible by "Transient FO".

3. *Authorization view (Fig. 3b)*: represents the flow of permissions or authorizations, how they are delegated from one actor to another. We distinguish between delegation of *authority* and delegation of *authority to delegate*.

   Delegation of *authority* shows authorizations given by an actor to another for one or more intangible resources, on specific *operations*: *modify* (M), *produce* (P), *use* (U), and *distribute* (D). An authorization can be limited to a *scope*—a set of goals—that determines the purpose for which authorization is passed. We assume that the authorizations start from the owner of the resource(s). Ownership relation is represented as a double-headed arrow from the role to the intangible resource. For instance, in the handover scenario, the Aircraft Operator owns the resource "IFPL" and authorizes ACC to read (use: U) and distribute (D) IFPL in the scope of the goal "Control".

   The delegation of *authority to delegate* implies that the delegatee can further delegate the received authorization, and subsumes the first type of authorization.

2.3 Expressing Security Needs

SecCo supports the following security needs:

- *Non-repudiation*: in a goal delegation, the delegator wants to prevent the delegatee from challenging the validity of the delegation.

- *Redundancy*: in a delegation, the delegator wants the delegatee to adopt redundant strategies for the achievement of the delegated goal. He can either use different internal capabilities, or can rely on multiple actors.
- *No-delegation*: the delegator expresses a security need over the delegation that requires the delegatee not to further delegate goal fulfilment. Such requirement is closely related to *trust*: the delegator actor trusts *that* specific delegatee actor for some goal, and does not trust other actors the delegatee might want to involve.
- *Non-disclosure*: when authority over a resource is granted without transferring authority to delegate.
- *Need-to-know*: when delegation of the authority to delegate is restricted to a goal scope. The actor granting the authority enables the second actor to delegate permission to others as long as other actors conduct operations on the resource within the specified scope.
- *Integrity*: when an actor does *not* delegate the authority to modify a resource.

Considering the description of security needs, we can say that they are expressed either over delegations or authorizations. This is in compliance with our view of taking an interaction-oriented approach for identifying security issues. The first group represents constraints actors might want to impose over their interactions, especially when one is relying on another to get things done (goal delegations). The second group considers security issues that arise due to permission flows and information exchanges (authorizations and resource provisions).

Referring to our running example, we can illustrate how some of these security needs are supported by SecCo. In the new SWIM environment, **(Ex1)** SWIM infrastructure would want to ensure *non-repudiation* of "Replica updated with shoot info" when delegating it to the adjacent ACC. On the other hand, as the information contained within "FO" is critical, the Aircraft Operator would express an *integrity* security need when providing ACC with "IFPL" **(Ex2)**. Finally, the Aircraft Operator wants to ensure that "IFPL" information (intangible resource) is used to "Control" by the ACC, expressing in this way a *need-to-know* security need **(Ex3)**.

2.4   Deriving Security Requirements in Terms of Commitments

SecCo represents security requirements as commitments between actors. We are reasoning on a role-based perspective, since we do not know who the actual participants at run-time are going to be. Therefore the commitments are between roles, implying that at run-time the actual agents playing those roles, are expected to make and comply with those commitments. Whenever a security need is specified over an interaction, say over a goal delegation, by the delegator, the delegatee is expected to make a commitment on the opposite direction for that security need, promising it will fulfill it (similarly for resource provision, or granting authorization). If all agents playing those roles comply with their commitments, the security needs will be guaranteed.

Security requirements are automatically derived from the business view. We sketch some security requirements derived from the scenario in Section 2.3 related to the security needs Ex1-Ex3. In the commitments below, debtor and creditor are roles, whereas antecedent and consequent are propositions.

Ex1. The non-repudiation security need results in a commitment from the adjacent area control center (aacc) to SWIM infrastructure (swim) that, if goal "Replica updated with shoot info" is delegated to (aacc), it (aacc) will not repudiate the delegation:
C(aacc, swim, d_1 =delegate(swim,aacc,Replica updated with shoot info), nonrepudiation(d_1))

Ex2. The integrity security need expressed by the Aircraft Operator (ao) results in an unconditional commitment made by ACC (acc) to (ao) that IFPL information will not be modified:
C(acc, ao, $\top$, integrity(IFPL))

Ex3. The need-to-know security need results in a commitment from the ACC (acc) to Aircraft Operator (ao) that it will not access the IFPL unless it is used for the goal "Control":
C(acc, ao, need-to-know(IFPL, Control, u $\land$ d))

3   Transferring SecCo Requirements to BPMN

The modelling presented in section 2 relates to business and/or operational modelling using a very simple language (in terms of concepts and notation) to express business/operational goals. It is easily understandable and accessible to decision makers who are not security experts. The modelling captures only what is important for the business or operation (i.e. goal-level), not how this business or operation needs to be conducted (i.e. process-level). Compared to BPMN, SecCo is therefore at a higher level of abstraction. We will now show how the derived commitments representing security requirements can be annotated into BPMN. We do this to guide the process modelling, but also to make these commitments a part of the specifications themselves.

BPMN 2.0 has four different diagram types, where the conversation diagram gives the most abstract view [18]. Its purpose is to give an overview of intercompany processes between several partners. Hence, we can annotate to which conversations and related participants the SecCo requirements apply. This is shown in figure 4, where SWIM, the flight pilot, the controlling ACC and the adjacent ACC need to co-operate in order to achieve a hand-over. Here, all three commitments (Ex1, Ex2 and Ex3) must be taken into consideration. BPMN participants can be mapped directly towards the SecCo actors, and conversations towards top goals. The security annotation has been manually added to the hand-over conversation guided by the ATM top-level goal. However, these security annotations might be too coarse grained in many situations, so we might have to dive a bit deeper to make the commitments more explicit.

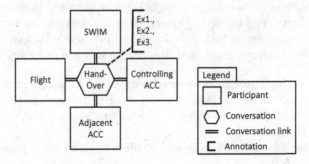

Fig. 4. A high-level conversation diagram for the handover scenario

The more detailed interactions can be represented using choreography or collaboration diagrams of BPMN. With choreographies, we are not interested in the partners' internal processes, but mainly the message exchange between them. According to Allweyer [19], choreographies are better than collaborations as a "basis for agreements and contracts between parties". In figure 5, we have created a choreography diagram for the hand-over scenario. First, the controlling ACC initiates a message exchange with SWIM when one of its flight is getting close to the airspace border and releases control over the FO. SWIM identifies which adjacent ACC to contact and relays the hand-over request to this site (Ex2 applies here). Notice that there are two logical outcomes of this last message exchange:

1. If the adjacent ACC refuses (this could be due to capacity problems), SWIM must inform the previously controlling ACC about this so that it can take back the control. The internal process of the controlling ACC (not shown in this figure) would then be to contact the flight and change the business trajectory of the FO. The process of requesting hand-over to another ACC would then be repeated.
2. The other outcome is that the adjacent ACC accepts the hand-over request. The following choreography would then be between the message exchange of these three parties related to the change of controlling ACC role.

4   Discussion and Further Work

The SecCo framework is meant to be an easy and intuitive way of obtaining security specifications in terms of formal commitments based on expressed security needs. It targets a non-scientific and non-technical population, such as commerce, marketing, pre-sale and business development staff of an organization. In this paper we have, through a scenario extracted from an industrial case study, shown the creation of commitments, and then (manually) transferred these commitments to BPMN models by system designers. Non-technical staff, mainly business people or development engineers, offers support to identify the security properties using SecCo (see figure 6). At the time being, the process

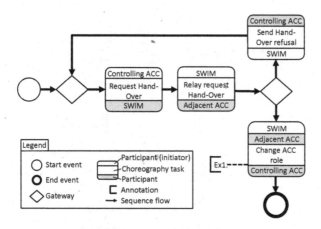

Fig. 5. A choreography diagram of the hand-over scenario

of mapping security specifications to security properties for business processes and the annotation of business process models with security properties is done manually.

In practice, our approach is not a one-way flow, as one often will identify new security goals when creating business processes (or the business processes might already exist beforehand). Another challenge is that of preserving a distinct separation between these two modelling activities. For instance, there is a danger that people try to express too much of the *process* with SecCo. This is not the intention here, and SecCo is not a process or business-oriented language, it operates at a higher level of abstraction and as a result does not contain enough constructs to have the same expressive power as for instance, BPMN. With SecCo we are stating what is important, and what needs to be protected.

Associated to the SecCo modelling notation is also a methodology that guides the modeller in eliciting and capturing the precise security criteria (including, but not limited to confidentiality, availability and integrity) that apply to the goals and/or resources that need protection.

We are currently working on the transformation of the security requirements as expressed with SecCo towards lower level languages aiming at service engineering. The commitments represent a powerful concept that should allow to enact the security at runtime through mechanisms such as security-by-contract. The transformations are not yet finalised as we are also analysing the necessity to include some risk assessment steps between the SecCo modelling and the lower level modelling, including BPMN. The BPMN examples shown in this paper are conversation and choreography diagrams, but for finer-grained commitments, it would be natural to also make use of collaboration and process diagrams, for instance to add commitments related to tasks or data object within a process.

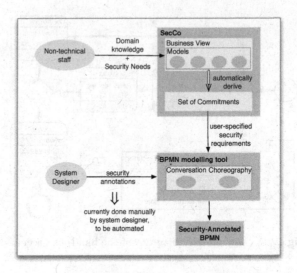

Fig. 6. Our approach to security-annotated BPMN

5   Conclusions

The need to take into account security issues when modelling business processes has been acknowledged by different research works, providing extensions to, for instance, BPMN [3,2,6] for security configurations. These approaches show the necessity to enrich BPMN annotation to support the specification of security requirements. However, existing approaches lack of the perspective of the security analyst as well as of a thorough analysis of the organizational setting. Security requirements are expressed considering traditional security properties and mechanisms.

In this work, we presented an approach to derive security requirements by modelling the organizational objectives of the involved parties and the social interactions that emerge between them. Our modelling framework allows to make a thorough analysis of the organizational setting, following the perspectives of different participants, their business goals and the interdependencies among them. The framework allows the various interacting parties to constrain the interaction by expressing security needs, which are later operationalized in security requirements via social commitments. It is in this latter concept that resides the strength of our approach.

Acknowledgements. This work has been partially supported by the EU-FP7-IST-IP-ANIKETOS and EU-FP7-IST-NOE-NESSOS projects.

References

1. Aguilar-Saven, R.: Business process modelling: Review and framework. International Journal of Production Economics 90(2), 129–149 (2004)
2. Wolter, C., Menzel, M., Meinel, C.: Modelling security goals in business processes. Modellierung 127, 201–216 (2008)
3. Rodríguez, A., Fernández-Medina, E., Piattini, M.: A bpmn extension for the modeling of security requirements in business processes. IEICE Transactions on Information and Systems 90(4), 745–752 (2007)
4. Firesmith, D.G.: Security Use Cases. Journal of Object Technology 2(3), 53–64 (2003)
5. Backes, M., Pfitzmann, B., Waidner, M.: Security in Business Process Engineering. In: van der Aalst, W.M.P., ter Hofstede, A.H.M., Weske, M. (eds.) BPM 2003. LNCS, vol. 2678, pp. 168–183. Springer, Heidelberg (2003)
6. Menzel, M., Thomas, I., Meinel, C.: Security requirements specification in service-oriented business process management. In: 2009 International Conference on Availability, Reliability and Security, pp. 41–48. IEEE (2009)
7. Pavlovski, C., Zou, J.: Non-functional requirements in business process modeling. In: Proceedings of the Fifth Asia-Pacific Conference on Conceptual Modelling, vol. 79, pp. 103–112. Australian Computer Society, Inc. (2008)
8. Cardoso, E., Almeida, J., Guizzardi, R., Guizzardi, G.: A method for eliciting goals for business process models based on non-functional requirements catalogues. International Journal of Information System Modeling and Design (IJISMD) 2(2), 1–18 (2011)
9. Sindre, G., Opdahl, A.: Eliciting security requirements with misuse cases. Requirements Engineering 10(1), 34–44 (2005)
10. Jürjens, J.: UMLsec: Extending UML for Secure Systems Development. In: Jézéquel, J.-M., Hussmann, H., Cook, S. (eds.) UML 2002. LNCS, vol. 2460, pp. 412–425. Springer, Heidelberg (2002)
11. Sindre, G.: Mal-Activity Diagrams for Capturing Attacks on Business Processes. In: Sawyer, P., Heymans, P. (eds.) REFSQ 2007. LNCS, vol. 4542, pp. 355–366. Springer, Heidelberg (2007)
12. Greiner, U., Lippe, S., Kahl, T., Ziemann, J., Jäkel, F.W.: Designing and implementing cross-organizational business processes-description and application of a modelling framework. Enterprise Interoperability, pp. 137–147 (2007)
13. Singh, M.P.: An Ontology for Commitments in Multiagent Systems: Toward a Unification of Normative Concepts. Artificial Intelligence and Law 7(1), 97–113 (1999)
14. OASIS: Reference Architecture Foundation for Service Oriented Architecture, Version 1.0, Organization for the Advancement of Structured Information Standards (2009)
15. Aniketos: Deliverable 6.1: Initial analysis of the industrial case studies (2011)
16. Yu, E.: Modelling Strategic Relationships for Process Reengineering. PhD thesis, University of Toronto, Canada (1996)
17. Bresciani, P., Perini, A., Giorgini, P., Giunchiglia, F., Mylopoulos, J.: Tropos: An agent-oriented software development methodology. Autonomous Agents and Multi-Agent Systems 8(3), 203–236 (2004)
18. Number:formal/2011-01-03, O.D.: Business process model and notation (bpmn) version 2.0 (2011)
19. Allweyer, T.: BPMN 2.0. BoD (2010)

Applied Knowledge Transfer to European SMEs by Expertise Networks Using Mixed Reality

Eberhard Blümel, Helge Fredrich, and Andre Winge

Fraunhofer Institute for Factory Operation and Automation IFF,
Sandtorstrasse 22, 39106 Magdeburg, Germany
{eberhard.bluemel,helge.fredrich,andre.winge}@iff.fraunhofer.de

Abstract. Our modern industrial and service society is shaped by innovations, which are creating new technologies, products and technical systems, on the one hand, and professional services, on the other hand, in order to develop new markets and create future-proof jobs. However, demographic development indicates that a large proportion of older and experienced employees will be retiring, while the number of high school graduates is diminishing. In the medium-term, this parallel development is going to cause a shortage of engineers and skilled labor. One particular challenge is to make technological options utilizable for learning and incorporate them in companies directly and in the inter-company vocational training. The paper describes on the basis of two industrial case studies the utilization of mixed reality technologies as well for education and training as for technical knowledge transfer. The required technological and the didactical basics will be explained. The paper concludes with a best practice approach for transfer of expertise from research organizations to the processing industry based on the "German-Baltic Expertise Network for Virtual and Augmented Reality" project.

Keywords: Mixed Reality, Knowledge Transfer, Technology Based Training.

1 Working and Learning in Real and Virtual Environments

Technologies such as 3-D visualization, simulation, digitization, virtual reality (VR) and augmented reality (AR) hold a key position in today's information society. These technologies are employed whenever information on, knowledge of and experience with complex systems is transferred.

Virtual reality is a high-end human-computer interface that links real-time simulation and interactions through multi-sensory channels (sight, hearing, touch, smell and taste) ([5]). In its ultimate form, virtual reality enables humans to become part of and to act in a computer generated environment.

In addition to "pure" virtual reality, mixed forms exist, which are subsumed under the term mixed reality. Mixed reality denotes environments or systems, which combine the real world and virtual reality with each other. In this sense, reality and virtual reality constitute the extremes in a reality-virtuality continuum. The approaches produced are discussed in relation to learning systems in detail in ([4]).

L. Niedrite, R. Strazdina, B. Wangler (Eds.): BIR 2011 Workshops, LNBIP 106, pp. 90–101, 2012.
© Springer-Verlag Berlin Heidelberg 2012

Bruns speaks of *mixed reality* when the boundary between the real and virtual parts of a system can be freely drawn user-centrically.

Forms of mixed reality are produced by enriching the real world with virtual components for the purpose of studying real objects (*augmented reality*) or by enriching the virtual world with real components for purposes of examining the virtual world (*augmented virtuality*).

Efficient support of qualification and training in the field requires VR work systems that integrate the aforementioned virtual technologies. It is crucial that the design and simulation tools implemented in the process chain have coordinated interfaces and thus data is consistently integrated.

In this form, virtual reality is well on its way to becoming an integral part of corporate operations as an information and communication technology. For qualification and training in the field, this means that real work systems for teaching and learning will increasingly be supplemented or replaced by VR work systems. This will necessitate incorporating didactic methods in VR/AR technology development concepts (see [3]).

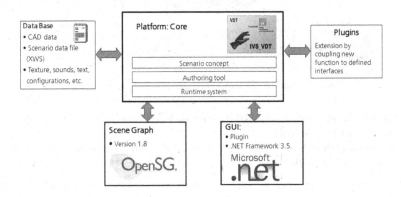

Fig. 1. VDT platform architecture

The Fraunhofer IFF's VDT Platform (Fig. 1) is a software platform that facilitates interaction with realistic virtual products, machinery and plants on the basis of immersive 3-D virtual environments. Fields of application for the VDT Platform include product and process development, and education and training.

This new technology enables trainers to conduct and individual trainees or teams of trainees to partake of theoretical and practical training on complex models in distributed environments without having to revert to real objects. The visualizations have great recognition value, simulations of a product's or plant's performance are realistic and users have options to interact realistically. Numerous cross-industry solutions have been developed for virtual interactive learning platforms for different training and educational objectives ([1], [2], [8], [9]).

2   Knowledge Transfer to Industry

The creation of VR training solutions and their implementation in operations requires specialized know-how from different fields, e.g. engineering, didactic methods for technical training and VR technology. Since small and medium-sized enterprises (SME) often lack all of this expertise, the Fraunhofer IFF developed a concept to transfer knowledge from VR training systems to industry and successfully tested it with the involvement of SMEs, educational institutions and research organizations.

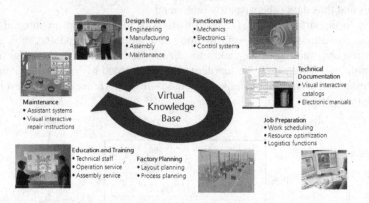

Fig. 2. Virtual reality supports the entire product life cycle

The goal is the practically oriented transfer of VR technologies to companies in the processing industry (Figure 2).

Professionally supported implementation of VR technologies based on work and demands enables SMEs to,

- already realistically represent virtually functioning new products during development and organize and optimize subsequent operations (manufacturing, assembly, operation, servicing/maintenance) during product development and qualify potential staff,
- restructure existing operations, involve staff in organization and already qualify them during development,
- qualify staff during operations planning and CNC programming and train them to operate equipment without affecting the real manufacturing operation.

In the project ViReKon being supported with funds from the the European Union and the State of Saxony-Anhalt, the Fraunhofer IFF is collaborating with training centers to create virtual training scenarios to qualify SMEs' staff. The methodological approach to knowledge transfer entails the following phases:

- **Raising SMEs' awareness**
  to identify the potentials for applications of virtual reality technologies
- **Performing an operational potential analysis**
  to specify companies' needs and structure operational problems

- **Qualifying skilled labor and management**
  to impart basic knowledge about virtual reality and test new effective forms of basic and advanced training (combining real and virtual methods in qualification)
- **Developing VR tools**
  to test and evaluate concrete VR applications in companies.

3 Case Study: Mechatronics Engineer Training with a Mixed Reality System

Learning and Doing. Prospective electronics and mechatronics engineers attend at the Technologie- und Berufsbildungszentrum Magdeburg (tbz) a basic training course to learn how to unite mechanical and electronic components into complex systems and then, in a six-week course, how to control these mechatronic systems by programming stored program control (SPC) units. The tbz employs a model of a belt conveyor system to prepare trainees for the demands in the field.

However, it only represents a fraction of a large industrial plant, which is more complex in most cases. Thus, trainees often find it difficult to integrate what they have learned from the model into an overall engineering context and then to apply it to industrial practice. This is where one ViReKon subproject comes in [6]. VR provides additional support to transfer knowledge acquired on the model to the real system. It supplies trainees and trainers diverse options for programming and operation. For instance, trainers can launch particular fault scenarios for teaching and learning, thus confronting trainees with a multitude of operational scenarios and enabling them to improve their problem solving skills. Altogether, VR expands the range of training options. Since practice makes perfect, this is a useful tool for trainees.

Classroom Internships. Virtual technologies relocate a workplace to a classroom. The system is virtually on a PC and can be operated with a keyboard and mouse. 3-D CAD data serve the researchers at the Fraunhofer IFF's VDTC as the basis for virtualization. First, the data must be processed for a virtual environment, i.e. certain physical correlations and material properties must be implemented in the raw data because a virtual environment does not contain anything that really follows the laws of nature, e.g. gravity. Therefore, the researchers must recreate reality so to speak. Researchers at the Fraunhofer IFF use their VDT Platform to reproduce such logical physical correlations.

It reproduces the performance of machinery and plants perfectly. The VR model is coupled with a real programmable logic controller (PLC) in order to use a virtualized plant for qualification purposes. When the control is actuated, the VR model in the computer responds just like the plant would respond in reality. This enables testing control sequences and programmed parameters easily and safely. Any mistakes trainees make solely affect the virtual environment. This is a great advantage for trainees because, ultimately, nothing in the virtual world can be destroyed. Thus, trial and error are allowed again.

Practicing Safely. All trainees can learn independently while sitting before their own monitors with a real PLC on the desk next to them (Fig. 3). They can experiment, try out the widest variety of scenarios and program steadily increasing complexities. This boosts the quality of, vocational training. However, training in cyberspace considered supplementary and is not intended to replace trainees' work on real production equipment. In an initial step, the VR specialists from the Fraunhofer IFF implemented a simple model of a real sorting system, which had been designed at the institute beforehand. Thus, the CAD data for it were available. Petri dishes with bacterial cultures are transported by a conveyor. A gripper grasps them and transfers them to the removal station where a pipetting unit takes a sample and processes it further. On the monitor, the apprentice follows the operations in the virtual system; the control unit the trainee uses is real. Trainees can use it to explore the system's responses. Errors made during programming remain without consequences. After all, a virtual Petri dish cannot break [7].

Fig. 3. Trainees at the tbz learn on virtual models of real machines. Photo: Dirk Mahler

4   Case Study: Knowledge Transfer on and with Virtual Interactive Product Documentations

Introduction. Although many companies in the manufacturing sector have long since made digital technologies such as 3-D CAD an integral part and basis of product research and development, they are still not taking full advantage of the potential to integrate and consistently utilize the digital models they produce.

This use case demonstrates how the company Elektromotoren- and Gerätebau Barleben GmbH (EMB) was enabled to use digital development techniques and design models effectively in different stages of the product life cycle and thus to support continuously certain aspects of corporate operations.

EMB designs, manufactures and installs transformer protection systems and electronic ballasts. In close collaboration with its clients, EMB creates technically and economically optimal solutions and employs certified and proprietary procedures to manufacture them. EMB provides its clients support from conceptualization to the start of production and for maintenance and service.

Tools for product marketing and sales as well as instructional aids that introduce staff to the functions, operation and maintenance of products are limited at present. Crucial information on workplaces or modes of operation, for instance, is not easily imparted by conventional tools such as written documentation. Tools with extensive visualization and interaction options are more expedient.

EMB's bestselling product is a Buchholz relay, a safety device for high voltage transformers. In the past, EMB used a PDF document to present this product at trade shows or in sales talks and also to qualify operators. It explained the Buchholz relay's design in texts supported by geometries rendered from the 3-D CAD system.

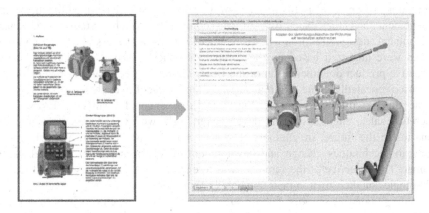

Fig. 4. A Bucholz relay from print to virtual interactive documentation

In the knowledge transfer project ViReKon (see below), EMB staff were qualified in a number of consecutive steps to convert digital models from their 3-D CAD system into virtual models and make them usable for a variety of intended purposes. Fig. 4 illustrates the situation before and after knowledge had been transferred.

Methodical Approach to Knowledge Transfer. The top-down-approach presented in in section 2 was selected to transfer knowledge about virtual reality technologies. Figure 5 visualizes the methodical approach to knowledge transfer implemented by the Fraunhofer IFF and its outcome.

This first required creating awareness among EMB's management and demonstrating the merits and potentials of VR use at a workshop. This was necessary to obtain management's willingness and support to implement these novel technologies. In small and medium-sized enterprises, such as EMB, in particular, innovations are basically supported by management since only they can take responsibility for the risks attendant with the implementation of new technologies.

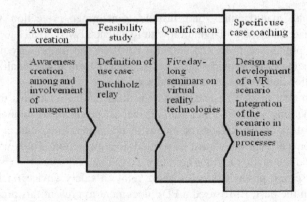

Fig. 5. Stages of knowledge transfer and the outcome

In the next step, a capability analysis of the company was performed together with management and the executives of the company's different units (e.g. sales, development, design and production). Fields of activity and use scenarios for virtual models were analyzed based on the company's concrete needs. Need for a virtual interactive product documentation of the Buchholz relay was identified, which ought to be used repeatedly in the different stages of the product life cycle.

The third step toward transferring knowledge entailed qualifying EMB staff, concretely sales, engineering and development staff, who would be employing VR scenarios in the future, in seminars. The staff was familiarized with the principles, interaction techniques, design and development of VR scenarios in a five daylong seminar. The objective of the seminars was to enable employees to use virtual reality technologies on their own in their company's operations.

Building upon this seminar, the attendees qualified were given coaching to develop a VR scenario collectively, which addressed and effectively solved the problems identified in the capability analysis.

Integrating VR Scenarios in Business and Training Processes. The decision to create virtual product documentation for a Buchholz relay was based on EMB's specific need to support operations in various stages of the product life cycle identified by the knowledge transfer capability analysis (see Figure 6).

Starting with the marketing and sales unit's requirements, a virtual model of the Buchholz relay was employed to develop a product explorer that enables salespeople to demonstrate the relay's construction, function and distinctive features vividly to customers. Virtual scenarios clearly benefit sale pitches, which previously relied solely on photos and a printed brochure. Moreover, given the sales unit's international orientation toward the Asian market, easily misunderstood texts are a less than ideal means of clear communication.

Whereas the marketing and sales unit solely needs and now communicates descriptive knowledge with the virtual product explorer, action-oriented knowledge must be supplied in other stages of the product life cycle. Important questions from customers and for the service unit include:

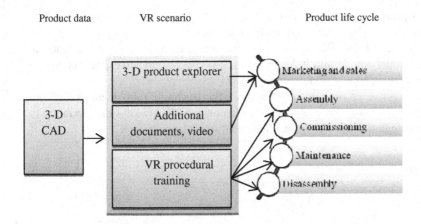

Fig. 6. Stages of the product life cycle supported by a VR scenario

- How is a Buchholz relay assembled and disassembled?
- How is a Buchholz relay put into operation and how is it maintained?
- How can its operational reliability be tested in different environments?

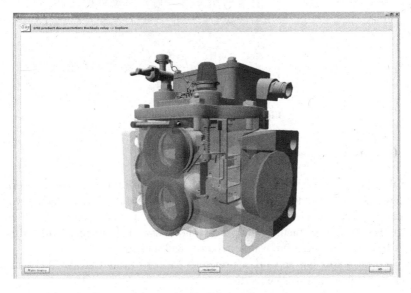

Fig. 7. Virtual interactive Buchholz relay product explorer

Texts fail to answer such questions well, especially because the documentation used has to be in a variety of languages.

The VR procedural training system does more than just present best practice solutions clearly. It also enables EMB to define its own manufacturer's standards, for instance, by presenting standard testing routines. Figure 8 pictures virtual product documentation for the assembly of a Buchholz relay.

The scenario can be viewed stereoscopically in anaglyph mode (cyan/magenta) to enhance the immersion. While it does have a few visual weaknesses, this system is more cost effective and was therefore employed.

Virtual interactive product documentation of the Buchholz relay is an example of knowledge transfer using VR technologies. Moreover, EMB now has the capability to use VR technologies to transfer knowledge about its own products.

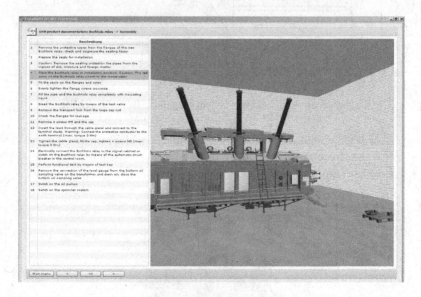

Fig. 8. VR procedural training

5   German-Baltic VAR Expertise Network

The goal of this project is the establishment of a German-Baltic expertise network for applied research of VR and AR. It will network the expertise of the partners involved from the countries of Germany, Latvia and Finland, pool researchers and users' experiences and transfer them to the processing industry and especially to SMEs for support the development of innovative products and services.

Each of the expertise network's principle partners from Germany, Latvia and Finland is contributing its own expertise:

- The Fraunhofer Institute for Factory Operation and Automation IFF specializes in applied virtual reality systems and is a member of the Federal Ministry of Education and Research's Virtual Technologies Innovation Alliance.
- The Sociotechnical Systems Engineering Institute SSII VIA specializes in methods of socio-technical simulation and is a member of the European Social Simulation Association.

- VTT Tampere specializes in VR systems for manual labor and is a member of the Finnish Forum for Intelligent Machines.

The overall network concept entails continuously interactively networking and widening the partners' expertise in the research fields of virtual and augmented reality, socio-technical simulation and customer-driven innovation to create VR based systems for customer-driven development of products and services.

The priorities in Phase 1 are the development and implementation of methods, actions and approaches:

- to systematically identify and present the expertise of the partners throughout the process chain of products and production systems (development, testing, manufacturing, commissioning and use),
- to pool expertise,
- to determine industry's needs and to disseminate offers of services and
- to develop the expertise network incorporating existing partner networks and other partners recruited for the expertise network.

International pilot projects in collaboration with SMEs are planned for Phase 2 and intended to deliver demonstrators of the expertise network's services.

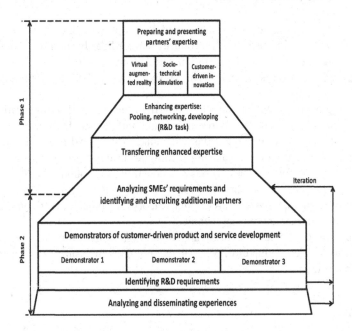

Fig. 9. Network concept

Figure 9 represents the interactive networking process over two phases. The aim of Phase 1 is to enrich the expertise of the initial partners IFF, SSII VIA and VTT by bundling their competences and to transfer the enhanced expertise to the industry.

The principle elements of Phase 1 of the concept are:

- preparing the network partners' expertise, beginning with the applicants,
- pooling, networking and widening the partners' expertise
- transferring expertise and experience to industry and research and
- identifying the demands of industry and especially SMEs.

A comparison of industry demands with the expertise on hand will deliver impetuses to identify other issues for research and development, to recruit new network partners in the countries involved and move on to the continuously interactive networking in Phase 2. The major aim of this phase is to initiate joint projects with the network partners to develop up to three demonstrators for customer-driven development of products and services using mixed reality technologies. The demonstrators are to be defined based on the requirements of the SME involved in the network. On the one hand they have to show up representative potentials for the use of mixed-reality technologies and on the other hand they will be used to identifying new R&D requirements.

6   Summary and Outlook

Virtual reality technologies have developed by leaps and bounds in recent years. Virtual reality can be used to reproduce extraordinarily complex reality. The Fraunhofer Institute for Factory Operation and Automation IFF is home to interactive high level VR environments that can be specially applied to a broad range of industrial training programs.

Digital engineering enables already today the almost seamless integration of real working systems and virtual environments and vice-versa. Hence, both the basic technological and economic conditions will make widespread use of interactive VR technologies in basic and advanced vocational training of technical specialists possible in the near future. These processes constitute the foundation for researching the didactic and technical potentials of implementing VR systems and their potentials for education. On this basis a conceptual theory is being worked on to research learning actions in real and virtual technical systems.

International expertise networks are emerging, which are disseminating and continuing to the development of VR/AR technologies to assure their acceptance by international user.

References

1. Belardinelli, C., Blümel, E., Müller, G., Schenk, M.: Making the virtual more real: research at the Fraunhofer IFF Virtual Development and Training Centre. Journal Cognitive Processing, 217–224 (2008)
2. Blümel, E., Haase, T.: Virtual Reality Platforms for Education and Training in Industry. In: Grundspenkis, J., Kirikova, M., Manolopoulos, Y., Novickis, L. (eds.) ADBIS 2009. LNCS, vol. 5968, pp. 1–7. Springer, Heidelberg (2010)

3. Blümel, E.: Stand und Entwicklungstrends des Einsatzes von VR/AR-Techniken für Qualifizierung und Training im Arbeitsprozess. In: e.V (Hrsg.): Kompetenzentwicklung in realen und virtuellen Arbeitssystemen, pp. 241–244. GfA Press, Dortmund (2007)
4. Bruns, F.W.: Lernen in Mixed Reality. In: Kompetenzentwicklung 2003, pp. 71–112. ABWF, Waxmann (2003)
5. Burdea, G., Coiffet, P.: Virtual Reality Technology, 2nd edn. John Wiley & Sons Inc. (2003)
6. Reek, T., Winge, A.: Realistic virtual systems to improve vocational training. In: Achievements and Results 2009 Annual Report of the Fraunhofer Institute for Factory Operation and Automation IFF Magdeburg, Magdeburg, pp. 96–97 (2009)
7. Reek, T., Winge, A.: Qualification in Cyberspace. In: IFFocus 2009, Magdeburg, pp. 16–19 (February 2009)
8. Schenk, M., Blümel, E., Schumann, M., Böhme, T.: Virtuelle Werkzeugmaschinen real gesteuert. wt Werkstattstechnik online 96(7/8) (2006)
9. Schenk, M., Blümel, E.: Lernplattformen zum Anlauf und Betrieb von Produktionssystemen. Industriemanagement – Zeitschrift für industrielle Geschäftsprozesse, Heft 3, 23–26 (2007)

Enterprise SPICE Based Education Capability Maturity Model

Antanas Mitasiunas[1] and Leonids Novickis[2]

[1] Vilnius University, 3 Universiteto Street, Vilnius, LT-01315, Lithuania
[2] Riga Technical University, 1 Kalku Street, Riga, LV-1658, Latvia
antanas.mitasiunas@maf.vu.lt, lnovickis@gmail.com

Abstract. In the context of knowledge society, education became one of the most critical systems. The quality of all other systems strongly depends on the quality of education system as never before. The purpose of this paper is to address the problem of quality of education system. An approach to solve this problem is based on the main assumption that education is a process oriented activity. According to this approach, product quality can be achieved by the means of process quality – process capability. Introduced here, SPICE conformant education process capability maturity model is based on process capability maturity modeling elaborated by world-wide software engineering community during the last 25 years, namely ISO/IEC 15504 that defines the capability dimension and the requirements for process definition and domain independent integrated model for enterprise-wide assessment and improvement Enterprise SPICE. A participative approach is proposed for education process assessment and improvement.

Keywords: Education process, capability maturity model, SPICE, Enterprise SPICE.

1 Introduction

It is possible to observe that in principle software engineering evolution takes the same road as traditional engineering. More than a century ago, the engineering disciplines realized that accidents like sank ships and collapsed bridges occur more and more rarely because their design procedures are able to specifically enumerate the parameters and tolerance levels. Nowadays the engineers are equipped with tools and methods to understand the consequences of these specifications and to design accordingly so that the production and manufacturing processes became reliable, predictable and efficient.

Some three decades ago, software developers started to seek for established and confirmed procedures and solutions to cope with software crisis that was caused by recurrent exceeding of project cost and schedule as well as failure of functionality and quality. Inspired by traditional engineers, software engineering community has developed standards and models such as ISO/IEC 15504 and CMMI that have been used by numerous software organizations around the world for guiding tremendous

L. Niedrite, R. Strazdina, B. Wangler (Eds.): BIR 2011 Workshops, LNBIP 106, pp. 102–116, 2012.
© Springer-Verlag Berlin Heidelberg 2012

improvements in their ability to improve productivity and quality. The concept of software process capability, which expresses process predictability, became an efficient working tool for process and product quality management.

The results of software engineering in terms of software process are generalized to any process capability assessment and improvement. In their turn, other "soft" engineers, e.g. innovation, follow pioneering way of software engineers. Software engineering being an extremely creative activity has been able to express it in process oriented terms. Developed and validated enhanced innovation and technology transfer process capability maturity model [1, 14] is another successful confirmation of the possibility to express in process oriented terms such creative activity as innovation.

The purpose of this paper is to provide a new methodology for capability maturity modeling, to develop ISO/IEC 15504 conformant education process capability maturity model EduSpice as a core element of the approach proposed and to introduce a participative approach to education capability assessment and improvement.

The state of the art in process capability maturity modeling and education process modeling is provided in the Sections 2 and 4. The Sections 3, 5 and 6 contain authors' contribution to process capability maturity modeling and education process assessment and improvement. The last Section concludes paper results achieved and provides future work to be done to complete the solution of the problem addressed.

2   Motivation and Capability Maturity Modeling

Education process capability maturity model, introduced here, is based on process capability maturity modeling elaborated by a world-wide software engineering community. Software engineering community has considerably contributed to the state of the art of process modeling. The numerous attempts to solve the software crisis applying technological and methodological approaches were not successful. Consequently software engineers turned to the software development organizational issues aiming to keep software projects within planned scope, schedule and resources.

This approach is based on the assumption that product quality can be achieved by the means of process quality – process capability. High process capability cannot be established at once during the launch of activity. Process capability can be improved applying iterative procedure of process capability assessment and improvement.

Process capability is related to process predictability. Organizational maturity expresses the way organization activities are performed. The idea of maturity expresses the improvement path of organization activities to achieve better results. Process capability concept enables to measure the state of performance of organization's activities and to plan individual steps for processes capability improvement.

The research in this area is based on ideas originated from capability maturity models (CMM) developed since 1987 by Software Engineering Institute (SEI) of Carnegie Melon University. These models have evolved into CMMI version 1.3 [2-4] known as CMMI for Development, CMMI for Acquisition and CMMI for Services.

In parallel, the international community has developed an international standard for process assessment ISO/IEC 15504: Process assessment framework, also known as project SPICE (Software Process Improvement and Capability dEtermination) initiated by the Ministry of Defence of UK in 1991 [7, 8].

ISO/IEC 15504 represents the third generation of process capability maturity models that refer to an external process reference model. The process capability assessment framework is defined in the normative part of ISO/IEC 15504-2.

In this context, an approach taken by ISO/IEC 15504 [7, 8] referring to the external process reference model is particularly important. It enables to extend model's application area outside the software engineering. External process reference model must satisfy requirements of process definition in terms of process purpose and outcomes.

Third main source in process capability maturity arena is iCMM v2.0 (integrated Capability Maturity Model), leading to the issues of model integration and architecture representation, developed by US Federal Aviation Administration in 2001. It influenced a lot the current state of CMMs area [6] and is along the same lines as ISO/IEC 15504 (SPICE) and CMMI models. Based on external process reference model approach, the convergence of SPICE and iCMM models is possible and, in fact, it is completed as Enterprise SPICE initiative, i.e. the model FAA iCMM plays the role of baseline in the development of SPICE based Enterprise Process Reference Model and Process Assessment Model. Enterprise SPICE model consists of Process Reference Model supplemented by Process Assessment Model. Enterprise SPICE has been developed by a joint effort of more than one hundred experts representing 31 countries from all continents. Enterprise SPICE is the most challenging process capability assessment and improvement initiative for the last several years. The first stage of Enterprise SPICE [5] project is completed and the draft of the future standard is publicly available.

Hundreds of various generic and specific organizational maturity models have been developed. These models mainly provide the characteristics of maturity levels. However, very few of them provide a decomposition of activity modeled as a collection of processes defined in minimal terms, namely, a process name, a process purpose and the process outcomes.

3   New Approach to Capability Maturity Modeling

The main idea of this work is to take an attempt to decompose the education activity in a set of single processes and their performance descriptions. The creative aspect of education activity is often provided as an argument against such approach. Of course, creativity cannot be modeled by process based notions. The question is whether education is really a completely creative activity. If yes, then a process oriented approach is indeed not suitable. In the following, we will argue that this is not the case.

Consider that software engineering is also an extremely creative activity, however it has been expressed in process oriented terms. Developed and validated enhanced innovation and technology transfer process capability maturity model [1, 14] is another successful confirmation of the possibility to express in process oriented terms such creative activity as innovation.

The paper [11] describes an analogy between process improvement in software development and process improvement in education, and provides arguments that the process orientation for education is even more important than for software engineering: skilled software engineers may neglect good software development practices but they can still produce a good product at the end. The process by which software is developed is not directly visible in the quality of the end product. Teachers, however, can influence the end product of their work only indirectly. On the large extent the final learning outcomes are not up to them but up to the students. All a teacher can do is to perform the process of teaching the best he can. The process is the only tool he has.

The successful results of an education process modeling are reported by a number of researchers and a particularly deep research is provided in [17] that supports the hypothesis that generic educational process model structure for higher education institutions can be established.

The provided arguments encourage the creation and validation of education capability maturity model. Based on the analytical study provided in the Section 2, a new methodology for capability maturity modeling is proposed. Such methodology is applicable for the creation of an ISO/IEC 15504 conformant continuous representation capability maturity model.

ISO/IEC 15504 introduces the concepts of a capability measurement framework and of an external process model. This enables to limit the effort for the creation of the capability maturity model: only the creation of a SPICE conformant external process model is needed and existing capability dimension can be reused.

In addition to this, Enterprise SPICE that is a generic SPICE conformant and a domain independent external process model is developed. Enterprise SPICE model consists of Primary, Organizational and Support process categories.

Enterprise SPICE being domain independent is defined at a quite abstract and high granularity level. In order to express domain dependent issues, the processes of Primary category should be defined at smaller granularity level. The processes belonging to Organizational and Support process categories are not domain sensitive and can be reused.

Therefore, the development of SPICE conformant capability maturity model can be restricted by the development of Primary category process descriptions.

The application of provided methodology enables to develop education process capability maturity model which is a ISO/IEC 15504 conformant model that reuses ISO/IEC 15504 capability framework. It provides Primary processes category of the education process dimension that satisfies the requirements of the Process Reference Model established by ISO/IEC 15504. Organizational and Support process categories can be reused from Enterprise SPICE process dimension.

In addition to education process reference model, education process assessment model can be created too. Such process assessment model ensures the possibility to assess capability of education of various institutions, to define processes capability profile, to define target processes capability profile and to update education practices to achieve target processes capability profile.

Education process reference model should be more abstract than a process assessment model. However a process assessment model should be more abstract than a real education institution's activity model. A unique assessment model must be suitable to assess and represent, in unique terms, the assessment results of various institutions. On the other hand, the granularity of an assessment model should be sufficiently small to achieve comparable assessment results and to avoid too big assessment mistakes.

So, three levels of abstraction of the process dimension can be distinguished:

- Process Reference Model – identification of processes defined in minimal terms, namely, a process name, a process purpose and the process outcomes;
- Process Assessment Model – in addition to process description within Process Reference Model, it contains the description of Base Practices and, possibly, the Work Products. Successful performance of base practices ensures the achievement of the process purpose and the process outcomes. Process Assessment Model can be understood as the collection of best practices related to education that is used as a reference standard for structuring, assessment, comparison and improvement of the education institution's activity;
- Activity model – more detailed description of the real education activity performed by a particular institution.

So, education capability maturity model can be understood as codifying of process oriented knowledge. Process capability maturity modeling can be treated as a method, system of notions, "language", tools, best practices, etc. It allows the knowledge systematization of process oriented activity and the description of the real education activity performed by particular institution. Education capability maturity model can be applied for an assessment of education process capability performed by institution; exchange of best practices contained within education activity model; definition of target education process capability profile based on assessment results and performance goals; and improvement of education activity to reach target process capability profile using the available best practices.

4   Education Process Modeling Related Work

The idea of a capability maturity modeling for education is not new. Most of contributions are based on organizational maturity modeling, i.e. on a staged representation of capability maturity models. From an application point of view, most of such models are related to information technology usage in education: e-learning, distance education and on-line education. An education process itself can be understood differently, with different stress on particular processes like teaching, learning, environment for teaching and/or learning and assessment.

An approach to codify process oriented knowledge for activity modeling is based on the 25 years old successful experience of Software Engineering community in software development process modeling. At first sight, software development is a completely creative activity. However it was modeled by tens of processes, hundreds of practices and work products. Of course, there are creative elements but they do not eliminate process oriented approach as a whole.

Computing Education Maturity Model (CEMM) [11] is inspired by SEI CMM and can be used to rate educational organizations according to their capability to deliver high quality education on a five level scale. Therefore CEMM can be used in order to improve an institution's capability by implementing the best practices and organizational changes.

The e-learning Maturity Model (eMM) [13] has had a long evolution and one of its latest versions is based on early version of Software Process Improvement and Capability dEtermination (SPICE) [8]. The result is a framework for e-learning maturity evaluation, which has been applied to the e-learning systems of several New Zealand universities.

An engineering education capability maturity modeling is addressed by several researchers. An idea of such modeling as a general strategy to overcome the lack of quality standards in the education sector is expressed by P. Jalote [9]. He addressed the need but not the implementation. The paper [15] proposes an Engineering Education Capability Maturity Model designed to improve the process of tracking, assessment and improving engineering students' capabilities in technical writing and oral communication skills, problem solving skills, interdisciplinary team collaboration skills, leadership skills, ethics and creativity. An Engineering Education Capability Maturity Model is an adaptation of an integrated process improvement model used in software systems engineering. This paper proposes three CMM-based models for improving the process capability of the engineering institution, the engineering faculty, and the engineering student. The Process Management Model for Higher Education (PMMHE) [10] is also related to the improvement process in engineering education process of the institutions of higher education. This paper discusses the process of learning as a competences certification model that impacts administrators, educators, students and alumni. The development of the Capability Maturity Model for Engineering Education System (E²-CMM) [12] is also inspired by Capability Maturity Model (CMM) used in software engineering. E²-CMM can be used in order to improve an institution's capability by implementing the best practices and organizational changes.

The Maturity Model for Process of Academic Management [16] presents a methodology for assessing the maturity of academic process management in private institutions of higher education for Brazilian market, and globally.

5   Education Capability Maturity Model - EduSpice

Education process assessment and improvement is completely based on education capability maturity model as a core tool for quality management. An idea is to build a new SPICE conformant Education capability maturity model called EduSpice as an external Process Assessment Model according to requirements [7] using Enterprise SPICE capability maturity model, that refers to the capability framework defined in the normative part ISO/IEC 15504-2. PRM EduSpice consists of Primary,

Organizational and Support process categories. Primary process category is based on results provided in [17] and consists of 10 processes. Organizational and Support process categories are reused from [5].

Identified in [17] generic processes for higher education institutions are: Reflective Research, Course Development, Production, Distribution, Academic Student Support, Assessment, Registration and Education Support System. These generic processes together with Course Delivery process and Learning process compose Primary process category.

According to ISO/IEC 15504-2, requirements for PRM process description must be done in minimal terms of process purpose and outcomes that are achieved as a result of process successful implementation. In addition to PRM Process assessment Model of EduSpice contains a set of indicators that explicitly addresses the purpose and outcomes, as defined in the PRM, and that demonstrate the achievement of the process attributes within. Description of EduSpice processes that belong to Primary process category is provided in Table 1 below.

Table 1. EduSpice Primary process category

EDU.1. Reflective Research	
Purpose	**Outcomes**
To gain knowledge of a course topic and an approach to its teaching	1) State-of-the-art in the topic is captured; 2) Main sources are identified; 3) Approaches to course teaching are analyzed; 4) Approach to course teaching is selected or developed.
Base Practices	
EDU.1.BP1: Define course topic. [Outcome 2]	
EDU.1.BP2: Identify main sources. [Outcome 2]	
EDU.1.BP3: Analyze sources identified. [Outcome 1]	
EDU.1.BP4: Understand the state-of-the-art of research. [Outcome 1]	
EDU.1.BP5: Identify teaching material available. [Outcome 3]	
EDU.1.BP6: Analyze approaches to course teaching. [Outcome 3]	
EDU.1.BP7: Select most suitable approach to course teaching. [Outcome 4]	
EDU.1.BP8: Develop new approach to course teaching if necessary. [Outcome 4]	
EDU.2. Course Development	
Purpose	**Outcomes**
To develop course and study material	1) Course structure and delivery is planned; 2) Learning outcomes are defined; 3) Course description is developed; 4) Course visualization and facilitation materials are prepared; 5) Course texts are collected and/or developed; 6) Course supporting practices are designed; 7) Material for supporting practices is developed.

Table 1. (*continued*)

Base Practices
EDU.2.BP1: Define learning outcomes of the course. [Outcome 2]
EDU.2.BP2: Plan course structure and delivery. [Outcome 1]
EDU.2.BP3: Develop course description. [Outcome 3]
EDU.2.BP4: Prepare course slides or other facilitating materials. [Outcome 4]
EDU.2.BP5: Prepare course texts for reading. [Outcome 5]
EDU.2.BP6: Plan supporting practices. [Outcome 6]
EDU.2.BP7: Design supporting practices. [Outcome 6]
EDU.2.BP8: Develop material for supporting practices. [Outcome 7]

EDU.3. Production	
Purpose	**Outcomes**
To produce study material and prepare study environment	1) Course handouts are multiplied or made available for distribution; 2) Course texts are printed or prepared in electronic form; 3) Exemplar textbooks are acquired; 4) Work places for supporting practices are installed, adapted and/or developed; 5) E-mail boxes and user accounts are created.

Base Practices
EDU.3.BP1: Assess the needs for study material and environment. [Outcomes 1-5]
EDU.3.BP2: Produce study handouts or materials in electronic media. [Outcome 1]
EDU.3.BP3: Print course texts or prepare document processors based documents. [Outcome 2]
EDU.3.BP4: Acquire most relevant textbooks and collect main references to available resources. [Outcome 3]
EDU.3.BP5: Develop requirements for work places of supporting practices. [Outcome 4]
EDU.3.BP6: Ensure availability of work places for supporting practices according to requirements. [Outcome 4]
EDU.3.BP7: Ensure access to IT infrastructure for course studies. [Outcome 5]

EDU.4. Distribution	
Purpose	**Outcomes**
To provide course study material and access to facilities to the students	1) Electronic information is published in the Internet; 2) Textbooks and course texts are made available to the students; 3) E-mail boxes and user accounts are assigned and activated; 4) Credits for use of facilities are allocated and delivered; 5) Software licenses and access are ensured.

Table 1. (*continued*)

Base Practices
EDU.4.BP1: Publish course study related material in the Internet. [Outcome 1]
EDU.4.BP2: Make available relevant textbooks and course texts to the course students. [Outcome 2]
EDU.4.BP3: Prepare and distribute e-mail boxes and user accounts data to their holders. [Outcome 3]
EDU.4.BP4: Deliver credits for the use of study facilities. [Outcome 4]
EDU.4.BP5: Ensure study software licenses and access rights for the students. [Outcome 5]

EDU.5. Course Delivery

Purpose	Outcomes
To present course material to the students to facilitate achievement of learning outcomes.	1) Mission and purpose of academic program are articulated; 2) Concepts and principles of the course topic are introduced; 3) Course core knowledge is delivered; 4) Students' target skills and abilities are clarified; 5) Intermediate learning results are monitored; 6) Supporting practices are performed and the students are trained.

Base Practices
EDU.5.BP1: Introduce the mission and purpose of study program in the context of local and global labor market. [Outcome 1]
EDU.5.BP2: Stress on concepts and principles of the course topic. [Outcome 2]
EDU.5.BP3: Clarify target knowledge, skills and abilities of the course to the students. [Outcome 4]
EDU.5.BP4: Provide core knowledge items of the course. [Outcome 3]
EDU.5.BP5: Integrate knowledge items and supporting practices to elaborate students' skills and abilities. [Outcome 3]
EDU.5.BP6: Monitor intermediate learning outcomes. [Outcome 5]
EDU.5.BP7: Ensure supporting practices performance. [Outcome 6]
EDU.5.BP8: Supervise supporting practices performance. [Outcome 6]

EDU.6. Academic Student Support

Purpose	Outcomes
To provide academic support to the students	1) A strategy for academic student support is developed; 2) Responsibility for students' support is assigned; 3) Scenarios for students' support are established; 4) Students' academic support is provided; 5) Students' academic problems are identified, recorded and classified; 6) Students' academic problems are analyzed and assessed to identify acceptable solutions; 7) Proposals to address students' academic problems are provided.

Table 1. (*continued*)

Base Practices
EDU.6.BP1: Develop strategy for academic student support. [Outcome 1]
EDU.6.BP2: Assign responsibility for academic student support. [Outcome 2]
EDU.6.BP3: Establish students' support scenarios. [Outcome 3]
EDU.6.BP4: Provide students' academic support. [Outcome 4]
EDU.6.BP5: Identify, classify and record students' academic problems. [Outcome 5]
EDU.6.BP6: Analyze students' academic to address their resolution. [Outcome 6]
EDU.6.BP7: Provide proposals to address students' academic problems systematically. [Outcome 7]

EDU.7. Assessment	
Purpose	**Outcomes**
To assess students' work and propose teaching improvements	1) Assessment instruments and methods are identified and described; 2) Criteria for learning success are established; 3) Assessment activities are performed; 4) Findings from assessments are analyzed; 5) Changes to enhance education quality are proposed.

Base Practices
EDU.7.BP1: Identify assessment methods. [Outcome 1]
EDU.7.BP2: Describe requirements for assessment instruments. [Outcome 1]
EDU.7.BP3: Establish criteria for learning outcomes assessment. [Outcome 2]
EDU.7.BP4: Assess learning outcomes achievement. [Outcome 3]
EDU.7.BP5: Identify findings of learning outcomes assessment. [Outcome 4]
EDU.7.BP6: Analyze assessment results. [Outcome 4]
EDU.7.BP7: Propose improvements for course definition, preparation and delivery. [Outcome 5]

EDU.8. Education Support System	
Purpose	**Outcomes**
To record, process and deliver education related information	1) Requirements for education system support (ESS) are established and maintained; 2) An infrastructure is established and maintained to support information needs at individual (student, teacher, employee), department, faculty and institution level; 3) Information is stored and protected from loss, damage and unwarranted access; 4) Timely access to relevant information is available to those that need it.

Table 1. (*continued*)

Base Practices
EDU.8.BP1: Establish and maintain requirements for ESS. [Outcome 1]
EDU.8.BP2: Establish and maintain infrastructure to support education information needs at all levels concerned according to ESS requirements. [Outcome 2]
EDU.8.BP3: Ensure ESS information storage and protection. [Outcome 3]
EDU.8.BP4: Transfer education process related information based activities to electronic environment. [Outcome 2]
EDU.8.BP5: Ensure ESS information availability to all authorized education process participants. [Outcome 4]
EDU.8.BP6: Ensure legal value of ESS electronic documents equal to handwritten documents. [Outcome 4]

EDU.9. Registration	
Purpose	**Outcomes**
To register and enroll the students	1) Studies candidates' applications are accepted; 2) Studies candidates' applications are proceeded; 3) Studies agreements are concluded; 4) Financial arrangements are completed; 5) Initial package for new comers is provided.

Base Practices
EDU.9.BP1: Accept study candidates' applications using various forms of information media. [Outcome 1]
EDU.9.BP2: Proceed applications of studies candidates using education support system. [Outcome 2]
EDU.9.BP3: Analyze and report applications ratings. [Outcome 2]
EDU.9.BP4: Prepare and conclude studies agreements. [Outcome 3]
EDU.9.BP5: Arrange financial obligations of enrolled to studies. [Outcome 4]
EDU.9.BP6: Provide initial packages to enrolled students. [Outcome 5]

EDU.10. Learning	
Purpose	**Outcomes**
To facilitate transformation of course information to students' knowledge, skills and abilities	1) Human and academic contacts between students and faculty are encouraged; 2) Reciprocity and cooperation among students are supported; 3) Active learning is encouraged; 4) Prompt feedback on learning progress is given; 5) Time on learning tasks is emphasized; 6) High expectations on learning success are communicated; 7) Divers talents and ways of learning are respected.

Table 1. (*continued*)

Base Practices
EDU.10.BP1: Encourage academic and human contacts between students and faculty. [Outcome 1]
EDU.10.BP2: Support cooperation and reciprocity among students. [Outcome 2]
EDU.10.BP3: Encourage active learning. [Outcome 3]
EDU.10.BP4: Give feedback on learning progress. [Outcome 4]
EDU.10.BP5: Assess the time needed to complete learning tasks. [Outcome 5]
EDU.10.BP6: Communicate high expectations on learning outcomes. [Outcome 6]
EDU.10.BP7: Respect various talents and ways of learning. [Outcome 4]

6   Education Process Assessment and Improvement

Traditional approach to process capability assessment and improvement foresees formal assessment performed by external assessor or assessment team and preparation of assessment report including recommendations for process capability improvement. Such an approach suits well for process capability determination that is dedicated for external use. However it is not sufficient for internal process improvement – it is much easier to perform processes that are defined internally by the institution rather than those defined outside.

In this section a participative approach to process assessment and improvement is introduced. According to participative approach, process improvement program consists of 6 steps and in addition to formal assessment it includes the development of education institution's activity model.

Step 1. Development of the institution's education activity process oriented model, by using terms and notions that are used in daily work, based on participative approach. Any institution or enterprise performs certain activity. However in many cases this activity is not documented, exists in the mind of employees only, is not understood as a collection of some processes and is not expressed by a common vocabulary dedicated to describe the activity and to transfer knowledge and/or experience on it. Process activity model should be done applying participative approach by the personnel as the process owner, guided by a competent consultant using wording and vocabulary as it is used in daily activity.

Step 2. Mapping of institution's activity model developed in Step 1 with developed standard education process capability maturity model. Process activity models are different in different institutions. Process capability assessment should be performed using a unique process assessment model to ensure comparability of process capability assessment results. Therefore processes defined in process activity model should be mapped to process assessment model to define the process assessment scope in standard terms. The mapping result is a collection of process assessment processes that overlap with activity model's processes.

Step 3. Guided self-assessment of institution's education process capability and conceiving of actual capability profile. Guidance is needed to receive comparable assessment results. Self-assessment approach is needed to make institution's personnel true owner of the process definition. Evidence to establish process capability will be found in process activity model, Work Products created in real activity and personnel interviews. The results of the institution's education process capability assessment will be produced as a process capability profile. Processes capability will be assessed at first at capability level 1, i.e. to what extent process is performed, process goals and process outcomes are achieved. The processes fully performed at capability level 1 can be assessed at higher capability levels.

Step 4. Definition of institutions' education process target capability profile based on institution's performance goals. It is a creative work to define target process capability profile based on institution goals and strategy. One institution can decide to improve the processes that have the lowest capability. The decision of another institution can be to stress on core business processes and to improve further the best processes in order to reach a higher capability level. The main problem that should be addressed is to link institution's goals and strategy with processes and their capability.

Step 5. Update of institutions' education activity model developed in Step 1 to achieve target capability profile defined in Step 4. Institution will improve process capability based on target profile done in terms of standard process assessment model however an institution will continue an activity based on the same wording and vocabulary, i.e. it will apply the same or updated activity model. Application of a process capability maturity model does not mean the rejection of current activity model and the shift to the standard process assessment models. Process assessment model is the management tool for process capability improvement only. Using this tool an institution acquires the knowledge indicating where the institution is and where it wants to go. Thereby the institution can define the appropriate road to achieve the desired goal, i.e., to define improved activity model based on the model developed in Step 1 to achieve target capability profile.

Step 6. Act according to updated education activity model and go to the Step 2 for continuous iterative improvement.

If the process capability improvement is included into education process, education will definitely achieve the needed quality independently of the initial stage of the institution's education process capability.

7   Conclusions and Future Work

The paper provides the following new results in process capability maturity modeling and education process capability assessment and improvement:

1) A methodology for SPICE conformant process capability maturity modeling based on ISO/IEC 15504 capability framework and Enterprise SPICE domain independent external process model is proposed;

2) Based on the proposed methodology, a SPICE conformant Process Assessment Model of Education capability maturity model called EduSpice is developed;
3) A participative approach to education process capability assessment and improvement is introduced.

Following remaining future work should be done: validation of the Education capability maturity model EduSpice by assessing experimentally the education process capability in higher education institutions.

References

1. Boronowsky, M., Woronowicz, T., Mitasiunas, A.: BONITA – Improve Transfer from Universities for Regional Development. In: The Proceedings of the 3rd ISPIM Innovation Symposium held in Quebec City, Canada, vol. 7, pp. 978–952 (2010) ISBN: 978-952-265-004-7
2. CMMI-ACQ. CMMI for Acquisition, Version 1.3. Software Engineering Institute (2010)
3. CMMI-DEV. CMMI for Development, Version 1.3. Software Engineering Institute (2010)
4. CMMI-SVC. CMMI for Services, Version 1.3. Software Engineering Institute (2010)
5. Enterprise SPICE An Integrated Model for Enterprise-wide Assessment and Improvement. Technical Report - Issue 1. The Enterprise SPICE Project Team, 184 psl (2010), http://www.enterprisespice.com/page/publication-1
6. Ibrahim, L., Bradford, B., Cole, D., LaBruyere, L., Leinneweber, H., Piszczek, D., Reed, N., Rymond, M., Smith, D., Virga, M., Wells, C.: The Federal Aviation Administration Integrated Capability Maturity Model FAA-iCMM for Enterprise-wide Improvement. Federal Aviation Administration, U.S. (2001)
7. ISO/IEC 15504-2. Information Technology – Process Assessment – Part 2: Performing an Assessment. International Standards Organization (2003)
8. ISO/IEC 15504-5. Information Technology – Process Assessment – Part 5: An Exemplar Process Assessment Model. International Standards Organization (2006)
9. Jalote, P.: Needed: a Capability Maturity Model for Engineering Education. The Economic Times India
10. Llamosa-Villalba, R., Aceros, S.E.M.: Process Management Model for Higher Education. In: IEEE EDUCON Education Engineering 2010 – The Future of Global Learning Engineering Education, Madrid, Spain, pp. 1955–1963 (2010)
11. Lutteroth, C., Luxton-Reilly, A., Dobbie, G., Hamer, J. A Maturity Model for Computing Education. Department of Computer Science, The University of Auckland, http://crpit.com/confpapers/CRPITV66Lutteroth.pdf
12. Manjula, R., Vaideeswaran, J.: A New Framework for Measuring the Quality of Engineering Education System Using SEI-CMM Approach – (E^2-CMM). International Journal of Software Engineering & Applications (IJSEA) 2(1), 28–43 (2011)
13. Marshall, S., Mitchell, G.: Applying SPICE to e-Learning: An e-Learning Maturity Model? In: ACE 2004: Proceedings of the Sixth Conference of Australasian Computing Education, pp. 185–191. Australian Computer Society (2004)
14. Novickis, L., Lesovskis, A., Mitasiunas, A.: Technology Transfer Model and Web-based Solution for Transport Logistics Service Providers. In: Proceedings od the European Computing Conference (ECC 2011), Paris, France, pp. 132–136 (2011)

15. Petrie, M.M.L.: Towards an Engineering Education Capability Maturity Model. In: Proceedings of the American Society for Engineering Education Annual Conference & Expositions (2004), http://soa.asee.org/paper/conference/paper-view.cfm?id=19350
16. Silva, D.F.A., Cabral, R.B.: Maturity Model for Process of Academic Management, http://daniels.com.br/wordpress/wp-content/uploads/2011/01/Maturity-Model-for-Process-of-Academic-Management.pdf
17. Van der Merwe, A.J.: Towards a Reusable Process Model Structure for Higher Education Institutions, dissertation of Doctor of Philosophy in Computer Science at the University of South Africa, http://uir.unisa.ac.za/bitstream/handle/10500/653/00thesis.pdf?sequence=5

Intellectual Ability Data Obtaining and Processing for E-Learning System Adaptation

Vija Vagale and Laila Niedrite

Faculty of Computing, University of Latvia, Raina boulv. 19, Riga, Latvia
vija.vagale@du.lv, laila.niedrite@lu.lv

Abstract. In this article authors describe how an e-learning system can obtain data about learner, so that later it could offer individual content for each learner, based on the obtained data. Authors also describe how the Learning Management System (LMS) Moodle has adapted a standard quiz module interface for testing elementary school students and how students' individual abilities could be measured more efficiently, for example, by measuring mathematical reaction time. For obtaining necessary testing results and partial processing a new module (TAnalizer) is offered, which is adapted to the Moodle environment. With this module one can gain precise data about each student's testing process and students' test results.

Keywords: E-Learning, User Model, Adaptation, Individualization, Customization, Personalization.

1 Introduction

E-learning is a process, which integrates digitally offered content, services and support. It includes intensive Information and Communication Technology (ICT) usage in order to promote and radically transform the learning process.

When combining e-learning with an individual approach to the learner, an adaptive system that can adapt to each user's features and needs is obtained. In case of the big number of learners individual approach requires very much time and material resources that is why it is practically impossible. Adaptive e-learning system usage in the learning process significantly increases the quality of learning.

The adaptation process of the system is based on data about users. The easiest way how to gain data, it is to interview and test the learner. While testing the goal and questions must be clearly defined, so that later by processing data gained in testing the result would be specific to characterizing magnitude of an individual person.

In this article authors offer a solution on how testing could help to gain individual intellectual ability characterizing magnitudes of the learner. Section 2 reveals concepts used in the article: customization, personalization and adaptation. In section 3, authors offer the most popular Learning Management System (LMS) Moodle adaptation opportunity review. Section 4 describes an adaptation process of the e-learning system for testing students, as well as testing process and testing result acquisition to investigate the scholar mathematical reaction time (MRT), followed by the analysis of gained

L. Niedrite, R. Strazdina, B. Wangler (Eds.): BIR 2011 Workshops, LNBIP 106, pp. 117–129, 2012.
© Springer-Verlag Berlin Heidelberg 2012

results. Section 5 indicates how experiment results can be used for the other adaptation cases. Finally, section 6 provides the concluding remarks.

2   System Individualization Types

This work gives an overview about two individualization types that depend on who initiates it: (a) customization and (b) personalization (Fig. 1)

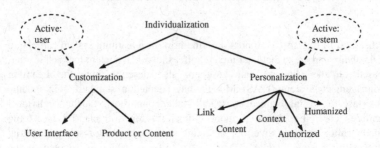

Fig. 1. Interaction of concepts used in the scientific work

In the first part of this section authors provide an explanation of customization, but in the second part the author offers definitions of personalization and adaptation.

2.1   Customization

Customization is the process, where a user takes an active part and controls adaptation of the system environment. A user indicates to computer his/her desires, it means that he/she *configures user interface* and *makes his/her own profile* by adding, taking off and moving elements.

Customization is divided into two types by options given to a user (Fig. 1):

- Customization of the user interface (UI);
- Customization of the product/content offered by the system.

Interface customization is a system functionality that allows a user to adapt system interface for his/her habits and desires. The most popular interface customization example is when the user can change color, background/pictures, layout, font size, icon size and even cursor style preferences. UI customization examples are the following: adaptive operating system interface, iGoogle, My Yahoo!, Pageflakes, Pearltrees.

Product/content customization is a system functionality that provides a possibility to choose delivered content or product. For example, Internet shops, such as eBay.com.

2.2   Personalization

Unlike customization, in personalization users are passive or with a very small control options. In this case, the system monitors, analyzes and reacts to users' behavior.

Many scientists have researched different types of the system personalization. Mostly, there are five personalization categories that are more frequently used, depending on the way how personalization is ensured: link, content, context, authorized and humanized personalization. A wide range of the personalization categories is shown in reviews in the following sources [12, 17, 19, 21].

In fact, between customization and personalization concepts there is no direct borderline. This difference is analyzed in [5].

Personalization can be ensured by the content adaptation or system visualization. In the e-learning environment a personalized system is interpreted as: (a) an adaptive system, where a user can adapt system behaviour for his/her needs, (b) an adaptive system, where automatical system adaptation takes place according to user needs without any request of the user for adaptation.

An adaptation process is based on the knowledge about the user. All data about the user is saved in the user module. A user module gives opportunity to differentiate users and provides an opportunity for the system to adapt its reaction depending on the user module [2].

In the adaptation process system performs three activities: collects information about user, creates a user model and adapts itself for a specific student. This structure is offered by Brusilovsky aud Maybury [2]. Moreover, Weibelzahl and Weber offer other models [22]: namely, Benyon and Murray model, Oppermann model, and Jameson model.

3   Moodle Personalization Opportunity Descriptions

Testing is one of the ways how to explore student's activity reaction time. In the educational system of Latvia employees widely use three online environments for designing tests: (1) Google environment surveys/questionnaires, (2) GENEXIS environment and (3) Moodle environment.

For this research it is necessary to make a large number of tests to gain precise time measurements that is why testing was included in the Moodle system. Moodle testing environment is broadly available and it gives opportunities to create simple quiz questions with easy collection of quiz results and processing, and also adapt the user interface for children features.

Nowadays the Open Source LMS Moodle is one of the most popular LMSs in the world [1, 7, 8, 11, 14]. Moodle is widely used in all levels of educational system in Latvia [20]. Many projects financed by the European Union help to raise the competence of the educational system in Latvia based on the Moodle system [15, 21].

There are good instructions and templates for programming, and a well-documented API [11] for Moodle. Its architecture is good for expanding, implementation, internationalization and inter-operability. Also, it has support of the community [1].

3.1   Integrated Solutions of Moodle Personalization

Personalization based on the roles and policy. Moodle offers user policies and roles, which provide different rights and opportunities depending on the given role. For ensuring user policy, one can use groupings and groups.

Accumulation of the necessary data for personalization and customization. Each user has his/her own profile, where he/she can fully or partly change the information about himself/herself. Each user can see his/her course grades. System collects data about user activities.

Personalized approach for teachers to display the course information. This approach allows displaying such information like course settings, design, and content. Setting of each learning course allow to change course parameters, to fill in the course with content, to choose resources and activities which can be used in the course, to change the course design by choosing it from the already given design list, to enroll a specific student to a certain course, and to change the user roles.

3.2   A Review of the Related Works on Moodle Personalization

Moodle is a Modular Object-Oriented Dynamic Learning Environment. This means that the system is built from separate modules, which make this system easy to adapt. It is possible to create different modules for specific needs with programming technologies such as PHP, MySql and JavaScript.

Moodle adaptation examples are displayed in the following works:

- *Moodle_LS System.* This system combines Moodle and LS-Plan sequence engine creating a new Moodle expanded version called Moodle_LS [9, 10]. Module has three main functions: it models learner according to his knowledge and learning styles, produces special course, and continues adapting the course during the learning process.
- *Module Learning Annotating for Moodle (LAM).* LAM module has provided an opportunity to attach annotations to the learning materials. Learners can view the materials directly online via Moodle and mark up annotations they want [11]. They can also see not only their annotations, but also other learners' notes. Users have also an opportunity to manage their annotations.
- *Agent-based personalization algorithm.* This algorithm is based on "the agent system, where every agent represents a single Sharable Content Object (SCO) of the available courses in the platforms' database. The algorithm works using connections between agents to exchange information about learners' progress and history of learning" [16].
- *"Activity locking" module.* This module determines activity path based on teacher-defined conditions [3, 18]. System also provides personalized learning path for each student considering his/her learning style, previous knowledge, learning speed and students' designed activities.
- *Metamodel* for adaptive courses is based on the Felder-Silverman learning style model [6]. Metamodel consists of different components, which can be combined to gain individualized course content. It provides different learning styles for learners. This model includes learning for the intuitive learners.

In the above mentioned cases for Moodle adaptation there was no research like this work, where adaptation solution of quiz environment of the Moodle system would be considered for learning process needs.

4   Description of the Experiment

Prior to offering an adapted content, system must get to know the user, i.e. system must diagnose his/her intellectual potential and competence levels. *Humans' ability* is psychical or physical property, which regulates his/her behavior; unconditioned and conditioned communication system, which is suitable for some activities. Abilities are distinguished in common and special. Common abilities are more universal, but special abilities are related to one field of the activity (for example, mathematical abilities). Persons' intellectual activity reaction time measurement is called *mental chronometry* [4, 13].

4.1   Measured Magnitudes

Mathematical reaction time (MRT) is defined as a random variable depending on two main factors - the individual and the problem type. MRT is a part of the total question response time. Total question response time is the time from question appearance moment till answer reception moment (Fig. 2). These measurements are too complicated that is why it is accepted that MRT is the time of the complete answer the question.

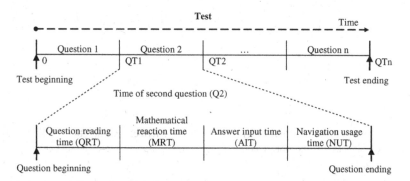

Fig. 2. Time distribution for whole test and for one of its questions. QT1 is the time from the quiz start till the first response to the question, QTn – the time of the quiz. For the second question QT1 is the time when question begins and QT2 – the time when the question ends.

4.2   Adaptation of Experimental Environment

Moodle standard testing interface was not suitable for the students who took part in the research and were from 10 to 16 years old. By following teachers' recommendations and using software given opportunities Moodle testing environment was changed based on such principles as:

• *Information adaptation for students of a specific age;*

Test questions were formulated precisely and clearly, using small amount of text and easy-to-understand language (Fig. 3b);

• *Removing elements which distract attention;*

In order not to distract attention from the test questions, all the standard test page elements in the testing environment interface were taken off leaving only test question, answer choice or input window and passage to the next question. The background color was changed and input and output font size was increased, so that children would not get tired and would perceive the information easier (Fig. 3a);

• *Full test question, answer and navigation fitting in one screen;*

To gain precise time measurements in the each test page only one question was shown fitting into one screen pictures, answer window and navigation icon (if necessary). Screen sizes of the computers in school classes where the testing process took place were taken as a default value.

• *Navigation (passage to the next question) simplification;*

In the standard test page there are two navigation bars – before and after the question. In each navigation bar one can see all question numbers and by clicking on them one can easily navigate to any question of the test. For the sake of simplicity, navigation bar location and appearance in the test module was changed. In the adapted version navigation to the next question is possible only by pressing "Next", which is located below the test answer input window. This version preserves the logical sequence of the way the student works in the test page (Fig. 3b).

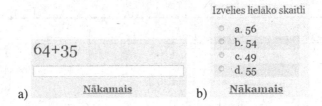

Fig. 3. Examples of the test questions with adapted interface: a) question "64+35" about "Arithmetical activities", b) question "Choose biggest number" about "two-digit number comparing"

• *Allowance to fill the test for one student only once and prohibition to return back to the previous question.*

To gain precise measurements and answers an opportunity to return back to the previous question was taken off. After unique test fulfillment an opportunity for the student to do this test again was taken off.

4.3   Experiment Process

The experiment was done in one of the Daugavpils basic schools in Latvia from April till May 2010. In general, 270 scholars from 12 classes were tested. Their age was from 10 till 16 years. Each participant has performed a certain number of tests: (a) two big overall tests with 50-55 questions in each test, (b) a number of short specialized tests with 5-10 questions in each test.

Testing process took place in one classroom, in the morning, from 8:00 till 14:00. 13 scholars participated in each testing activity. Duration of each testing activity was 40-50 minutes.

At the beginning of testing all students opened one test and each of them read the questions and filled in the answers from the standard keyboard. Using opportunities offered by the e-learning system and specialized software developed for this experiment, the following data was recorded: (1) time between question page opening and answer input (MRT) (measured in seconds); (2) the correctness of the answers (correct/incorrect).

In the testing process the following question types were used [4]:

1. *Testing of elementary mathematical skills (skills are connected with knowledge gained at school):* three-digit number comparing (Fig. 3b), searching for regularities (Fig. 4d), arithmetical progressions (Fig. 4a), geometrical progressions, arithmetical operations (Fig. 3a), finding the missing number from 1 till 10 (Fig. 4b), and determining the number of options (Fig. 4c).

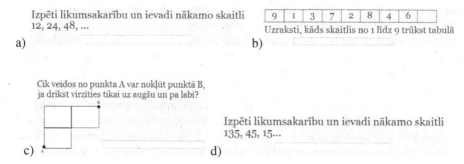

Fig. 4. Examples of mathematical elementary skill testing questions: a) "Find regularity and input the next following number" about "Arithmetical progression", b) "Write which number is missing in the table from 1 to 9" about "Finding of the missing number", c) "In how many ways it is possible to get from point A to point B, if you can move only up and to the right?" about "Determining the number of options", and d) "Find regularity and input the following number" about "Searching for regularities"

2. *Elementary mathematical skill testing (skills are not connected with knowledge gained at school).* For example, skill to count items on the screen fast (Fig. 5).

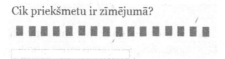

Fig. 5. Question "How many items are shown in the picture?" tests the skill to count items on the screen fast

3. Special/control questions. Determining keyboard usage speed (Fig. 6a), recognizing objects (Fig. 6b), and literacy (Fig. 6c).

Kāds dzīvnieks ir attēlots zīmējumā?

Uzraksti skaitli 1111

a. zirgs
b. briedis
c. govs
d. āpsis

Izvēlies atbildi *"dzeltens"*

1. sarkans
2. balts
3. dzeltens
4. zils

a)   b)   c)

Fig. 6. Examples of special questions: a) determining keyboard usage speed – "Write number 1111", b) recognizing objects – "Which animal is shown in the picture?", and c) checking literacy - "Choose the answer "yellow" "

Mathematics teachers worked out all test questions. They also collected the questions, divided them into types, and adapted them to the defined age group.

4.4   Gathering and Collecting of the Experiment Results

It is possible to view results gained during the testing process in Moodle system in two ways: (1) by discharging results of all attempts in a specific course; (2) by viewing detailed information about each test question.

In the first case, results of all attempts are output in one common table about all users showing the start and finish time of the test, total test time, total points, and points for each question. In this version this is not foresaw test attempt filtration about specific criteria, for instance, testing date or user.

In the second case, information about specific users' specific question is output in a separate window and shows question text, input answer, question appearance time and question window closing time. In this case there is no foreseen opportunity to save detailed information about each test question in the file or to export results in one table for one user about all test.

TAnalizer Module. In Moodle system a built-in Quiz module is not enough to gather and collect all necessary data. That is why a new module was developed, which collects and shows more complete information about the asked test questions, students' input answer and time spent in seconds for each test question.

TAnalizer module can be installed as a standard Moodle module and can be added in any course as a new activity. This module has more functions (Fig. 7). It *selects* necessary test attempt, *selects* necessary data, *processes* collected test data, *saves* processed data, *filter* data and *generates* report, which can be exported in the .txt or .xls formats. Obtained data can further be processed with Microsoft Excel, SPSS or Magma software.

TAnalizer module works similar to Quiz Module but unlike standard module TAnalizer gains and gathers more complete information about test attempts and saves necessary data for processing in a created additional table. Module collects data about Quiz Attempts for a specific course.

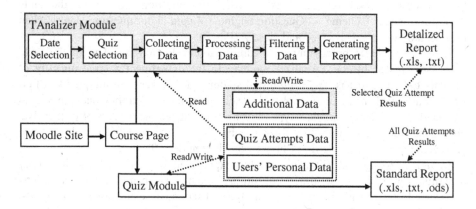

Fig. 7. TAnalizer Module interaction with existing Moodle components

Test attempt selection. Moodle system is based on the user role policy (section 3.1), so, first of all, the module is searching for an appropriate system user (for example, "student") identifier, instead of outputting all the test attempts. Then, the system searches for all appropriate courses quiz attempts after identifying the user and the course. The module user (teacher) is offered to choose test date and only then the user can choose the accomplished name of the test.

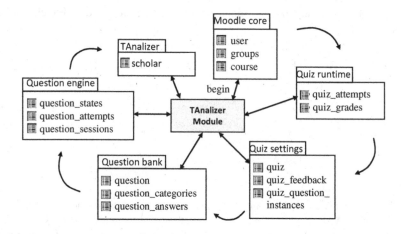

Fig. 8. TAnalizer module interactions with Moodle system table schemes and module self-created table "Scholar"

Data collecting. A created module collects data from the original tables, where the system stores results of test attempts. After choosing the date and the name of the testing follows collection of data on the respective attempt. From the table "Quiz" (scheme – "Quiz settings") one gained results of the chosen test attempt, from the table "Question" (scheme – "Question bank") – question type, from the table "Question_states" (scheme – "Question engine") – data about question states (when the question was opened, saved and closed) (Fig. 8).

By collecting and processing data additional information is saved in the table "Scholar" created by the TAnalizer module. In the experiment a large quantity of scholars took part that is why each tested student had his/her own unique identifier, which was saved in the additional table "Scholar". In the identifier one can see an indicated class number and class type (a or b). It facilitated the process of further data processing. Identifier conformity for a specific student was indicated in the module generated report by clicking the "Show Users" button (Fig. 9).

Data processing and filtration. In this experiment one of the most important magnitudes was a precise time acquisition, which was spent for answering test questions. In the testing environment interface all redundant elements were taken off (section 4.2) that is why the module employs system's window appearance of a fixed question and closing time, and calculates difference between these magnitudes. The time consumed for the question in seconds can be viewed (Fig. 9 column F) or can be saved into a file (a module generated report) by clicking buttons "Save Times to TXT" or "Save Times to Excel".

Generating report. Collected data is processed and filtered to gain and output the report about quiz attempts, which shows information about the student (name, surname, grade), test (name, points, beginning time, end time, total time), and every quiz question (number, text, inputted answer, points, end time, total question time) (Fig. 9). It is possible to save the obtained report in different ways: save all report data, save only test times or test points. Results can be exported to Excel and TXT formats.

A	B	C	D	E	F
NrQ13	TekstsQ13	AtbildeQ13	PunktiQ13	LaiksQ13	LStarpQ13
13	58–39	18	0	1272438178	12
13	58–39	19	1	1272438240	8
13	58–39	11	0	1272438223	7
13	58–39	19	1	1272438220	12

Save All to Excel	Save Times to Excel	Save Points to Excel
Show Users	Save Times to TXT	Save Points to TXT

Fig. 9. Here one can see a part of TAnalizer generated report page about the results of the 13th question. Column A shows the number of the question, B – the question text, C – students' answer to this question, D – obtained points, E – time in the seconds when the answer was given (QT13), and F – the calculated time which was spent on this question (Q13).

Created module fits very well in Moodle system, expanding the already existing opportunity to obtain process and to use results of the testing process. In combination with Quiz Module, TAnalizer module can be used to obtain data, which characterizes not only individual MRT, but also other intellectual abilities.

Gained Data Analysis in the Experiment. In the experiment during the processing of the test results we obtained more detailed results:

- *Data about e-learning system user as an individual person.* In the experiment we used mathematical form question that is why in this case we obtained data, which describes mathematical reaction time. Results describe mathematical thinking strength sides and foibles of an individual person.
- *Data about class in general.* By collecting testing results in one class the total development level was shown in a respective class, as well as an average level of all students, points of the students with the highest and the lowest results, and differences between the biggest and the smallest MRT in the class.
- *Data that describes gender differences,* taking into account the age of children. Boys' average MRT indicator is lower (better) than girls' average MRT (worse); bigger difference is seen starting from the 7th form (13-14 years) [4].
- *Data that describes educational program in general.* The experiment showed that in national minority schools student's MRT is lower (better) than that of a student of the general program [4].

An adaptive system ensures learning process that is why there is a necessity for data, which describes a system user and magnitudes that characterize his/her mathematical abilities. It would be interesting, if adaptive system would offer a user adapted course content, taking into account also individual's gender and age.

5   The Usage of the Experiment Results for Other Adaptation Cases

In the described experiment we have obtained data, which describes individual person's specialized abilities, i.e. mathematical abilities. It is possible to research also other person's characterized magnitudes (general abilities) in a similar way. Indicators of intellectual abilities are necessary for system adaptation.

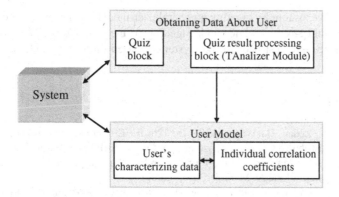

Fig. 10. A component used in the experiment including the structure of the adaptive system

Based on the approach on the adaptive systems [2], a system intervenes in three stages of the adaptation process: the data about user extraction, user's module creation, and the adaptation process. Fig. 10 shows how the adaptive system structure includes described experiment components. To obtain data about the user the authors used "Quiz block" and "Quiz result processing block". In this experiment "Quiz block" is Moodle system Quiz module with questions from the Question bank, but "Quiz result processing block" is created as a TAnalizer module.

In the user model the system must be based on the "User's characterizing data" block and "Individual correlation coefficients". In the "User's characterizing data" the data is stored that is acquired from the "Quiz result processing block" based on data gained in the testing process. In the "Individual correlation coefficients" block one can find data, which characterizes individual person's feature (physiological or other) and affects test results.

To individually test other abilities, "Quiz block" content must be changed using other quiz questions.

6   Conclusions

In the experiment the authors describe the process and testing results of the obtained data, which may be used for describing a user and for making the user model of an adaptive system.

In the experiment the authors describe the processes which are possible to use for researching other individuals' abilities.

The analyzed data indicates that the characterized magnitudes of an individual, which are obtained in testing process, are very important. During the result processing the data that is typical for some individual person group (grouping, for example, by individual features) appeared. By processing data, one can acquire correlation coefficients that indicate a connection of a person's ability with his/her physiological features. The usage of such data in the process of creation of user models of adaptive systems would lead to more precise results than the usage of individual attributes only.

In an adaptive system by creating a general user model the usage of the correlation coefficient would ensure a better understanding of the user model. More qualitative adaptation is ensured just because the system is based on a user model that is more precise.

References

1. Al-Ajlan, A., Zedan, H.: Why Moodle. In: 12th IEEE International Workshop on Future Trends of Distributed Computing Systems, pp. 58–64. IEEE Press, Washington (2008)
2. Brusilovsky, P., Maybury, M.P.: From Adaptive Hypermedia to the Adaptive Web. Communications of the ACM 45(5), 30–33 (2002)
3. Castello, J., Leris, D., Martinez, V., Sein-Echaluce, M.L.: Personalized Learning On The Moodle Platform Using The CICEI Conditionals: Support Course In Mathematics. In: INTED 2010, pp. 277–282. IATED Press, Valencia (2010)

4. Daugulis, P., Shapkova, A.: Research of Mathematical Reaction Time of Schoolchildren for Improving Mathematical Education. In: Daugulis, P. (ed.) 11th International Conference Teaching Mathematics: Retrospective and Perspectives. Daugavpils (2010)
5. Eirinaki, M., Vazirgiannis, M.: Web Mining for Web Personalization. ACM Transactions Internet Technology 3, 1–27 (2003)
6. Graf, S.: Adaptivity in Learning Management Systems Focussing on Learning Styles. PhD Thesis. Vienna University of Technology, Austria (2007)
7. Graf, S., List, B.: An Evaluation of Open Source E-Learning Platforms Stressing Adaptation Issues. In: 15th IEEE International Conference on Learning Technologies, pp. 163–165. IEEE Press, Ischia (2005)
8. Hauger, D., Köck, M.: State of the Art of Adaptivity in E-Learning Platforms. In: 15th Workshop on Adaptivity and User Modeling in Interactive System, pp. 355–360. LWA Press, Halle (2007)
9. Limongelli, C., Sciarrone, F., Vaste, G.: Personalized e-Learning in Moodle: the Moodle_LS System. Journal of e-Learning and Knowledge Society 7(1), 49–58 (2011)
10. Limongelli, C., Sciarrone, F., Temperini, M., Vaste, G.: Adaptive Learning with the LS-Plan System: a Field Evaluation. IEEE Transactions on Learning Technologies 2(3), 203–215 (2009)
11. Lin, H.-T., Wang, C.-H., Lin, C.-F., Yuan, S.-M.: Annotating Learning Materials on Moodle LMS. In: ICCTD 2009, pp. 455–459. IEEE Press, Kota Kinabalu (2009)
12. Ling, M.: Web Content Personalization and Task Complexity in e-Commerce Decision Making. Ph.D. dissertation. ETD collection for University of Nebraska, Lincoln (2006)
13. Meyer, D.E., Osman, A.M., Irwin, D.E., Yantis, S.: Modern Mental Chronometry. Biological Psychology 26, 3–67 (1988)
14. Moodle statistics, http://moodle.org/stats/
15. Raising competence of professional education teachers, http://profizgl.lu.lv/
16. Rauch, L., Andrelczyk, K., Kusiak J.: Agent-based Algorithm Dedicated to Personalization of e-Learning Courses. In: 20th EADTU, Lisbon (2007)
17. Rossi, G., Schwabe, D., Guimar, R.: Designing Personalized Web Applications. In: 10th International Conference on World Wide Web, pp. 275–284. ACM Press, New York (2001)
18. Rubio Reyes, B., Galan Moreno, M., Ocon Carreras, A., Delgado Cejudo, G., Rubio Royo, E.: Some Technological Solutions To Improve The Efficiency And Management of Learning Using Moodle Platform. In: INTED 2010, pp. 354–360. IATED Press, Valencia (2010)
19. Sehring, H., Bossung, S., Schmidt, J.: Active Learning By Personalization – Lessons Learnt from Research in Conceptual Content Management. In: 1st International Conference on Web Information Systems and Technologies, pp. 496–503. INSTICC Press, Miami (2005)
20. Vagale, V.: Utilization of CMS in Educational System in Latvia. In: 6th International Conference, Person. Color. Nature. Music, pp. 262–269. Saule Press, Daugavpils (2009)
21. Teachers of general education further education, https://talakizglitiba.visc.gov.lv/visp/
22. Weibelzahl, S., Weber, G.: Evaluating the Inference Mechanism of Adaptive Learning Systems. In: Brusilovsky, P., Corbett, A.T., de Rosis, F. (eds.) UM 2003. LNCS (LNAI), vol. 2702, pp. 154–162. Springer, Heidelberg (2003)
23. Won, K.: Personalization: Definition, Status, and Challenges Ahead. Journal of Object Technology 1(1), 29–40 (2002)

Perceived Social Influence in Watching Online Theory Presentations

Frank Goethals

IESEG School of Management (LEM-CNRS), 3 Rue de la Digue, 59000 Lille, France
f.goethals@ieseg.fr

Abstract. This paper investigates the intent of students of a Paris business school to watch online theory videos. The research model builds upon the UTAUT and extends it with other antecedents of the behavioral intention. Using 379 filled out questionnaires, the significance of the new constructs is shown. We also develop a new way to measure the perceived social influence. While the social influence is insignificant when measured in the classic way, it is significant when using our richer measure.

Keywords: Theory videos, online learning platform, acceptance, perceived social influence.

1   Introduction

Thanks to the proliferation of online social networks such as Facebook, social networks are getting more and more attention in research. Top ranked journals often publish papers on Social Network Analysis (SNA). Omega for example paid attention to SNA in [1] and the European Journal of Information Systems published similar research in [2]. In this paper we intend to link knowledge on social networks to another important field of IS research: the acceptance of an information system.

Research on IS acceptance has been very prolific. The most recognized model today is the UTAUT (unified theory of acceptance and use of technology) [3], which builds upon the TAM (Technology Acceptance Model, [4]) and many other theories (such as the Theory of Planned Behavior [5] and the Theory of Reasoned Action [6]). Social Influence is one of the four key antecedents of Behavioral Intention in the UTAUT. The constructs in the UTAUT, including the social influence, are measured through a survey. In this paper we investigate whether the classic way of measuring the social influence through a number of survey items reflects the social influence that is detected on the basis of knowledge of a person's network.

Our research was done in the context of the acceptance of a feature of an Online Learning Platform. Students at IESEG School of Management were asked to watch online theory videos before attending some class sessions. More specifically, in each of the Bachelor years, students had one class in which online movies were included. Professors noticed that students had not always watched the movie when coming to class, leading to questions about students' acceptance of the video feature of the

L. Niedrite, R. Strazdina, B. Wangler (Eds.): BIR 2011 Workshops, LNBIP 106, pp. 130–142, 2012.
© Springer-Verlag Berlin Heidelberg 2012

online learning platform. A survey was set up to gather data to measure the applicability of the UTAUT and some additional constructs that were identified on the basis of literature on antecedents of student satisfaction with offline classes. Our research, presented at the BIR 2011 conference, pointed out that these new constructs are valuable [7]. Here we extend that research by measuring the social influence construct in a different way. Moreover, we apply the model to a different group of students from [7], testing the model in a different population.

In the next section we review the theory on technology acceptance and we develop our research model. After that we explain our research method. Next the research results are presented and we discuss the findings.

2   Literature Review and Research Model

As stated above, the unified theory of acceptance and use of technology (UTAUT) [3] builds upon the TAM (Technology Acceptance Model, [4]) and many other theories (such as the Theory of Planned Behavior [5] and the Theory of Reasoned Action [6]) and is considered in modern literature as a more complete model.

The UTAUT unifies general determinants of system appreciation (e.g. performance expectancy, facilitating conditions and effort expectancy) with individual-related variables such as gender, age or experience using the system and social influences. The key dependant variables of behavioral intention and use behavior can be respectively defined as "the degree to which a person has formulated conscious plans to perform or not perform some specified future behavior" [8] and the frequency, duration, and intensity of a student's interactions with a particular system [9]. Recent research on online learning platform acceptance tested the applicability of the UTAUT constructs in this particular field. Using data of 45 participants in an executive MBA program in China, it was shown that perceived usefulness has a direct effect on the use of a virtual learning environment [10]. The other variables in their model, perceived ease of use and social norm were insignificant antecedents of the use behavior. However, that research does not include 'behavioral intention' as a mediating construct between the perceived usefulness, perceived ease of use and social norms on the one hand and 'use behavior' on the other hand. In line with the UTAUT, most research confirms the fact that the intention to use plays a mediating role. Given the fact that prior research showed a clear postive relation between behavior intention and use behavior [3], our goal (in contrast to that of [10]) is to get more insight into antecedents of intention to use. From this viewpoint, it is valuable to note that Wang et al. [11] applied the UTAUT in a study in Taiwan with a mixed sample of full time students and employees and found that effort expectancy, performance expectancy and social influence were significant antecedents of the intent to use a mobile learning platform.

Much research on online learning platforms (OLPs) acceptance focused on the acceptance in the context of pure online classes; where the OLP is not merely a complement to offline classes but is the only means used for teaching [12, 13]. Such research intends to support an entire new business model of distance learning. Chiu and Wang [13] for example investigated antecedents of students' intent to enroll for new online classes after haven taken an online class. Others investigated the acceptance of online learning platforms by employees who have to take classes to be eligible for promotion [14, 15, 16]. Grant and Danziger [14] for example applied the UTAUT (without making modifications to the model) and found that performance expectancy, effort expectancy and social influence indeed were significant antecedents of the intent to use the system. In contrast to such studies, we investigate the use of the online system as a complement to offline classes.

Prior research on OLP acceptance investigated the acceptance by instructors [17]. Others focus on the students' acceptance and this is also the focus of our paper. We also note that prior research in this field usually investigates the use of a complete platform, rather than the use of a specific feature of the platform. Studying the former level is interesting but tends to hide relevant elements in the acceptance process. For example, often students can hardly choose to use the system or not because they have to download the manual from the class' website. Still, use of the system is then limited to a number of features and some features are not used. The latter is not investigated in such studies. In our study, we focus on the intent to use a single (new) feature of the online learning platform, rather than the intent to use 'the online learning platform'.

In [7], the paper that was presented at the BIR 2011 conference, we have developed the model that is shown in Figure 1. Hypotheses H1 till H9 are directly derived from the UTAUT. They involve well known constructs such as performance expectancy (PE), effort expectancy (EE) and social influence (SI) and the moderating effects of gender and voluntariness. These are considered to be well known antecedents of behavioral intention (BI) and their role in terms of OLP acceptance has been shown before. H10 to H17 relate to constructs that received very little attention in the past. First, H10 concerns the 'Perceived Content Usefulness' construct, which refers to the perceived usefulness of the contents of the video, rather than the usefulness of using a video system as such (which is part of the classic 'performance expectancy' construct). This construct could be translated to a traditional work setting in the sense that user may (or may not) understand well why it is important to enter some data in a system. Often the data someone has to enter is only useful for another person, but the person who enters the data does not know what the other person is using the data for exactly. This may lower his/her intention to enter the data. H12 refers to the enjoyment or pain that is experienced when using the system. If the person on the videos has an irritating voice, students will have a lower intent to watch the movies in the future. If the movies are fun, students will have a higher intent to watch future movies. H13 concerns that fact that facilitating conditions should not be seen merely as a direct antecedent of real use behavior (as in the UTAUT). The facilitating conditions can also change the intent to use the system. The 'job experience' construct in H14 is a proxy for the person's flexibility to start using a new system. The longer someone did the task without using the system, the more resistance the person will have against system usage. In context of the online learning platform, this was measured through the academic year in which the student is enrolled. H15 to H17 concern moderating effects of the job experience on performance expectancy, effort expectancy and social influence.

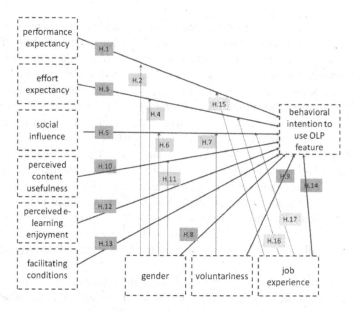

Fig. 1. Antecedents of Behavioral intention to use an OLP feature (online theory videos)

In this paper we test the same model as in the BIR conference paper [7], but here we use a different dataset and we measure the Social Influence construct in a very different way. We note that Social Influence is usually measured by asking respondents direct questions such as 'people who are important to me think that I should use the system' [3], but studies did not yet operationalize the construct to the extent that relations between influencers and influencees are measured. More specifically, we investigate the relationship between students and we link the behavioral intention to use the OLP feature to the student's friends' behavioral intention to use the OLP feature. Two basic assumptions underlying SNA are respected in our research: actors and their actions are interdependent rather than independent and fully autonomous; and relational ties between actors evidence the generation and transfer of knowledge [18].

3   Research Setup

In this section we describe the research setting, the research method and the research instrument that were used to empirically test the model.

3.1   Research Setting

The research model was tested in the Paris campus of a French Management School. The school uses a rich OLP where students can download manuals, upload assignments, have discussions, etcetera. For the academic year 2010-2011, in each student year one professor redesigned a class by moving theory lessons online.

This way, students can study theory at their own speed and professors have more time in class to help students doing exercises. In first Bachelor it concerned the 'Business Exploration' class, in second year the class on Sales Techniques and in third year the course of Management of Information Systems. During those lessons, students were asked by their respective professors to watch movies before (almost) every session. The movies were available on the OLP and ranged from 25 minutes to 50 minutes. Professors gave instructions at the end of each class and highly recommended to use the system as a complement to the course. For example, one movie in the MIS class explained the use of SQL (Structured Query Lanaguage). The professor then stated in class (in session 4) that the next session (session 5) would be devoted to exercises on SQL. Watching the movies would make offline sessions more valuable to students, giving the movies a mandatory character. Still, students who had not watched the movie were not denied access to the class, making the decision to watch the movie more voluntary. After having logged-in to the system, students can watch the movies as often as they like and professors can keep track of students' activity along the process.

The unit of analysis in this study is an individual Bachelor student, that is, a potential user of the new system and watcher of the videos. The sampling frame consisted of all students in their Bachelor degree. There were 379 students in the sample.

3.2   Research Method and Research Instrument

At the end of the semester, students were asked to fill out a survey on paper. This happened during a class in order to increase response rates. The class where the survey was done was usually different from the class concerned so that the presence of the professor could not influence answers. The questions that were used in the survey are included in the Appendix. The questions were based on prior questionnaires and adapted to our setting. A seven-point Likert scale was used to measure all constructs. Behavioral intention was measured primarily using items from Venkatesh et al. [3]. The items were then adapted (e.g. for the MIS class) into: (1) I intend to watch online videos in the future if they are included in a class of MIS; (2) I predict I would watch online videos in the future if they were included in a class of MIS; and (3) I plan to watch online videos if they are included in a class of MIS. This resulted in a Cronbach's alpha of 0.941.

Concerning the independent variables, the performance expectancy, effort expectancy, social influence and facilitating conditions scales were also adapted from Venkatesh et al. [3]. After testing for Cronbach's alpha, six items were retained to measure performance expectancy (alpha = 0.932) and for effort expectancy (alpha = 0.787), four items were retained to measure facilitating conditions (alpha = 0.748) and four items to calculate the social influence according to the way it was done in prior studies [3] (alpha = 0.733). We note we thus also measured the social influence in the classic way, to enable a comparison with our new way of measuring social influence (see below).

Furthermore six items were used to measure perceived e-learning enjoyment (alpha = 0.788) and five items to measure perceived content usefulness (alpha = 0.824).

The items for the latter two constructs were mainly derived from Giangreco et al.'s research on training evaluations [19]. All internal reliability coefficients were thus well above the 0.70 threshold recommended by Nunnally [20]. To enable the reader to interpret the statistical results presented below, we clarify that a higher score on some construct means that:

- the system is perceived as more useful (performance expectancy),
- the system is easier to use (effort expectancy),
- the facilitating conditions are satisfied,
- more social pressure is perceived to use the system,
- the system is more enjoyable (e-learning enjoyment), and
- the content is perceived as more useful.

Gender was coded as 1 for males and 2 for females. The 'job experience' in this case was measured through the year in which the student is enrolled. It should be noted that the success rate of students at the school is around 90% (thanks to severe entrance exams) so that there are very few students that retake the year. The student year is thus a very good proxy of the job experience. Moderating effects were calculated by using the mean-centered values of the variables.

To measure the social influence in another way, we asked the students to write down the names of friends in the class of which they think they undergo an influence in terms of online video platform usage. We also asked students to write down the intensity of the impact that friend had on him/her. We then calculate the New Social Impact (NSI) by multiplying the friends' intent to watch the movie with the weight that was given to the relationship with the friend, and dividing this product by the number of friends the student mentioned. By asking students about who is influencing them, we identify the people that are *perceived* as influencing the student. One could hypothesize this should give the same result as the use of the classics Social Impact construct as measured in the UTAUT, as that construct also concerns the *perceived* social impact. More specifically, Social influence (SI) was defined as 'the degree to which an individual perceives that important others believe he or she should use the system' [5].

The survey instrument was pretested with two students from each year. Only minor changes were needed after the pretest.

4   Research Results

Table 1 shows the results of the regressions (run in SPSS v19). The left pane shows the results when applying the concepts of the normal UTAUT that can be applied in this context (Model A). The pane in the middle shows the extension of the UTAUT with our new constructs, without changing the way social influence is measured (Model B). The right pane shows our extended UTAUT model with the new social impact measure instead of the old social impact measure (Model C). The R^2 of the UTAUT is remarkably low on our dataset (0.293), showing the importance of looking for different constructs in different settings. (We will not discuss the results of the UTAUT model test here, as many prior research already confirmed the significance of the antecedents of the Behavioral Intent in the UTAUT.) The new models (Model B and Model C) both have a considerably higher R^2 of 0.398. All new constructs are significant at p = .05. The higher the year the student is in, the lower his intent is to watch the online movies, showing resistance of the senior student and less motivation of senior students to work to pass a class (confirming H14). The higher the e-learning enjoyment is, the higher the intent is to watch the movie (confirming H12). Similarly, if the perceived usefulness of the content of the video is higher, the student's intent to watch the theory movie will be higher as well (confirming H10). Finally, the facilitating conditions seem to play a role indeed, in the sense that problems with slow internet connections and the like not only prevent students from watching the movie (impacting directly on the use behavior) but also lower their intent to watch the movies (confirming H13).

Table 1. Test results of the linear regressions for three different models. β is the standardized coefficient. (MF = multiplicatory factor)

	Model A: Original UTAUT		Model B: Extended UTAUT (classic SI)		Model C: Extended UTAUT (new SI)	
R^2 adjusted	0,293		0,398		0,398	
	β	p-value	β	p-value	β	p-value
Performance expectancy (PE)	.127	.010	-.001	.990	-.015	.771
Effort expectancy (EE)	.413	.000	.191	.001	.193	.001
Social influence (SI)	.034	.500	-.045	.355	-.104	.017
Gender	.003	.943	-.003	.950	.002	.957
Voluntariness	.123	.008	.079	.070	.067	.119
MF voluntariness x SI	.066	.135	.054	.186	-.036	.398
MF gender x SI	-.070	.156	-.095	.051	-.022	.610
MF gender x PE	-.047	.331	-.009	.852	-.017	.719
MF gender x EE	.030	.540	.065	.203	.044	.382
Year			-.106	.016	-.103	.018
MF year x PE			.028	.609	.036	.495
MF year x EE			-.024	.639	-.010	.840
MF year x SI			.039	.422	-.020	.635
E-learning enjoyment			.212	.000	.201	.001
Perceived Content Usefulness			.235	.000	.227	.000
MF gender x PCU			-.072	.164	-.104	.039
Facilitating conditions			.131	.009	.119	.019

Model B and Model C have the same R^2, but two more variables are significant in Model C. Interestingly, while the social influence that was measured in the classic way was insignificant (see Model A and Model B), the new way of measuring the perceived social influence turns this construct into a significant antecedent of the behavioral intention to use the system. The effect is negative, what means that, if a student's friend intends to watch a theory movie, the student is less likely to watch the movie himself. The moderating effect of gender on the impact of the perceived content usefulness on the behavioral intention is also significant. The moderating effect (with a negative sign) shows that the usefulness of the content is more important for males than for females.

5   Discussion

All new constructs are significant, with betas that are at least as big as the classic UTAUT constructs. This shows the high relevance of our new constructs. This is confirmed by the sharp increase in the R^2. The fact that the social influence becomes significant in Model C is interesting. First, it seems counter-intuitive to see that the effect is negative. If a student's friends intend to watch a movie, the student is less likely to watch the movie. While one might expect the opposite, the reasoning of students seems demotivating for professors. If the movie concerns theory (e.g. on ER diagrams or SQL) on which exercises will be made, students believe that a friend will be able to explain them swiftly the theory in class at the moment the theory is needed. If the movie concerns a topic on which there will be a discussion in the next session, students believe that if their friends watched the movie, their friends will keep the discussion going and will reply to questions, so that they can sit in class without the professor noticing the student did not watch the video. Further research is needed to confirm this perception. Secondly, the fact that social influence is significant in Model C, but not in the other models, shows that there is a real difference in the data that is gathered when students are asked questions such as 'people who influence my behavior think that I should use the online video system' from the data that is gathered if students are just asked who is influencing their intent to watch movies. While the former seems to point more in the direction of an *active* intent of a friend to *positively* influence a student to use the system, our way of measuring allows considering a more *passive* influence of a friend and an influence that may be *negative*. The standard questions that are used to measure social influence such as the one above, or 'people who are important to me think that I should use the online video system' can only get a score in terms of a positive influence, reaching from a very small positive influence to a very strong positive influence. The scale does not allow a person to notify that there was for example a very strong negative influence.

In the original UTAUT, 'experience' is included as a moderator between effort expectancy and BI and between social influence and BI. However, the experience variable there concerns the experience using the system, not the experience on the job, which is a very different construct. The latter is included in our model using the 'job experience' construct. Change management is thus more important in higher years than in lower years and seasoned students need more stimulus to use the new feature, in this case: to watch the online movies.

Perceived content usefulness was shown to have a significant, positive relation with the intent to use the system. While prior research on system acceptance had investigated to a big extent the usefulness of the system to do a job, the usefulness of the job in itself was neglected in important models such as the TAM and the UTAUT. For the evaluation of a new feature of an online learning platform, it is important to take into account whether that feature is used for a class in which students are generally very interested or not. It may be appropriate to test new features first in classes in which students are highly interested, to increase the general adoption rate of the new feature. Furthermore, it has to be noticed that the importance of PCU is higher for male students than for female students. Consequently, also the class' gender composition (percentage of males vs. females) has to be taken into account when evaluating the use of the new feature on the online learning platform. Increasing the PCU will have a bigger impact upon the intent to use the system for a male student population than for female students.

E-learning enjoyment has a very significant, positive relation with the intent to use the system. Students are more motivated to watch movies if the movies are presented in a more dynamic and convincing way, involve the student, motivate the student to learn, etcetera. Hence, the fact that watching the movies is important for students to get most out of the class is not enough to motivate students to watch movies: the movies also have to be perceived as giving enjoyment. This implies that making movies more dynamic and motivating is not optional, but something professors *have to* take into account. When talking to the professors that were involved, it became clear they had not considered enjoyment to be an important element at that point in time: they were too busy finding the right wording, deciding what content to put online and what content to keep in offline classes, and to get to understand the new online system. Future research should not only focus on the adoption of features of the platform by students, but also upon features adopted by professors. Professors seem to have focused first and for all on the features that seem useful (how can I show my content?), rather than enjoyable (e.g. adding animations and interactive quizzes).

Further research has to investigate whether our findings are also applicable in the context of pure online classes and in cases where the students are employees who take additional classes. Finally, we stress the fact that our research was conducted in a single institution and a single country and that the research needs to be replicated in other institutions and countries to guarantee the external validity.

6   Conclusions

This paper identifies constructs that can be added in a meaningful way to the UTAUT as antecedents of the Behavioral Intention. The new constructs are shown to be significant in the context of the acceptance of a feature of an online learning platform at a management school. The students are more likely to watch online theory movies if the perceived content usefulness is higher, the perceived e-learning enjoyment is higher and the facilitating conditions are better. Students in higher years (i.e., with more 'job experience') show a lower willingness to accept the new feature.

Finally, the social influence construct was measured in a different way from what is done in the UTAUT. While the social influence is not significant when measured in the classic way, it is significant when investigating the behavioral intention of a student's friends.

Acknowledgments. I would like to thank five students for their help in collecting the data for this research: Aurélien Caplan, Olivier Loquineau, Marine Billiot, Karine Toumazeau and Christophe Zanetto.

References

1. Biehl, M., Kim, H., Wade, M.: Relationships Among the Academic Business Disciplines: a Multi-method Citation Analysis. Omega 34(4), 359–371 (2006)
2. Vidgen, R., Henneberg, S., Naudé, P.: What Sort of Community is the European Conference on Information Systems? A social network analysis 1993-2005. European Journal of Information Systems 16(1), 5–19 (2007)
3. Venkatesh, V., Morris, M.G., Davis, G.B., David, F.D.: User Acceptance of Information Technology: Toward a Unified View. MIS Quarterly 3(27), 425–478 (2003)
4. Davis, F.: Perceived Usefulness, Perceived Ease of Use, and User Acceptance of Information. MIS Quarterly 3(13), 319–339 (1989)
5. Taylor, S., Todd, P.A.: Understanding Information Technology Usage: a Test of Competing Models. Information Systems Research 6(4), 144–176 (1995)
6. Karahanna, E., Straub, D.W.: The Psychological Origins of Perceived Usefulness and Ease of Use. Information and Management 35(4), 237–250 (1999)
7. Loquineau, O., Caplan, A., Toumazeau, K., Zanetto, C., Billiot, M., Goethals, F.G.: On the Intention to Use an Online Learning Platform Feature. Scientific Journal of Riga Technical University 43, 92–98 (2011)
8. Warshaw, P., Davis, F.: Disentangling Behavioral Intention and Behavioral Expectation. Journal of Experimental Social Psychology, 213–228 (1985)
9. Sykes, T.A., Venkatesh, V., Gosain, S.: Model of Acceptance with Peer Support: a Social Network Perspective to Understand Employees' System Use. MIS Quarterly 33(2), 371–393 (2009)
10. Raaij, E.M., Schepers, J.J.L.: The Acceptance and Use of a Virtual Learning Environment in China. Computers & Education 50(3), 838–852 (2008)
11. Wang, Y.S., Wu, M.C., Wang, H.Y.: Investigating the Determinants and Age and Gender Differences in the Acceptance of Mobile Learning. British Journal of Education Technology 40, 92–118 (2009)
12. Joo, Y.J., Lim, K.Y., Kim, E.K.: Online University Students' Satisfaction and Persistence. Computers & Education 57(2), 1654–1664 (2011)
13. Chiu, C.-M., Wang, E.T.G.: Understanding Web-based Learning Continuance Intention: the Role of Subjective Task Value. Information & Management 45(3), 197–201 (2008)
14. Grant, R., Danziger, J.: Corporate e-Learning: Exploring Implementation and Outcomes. Thesis, The CRITO Consortium (2007)
15. Gunawardana, K.D., Ekanayaka, S.: An Empirical Study of the Factors that Impact Medical Representatives' Attitude toward the Intention to Use m-Learning for Career Development. Sasin Journal of Management 15(1), 26 (2009)

16. Grant, R., Danziger, J.: Exploring the Corporate Benefits and Employee Adoption of Corporate e-Learning. IT in Business (2005)
17. Daim, T.U., Blanton, S., Nuri Basolglu, A., Ding, A.: Exploring Information Technology Adoption in the Classroom : Case of Online Learning Technology. International Journal of business information systems 7(3), 327–340 (2011)
18. Wasserman, S., Faust, K.: Social Network Analysis: Methods and Applications. Cambridge University Press, Cambridge (1994)
19. Giangreco, A., Carugati, A., Sebastiano, A., Della Bella, D.: Trainees' Reactions to Training : Shaping Groups and Courses for Happier Trainees. International Journal of Human Resource Management 21(13), 2468–2487 (2010)
20. Nunnally, J.C.: Introduction to Psychological Measurement. McGraw-Hill, New York (1970)

Appendix: Survey Instrument

1. Please enter your first and last name in capital letters
2. Birthdate: DD/MM/YYYY
3. 1) IESEG student or 2) International – Exchange student
4. What is your gender (M, F)?
5.a. Network 1: List the names of your closest friends (up to seven) in IESEG. Mention their IESEG year and grade the intensity of your relation. A = we are together most of the day; B = we meet once a day for a short talk; C= we meet a few times every week; D = we meet once a week.
5.b. Network 2: List up to seven people of which you think you generally influence their learning at IESEG. Also mention how big you think your impact is. (A= major impact, E=minor impact)
5.c. Network 3: List up to seven people who influence your usage (or non-usage) of the online video system and grade the intensity of this influence (A = major influence -> E = minor influence). This influence can be both 'active' (e.g. by saying you need (not) to watch the videos) and 'passive' (e.g. by saying that they did (not) watch the videos). Write A for active or P for passive. Also mention whether the influence was rather positive (i.e. to watch the movies) or rather negative (i.e. not to watch the movies). Write a + or a - sign.

Grade from 1 to 7.
(1=Totally disagree < 2 < 3 < 4=Neutral < 5 < 6 < 7=Totally agree):

6. Items related to Interest in the class:
   Before the Management of Information systems class by F. Goethals, I was interested in the topic of that class.
   Before that class I was interested in using an online video system to watch online classes.
7. Items related to perceived e-learning enjoyment
   Overall, I enjoy the online video system
   I enjoy the flexibility in organizing my time
   The video content is presented in a dynamic and convincing way

I felt involved

I feel like the duration of an online movie was appropriate

I was motivated (either online or offline) to do my best to learn

8. Items related to performance expectancy

Using the online video system increases my productivity

Using the online video system helps me understand the course content better

I think that using the online video system would help me to succeed the course

I think the online video makes the entire class more efficient

Using the online movie system allows me to learn more quickly

The speed of the presentation was OK for me to understand the material

9. Items related to effort expectancy

Overall, the online video system is easy to use

The way you interact with the online video system is clear and understandable

Learning to operate the online video system is easy for me

It is easy to concentrate while watching to the video

The effort I made to learn something was appropriate

It is easy to get the system to do what I want it to do

10. Items related to social influence

People who influence my behavior think that I should use the online video system

People who are important to me think that I should use the online video system

In general, IESEG has supported the use of the online video system for my studies

People at IESEG who use the system have generally good grades

My teacher explained the reason for using the online system in this class

11. Items related to behavioral intention

I intend to watch online videos in the future if they are included in a class on Management of Information systems

I predict I would watch online videos in the future if they were included in a class on Management of Information systems

I plan to watch online videos in the future if they are included in a class on Management of Information systems

12. Items related to facilitating conditions

The frequency at which I have to watch the videos is appropriate

For practical reasons, the duration of individual videos was too long

The video was well structured

The video system is compatible with the systems I normally use (eg: browsers, mac etc)

I had all resources necessary to watch the video (e.g.: internet connection)

I had the knowledge that is necessary to be able to work with the movie system

13. Items related to perceived usefulness

The contents of the movies were useful for my future career

The contents fitted my prior knowledge of the topic

The topics of the movies were interesting

I understood the importance of this topic in the IESEG curriculum

Together with the offline classes, there is a good balance between theory and practice in this course

14. Item related to voluntariness of use

When online videos are available along the course, do you feel like it is mandatory to watch them?

15. Items related to use behavior

When a new video is supposed to be watched before the next offline class session, I watch the video... (1=not at all, 2=only before the exam, 3=in few cases before next offline session, 4=in most cases before next offline session, 5=at least partly before next offline session, 6=always before next offline session)

How many minutes do you on average spend on watching an individual video ? (Write a number in minutes)

16. When did you take the class on Management of Information systems? (Write 1 if it was during the 1st semester or write 2 if it was during the 2nd semester)

17. Do you have any comments?

The Conceptual Framework for Integration of Multiagent Based Intelligent Tutoring and Personal Knowledge Management Systems in Educational Settings

Janis Grundspenkis

Department of Systems Theory and Design, Riga Technical University,
1 Kalku Street, Riga, LV-1658, Latvia
Janis.Grundspenkis@cs.rtu.lv

Abstract. Requirements of the information age causes new challenges for universities – necessity to change teaching and learning process to ensure that students be able to interpret non-standardized information for problem solving and decision making and have skills of effective turning their knowledge into action which is a requisite that graduates from universities will be innovative and will become so called knowledge workers. The purpose of the paper is to attract educators' attention to the potential of getting synergy effect from integration of intelligent tutoring and knowledge assessment systems with personal knowledge management systems. The conceptual framework is based on multiagent paradigm and the novel approach how to support student-centered individualized study process using traditional modules of intelligent tutoring systems (ITSs): tutoring, student diagnosis and domain knowledge modules is described. The conception of graph based pedagogical model is given as well as implementation aspects of two systems (a part of the framework) – the intelligent tutoring system MIPITS and the intelligent knowledge assessment system IKAS are overviewed.

Keywords: Intelligent tutoring system, intelligent knowledge assessment system, personal knowledge management system, multiagent system.

1 Introduction

In information age for organizations to keep competitiveness it is more important to concentrate more on knowledge than on production of material things, i.e. knowledge becomes the most important asset of organizations and individuals as well. Universities also should take this trend towards the knowledge society into account. Nowadays universities face new challenges – how to organize educational process in such a way that graduates will become so called knowledge workers in full sense of this term. It means that students are able to interpret non-standardized information for problem solving and decision making, they have skills of innovations closely connected with effective turning information into actions. Universities have potential for reaching this goal by focusing on knowledge intensive processes both in education

L. Niedrite, R. Strazdina, B. Wangler (Eds.): BIR 2011 Workshops, LNBIP 106, pp. 143–157, 2012.
© Springer-Verlag Berlin Heidelberg 2012

and research activities. As it is underlined in [1] the information and knowledge assets (intellectual capital), i.e. knowledge that can be converted into value, makes great potential for all forward looking organizations but only in case if latter utilizes it well. At the same time universities as other typical service organizations are information rich and knowledge poor because their most valuable knowledge is tacit knowledge [2] which mainly resides in human brains. As a rule, a certain amount of this knowledge each day is lost for the university when its teachers and researchers go home and a significant part of this knowledge is lost forever if a staff member quits work. Practically the only feasible way out of this situation is to turn tacit knowledge into explicit (formalized) knowledge.

The purpose of this paper is to attract attention to the potential of integration of intelligent tutoring and knowledge assessment systems with organizational, and in particular, personal knowledge management systems which capture explicit knowledge. This, in its turn, allows universities to maintain and develop their intellectual capital and to face new challenges by introducing student-centered individualized teaching process and reach the needed learning outcomes.

The rest of the paper is organized as follows. The next section gives motivation which inspires to start the development of the framework. In the third section the traditional architecture of intelligent tutoring systems (ITSs) is shortly overviewed. In the fourth section the conceptual framework for integration of four systems mentioned above is described. The fifth section gives a conception of graph based pedagogical model which supports a tutoring module of ITS. The architecture of already implemented multiagent intelligent tutoring system MIPITS and intelligent knowledge assessment system IKAS shortly are discussed in the sixth section. Conclusions summarize the proposed framework and outline some directions of future research.

2   Motivation of the Work

Artificial intelligence and knowledge management are two research fields that are directly related to acquisition, capturing, processing, usage and dissemination of explicit knowledge. Analysis of many available sources of literature reveals rather strange situation. On the one hand parallel with the promotion of education process by advanced information and telecommunication technologies (ICTs) during last decades a lot of approaches, methods, methodologies, systems and environments have been proposed, developed and implemented under the umbrella term of technology-based learning [3]. Almost at the same time different modes of distance learning (e-Learning, m-Learning, Web-based learning, etc.) and blended learning became widespread practice. All these approaches have undeniable, well-known advantages but despite them it is needed to point at the main drawback – corresponding systems and environments cannot generate personalized learning materials and objective or subjective tests which ensure adaptation to psychological characteristics and learning styles of individual learners [4], [5]. Moreover, with the dissemination of distance learning knowledge assessment has become a constant concern [6]. At least partly the abovementioned drawbacks may be eliminated by ITSs. These systems are more adaptive because they simulate a teacher who carries out individualized tutoring by using domain and pedagogical knowledge as well as knowledge about a learner [7]. ITSs to the certain extent can adapt learning materials, generate tasks and problems from the domain knowledge, assess a learner's knowledge and provide informative feedback [8]. It is worth to stress that all these tutoring systems are based on explicit knowledge and thereby using them universities can maintain and develop their intellectual capital and to feel relatively safeguarded against changes of academic staff.

On the other hand concerning the usage of knowledge management (KM) in education the situation is not so promising as in case of tutoring and knowledge assessment systems. There are quite a lot of tools that support research which universities can utilize on personal, group, intra-university and inter-organizational levels [9]. The greatest part of systems that support research are used for search of literature, scientific data processing and scientific knowledge sharing. The "NetAcademy" approach [10] and ontology oriented KM that helps to handle scientific data [11] are only two examples. Unlike research, applications of KM ideas in education are incredible unnoticed and undeveloped. Practically only one proposal of training system on the basis of KM was found in literature [12] authors of which described two models: a problem-guided and a KM-guided training model. Reasons why education community has paid so little attention to the potential of KM are unclear. May be it is because studies in KM mainly focus of organizational knowledge captured in corporate and/or organizational memory [13], [14], [15] and on the use of advanced ICTs for the development and implementation of knowledge management systems (KMSs). However, KMSs initiatives in organizations have often run into difficulties due to the fact that their development is time and resources consuming [16], [17]. For universities these difficulties are even harder because the greatest part of their knowledge is tacit knowledge. Research on causes of problems has shifted the closer attention to the human dimension of KM because among others, one cause (possible the main one) of implementation problems is expansion of individual's personal tacit knowledge to explicit knowledge of organization as a whole. Only recently research on personal knowledge management (PKM) skills and practices emerged [18]. Tsui [19] defines PKM as a collection of processes that an individual needs to carry out in order to gather, classify, store, search and retrieve knowledge in his/her daily activities. Barth [20], in his turn, gives much shorter definition of PKM as taking responsibility for what you know, who you know, and what they know thus meaning that PKM is not geared just on individual, but it is more focusing on collaboration between knowledge workers including also creation of communities of practice for knowledge sharing and subsequently for knowledge creation. So PKM is not only the important success factor in organizational KM but it may be remarkably relevant factor for support of individualized learning as well because using PKM systems (PKMSs) at individual level universities can maintain and develop their intellectual capital.

Summarizing, integration of ITSs, intelligent knowledge assessment systems (IKASs), PKMSs and organizational KMSs may give the synergy effect in supporting effective knowledge intensive education and research processes at universities.

3   An Overview of Traditional Architecture of Intelligent Tutoring Systems

Research in the domain of ITSs has been carried out for over 30 years since the earliest SCHOLAR system for teaching South America's geography appeared [21]. Following systems (due to the scope of this paper they are not listed; see [22]) established main principles and traditional architecture of ITSs which consists of four modules – communication, tutoring, domain knowledge and student diagnosis module where the last three modules are supported by pedagogical, expert and student model, correspondingly as it is shown on Fig. 1. The communication module or interface is responsible for interaction between system and its users controlling screen layouts, interaction tools, and so on. The tutoring module handles teaching strategies and instructions needed to control a learning process by selection, sequencing and presentation of material that is most suitable for an individual learner. This is supported by a pedagogical model which uses not only built-in learning strategies but also information received from the student diagnosis module. The primary task of latter is to infer the student model containing information about the current level of learner's knowledge (what he/she has learned, what are mistakes and misconceptions, etc.), his/her psychological characteristics, past experience, learning styles, feedback and help priorities, etc. In traditional architecture of ITS knowledge assessment is carried out by the student diagnosis module, too. It compares students' solutions with experts' ones and gives an assessment. The domain knowledge module concerns objects and their relationships taught by the ITS. This module is based on the expert model containing knowledge of problems and their correct solutions.

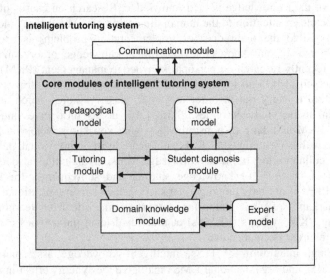

Fig. 1. Traditional architecture of ITS

The proposed conceptual framework is based on multiagent paradigm. So it is rational shortly to describe intelligent agents possibly used in ITSs (as the analysis of various already implemented ITSs shows [22] these agents in different combinations are commonly used). Agents of tutoring module evaluate, update and generate curriculum, implement different teaching strategies and/or generate and present feedback, explanation and help. Usually this module consists of several teaching strategy agents (if alternative strategies are built in a pedagogical model), a curriculum agent, and a feedback and explanation agent. The domain knowledge module includes agents-experts that solve problems and tasks related to the subject matter and examples. As a rule, for each problem and task a specific agent-expert is needed. The main purpose of agents comprising a student diagnosis module typically is evaluation and updating of information concerning a particular learner. This information is related to his/her cognitive states and psychological characteristics, mistakes and their causes, as well as to all information that could be useful for adaptation of learning process. So conclusion is that possible agents of student diagnosis module are a psychological agent (for building a profile of learner's psychological characteristics such as learning preferences and style, personality traits, etc.), a knowledge evaluation agent (for determining and registering learner's mistakes and their causes), a cognitive diagnosis agent (for building model of learner's current knowledge level and skills based on assessment) and an interaction registering agent (registering a history of learner's interaction with a system).

4   The Conceptual Framework for System Integration

The conceptual model of our approach which is based on idea that in educational settings there are two sets of knowledge workers, namely, teachers and students who are supported by ICTs technologies and tools, first was described in [23]. This model describes how knowledge workers are embedded into a KM environment. The initial model till now has been essentially modified and using the systems approach the two layer framework has been developed which is shown in Fig. 2.

At the system's layer all four systems: university's KMS, a set of PKMSs, ITSs and IKASs are integrated. Actually at the moment only two systems from those shown in Fig. 2 have been implemented using multiagent paradigm – the intelligent tutoring system MIPITS [24] and the intelligent knowledge assessment system IKAS based on concept maps [25], [26], [27]. So the second layer is the multiagent layer.

Development of other two systems (university's KMS and PKMSs) are behind. Only the first steps have been done toward university's KMS. It is clear that development of KMS for the whole university requires much more workforce than has one research group, therefore in this paper the view stated in [17] is accepted: each organization already has some rudimentary parts of KMS even before planning to develop its KMS. So one may assume that such parts also are in RTU.

In result of research on PKMS of knowledge worker the conception of agent based PKMS has been developed [28], [29]. The agent based PKMS consists from a set of agents which constitutes a knowledge worker's environment. Conditionally these agents are located in three circles. Selection of agents to large extent is based on publications [30], [31].

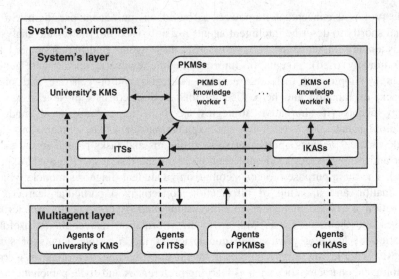

Fig. 2. Two layers of conceptual framework

The internal circle includes the following personal agents: search, assistant, filtering and workflow agents. The next circle has internal communication agents: messaging, team, cooperative, collaborative agents and communication facilitators. Agents for access to external systems are network, database, connection and access agents, network software distribution agents and intelligent Web agents. This external circle of agents may play the most important role in the knowledge worker's PKMS because nowadays the Web is the richest source of data, information and knowledge accessible for any user who needs it for his/her educational purposes. Unfortunately at the time being the Web contains a lot of data, structured data such as structured documents and online databases, simple metadata but not so many formal knowledge representations encoded using different languages and practically unconnected ontologies [32]. The challenging and promising research field called Web Intelligence [33] is directly aimed at this problem. During the last decade when practical usage of relatively simple agents started significant steps towards the development of a cybercivilization where agents will help efficiently by providing uniform access to the Web resources, in particular, Semantic Web have been made. The future evolution of suitable agents for PKMS is connected with knowledge agents and teams of agents. The first ones will be able to learn from their environments and from each other, will have access to any types of information and knowledge sources and will be able to manipulate information and knowledge in order to answer queries posed by humans and other knowledge agents. Teams of agents, in their turn, will be able to search Web sites, heterogeneous databases and knowledge bases, and work together to answer queries that are outside the scope of any individual intelligent agent. These agents will execute searching in parallel, showing a considerable degree of natural language understanding, using sophisticated pattern extraction, graphical pattern matching and context-sensitive search. So, in future more and more activities now performed by humans will be done by intelligent agents and multiagent systems in this way making PKMSs more and more intelligent. In reality a lot of work should be done within the proposed framework to implement a PKMS which to some extent comes closer to the abovementioned abilities of agents. Only the first prototype of messaging agent based on mobile devices has been implemented [34]. Several personal agents for knowledge worker's PKMS are under the development.

5   Conception of Graph Based Pedagogical Model

A tutoring module is responsible for providing the knowledge infrastructure to adapt teaching and learning process to needs and characteristics of each individual learner. Commonly as it is described in Section 3 this module tailors appropriate learning activities and selects proper methods and strategies for teaching, i.e. it provides instructions, offers a variety of materials with different media and alternative modes of explanation. The purpose of the proposed framework is to extend the functionality of tutoring module to make it more flexible. The final goal is implementation of intelligent tutoring module which tailors individual study programme by adapting the modularized curriculum structure, selects the suitable learning strategy for each study course, advises additional work by giving feedback (explanation, hints and help) and supplies a learner with learning objects given in a preferable form. This goal corresponds with main advantages of ITSs – support of individual teaching and learning, i.e. potency of personalized instruction delivery and knowledge assessment which means that a system adapts itself to different categories of students.

The main objective of any ITS is its intelligence, i.e. ensuring of adaptive teaching methods including adaptive knowledge assessment and feedback [35]. That is why the most part of already developed ITSs, for example, [36], [37] are focused on this aspect. Another aspect of adaptation – development of individual curricula corresponding both to students' preferences and interests and to the needs of industry is somewhat disregarded. Practically it means the development of flexible individual curriculum in which the well known Bloom's taxonomy [38] is taken into account for each particular study course (each of the outcome based learning objectives was processed for level of skills based on the Bloom's taxonomy [39]).

To fill out the abovementioned gap a novel approach of the usage of the 4-tuple of AND-OR graphs $<G_1, G_2, G_3, G_4>$ is proposed on which a pedagogical model is based. The focus is on the scenario in which learners start personalization with choosing the sequence of study courses to build their individual study plan. This first personalization phase is based on graph $G_1(V_1, Q_1)$ which is a tree representing a hierarchy without crosslinks. Semantics of hierarchical levels are the following: a root node (zero level node) represents the name of the study programme, the first level nodes represent study years while the second level nodes correspond to semesters. Links between an ancestor node and its descendants at these levels correspond to logical AND because all defined years and semesters are required for graduation. Nodes at the fourth level represent traditional modularized curriculum structure, namely, mandatory courses, restricted electives and free-choice courses. Links between nodes of last two levels may correspond to logical AND (students must take all mandatory courses) or to logical OR (only limited number of restricted electives and free-choice courses are needed). Each node has a label denoting corresponding number of ECTS (credit points).

The next graph $G_2(V_2, Q_2)$ is constructed for each study course and represents its structure. The root node gives the name of the course and its descendants represent topics with prerequisite relationships between topics. The third level reflects the structure of each topic, namely, how it is taught (lectures, practical seminars, laboratory works and/or individual works). If links of a graph $G_2(V_2, Q_2)$ correspond to logical OR then students have alternative ways how to acquire knowledge of the topic. For example, the topic may be taught in form of laboratory or individual work. Besides nodes may have labels indicating at what level of Bloom's taxonomy the topic should be learned. So each student can personalize his/her level of knowledge of particular topic depending on his/her specialization and interests.

The third step is mapping of each topic to the corresponding concept map (CM) [40] which is a semi-formal knowledge representation tool visualized as a graph $G_3(V_3, Q_3)$. This graph consists of finite, non-empty set of nodes V_3 representing taught concepts and a finite, non-empty set of arcs Q_3 representing relationships among concepts. Diversity of graphs representing CMs and, as a consequence, determining different types of tasks is described in [41]. Each concept is connected with corresponding third level nodes of graph $G_2(V_2, Q_2)$. Thus students can personalize the ways how they wish to acquire knowledge about the particular concept.

The last graph is $G_4(V_4, Q_4)$ the root node of which represents each concept of graph $G_3(V_3, Q_3)$ and arcs connect this root node with nodes representing learning objects (LO) which are available to acquire knowledge about this concept. According to the standards, for example, SCORM [42] a LO is an entity that contains information on study content. According to [42], [43] LOs can be non-digital or digital, they may be presented in different forms (text, video, audio, etc.), used repeatedly in different courses, may be modular, interconnectable, dividable, combined in different ways and easy integrated in different courses. So they have a great potential for personalization of learning but the real effectiveness depends on quality of student model (due to the scope of the paper this aspect is not discussed). Summarizing, lets point that selecting paths traversing nodes of graph sequence G_1, G_2, G_3 and G_4 students have different ways how to personalize their study process and find one which is more appropriate for them. Other aspects of personalization of study process implemented in intelligent knowledge assessment system IKAS are described in the next section.

6   Architecture of Developed Intelligent Systems MIPITS and IKAS

Analysis of known agent based ITSs confirms that they all have been developed for specific study courses [7]. The MIPITS system has been developed for the study course "Fundamentals of Artificial Intelligence". The implemented part of this course contains such topics as search algorithms and two-person games where practical skills of problem solving are very important. So the system offers learning materials, generates practical problems and gives feedback to a learner about his/her solution evaluating his/her knowledge. MIPITS is realized according to the ITS development methodology MASITS [44] supported by the corresponding tool which is implemented in JADE platform (http://jade.tilab.com). In general the architecture of MIPITS corresponds to the traditional architecture of ITSs described in Section 3 but its special feature is an open holonic multiagent architecture (see Fig. 3).

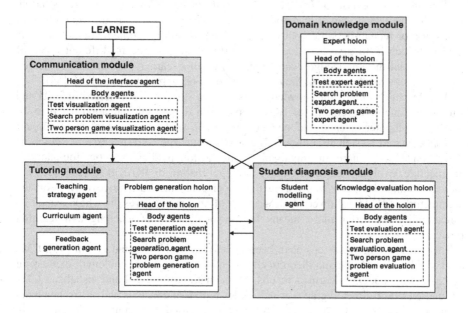

Fig. 3. The architecture of MIPITS

The architecture consists of higher level agents representing all four modules of ITS. All higher level agents can be implemented as holons [45]. Each holon consists of one head agent and a number of body agents. The head of the holon is responsible for communication outside the holon and coordination of all body agents. There are open and closed holons in MIPITS. Open holons are composed of the head and certain type of body agents which number and exact instances are not known during the design of the system and can be changed during its maintenance and runtime in that way ensuring modification of system's functionality. The body agents register their services at the directory facilitator agent which, in its turn, is used by the head of open holon to find actual body agent. Closed holons are composed of agent instances specified during the design of the system and afterwards can not be changed.

The communication module is implemented as the interface agent which in only agent interacting with a learner. The tutorial module consists from four agents. The teaching strategy agent is responsible for provision of learning material of each topic. The curriculum agent creates a personalized curriculum when a learner has registered in the system. The problem generation agent is responsible for generation of all types of problems built-in the system and adaptation of them to the knowledge level and preferences of learner. The domain knowledge module is implemented as the expert agent responsible for solving all types of problems. The student diagnosis module includes the student modelling agent and the knowledge evaluation agent. The first of mentioned agents creates, updates and provides the student model if any other agent requests for it. The knowledge evaluation agent finds a learner's mistakes by comparing his/her solution with the expert agent solution.

The tutoring scenario of MIPITS consists from the following steps: registration, login, the theoretical step with purpose to give a learning material allowing a learner to acquire or repeat theoretical knowledge of the topic, the problem solving step the goal of which is to give a learner an opportunity to practice in different types of problems, and the knowledge evaluation step when a learner's solution is evaluated and after that a feedback about the result is given. For more details see [24], [44].

The design of intelligent knowledge assessment system IKAS started in 2005 and since that time five versions of IKAS have been developed and approbated in 16 different computer science and pedagogical study courses. The goal is to support student-centered systematic knowledge assessment and self-assessment which is based on CMs. There are available quite a lot publications on foundations, architecture, evolution of functionality and approbation of IKAS ([7], [25], [27] are only few examples). For this reason the paper gives only a short overview on the architecture of IKAS followed by description of new research results which extend its functionality and offer more means for personalization of teaching and learning process.

CMs as a pedagogical tool have been developed by Novak and Govin [40]. CMs are a viable, computable and theoretically sound solution to the problem of expressing and assessing student's learning results. Mathematically defined and visualized CMs are undirected or directed graphs which nodes represent concepts and arcs relate pairs of nodes. Arcs may have weights (teacher's specified importance of relationship between two concepts) and/or linking phrases specifying the kinds of relationships. Till now CMs are more frequently used as a tutoring tool and much less as a knowledge assessment tool. The framework for conceptualizing CMs as a potential knowledge assessment tool is worked out in [46]. The authors define assessment as combination of task given to a student (variations: task demands, task constraints, task content structure), response format (variations: response mode, characteristics of response format) and a scoring system (general strategies: score components of student's CM, compare student's and expert's CMs, use combination of previous two). The important factor for developers of IKAS is that contrary to ITSs each of which is limited by specific of a study course, a CM based knowledge assessment system is independent from a content of particular study course. Actually the IKAS may be considered as a shell in which only needed CMs must be stored.

The developed IKAS has two groups of users – teachers and learners (students). Both are supported by corresponding modules. The teacher's module ensures the construction of expert's CMs. The learner's module includes tools supporting solution of CM tasks and representation of feedback. The third module is the administrator's module (not shown in Fig. 4) which manages data about users and study courses. The core of the IKAS architecture depicted in Fig. 4 is the intelligent knowledge assessment agent implemented as a multiagent system consisting from communication, interaction registering, knowledge evaluation agents and the agent-expert.

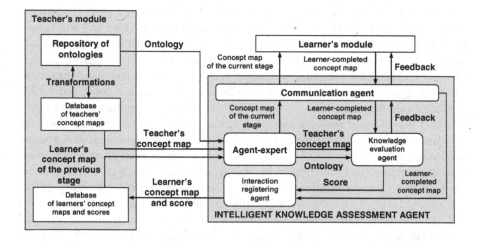

Fig. 4. The architecture of IKAS

The agent expert forms a CM of a current stage using a teacher's CM and a learner's CM of previous 'stage, and passes it to the communication agent for visualization. The agent-expert also delivers a teacher's CM and corresponding ontology to the knowledge evaluation agent for comparison. The communication agent perceives the learner's actions and is responsible for the output of feedback received from the knowledge evaluation agent. The latter compares a learner's CM with the teacher's CM and a corresponding ontology, and recognizes synonyms and several patterns (correct or incorrect) for learner's solution. Patterns of solutions are subgraphs such as, for example, a learner's defined relationship exists in a teacher's map but the type of relationship is incorrect. The interaction registering agent after receiving a learner's solution and its assessment stores them in a database.

The IKAS has capacity for adaptation to each learner's current knowledge level. This is achieved by changing the degree of task difficulty (the latter can be initialized by a learner or by the system) or by changing the form of feedback and help. The IKAS offers the definition, the short description or the example of concept and allows to ask the system to give explanation of concept, to check a proposition's correctness or to decrease the task difficulty inserting additional concepts into a CM.

Practical usage of IKAS confirms that a student model has extreme importance for achieving high degree of adaptivity to different knowledge levels, preferences and learning styles of students. At the moment a student model contains five data sets: general data about students, data about their knowledge level and mistakes, psychological characteristics, student priorities among alternative choices (used language and explanation priorities) and statistical data on explanation frequency asked by students. For further improvements of student model a conception and architecture of multiagent based user modelling shell AGENT-UM is worked out [47]. The architecture and working principles of the shell in general are based on key principles introduced by Alfred Kobsa for User Modelling System [48]. At the same time the designed shell incorporates new features. It will have GUI for the end user in order to provide possibilities to view, fill out and edit his/her model and will consist from four agents: the stereotypes manager (provides the personal inference agent with specific stereotypes, analyzes adequateness and modifies them if necessary), the tests manager (provides the user models manager with specific tests and questionnaires to get information about learner's knowledge level of the particular topic and his/her learning style), the user models manager (sends and displays specific user models to a user and provides the personal inference agent with specific user model) and the personal inference agent (receives information about user interaction with a target application, asks the user models manager for current assumptions about a user, infers new assumptions and tells them to the user models manager, sends current assumptions to a target application). It is foreseen that in case if biofeedback sensors and effectors will be available for user's emotion and psychological state observation then the fifth agent, namely the state monitoring agent which main purpose is to find appropriate motivation strategy for a user will be implemented, too. Thus the usage of AGENT-UM shell will solve student modelling tasks which are prerequisite for implementation of cognitive diagnosis agent of ITS.

Research on how to extend the use of ontologies in IKAS (not only for identification of synonyms) started with development of algorithm of OWL ontology transformation into CM [49]. In addition the algorithm for transformation of CMs into OWL ontology, the algorithm for supporting a teacher in learning material authoring based on the idea that LOs are not for isolated concepts but correspond to subgraphs of CM, and the algorithm for a study course and a personalized learning path compilation is created. The corresponding tools are implemented and integrated in the IKAS as well as the tool MergeUtil for handling files with merged ontologies (the purpose of ontology merging is possibility to check are topics and/or study courses connected or not) [50]. These results allow to get CMs from already developed ontologies, to extend a self-assessment mode offering learning materials after students' answer evaluation for remediation of detected errors and misconceptions, to merge CMs for a study course, a module or a whole study programme audit.

7   Conclusions

In this paper the conceptual framework for integration of four systems, namely ITSs, IKAS, PKMS and organizational KMS is proposed. The main purpose of the paper is to attract attention of educators that implementation of the proposed framework not only may produce a synergy effect of teaching and learning process but also may allow universities to maintain and develop their intellectual capital in the form of explicit knowledge. Implementation of the framework is based on multiagent paradigm which enables building of open architecture systems and ensures development flexibility concerning their functionality. Definitely a lot of work should be done to reach the final goal of implementation and usage of framework. Future research is focused on agent-based Web services, applications of Web Intelligence for ITSs and knowledge assessment systems, and semantic search of learning objects.

References

1. Apshvalka, D., Grundspenkis, J.: Making Organizations to Act More Intelligently in the Framework of the Organizational Knowledge Management System. In: Scientific Proceedings of Riga Technical University. 5th Series, Computer Science, Applied Computer Systems, vol. 17, pp. 72–82. RTU Publishing House, Riga (2003)
2. Nonaka, I., Takeuchi, H.: Knowledge Creating Organizations. Oxford University Press, New York (1995)
3. Anohina, A.: Analysis of the Terminology used in the Field of Virtual Learning. Journal of Educational Technology & Society 8, 91–102 (2005)
4. Computer Assisted Assessment. Using Computers to Design and Deliver Objective Tests, http://etudeedl.free.fr/annexes/assess.pdf
5. Lukashenko, R., Anohina, A.: Knowledge Assessment Systems: An Overview. In: Scientific Proceedings of Riga Technical University. 5th series, Computer Science, Applied Computer Systems, vol. 38, pp. 25–36. RTU Publishing House, Riga (2009)
6. da Rocha, F.E.L., da Costa Jr., J.V., Favero, E.L.: An Approach to Computer-Aided Learning Assessment. In: Third International Conference on Concept Mapping, Tallinn and Helsinki, September 22-25, pp. 170–177 (2003)
7. Grundspenkis, J.: MIPITS and IKAS – Two Steps towards Truly Intelligent Tutoring System Based on Integration of Knowledge Management and Multiagent Techniques. In: International Conference on e-Learning and the Knowledge Society (e-Learning 2010), Riga, Latvia, August 26-27, pp. 22–39. JUMI, Riga (2010)
8. Brusilovsky, P., Peylo, C.: Adaptive and Intelligent Web-Based Educational Systems. International Journal of Artificial Intelligence in Education 13(2-4), 156–169 (2003)
9. Kirikova, M., Grundspenkis, J.: Towards Knowledge Management Oriented Information System: Supporting Research Activities at the Technical University. In: Magyar, G., Knapp, G., Wojkowski, W., Wojkowski, W.G., Zupančič, J. (eds.) Advances in Information Systems Development: New Methods and Practice for the Networked Society, vol. 1, pp. 135–145. Springer US (2007)
10. Lincke, D.-M., Shmidt, B., Schubert, P., Selz, D.: The NetAcademy – A Novel Approach to Domain-Specific Scientific Knowledge Accumulation, Dissemination, and Review. In: Thirty-First Annual Hawaii International Conference on System Sciences, vol. 2, pp. 131–140. IEEE Computer Society, Washington, DC, USA (1998)
11. Zhao, Z., Belloum, A., Sloot, P., Hertzberger, B.: Agent Technology and Scientific Workflow Management in an E-Science Environment. In: 17th IEEE International Conference on Tools with Artificial Intelligence, Hong Kong, China, November 14-16, pp. 19–23. IEEE Computer Society (2005)
12. Chu, H.-C., Chen, Y.-M., Wen, C.-C.: A Knowledge Management Framework for Case-Based E-Learning. In: Nunes, M., McPherson, M. (eds.) IADIS International Conference e-Learning 2008, Amsterdam, The Netherlands, July 22-25, pp. 68–75 (2008)
13. Brooking, A.: Corporate Memory: Strategies for Knowledge Management. International Thomson Business Press, London (1999)
14. Walsh, J.P., Ungson, G.R.: Organizational Memory. Academy of Management Review 16(1), 57–91 (1991)
15. Grundspenkis, J.: Concepts of Organizations, Intelligent Agents, Knowledge, Learning and Memories: Towards an Inter-Disciplinary Knowledge Management. In: Wang, K., Grundspenkis, J., Yerofeyev, A. (eds.) Applied Computational Intelligence to Engineering and Business, pp. 172–191. RTU Publishing House, Riga (2001)

16. Tiwana, A.: The Knowledge Management Toolkit, 2nd edn. Prentice-Hall, New-Jersey (2002)
17. Maier, R.: Knowledge Management Systems. Springer, Heidelberg (2004)
18. Apshvalka, D.: Personal Knowledge Management. In: Remenyi, D. (ed.) 11th European Conference on Information Technology Education (ECITE), Amsterdam, Netherlands, November 11-12, pp. 17–22 (2004)
19. Tsui, E.: Technologies for Personal and Peer-to-Peer (P2P) Knowledge Management. CSC Leading Edge Forum Technology Grant report (2002)
20. Barth, S.: The Power of One. In: Knowledge Management Magazine, http://www.quantum3.co.za/KMM%20Article%20Dec2000.htm
21. Carbonell, J.R.: AI and CAI: An Artificial Intelligence Approach to Computer Assisted Instruction. IEEE Transactions on Man-Machine Systems 11(4), 190–202 (1970)
22. Grundspenkis, J., Anohina, A.: Agents in Intelligent Tutoring Systems: State of the Art. In: Scientific Proceedings of Riga Technical University. 5th series, Computer Science, Applied Computer Systems, vol. 22, pp. 110–121. RTU Publishing House, Riga (2005)
23. Grundspenkis, J.: Conceptual Framework for Integration of Multiagent and Knowledge Management Techniques in Intelligent Tutoring Systems. In: Vasilecas, O., et al. (eds.) Information Systems Development. Advances in Theory, Practice, and Education, pp. 207–216. Springer Science + Business Media (2005)
24. Lavendelis, E., Grundspenkis, J.: MASITS Methodology Supported Development of Agent Based Intelligent Tutoring System MIPITS. In: Filipe, J., Fred, A., Sharp, B. (eds.) ICAART 2010. CCIS, vol. 129, pp. 119–132. Springer, Heidelberg (2011)
25. Anohina, A., Grundspenkis, J.: Prototype of Multiagent Knowledge Assessment System for Support of Process Oriented Learning. In: 7th International Baltic Conference on Databases and Information Systems, Vilnius, Lithuania, July 3-6, pp. 211–219. IEEE Operations Center, Lithuania (2006)
26. Grundspenkis, J.: Development of Concept Map Based Adaptive Knowledge Assessment System. In: IADIS International Conference on e-Learning, Amsterdam, The Netherlands, July 22-25, pp. 395–402 (2008)
27. Grundspenkis, J.: Concept Maps as Knowledge Assessment Tool: Results of Practical Use of Intelligent Knowledge Assessment System. In: IADIS International Conference "Cognition and Exploratory Learning in Digital Age" (CELDA 2009), Rome, November 20-22, pp. 258–266. IADIS Press (2009)
28. Grundspenkis, J.: Intelligent Agents and Knowledge Management Perspectives for the Development of Intelligent Tutoring Systems. In: 9th International Conference on Enterprise Information Systems (ICEIS 2007), Funchal, Madeira, Portugal, June 13-16, pp. 380–388 (2007)
29. Grundspenkis, J.: Knowledge Creation Supported by Intelligent Knowledge Assessment System. In: 12th World Multi-Conference on Systemics, Cybernetics and Informatics, Orlando, Florida, USA, June 29-July 2, vol. VII, pp. 135–140 (2008)
30. Knapik, M., Johnson, J.: Developing Intelligent Agents for Distributed Systems. McGraw Hill, New York (1998)
31. Ellis, C., Wainer, J.: Groupware and Computer Supported Cooperative Work. In: Weiss, G. (ed.) Multiagent Systems. A Modern Approach to Distributed Artificial Intelligence, pp. 425–458. MIT Press, Massachussetts (2002)
32. Martin, P.: Knowledge Representation, Sharing and Retrieval on the Web. In: Zhong, N., Liu, J., Yao, Y.Y. (eds.) Web Intelligence, pp. 243–276. Springer, Heidelberg (2003)
33. Zhong, N., Liu, J., Yao, Y.Y. (eds.): Web Intelligence. Springer, Heidelberg (2003)

34. Osis, K., Grundspenkis, J.: Advancements in Smartphone Technology and Applications in Personal Knowledge Management. In: International Technology, Education and Development Conference (INTED 2010), Valencia, Spain, pp. 4840–4851 (2010)
35. Chakraborty, S., Roy, D., Basu, A.: Development of Knowledge Based Intelligent Tutoring System. In: Sajja, P.S., Akerkar, R. (eds.) Advanced Knowledge Based Systems: Model, Applications & Research, vol. 1, pp. 74–100 (2010)
36. Cardoso, J., Bittencourt, G., Frigo, L.B., Pozzebon, E., Postal, A.: MathTutor: A Multi-agent Intelligent Tutoring System. In: 1st IFIP Conference on AI Applications and Innovations, WCC 2004, Toulouse, France, August 22-27 (2004)
37. Liegle, J.O., Woo, H.G.: Developing Adaptive Intelligent Tutoring Systems: A General Framework and Its Implementations. In: Proceedings of Information Systems Education Conference (ISECON), Philadelphia, PA (2000)
38. Anderson, L.W., Krathwohl, D.E., Bloom, B.S.: A Taxonomy for Learning, Teaching and Assessing: A Revision of Bloom's Taxonomy of Educational Objectives [Abridged]. Addison Wesley Longman, New York (2000)
39. Kamali, R., et al.: A Curriculum Model Based on the SIGITE Guidelines. Journal of Information Technology Education 6, 363–371 (2006)
40. Novak, J.D.: Learning, Creating, and Using Knowledge: Concept Maps as Facilitative Tools in Schools and Corporations. Lawrence Erlbaum Associates, Mahwah (1998)
41. Grundspenkis, J.: Usage Experience and Student Feedback Driven Extension of Functionality of Concept Map Based Intelligent Knowledge Assessment System. Communication and Cognition 43(1&2), 1–20 (2010)
42. Institute of Electrical and Electronics Engineers. Draft Standard for Learning Object Metadata. IEEE 1484.12.1 (2002)
43. Silveira, R.A., Gomes, E.R., Viccari, R.M.: Intelligent Learning Objects: An Agent Approach to Create Reusable Intelligent Learning Environments with Learning Objects. Springer, Heidelberg (2006)
44. Lavendelis, E.: Open Multi-agent Architecture and Methodology for Intelligent Tutoring System Development. Doctoral thesis, Riga Technical University, Riga (2009)
45. Fischer, K., Schillo, M., Siekmann, J.: Holonic Multiagent Systems: A Foundation for the Organisation of Multiagent Systems. In: Mařík, V., McFarlane, D.C., Valckenaers, P. (eds.) HoloMAS 2003. LNCS (LNAI), vol. 2744, pp. 71–80. Springer, Heidelberg (2003)
46. Ruiz-Primo, M.A., Shavelson, R.J.: Problems and Issues in the Use of Concept Maps in Science Assessment. Journal of Research in Science Teaching 33(6), 569–600 (1996)
47. Lukashenko, R., Grundspenkis, J.: A Conception of Agents-Based User Modelling Shell for Intelligent Knowledge Assessment System. In: IADIS International Conference e-Learning 2009, Algarve, Portugal, June 17-20, pp. 98–104 (2009)
48. Kobsa, A.: Generic User Modelling Systems. User Modelling and User-Adaptive Interaction 11(1-2), 49–63 (2001)
49. Grundspenkis, J., Graudina, V.: Concept Map Generation from OWL Ontologies. In: 3rd International Conference on Concept Mapping, Tallinn, Estonia, September 22-25, pp. 173–180 (2008)
50. Graudina, V.: Investigation and Implementation of Integration of Knowledge Cartography Techniques and Intelligent Concept Map-Based Knowledge Assessment System. Doctoral thesis, Riga Technical University, Riga (2011)

Evaluation of Engineering Course Content by Bloom's Taxonomy: A Case Study

Andrejs Romanovs[1], Oksana Soshko[1], Yuri Merkuryev[1], and Leonids Novickis[2]

[1] Department of Modelling and Simulation, Riga Technical University,
1 Kalku Str., Riga, LV-1658, Latvia
[2] Division of Applied Computer Systems Software, Riga Technical University,
1 Kalku Str., Riga, LV-1658, Latvia
{rew,oksana,merkur}@itl.rtu.lv, lnovickis@gmail.com

Abstract. The paper presents a case study focused on evaluation of the engineering course "Logistics information system" content according to the cognitive domain of Bloom's taxonomy model. Authors introduce experience in elaborating course content, including description on the course teaching methods, outcomes, activities, and assessment system. Bloom's learning outcomes model is described as an essential element in improving course quality. The paper could be considered as the experience sharing with colleagues working on engineering courses development and assessment.

Keywords: Engineering course content, Bloom's taxonomy, logistics information systems.

1 Introduction

Nowadays the academic society is involved in the process of forming a totally new educational system which however, does not have a clear form. Common trends related to application of information and telecommunication technologies as well as promotion of modular courses show a perspective of creating virtual universities where students can pick up different courses supplied by globally spread educational institutions in order to meet their educational goals. In this context, harmonization of educational system according some common standards has a high priority in every higher school. This will allow achieving both enhancement of existing educational processes and settling a basis for new developments in educational space.

Enhancement of curriculum and course contents is a regular function of all academic stuff involved in teaching. However, now actual is a systematization of this process according to some general models, as for example Bloom's taxonomy model of learning outcomes which is popularized among plenty of educational issues.

The topicality of above mentioned in a field of engineering studies formed a goal of the current paper as sharing academic experience in "Logistics Information System" (LIS) course content developing as well as presenting a new approach of course content elaboration by means of Bloom's taxonomy. This is an obligatory course within "Information technology" Master curriculum in the faculty of Computer

L. Niedrite, R. Strazdina, B. Wangler (Eds.): BIR 2011 Workshops, LNBIP 106, pp. 158–170, 2012.
© Springer-Verlag Berlin Heidelberg 2012

science and information technologies at Riga Technical University. The rest of the paper is structured as follows. First, detailed introduction into the course is presented. Then, the empirical experience of authors' findings on improving course content based on Bloom's taxonomy is summarized. Finally, current challenges which academicians can face with during the process of course evaluation and enhancement are discussed.

2   Introduction to Logistics Information System

2.1   LIS Syllabus

The LIS course is aimed at providing students with high level knowledge, skills and competencies in Logistics Information Systems through the integration of theory and practice. The course focuses on the application of information technologies to logistics management. It is divided into two parts: Logistics Information Technologies and Logistics Information Systems. Due to the high correlation between both of them, information technology applications in logistics management should be first explored before going deeply to the subject of Logistics Information Systems, which in turn are applications of appropriate information technologies to the realization of logistics functions. However, the important point is to observe information technologies in the context of logistics management. Fig. 1 explains the LIS course main components.

As shown in Fig. 1, the course is structured into several blocks. It starts with a course overview block. According to the first principle of andragogy which states that, as the learners need to know why learning is important and how learning will be conducted, the course structure, goals, outcomes and requirements must be discussed first. Moreover, a response to IT professional standards should be provided underlining the role of the LIS curriculum for getting a professional diploma of Master in Information Technology. This is normally done in interactive discussion sessions, if the number of students is not too great. Finally, the lecturer outlines the course structure, its goals and outcomes.

The second block of the LIS course covers the main topics in Logistics Information Technologies, such as Cargo Tracking Systems, Global Positioning Systems (GPS), Geographical Information Systems (GIS), Methods of Automotive Identification (Bar codes, RFID, Biometrics), Industrial Networks, Electronic Data Interchange, Mobile Technologies in Logistics etc. Actually, they all are sub-blocks within the main Logistics Information Technologies block. The sequence of the sub-block through the course is not precisely defined, and is flexible to any lecturer/students requirements. Along with this theoretical block, students are invited to improve their practical skills performing several labs, namely "GPS and GIS application for object positioning monitoring", "Cargo Tracking Systems Analysis", and "Radio Frequency Technology applications in Logistics"[1]. The evaluation test finalizes the block of Logistics Information Technologies and allows students to summarize and analyze it during preparation for the evaluation.

The next block of the LIS course is aimed at both exploring and introducing the variety of information systems in the context of logistics management. Several solutions are discussed in the fields of transportation logistics, inventory management, warehouse logistics, production etc. In each case the focus is on the functionality of the system for supporting related logistics functions. However, besides exploring the functionality, technical solutions are also discussed in order to underline the correlation between information technologies and information system. For example, when discussing every logistics information system, the following questions are debriefed: hardware (not only the common use like computer, fax, or whatever, but also GPS tracker, or RFID scanner), software, data transmission solutions (local network, Wi-Fi, mobile network, EDI etc.), and information technology (GPS, GIS, Biometrics, etc.). In parallel with lecturer's (and invited industrial partners' as well) presentations, students make their own presentations of different logistics information systems. This task is performed as team-work and is aimed at both enhancing students' professional competence and their group working skills. The block is finalised by evaluation tasks (see the section on evaluation for detailed explanation).

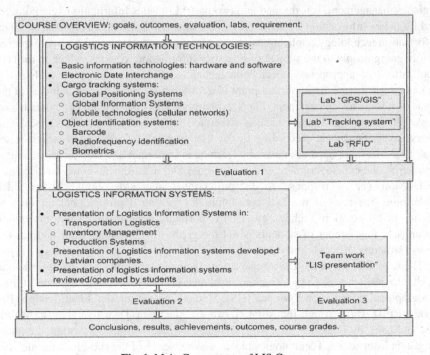

Fig. 1. Main Components of LIS Course

2.2   LIS Audience

The understanding of the students taking the course is a quite essential point in any educational process. Prior experience of the learner undoubtedly impacts on the process of learning, partly because students get their experience not only at university. The LIS course is developed for postgraduate students doing full-time Masters Studies in the field of Information Technology, so prior knowledge in information technologies and computer science is preferable. This cannot be regarded as a challenge because (1) professional competence in information technologies is presumed, when one is a student in the Faculty of Computer Science and Information Technology, and (2) the course in Logistics Information Systems is a logical enhancement of the course of Logistics Information Systems Basics which is part of the Bachelor's Curriculum.

The LIS course consists basically of postgraduate students whose average age is 22-24. Almost 90% of LIS students are employed either in private companies or in government organizations, which makes them to be extremely high demanded for qualitative learning and teaching processes. Most of the students work in the IT field, which gives them deeper professional skills. For that reason, lecturers need to be able to adjust course material to suit students experience and prior knowledge. Some features of LIS students noticed during the teaching experience are (1) students ask for concise information, (2) need more practical illustration, (3) share their own experience about subject, (4) prefer debriefing sessions to lesson, (5) prefer labs to lessons.

2.3   LIS Teaching Methods

According to our experience, a lecturer must organize the course providing a balanced learning experience using different learning methods, i.e., lectures, labs, discussions etc. To illustrate, during typical classroom lectures, conceptual and theoretical information (intuitive learning) should be supplemented with concrete, practical information (sensory style) expressed through lecturers comments and explanations. Pictures and diagrams of slides presented to visual learners must also be explained orally for verbal learners who seek explanations having words. Active learners prefer to do physical experiments and to learn by expressing themselves working in groups. They appreciate conducting lab exercises which can promote the students cognitive activities. For reflective learners, however, we provide tasks, such as evaluating different options (i.e., different cargo tracking options in the lab "Tracking system" exercise) and making analysis (of the data acquired in lab "GPS/GIS").

LIS employs lectures as the most used teaching method. This can be called a passive teaching method, where the lecturer has a major role. Lectures are mostly used in the Logistics Information Technologies block; however it still has some active learning elements such as debriefing, discussions and 5 minute activities done in pairs. The Logistics Information Technologies block is organized using workshops, seminars and team-projects. Here, both lecturers and students have active roles, so this block can be characterized as an active learning support block.

Laboratory exercises are traditional method of active learning. Labs can be used to facilitate the exploration and illumination of difficult concepts. Most importantly, labs can enhance the cognitive learning process, which is often referred to as the integration of theory with practice.

In fact, information technologies within LIS are not only the subject of teaching, but rather part of didactical tool aimed at demonstrating the power of IT in every field of application, such as logistics, education, entertainment and others [2]. The opportunity to learn information technologies/systems by applying them in studies allows students (1) to understand the basic principles of IT in Logistics (which is the aim of the course), and (2) to evaluate the variety of its applications for different solutions (which is the outcome of the course). This, according to Bloom's Taxonomy of Educational Objectives, can be explained as student growth through development of their intellectual skills and abilities.

2.4   LIS Student Evaluation

The student evaluation process is a critical challenge for every academic course. It should be realized in a way which:

1. allows adequate evaluation of student knowledge;
2. is effective for learning and can be used as learning element;
3. covers students personal character traits (for example, some of them perform better on tests, some benefit more in oral examinations, others do better writing essays).

Initially, the evaluation of students was conducted at the end of the course and was organized as an examination. In this, students choose a topic for discussion at random from a number of cards. After a brief preparation period, students present their topics and receive a grade. However, the shortcoming of this method is the limited number of questions students may answer in a limited time period. Due to that, since 2004 the examination processes has been supported by an on-line test which consists of more than 500 questions covering the main points in LIS. Students answered about 40-60 questions in a one hour time frame. This allowed the evaluation of a wider range of student knowledge and avoided any claims of unfair assessment. However, the main shortcoming of this is that examination at the end of the course usually leads students to postpone their studies to a few days before the exam.

To improve the evaluation by making it an assessment-for-learning, in 2009 a new evaluation system was implemented. The final grade for the course is derived from these three components, (1) a first evaluation after the "Logistics Information Technologies" block, (2) a second evaluation after the "Logistics Information Systems" block, and finally (3) a third evaluation for team-work at the presentation of the LIS system.

Each evaluation has its own weight and allows students to complete their final grade points during the semester. This can be called a portfolio assessment, in which students gather artifacts that illustrate their development over time. If a student is not satisfied with a final grade, it is always possible to improve the grade by taking a written examination which covers all course questions. The evaluation portfolio in the LIS course consists of:

- An on-line test with 60 questions which covers the block of Logistics Information Technologies (Evaluation 1 in Fig. 1);
- Written essays on three questions in the context of block Logistics Information Systems (Evaluation 2 in Fig. 1);
- Team-work and lecturer presentations of the Logistics Information Systems (Evaluation 3 in Fig. 1).

While there are still some shortcomings in the current evaluation, the new way of assessing students provides the following benefits:

1. motivates students to study during the course;
2. minimizes psychological stress during the assessment, by providing opportunity to improve the grade during next evaluations;
3. provides a variety of assessment methods way for students. This is an essential point for discussion in a pedagogical context, because there is no just one 'best' way of examining the students. Some of them being "slow-thinkers" would feel a lot of pressure due to time limitations during the test (in evaluation 1). Others might feel more comfortable going deeply into the subject (as is necessary in evaluation 2), and some like to give direct answers to precisely-defined questions;
4. supports both individual student work (and responsibility for the outcome) and team-work (where the responsibility for the evaluation is spread among all team workers).

The evaluation portfolio components may have differential weights which can be easily updated by the lecturer before the course is started.

3   Evaluating and Enhancing Course Content

3.1   Course Content Development

Information technology as well as any IT related subject is rapidly and fast developing field which requires a total control over the course subject and almost incessant revision it up to new trends. Being an interdisciplinary course, the content of "Logistics information System" is updated continuously toward actualities in both fields, i.e. logistics and information technologies.

A revision of the course content and course structure re-planning is usually done at three planning levels (see Fig. 2). Strategic revision is performed either to develop a new course or to update it up to new Master curriculum's goals. During this a description of the course is analyzed and course goals are updated to satisfy both Master Curriculum and industry requirements. Time horizon of strategic planning is usually 5 years.

Tactical revision is done once in three years. It analyzes course outcomes, teaching methods and tools. It results also in defining potential improvements needed to be implemented into course content. As illustration, the result of every tactical revision of LIS course is a decision on developing and implementation of new labs.

Operational revision is conducted frequently right before the course is run. It allows analyzing course activities, its duration, as well as evaluating the assessment system. Also, decisions within this stage are partly based on student evaluation of the course, see [1].

If summarize either curriculum or course content development and enhancement, it consists of several main steps. Model of course development is clearly presented in [3] by five steps, (1) translate course goals into measurable student outcomes; (2) determine levels of expertise required to achieve outcomes; (3) select both curriculum and classroom assessment techniques; (4)choose and implement instructional methods (course activities); and (5) conduct assessment and evaluate - are outcomes realized.

However this simply looking process is performed under a variety of requirements and restrictions, and usually should be done in a short time limit. Due to this a methodic help is needed sometimes to achieve the best quality in course development. However the main issue is not related to the lack of methodology, as in fact there a wide scope of literature on the subject of curriculum development. The challenge is focused in elaboration of a framework which (1) allows planning, evaluating and enhancing course content under a time limitation, (2) respects and follows pedagogical and educational aspects and (3) is intelligible for any academic personal despite their specialization and research field. This is more actual for technical studies where academic stuff involved into the teaching process has mostly empirical pedagogical skills. Forced to enhance curriculum quality they adopt engineering related methods and approaches into the process of curriculum development. Illustratively, Institute of quality Engineering of RTU presented a case study of using DMAIC methodology of Total Quality Management for developing Master and Bachelor Curriculums in "Total Quality Management" [4]. Another example from the same field of Totally Quality Management is presented in [5], presenting the application of QFD (Quality Function Deployment) in developing curriculums.

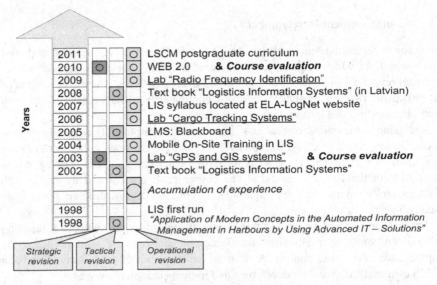

Fig. 2. LIS course revisions chronology

3.2   Course Content Evaluation According to Bloom's Model

Although the paper refers to the Bloom's taxonomy, the extended model of its cognitive domain presented by Anderson and Krathwohl [6] are applied now into harmonizing LIS course content. The novelty of Anderson is that they changed the name for each level from a noun to a verb, as the Fig.3 shows. Applying verbs in evaluation course outcomes and related activities made this model adoptable into teaching process among academics.

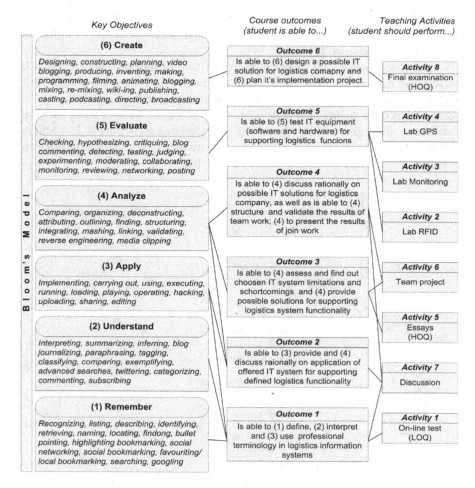

Fig. 3. LIS outcomes and teaching activities in a light of Bloom's model

As the Fig. 3 shows, the LIS course outcomes are structured according six Bloom's model's objectives, however expected outcomes may cover more than one objective, as for example an outcome "to understand, interpret and use professional terminology" summarizes key words from three levels of Bloom's knowledge model, i.e. remembering, understanding, and applying. Evaluation of activities could be done as referring to the related outcome, which is already evaluated in the light of Bloom's model (as it is done in Fig. 3). However, more efficient for course harmonizing is to evaluate course activities separately from outcomes, using same Bloom's model (see Fig. 4). Almost the same approach of course's outcomes and activities evaluation is presented in [7].

Within current paper application of Bloom's taxonomy is demonstrated for evaluation of course outcomes and teaching activities, although authors are inspired also by a case study on evaluation of final examination papers and questionnaires in light of Bloom's taxonomy by grouping all questions from examination papers into two categories, i.e. lower order questions (cover two lowest layers of Bloom's pyramid, i.e. knowledge and comprehension) and high order questions (cover the rest layer of Bloom's pyramid) [8].

Within current paper it is proposed to extend both evaluations numerically. LIS course activities and outcomes are analyzed and measured using a grade scale [0..2] based on the developed chart (Fig. 4) resulting in a proportional distribution of all Bloom's objectives among course activities and outcomes. Authors used following gradation of scale: 0 – activity (outcome) is not related to objective, 1 – activity (outcome) represents an objective partly, 2 – activity (outcome) is related to objective strongly.

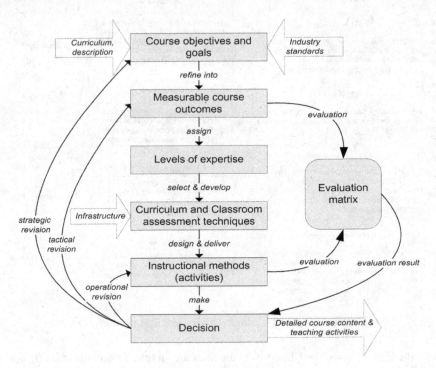

Fig. 4. Course development framework

To evaluate both outcomes and activities a matrix is used as presented respectively in Table 1 and Table 2. The measurement of teaching activities is performed by the academics involved into course teaching. Tables present a matrix which are formed by 8 activities (or respectively 6 outcomes) mentioned in Fig.3 and 6 Bloom's objectives (i.e. 1 – knowledge, 2 – comprehension, 3 – application, 4 – analysis, 5 – synthesis, 6 – evaluation).

Table 1. LIS Course's Activities Evaluation Matrix

	1	2	3	4	5	6
Activity 1	2	2	2	0	0	0
Activity 2	0	0	0	0	2	0
Activity 3	0	0	1	0	2	0
Activity 4	0	0	0	0	2	0
Activity 5	0	0	0	1	0	1
Activity 6	0	0	0	1	0	1
Activity 7	1	1	2	2	0	0
Activity 8	0	0	0	0	0	2
%	12	12	20	16	24	16

Table 2. LIS Course's Outcomes Evaluation Matrix

	1	2	3	4	5	6
Outcome 1	2	2	2	0	0	0
Outcome 2	0	0	2	1	1	0
Outcome 3	0	0	1	1	1	0
Outcome 4	1	1	0	1	1	1
Outcome 5	0	0	0	0	2	1
Outcome 6	0	0	0	0	1	2
%	13	13	21	12	25	16

It is recommended to perform outcomes evaluation by external colleague or industry partner, by this ensuring (1) external assessment of course content and (2) critical comments on a course improving. Moreover, to achieve a feedback from students, outcomes evaluation could be done based on results of student questionnaires. However at the moment, outcomes evaluation of LIS course is conducted by the academic stuff of department which operates the course.

The results of both measurements are than compared to show the difference between course's outcomes and activities in a light of Bloom's model's objectives (see Fig. 5).

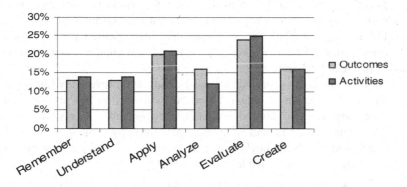

Fig. 5. Comparing results

As the chart shows there is some difference between outcomes and teaching activities evaluation in the light of Bloom's taxonomy, the difference is not critical. Though, author should admit that results presented in Fig. 5 were achieved as an output of iterative process on outcomes and activities analysis.

The conclusion of chart analysis is either the course content is harmonized or not. Idealized, the difference between outcome Oi and activity Ai within one objective is approaching zero value, $|Oi-Ai| \rightarrow 0$, $i \in [1..6]$. In this case a full harmonization between outcomes and objectives is obtained (it can be said that the course content is harmonized according to Bloom's model).

However, there are at least two challenges that the authors faced with. First one is related to the necessity of using etalon distribution for Bloom's objectives, which in its turn can vary depending on academic year the course is operated at. Within current page authors empirically evaluated "etalon" distribution based on own perception and academic experience, also addressing to some papers on same matter as an example [11]. The second challenge is associated with an estimation of allowed discrepancy Δi between outcome and activity for each objective of Bloom's model. During paper developing, it is assumed to be within 5%. As conclusion, to summarize above mentioned the following rule of course content harmonization can be defined:

$$\text{IF } \Delta i < 5\% \text{ THEN run\_the\_course}$$
$$\text{ELSE do\_course\_ revision \{strategic, tactical\}} \tag{1}$$

3.3   From Empirical Experience to Qualitative Research

The rationale of the use of qualitative research methods within current research now became evident, as the main outcome of the case study is evaluation of the course quality. In the context of qualitative research methods, current research can be considered as a case study focused on the particular academic course. This case study has iterative nature, as the course is given for students once per semester. After completing the course and collecting research data, some recommendations are done for improving course content, including activities (labs, seminars, assignments etc.). Following data collection methods are used:

1. Interviews are main data collection methods within this research. It allows performing course content revision in internal and external way.
2. Documents analysis is another important step focused on a revision and examination of labor market job vacancies and similar course descriptions available at Internet (external course evaluation).
3. Observations is secondary data analysis method however very important as it allows examination of obtained students skills during labs and seminars, i.e how they use the terminology, how they are able to operate with labs equipment etc. (internal course evaluation) by this providing deeper understanding about how course outcomes are achieved. Observation is conducted by lecturers and invited industrial partners.

As the result, the case study provides better understanding of (1) is there a need for updating the course outcomes and competencies (as well as activities), (2) is there a strong interconnections among the course outcomes and competencies, (3) what are students evaluations of the learning outcomes in a context of Bloom's model?

The particular interest is about students' questionnaires data analysis. Students are asked to complete questionnaires twice per course: in the beginning (first lesson after they are introduced to course content) and at the end of the course (after all the requirements and assessments are completed). They are invited to write respectively, (1) what they expect from course (i.e. "expectations": I would like to be able to do...), and (2) what are they able to do right after completing the course (i.e. "satisfaction"). They should write at least 10 sentences by using "probes" from the provided list of verbs. Those verbs in mixed way are picked from the Bloom's model.

Then, all the statements are analyzed and the distribution pattern of key verbs among Bloom's model categories is estimated. The opinion exists, and actually this is a current challenge of Bloom's model, that distribution pattern of Bloom's categories differs up to the student type. For example, it is evident that weight of first categories (LOTS, i.e. remembering, understanding, and applying) for pupils is higher than for students etc.

These are some interesting findings while conducting the case study:

- Students rather estimate themselves to be at first levels of Bloom's model (LOTS) despite that course activities are focused on higher levels (HOTS);
- Students "expectation" are more focused on first levels (LOTS), however "satisfaction" are evaluated to be at higher levels of Bloom's model;
- Top five verbs as "to search", "to discuss", "to explain", "to test", and "to use" are quite unrepresentative for engineers students;
- There are a set of verbs which students never use even these verbs are presented within course content.

4   Conclusions and Further Research

A global actuality of course content enhancement is discussed in the introduction of the paper; however topicality of this subject is more critical for new members of the European Society in the context of Bologna declaration. There is a variety of case studies on developing curricula and course content, however application of generalized framework for course content enhancement should be performed under some educational instructions to achieve the best quality of educational processes. The presented empirical case study focuses on evaluation of LIS course's content according to Bloom's cognitive learning model. It is easy to use, and is aimed at enhancement of the course content; however it is actually only an initial point for future research on this matter. Bellow some current issues of the conducted case study are discussed along with possible directions of future research:

- It is sometimes a real challenge for students to write down more than five sentences (both before and after the course) even there are three demonstrative examples in the questionnaires. The solution here could be a discussion with students about main outcomes of the course after completing the course (retrospective).

- What are the most appropriate key verbs for engineering courses? For this, engineering literature analysis should be performed.
- Is there any "benchmark" distribution pattern for Bloom's model categories? Here, the further research is related to conducting education literature review and discussing the topic with both industrial and academic experts.
- With years, ontology of some verbs has been changed (from 1956 when Bloom's model was first presented). For example "to search" spending hours in libraries is not the same as "to search" in Internet now. Sometimes it looks like a verb should be within another category than it was presented in the classic Bloom's model. Moreover, in different publication "probes" verbs sometimes are mixed within categories, i.e. same verb appears in more than one category. Here, the further work must be done in collaboration between engineers and educators; literature review may help as well.
- The analysis of students' answers is quite sensitive and time consuming as sometimes students written answers are not related directly to the course outcomes. To use the functionality of learning management system for student on-line interviewing could facilitate a process of student answers decoding, however the validations of students "statements" still will be necessary.

Acknowledgments. Authors express gratitude to Baltic-German University Liaison Office for funding LIS RFID laboratory enhancement under the project "Establishment of Training and Research Laboratory of Logistics RFID Technologies".

References

1. Romanovs, A., Soshko, O., Merkuryev, Y.: Information Technology Focused Training in Logistics. In: 9th IEEE International Conference on Information Technology Based Higher Education and Training, ITHET 2010, Turkey, Cappadocia, pp. 27–34 (2010)
2. Romanovs, A., Soshko, O., Lektauers, A., Merkuryev, Y.: Application of Information Technologies to Active Teaching in Logistic Information Systems. In: Grundspenkis, J., Kirikova, M., Manolopoulos, Y., Novickis, L. (eds.) ADBIS 2009. LNCS, vol. 5968, pp. 23–30. Springer, Heidelberg (2010)
3. Field-tested Learning Assessment Guide, STEM instructors WEB site. College Level One Team, http://www.flaguide.org
4. Salenieks, N., Janauska, J., Rudnevs, J., Civcisa, G., Liberts, G., Grislis, A.: Engineering / managerial education for international business knowledge in European small countries, pp. 6–14. LLU, Jelgava (2005)
5. Bier, I.D., Cornesky, R.: Using QFD To Construct a Higher Education Curriculum. Quality Progress 34(4), 64–67 (2001)
6. Anderson, L.W., Krathwohl, D.R.: A taxonomy for learning, teaching, and assessing: A revision of Bloom's Taxonomy of Educational Objectives. Longman, New York (2001)
7. Crowe, A., Dirks, C., Wenderoth, M.P.: Biology in Bloom: Implementing Bloom's Taxonomy to Enhance Student Learning in Biology. CBE Life Sciences Education, American Society for Cell Biology 7(4), 368–381 (2008)
8. Swart, A.J.: Evaluation of Final Examination Papers in engineering: A case study using bloom's taxonomy. IEEE Transaction on Education 53(2), 257–264 (2010)

Calculate Learners' Competence Scores and Their Reliability in Learning Networks

Martin Hochmeister

Electronic Commerce Group, Vienna University of Technology
Favoritenstraße 9-11/188-4, 1040 Vienna, Austria
martin.hochmeister@ec.tuwien.ac.at

Abstract. Intelligent tutoring systems rely on learner models in order to recommend useful learning resources. Learner models suffer from incomplete and inaccurate information about learners. In learning networks, learners share their knowledge and experiences online and collaboratively perform problem-solving tasks. In this paper, we present an approach that calculates learners' competence scores based on their contributions and social interactions in a learning network. We aim at more comprehensive and accurate learner models, which allow more suitable recommendations of learning resources. Competence scores range from 0 to 100 points, each associated with a confidence level representing the calculation's reliability. For evaluation, we conducted an experiment with 14 master students at university. The results show that our approach tends to underestimate competences, while it calculates 54% of the scores accurately. Student feedback suggests to apply our approach for recommending future courses as well as forming student groups.

Keywords: User Modeling, Competences, Confidence, Online Communities, Learning Networks.

1 Introduction

Intelligent tutoring systems recommend learning resources to learners based on their learner models. Learning resources include learning content, learning paths that may help navigating through appropriate learning resources or relevant peer-learners, with whom collaborative learning may take place [13]. Intelligent tutoring systems perform poorly until they collect sufficient information of learners. Such systems may improve their service by exploiting more comprehensive and accurate learner models.

In a collaborative learning environment two or more people learn or attempt to learn something together [6]. Problem solving is an activity that triggers learning mechanisms. Learning networks are a special kind of learning environments, where groups of people use the internet to collaborate in problem solving tasks [9]. The knowledge being exchanged as well as the interactions in such learner networks are promising sources for mining the competences of learners.

In this paper, we propose an approach that implicitly collects competence information about learners in a learning network based on both the knowledge

L. Niedrite, R. Strazdina, B. Wangler (Eds.): BIR 2011 Workshops, LNBIP 106, pp. 171–183, 2012.
© Springer-Verlag Berlin Heidelberg 2012

they share and the social interactions they are involved in. Learners' knowledge is determined by means of terms they use in their contributions. We further use data about social interactions between learners to qualify the proficiency level (from 0 to 100 points) of learners' knowledge. In particular, we are interested in *how we can calculate competences on an absolute scale* rather than a relative measure just comparing learners. Furthermore, we ask *how we can determine a confidence level estimating the trust in calculated competence scores.* In order to answer these questions, this paper contributes (a) heuristics as the base to determine the proficiency level on an absolute scale, (b) a method for competence scoring combining these heuristics and (c) a measure to evaluate the reliability of competence scores. We evaluated our approach by conducting a first experiment with master students in the course of a tutorial about knowledge management held at university. The results show that the proposed calculation method generally underestimates learners' competences. However, the students perceived the method to be useful for tasks like recommending future courses as well as forming learning groups.

The remainder of this paper is organized as follows. In Section 2, we review existing approaches focusing on expertise modeling. We proceed in Section 3 with devising heuristics and the calculation methods for competence scores and confidence levels. We conduct an empirical study for evaluation of our approach as described in Section 4. We conclude this paper in Section 5 and present ideas for future work.

2   Related Work

The reviewed approaches can be distinguished on the sources of evidence they consider for expert modeling. Some focus only on user-generated content, others concentrate on links between content items or users and the last group exploits both content and link structures.

Campbell et al. [4] present a method to rank experts based on email communication by analyzing content as well as network data. The texts of email messages are used to generate clusters of similar content, whereas the graph of message exchanges is used to calculate a ranked list of individuals. A network analysis method calculates an authority score depending on whether a person acts as an authority or as a hub in the network. Experts are finally ranked to a given topic based on authority scores.

In the context of software development, Mockus and Herbsleb [14] present a quantitative approach to measure expertise. The degree of expertise is measured by the number of expertise atoms (EAs) gained by submitting changes to specific deliveries, such as a change to the source code of a software subsystem. Each type of delivery has a certain amount of EAs assigned to it. To calculate the degree of a person's competence, the EAs collected by this person are compiled for a total score.

Demartini [5] proposes two methods to find experts by means of *Wikipedia*[1] resources. Demartini assumes that authors are competent about topics they describe. An article associated with a person is processed by means of the *Term Frequency and Inverse Document Frequency* (TF-IDF) measure resulting in an expert profile represented by a list of term vectors. Another method is based on the authority of *Wikipedia* articles obtained by analyzing the links between articles. The assumption is that the most linked documents have a higher authority and thus better reflect expertise.

Balog and De Rijke [2] automatically construct an expert profile based on documents from an organization's intranet. They assume that users are competent in a given knowledge area if their name appears in a document considered as relevant to the knowledge area in question. A competence score represents the sum of relevance scores of documents associated with a given person. A system using this method responds to a query about a certain knowledge area with a ranked list of experts sorted by their aggregated relevance scores.

Zhu et al. [17] extract named entities, representing persons and subject matter terms, and build a matrix of their co-occurrences related to documents. Extracted subject matter terms are presumed to indicate possible competences. Each of these person-competence pairs holds a value corresponding to the frequencies of co-occurrences found among all documents. Based on these values, they generate a ranked list displaying candidate experts holding a given competence.

ExpertiseRank is an algorithm processing structural information in a question-answer network [16]. It is based on the heuristic that if person B is able to answer A's question, and C answers B's question then C's expertise rank should be boosted, not only because C was able to answer a question, but because C answered a question of B who answered an other's question as well.

Dorn and Hochmeister [7] present a basic approach to quantify competences in online communities. They incorporate background knowledge to assign competences to competence fields. Terms extracted from users' contributions are matched with terms represented in a taxonomy. The top-level concepts in the taxonomy represent the various competence fields. Finally, the user is given a list of competence fields ranked by the number of exact term matchings.

The more advanced approaches we reviewed calculate scores to rank experts. Ranking implies that scores are calculated relative to the scores of other persons and thus do not reflect an individual's absolute expertise level. However, ranking of experts is useful, as long as we look for the best candidates in an organization. Ranking approaches can not determine whether a candidate has the required proficiency level to accomplish a particular task, for instance, when staffing a software development project team that requires professional java programmers rather than top experts. In addition, it is not desirable to contact the best ranked candidates all the time, since they could be better employed in more complex tasks rather than helping out on simple problems.

---

[1] http://www.wikipedia.org/

3   Quantify a Learner's Competences

Online communities provide different contribution types to share knowledge. We analyzed community-driven question-answering services like *Microsoft TechNet*[2] and *Yahoo! Answers*[3], forums like *Informatik Forum*[4] and an online community sharing bookmarks like *Delicious*[5]. We conclude that knowledge is mostly shared by simple structures including a title and a text body. Such artifacts may be tagged as well as rated. Users may respond to others either by comments or even longer texts.

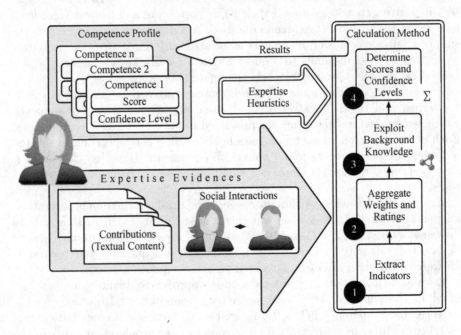

Fig. 1. Process of Competence Calculation

Based on these commonly used contribution types, we set up an online community for the purpose of collaborative learning. The community members are represented by master students, who share challenges they face during their everyday student life related to internet technologies. Students post challenges and build or refine solutions together with other students. We assume that terms used in constructing contributions as well as in discussing these contributions may indicate learners' competences. The contribution types include *challenges* describing a problem, *solutions* to solve challenges, *comments*, *tags* and *ratings*. Figure 1 shows the big picture of the proposed method.

---

[2] http://social.technet.microsoft.com/Forums/
[3] http://answers.yahoo.com/
[4] http://www.informatik-forum.at/
[5] http://www.delicious.com/

3.1   Weighting Contribution Types

We understand terms extracted from learners' contributions as indicators for learners' competences. Terms from one contribution type may reflect a higher and more reliable value for competence calculation than terms from another contribution type. Therefore, we examine each contribution type and represent its significance for competence calculation with weights in a range of [1,5]. Learners show competences when they apply certain skills while performing an action in a real-world situation. Reliable expertise statements depend on how easy an artifact is to fake [15]. Quality measures of *Wikipedia* articles associate the quality and integrity of articles with the expertise of their authors [11]. In this paper, we test the quality of a learner's contribution by whether the contribution can be rated by others or not. Table 1 lists the questions we used to systematically determine weights for each contribution type. As shown in Table 2, we used arrow symbols on a four-point-scale to answer these questions. For instance, the chance that *solutions* originate from experience (Qu.1) is very high whereas the chance to assume experience behind a *comment* is very low.

Table 1. Criteria for Examining Contribution Types

Questions	Heuristics
1. How far does the contribution originate from experience?	The more a contribution originates from experience the more valuable it is for expert profiling.
2. How promising is the contribution regarding the calculation of a maximum competence score?	The more action in problem-solving is involved and the more significant the occasion of contribution, the higher the level of expertise to measure.
3. How costly is the contribution to fake?	The harder a contribution is to to fake the more valuable it is for expert profiling.
4. How likely is the contribution of high-quality?	The higher the quality of a contribution is the more competent the author must be.

Learners post *challenges* based on problems they experience in a learning situation, for instance, during an exercise given in a tutorial. While authoring challenges, learners need to reflect the problem space profoundly. However, they are not able to solve the challenge, hence it is not possible to measure a maximum competence score by only considering challenges. Learners may easily fake challenges by copying and pasting text, but most of these cases will be revealed by other learners' ratings.

While constructing *solutions* learners reflect the problem as well as the solution space. Learners solving others' problems indicates that solvers may have superior expertise than the learners who post the problems [16]. Therefore, we

Table 2. Weighting Scheme

Question	Challenge	Solution	Comment	Tag	Rating
Qu.1: Experience	$\uparrow$	$\Uparrow$	$\Downarrow$	$\uparrow$	$\Uparrow$
Qu.2: Max Score	$\downarrow$	$\Uparrow$	$\Downarrow$	$\downarrow$	$\uparrow$
Qu.3: Fake	$\uparrow$	$\uparrow$	$\downarrow$	$\downarrow$	$\uparrow$
Qu.4: Quality	$\Uparrow$	$\Uparrow$	$\Downarrow$	$\Downarrow$	n/a
Weights	$\omega_{Ch} = 3$	$\omega_S = 5$	$\omega_{Co} = 1$	$\omega_T = 2$	$\omega_R = 4$

Probability: $\Uparrow$ ... very high, $\uparrow$ ... high, $\downarrow$ ... low, $\Downarrow$ ... very low

assume that a solution allows to measure the maximum possible score of a competence. A solution is rated by others and thus very costly to fake. Its quality with respect to completeness and accuracy is qualified by ratings as well.

Learners comment on others' contributions to help them refining their contributions, ask questions or just showing their opinion. Since the motivation behind *comments* is not definitely clear, they contain lots of noise that makes them difficult to interpret [1]. Since comments can not be rated, they represent an unreliable source for expertise extraction.

If learners find certain contributions interesting they can assign *tags* to them. This indicates that they must be somehow competent within the given topic, but we can not determine to which extent. Tags appear to be the most significant descriptive feature regarding multimedia content [1]. However, tags can not be rated, which makes them easy to fake.

Aggregated *ratings* represent a viable indication for high-quality contributions [3]. From the rater's view, ratings are easy to fake though. We assume that the majority of learners only rate others' contributions if they have strong self-confidence regarding their own experience in the given topic. Ratings are very costly to fake especially the higher the number of raters is. Learners being rated have to show true expertise by posting complete and accurate contributions otherwise users will respond with low ratings.

3.2   Calculate Absolute Competence Scores

The calculation of competence scores takes four steps as shown in Figure 1. At first, we use online text mining services, i.e., *OpenCalais Service*[6] and *Yahoo! Query Language*[7], to extract terms from a learner's contributions.

Secondly, we assign to each term a weight equal to the weight of the contribution the term was extracted from. For instance, we assign the weight ω_{Ch} to a term we obtained from a challenge. Equation 1 shows the calculation of an initial score for competence c of a given user u.

$$sc_{init}(u, c) = \omega_{contribType} \cdot r_{factor} \cdot \tag{1}$$

---

[6] http://www.opencalais.com/
[7] http://developer.yahoo.com/yql/

where r_{factor} is the contribution's rating score normalized to [1,2]. For instance, when using a 4-point rating scale, the highest possible rating score 4 results in $r_{factor} = 2$, where the lowest rating score results in $r_{factor} = 1$. If a term has a weight of 5 and the maximum average rating, the term receives an initial score of 10. We normalize this value to a score of 100 points. Terms originating from contributions not being rated obtain default rating scores. Due to this procedure, equal terms may receive scores from different contribution types. In this case, only the highest score will be considered for further processing.

At this stage, two problems occur. Firstly, we can not distinguish terms originating from the same contribution with respect to their level of generality. One term might indicate a specific competence whereas another term might represent a general competence. However, both terms received the same initial score. Secondly, terms may be identified that are not relevant to the domain of interest. We tackle these problems in the third step by introducing background knowledge in the form of a lightweight ontology. This ontology links competence concepts and structures them in a hierarchical order. We adopted the ontology already used in [10]. Terms associated with a learner are mapped to ontology concepts as shown in Equation 2. A term t indicating a competence c is mapped to an ontology concept o_c. This allows to eliminate terms not relevant to the domain of interest.

$$\mathcal{T} \to \mathcal{O} : t \mapsto sim_{Levenshtein(\%)}(t, o_c) > tr_{sim} . \tag{2}$$

where $t \in \mathcal{T}$ and $o_c \in \mathcal{O}$. $\mathcal{T}$ is the set of extracted terms and $\mathcal{O}$ the set of ontology concepts. Terms mapped to the ontology need to exceed the threshold value tr_{sim} otherwise they will be discarded. The function $sim_{Levenshtein(\%)}$ calculates the similarity between identified terms and the labels of ontology concepts based on the edit distance between two strings. The similarity function allows to further refine the initial score as shown in Equation 3.

$$sc_{init}(u, c) = \omega_{contribType} \cdot r_{factor} \cdot sim_{Levenshtein(\%)} . \tag{3}$$

In the fourth step, we tackle the problem regarding the different abstraction levels of terms. The ontology's hierarchical structure allows to align scores by propagating them from the bottom level up to the top level. We adopted the propagation approach presented by Kay and Lum [12]. A competence's final score $sc(u, c)$ results in the weighted sum of its children's scores as shown in Equation 4.

$$sc(u, c) = sc(u, c) + (1 - sc(u, c))\frac{\sum_{child \in \mathcal{C}_p} sc_{init}(u, child)}{|\mathcal{C}_p|} . \tag{4}$$

where $\mathcal{C}_p$ is the set of children of competence c. The scores are propagated level by level from the lowest child concept found during mapping up to the hierarchy's root concept.

3.3   Determine a Score's Confidence Level

A modeling task intrinsically has a degree of uncertainty, so does the calculation method proposed in Section 3.2. Therefore, we compute for each competence score a confidence level to further qualify the score. We propose two measures to estimate a score's confidence level. Both are finally combined into a total confidence measure.

The first measure is built on the assumption that only a top expert can accurately rate another top expert. Equation 5 shows the calculation of the confidence level for competence c based on the average raters' competence scores regarding c.

$$conf_{raters}(u, c) = \frac{1}{|\mathcal{R}_c|} \cdot \sum_{r \in \mathcal{R}_c} score(r, c) \, . \tag{5}$$

where $\mathcal{R}_c$ is the set of raters, which assessed another user's contributions indicating competence c.

Our second measure assumes that the more diverse learners' contributions are, the higher is the confidence in computed competence scores. For instance, the confidence in a competence score is higher if the user shows a certain competence in both a challenge and a solution rather than only submitting a challenge. Equation 6 formulates the calculation of this aspect utilizing the contribution weights determined in Section 3.1. The higher the contribution's weight is, the higher is the level of confidence.

$$conf_{diversity}(u, c) = \frac{\sum_{contrib \in \mathcal{C}_{u,c}} getWeight(contrib)}{\sum_{\omega \in \mathcal{W}} \omega} \, . \tag{6}$$

where $\mathcal{C}_{u,c}$ is the set of contributions submitted by user u involving competence c and $\mathcal{W} = \{\omega_{Ch}, \omega_S, \omega_{Co}, \omega_T, \omega_R\}$.

In Equation 7, we combine both confidence measures to the final confidence measure.

$$confidence(u, c) = \lambda \cdot conf_{raters}(u, c) + (1 - \lambda) \cdot conf_{diversity}(u, c) \, . \tag{7}$$

where λ controls the balance between the single confidence measures.

4   Evaluation

We conducted an experiment with 14 master students enrolled in a computer science program at university. In a tutorial about knowledge management we started an exercise lasting four weeks. Students were encouraged to participate in a learning network and share their experience regarding internet technologies. To make sure to collect enough data for evaluationd, students were required to submit at least three challenges and three corresponding solutions. Students were asked to take part in discussions as well as interacting with others via tagging and rating. Students could also provide solutions to others' challenges, which we called alternative solutions. Figure 2 illustrates the steps taken during evaluation.

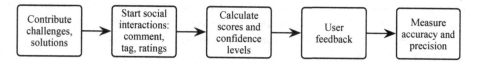

Fig. 2. Evaluation steps

As soon as students submitted a certain amount of contributions, the system calculated their learner models. We opened the learner models to the students for inspection, as shown on the left side in Figure 3. After a period of four weeks we asked the students to give feedback on the calculated scores as well as on the possible potential they see in the automatic calculation of competence profiles. We then measured both the score accuracy and the precision of identified competences.

We measured the scores' accuracy by how close the calculated scores lie together with a learner's self-assessment. Students were asked to give feedback on whether the calculated scores are (1) *lower* (2) *equal* or (3) *higher* than the scores they would self-assess. The right side in Figure 3 depicts the feedback form as presented to the students. This allows us to test if our method tends to either underestimate or overestimate a learner's competences.

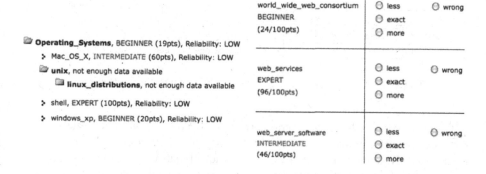

Fig. 3. Example of a Learner Profile and a Feedback Form

As for precision, students assess the proper identification of competences with respect to their contributions. Students mark competences as *wrong* if competences are not related to their contributions at all.

To evaluate the proposed confidence measure we assume that a valid calculation of confidence levels would result in higher levels for the feedback category *exact* compared to the categories *less* and *more*. Confidence levels for competences marked as *wrong* will not be analyzed.

For the first evaluation of our method, we took over the contribution weight settings from Table 2. A contribution has to be rated by at least two students otherwise the parameter r_{factor} is set to 1. Comments, tags and ratings can not be rated, for these contribution types r_{factor} is set to 1 as well. The similarity threshold is set to $tr_{sim} = 90$. Regarding the aggregation of confidence levels in Equation 7, λ is set to 70%.

We did not want to overexert users with displaying an overlong list of competences. Therefore, only competences exceeding a score of 20 points were displayed in a learner's profile.

4.1 Results and Findings

Figure 4 shows the amount of data collected during the four-week experiment cycle. Figure 5 displays the feedback of learners regarding the calculated competence scores.

Contributions submitted	
Challenges	59
Solutions	56
Alternative Solution	22
Comments	88
Tags	359
Ratings	243
Total	827
Competences calculated	1301
Competences assessed	246

Fig. 4. Data Statistics

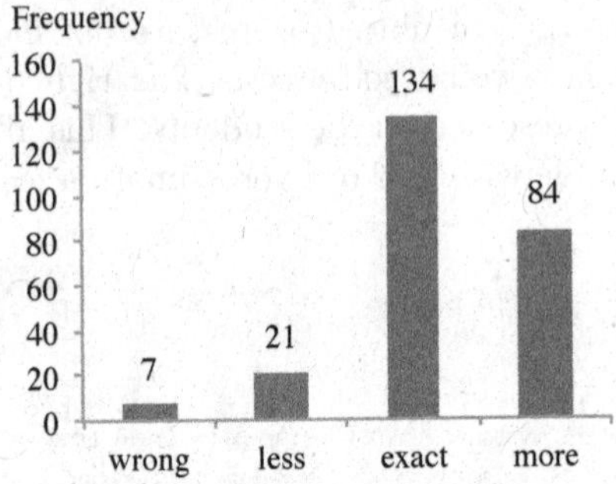

Fig. 5. Feedback Results

On average, we calculated 93 competence scores per student, where 18 competences were actually displayed for feedback (exceeded 20 points limit). Students felt accurately assessed in 134 of 246 calculations resulting in an accuracy rate of 54%. As for the rest of the calculated scores, our method underestimated learners' competences in 75% of the cases. This may be caused due to the fact that people usually tend to overestimate their competences [8]. Additionally, competence scores may be underrated because we only consider the highest weighted contribution type to determine a competence's score. At the moment, scores obtained from lower weighted contribution types are discarded. However, based on these first results, we are able to redesign and adjust our method for future experiments.

As shown in Figure 5, seven out of 246 displayed competences were classified as wrong. As for precision, this means that 17 out of 18 competences were identified properly resulting in a precision rate of 97%. This is a very promising percentage rate which proves the adoption of text mining web services to be a viable option for initial competence extraction.

A shortcoming of this study is that on average, we only collected 1.8 ratings per rate-able contribution type. Hence, many competence scores had to be calculated based on default rating values (pessimistic approach, low values). This is possibly another reason why students felt mostly underestimated by the system. Poor rating data affected the calculation of confidence levels as well. The results show throughout rather low confidence levels, which limit a serious interpretation. For future experiments, we have to make sure to collect enough rating data, for instance, by modifying the task design.

Asked after the potential of automatically generated learner profiles, students said that they can imagine to use their profiles as *a personal knowledge base* they can reflect on. Some said that our method could enhance the university's existing course dictionary tool to recommend future courses. Others think of using the learner profiles as the fundament of a *competence marketplace* where organizations and students get in touch regarding collaboration. Moreover, students guess that our method could support the gathering of students in learning groups.

5   Conclusion

Intelligent tutoring systems, recommending suitable learning materials to learners, suffer from poor learner models. State of the art approaches mainly generate a ranked list of candidate experts concerning a certain competence. In contrast to this relative measurement method, we proposed a method to calculate absolute competence scores of learners based on their contributions and social interactions in a learning network. We systematically determined weights for the various contribution types, which build the base for score calculation. The calculation method yields both competence scores and confidence levels to qualify a score's validity.

We conducted a first experiment with 14 university students to evaluate the scores' accuracy, the precision of identified competences and students' acceptance. Results show that 97% of competences were identified properly and 54% of competence scores were accurately calculated compared to students' self-assessments. The majority of the remaining competence scores were calculated lower compared to students' self-assessments. As for testing the calculation of confidence levels, we could not collect enough data for serious argumentation and thus need to change the study design for future experiments. Qualitative student feedback reveals that students perceived the computed competence scores as a useful base for recommending future courses as well as for the formation of learning groups.

Regarding future work, we plan to experiment with different weight settings and consider to automatically determine weights based on data mining techniques. The adoption of a more sophisticated approach for score propagation as well as the implementation of a TF/IDF measure for competence identification from various learners' contributions may improve the scores' accuracy. Considering the age of learners' contributions during confidence calculation seems interesting as well. The older the contributions are, the lower is the trust in competence scores obtained from them. Another idea for improvement involves further expertise heuristics. For instance, the fact that learners commenting one another, in particular at the beginning of a discussion thread, may inspire authors to revise their contributions. As a consequence, the contribution's quality may improve and thus boost the author's competence scores. Besides that, we want to compare our approach with approaches from literature, e.g., Zhang et al. [16], to highlight the potential of absolute competence scores.

Acknowledgments. This research is part of the project SeCoMine, which derives competences within an online-community based on user contributions and social interactions. SeCoMine is fully funded by the Österreichische Forschungsförderungsgesellschaft mbH (FFG) under the grant number 826459.

References

1. Almeida, J., Gonçalves, M., Figueiredo, F., Pinto, H., Belem, F.: On the quality of information for web 2.0 services. IEEE Internet Computing 14(6), 47–55 (2010)
2. Balog, K., De Rijke, M.: Determining expert profiles (with an application to expert finding). In: IJCAI 2007: Proc. 20th Intern. Joint Conf. on Artificial Intelligence, pp. 2657–2662 (2007)
3. Blooma, M., Chua, A., Goh, D.: Selection of the best answer in cqa services. In: 2010 Seventh International Conference on Information Technology, pp. 534–539. IEEE (2010)
4. Campbell, C., Maglio, P., Cozzi, A., Dom, B.: Expertise identification using email communications. In: Proceedings of the Twelfth International Conference on Information and Knowledge Management, pp. 528–531. ACM (2003)
5. Demartini, G.: Finding experts using wikipedia. In: Proceedings of the Workshop on Finding Experts on the Web with Semantics (FEWS 2007) at ISWC/ASWC2007, Busan, South Korea (2007)
6. Dillenbourg, P.: What do you mean by collaborative learning. In: Dillenbourg, P. (ed.) Collaborative-learning: Cognitive and Computational Approaches, pp. 1–16. Elsevier, Oxford (1999)
7. Dorn, J., Hochmeister, M.: Techscreen: Mining competencies in social software. In: The 3rd International Conference on Knowledge Generation, Communication and Management, Orlando, FLA, pp. 115–126 (2009)
8. Dunning, D., Heath, C., Suls, J.: Flawed self-assessment. Psychological Science in the Public Interest 5(3), 69 (2004)
9. Hiltz, S., Turoff, M.: What makes learning networks effective? Communications of the ACM 45(4), 59 (2002)
10. Hochmeister, M., Daxböck, J.: A User Interface for Semantic Competence Profiles. In: Konstan, J.A., Conejo, R., Marzo, J.L., Oliver, N. (eds.) UMAP 2011. LNCS, vol. 6787, pp. 159–170. Springer, Heidelberg (2011)
11. Hu, M., Lim, E., Sun, A., Lauw, H., Vuong, B.: Measuring article quality in wikipedia: models and evaluation. In: Proceedings of the Sixteenth ACM Conference on Conference on information and Knowledge Management, pp. 243–252. ACM (2007)

12. Kay, J., Lum, A.: Exploiting readily available web data for scrutable student models. In: Proceedings of the 2005 Conference on Artificial Intelligence in Education: Supporting Learning through Intelligent and Socially Informed Technology, pp. 338–345. IOS Press (2005)
13. Manouselis, N., Drachsler, H., Vuorikari, R., Hummel, H., Koper, R.: Recommender systems in technology enhanced learning. Recommender Systems Handbook, 387–415 (2011)
14. Mockus, A., Herbsleb, J.: Expertise browser: a quantitative approach to identifying expertise. In: Proceedings of the 24th International Conference on Software Engineering, pp. 503–512. ACM (2002)
15. Shami, N., Ehrlich, K., Gay, G., Hancock, J.: Making sense of strangers' expertise from signals in digital artifacts. In: Proceedings of the 27th International Conference on Human factors in Computing Systems, pp. 69–78. ACM (2009)
16. Zhang, J., Ackerman, M., Adamic, L.: Expertise networks in online communities: structure and algorithms. In: Proceedings of the 16th International Conference on World Wide Web, pp. 221–230. ACM (2007)
17. Zhu, J., Goncalves, A., Uren, V., Motta, E., Pacheco, R.: Mining web data for competency management. In: Proceedings of the 2005 IEEE/WIC/ACM International Conference on Web Intelligence, pp. 94–100. IEEE (2005)

Timely Report Production from WWW Data Sources

Marko Niinimaki[1], Tapio Niemi[1], Stephen Martin[2,*],
Jyrki Nummenmaa[3], and Peter Thanisch[3]

[1] Helsinki Institute of Physics, Technology Programme, CERN, CH-1211 Geneva 23,
Switzerland
{tapio.niemi;man}@cern.ch
[2] World Health Organization, Avenue Appia 20, 1211 Geneva 27, Switzerland
martins@who.int
[3] Department of Computer Sciences, FIN 33014 University of Tampere, Finland
{jyrki,pt}@cs.uta.fi

Abstract. In business intelligence, reporting is perceived by users as the most important area. Here, we present a case study of data integration for reporting within the World Health Organization (WHO).

WHO produces Communicable Disease Epidemiological Profiles for emergency affected countries. Given the nature of emergencies, the production of these reports should be timely. In order to automate the production of the reports, we have introduced a method of integrating data from multiple sources by using the RDF (Resource Description Framework) format.

The model of the data is described using an RDF ontology, making validation of the data from multiple sources possible. However, since RDF is highly technical, we have designed a graphical tool for the end user. The tool can be used to configure the data sources of a given report. After this, data for the report is generated from the sources. Finally, templates are used to generate the reports.

Keywords: Data integration, ontology, XML, RDF, OLAP.

1 Introduction

Reporting is the most important area of business intelligence (BI), with respect to both expenditure and perceived value by end users. For example, Microsoft carried out BI user profiling, estimating that at least 90% of BI usage involves reporting [13]. Almost every medium-to-large organization uses at least one BI reporting platform. However, as reports often involve data from several sources, preparing data for reports is an essential step in the process.

In this paper, we discuss report design and report production in general, but our case study of preparing data is humanitarian emergencies related country specific reports produced at the World Health Organization (WHO). Prior to automating the data preparation, the process involved manual tasks of locating and copying the data.

---

* The author is a staff member of the World Health Organization. The author alone is responsible for the views expressed in this publication and they do not necessarily represent the decisions, policy or views of the World Health Organization.

L. Niedrite, R. Strazdina, B. Wangler (Eds.): BIR 2011 Workshops, LNBIP 106, pp. 184–195, 2012.
© Springer-Verlag Berlin Heidelberg 2012

This paper is organized as follows: We present our case in Section 2. After that the related work is introduced in Section 3. Then, we explain the process of reporting in Section 4 and the foundation of the data collection and integration in Section 5. The actual method of data integration and its implementation, including the data sources used, as well as a description of how reports are generated, are presented in Section 6. Finally, Section 7 contains a summary and discussion of future work.

2 Case: Communicable Disease Epidemiological Profiles

Humanitarian emergencies expose affected populations to multiple risks: displacement, damaged infrastructure, loss of shelter, food insecurity, inadequate safe water and sanitation, increased exposure to disease vectors and reduced access to health care. These risks, both individually and cumulatively, have a negative impact on the health of these populations, making them more vulnerable to communicable disease. In such circumstances it is common to see rates of communicable disease and mortality above base rates by a factor of ten.

Since 2002 the Disease Control in Emergencies unit at the World Health Organization's Headquarters in Geneva has been producing Communicable Disease Epidemiological Profiles for emergency-affected countries. The aim of these profiles is to provide up-to-date information on the major communicable disease threats faced by the resident and displaced populations in emergency-affected countries. The information provided in these reports is designed to inform public health strategies and to help prioritize and coordinate communicable disease control activities among the multiple agencies working in such countries, to reduce the impact of communicable disease. The diseases included in the profiles have been selected because of their high burden or epidemic potential, or because they are (re)emerging diseases or important but neglected tropical diseases subject to global elimination or eradication efforts.

On average it takes six months to produce a country epidemiological profile absorbing considerable time and resources. At present, production is a multi-step process: it involves obtaining technical information from disease experts, writing, editing, formatting, proof reading and obtaining relevant clearance before publication electronically (in the PDF format) and in hard copy. Evaluation shows that these products have a long shelf-life and are used consistently over time. However the revision of these profiles to incorporate new data requires an identical production process and a similar investment of time and resources.

In a joint project between WHO and the Helsinki Institute of Physics, we have employed the ETL (Extract-Transform-Load) process in order to produce and revise country specific data in a timely fashion, taking into consideration a number of special requirements:

– The source of every piece of data must be possible to trace.
– The data can be public or restricted access. However, in the case of the latter, this would need to remain restricted accordingly.
– A well-defined schema or ontology does not necessarily exist for all data sources.
– No query or data definition language knowledge should be required from the users.

Based on these requirements, we have created a functional prototype of automated report generation by importing and harmonizing data from several sources. The data is imported directly into a word processing template from which the full reports can be generated in both PDF and hard copy.

3 Related Work

Reporting in general can be seen as presenting data, often in summarised or condensed form. In the context of data warehouses, Malinowski and Zimanyi define reporting as the process of extracting data from a database or a data warehouse and presenting it to users [14]. The motivation for reporting is seen as supporting decision making [6]. While there is a long tradition of report generation from numeric sources by aggregation (see e.g. [7]), producing reports automatically from textual sources is a more recent trend [16]. Reporting platforms, on the other hand, have been studied e.g. in [26].

Integrating data from different sources has been the subject of many studies, for a summary, see e.g. [12]. A study by Motro [17] describes a very similar problem to ours. In his work a virtual superview is created representing an integrated view to multiple databases. The user can query this superview and the system decomposes the queries to sub queries for each underlying database. After the query processing in individual databases, the results are combined taking care of possible conflicts such as inconsistent or missing data. For our purposes Motro's method is too complicated, since it requires detailed integration of the database schemata of the databases involved. Another problem with this method is a lack of support for heterogeneous databases. The problem of heterogeneous databases has been addressed by Reddy et al. [23] but their method, too, is heavy for ad-hoc type information. The approaches above are based on well-structured data sources following the network of relational data models while our needs are focused more on semi-structured data. This kind of data integration has been studied, for example, in the Tsimmis project [9]. The goal of the project was to develop methods and tools for integrating several structured or unstructured information sources. Moreover, Abiteboul has studied how semi-structured data can be queried [5]. He has identified several different situations related to, for example, the structure of data, database schema or a lack of it, and the distinction between the schema and the data.

Mohania and Bhide [15] study new trends in information integration. They describe context oriented information integration in which the schemata of information sources is not necessarily known but the approach is based on the context of users' queries. Another relevant concept for our study is the user centric information integration. It describes a common situation in which the data integration is made by the user, not the database administrator. There, a typical challenge is managing access rights to data.

A promising approach for data integration is based on Semantic Web technologies, where formalisms have been created to make the meaning of data more explicit by the use of ontologies. There, ontology-based data integration using RDF was possibly first mentioned by Bray [8]. On the other hand, Abiteboul et al. [4] present methods and systems for storing and accessing XML (eXtensible Markup Language) resources in the World Wide Web. RDF is most often expressed in the XML form [3].

Methods related to RDF have also been applied to query integration. Correndo et al. [11] study rewriting SPARQL (an RDF query language) queries. The input for the system is the query with the ontology used to formulate it and the target ontology or a data set. The output is a rewritten query using the target ontology.

Näppilä et al. [18] present a tool for construction OLAP cubes from structurally heterogeneous XML documents. They propose high-level query primitives that have been designed to work with structurally heterogeneous XML documents. In this way, the designer does not need to know the exact structure of the different documents used as source data. While this approach is promising, it is probably not quite ready for daily report production.

In our papers [22,21], we have presented a method and implementation to transform data sources into RDF format using "ontology mapping", and then uploading the data into an OLAP system for analysis. The benefit of the RDF intermediate step is that the correctness of the data source (and its transformation) can be checked against the RDF ontology. The ontology mapping uses well-known XSLT [27] methods for data transformation.

Concerning the presentation of data to end users and integrating it with existing reports, Witkowski et al. [28] presents a method using a spreadsheet office tool as a user interface to a relational database system. The system offers both a familiar interface and efficient data processing for the user.

4   Reports and Reporting

It is difficult to formulate a definition of what we mean by a report. However, the salient characteristics of reports and reporting applications can be summarised as follows:

A report extracts data from back-end data sources, uses business logic to convert the extracted data into useful information and presents the information in a meaningful way to a business decision-maker.

Existing business intelligence reporting products can handle a variety of back-end data sources (e.g. relational databases, OLAP cubes, XML files etc.), are flexible with regard to both the rendering (e.g. HTML, spreadsheet, etc.) and the output medium (paper or electronic) and facilitate a variety of usage patterns (interactive or passive) and report design representations (in program code or in a graphical design tool). The presentation of the report may be interactive. For example, the report may contain data that is only revealed in more detail if requested by the user, or some statistical computations might only be produced when the user requests them.

In everyday language, the term "report" refers simply to the output that the user sees. However, in practically all technical literature on reporting technology, the term "report" can also refer to the design of a report. Thus a report may be stored in a report design repository and run any number of times. Each time the report is run, the design of the report is re-used, but the information content of the report may vary. During each run, the current values of the input data items are retrieved from back-end data sources, such as databases, and used in producing the report output. The data in the data sources can change over time, but the report design changes less frequently.

It is useful to think of a report as comprising three parts.

- Data – The information about the data to be extracted from back-end data sources (or higher-level views) when the report is run.
- Layout – How the information is to be presented
- Properties (parameters, interactions, etc) – The selections and functionalities available for the usage of the report.

Users of reporting tools differ by the amount of expertise that they possess and by their role in the reporting cycle.

- Report consumers – The people who actually use the information in the report. They know about the business, but they do not necessarily know about the data.
- Power users – People who have some knowledge of the business and enough knowledge about the reporting platform to facilitate some degree of self-service.
- Report authors – These people typically have a limited knowledge of the business and an in-depth knowledge of the design facilities of the reporting platform.
- Reporting administrators – Typically they have a limited knowledge of the business. They have technical knowledge about the reporting platform as well as knowledge about the back-end data sources.

Typically, the report authors time is a very scarce resource. Some organizations use business analysts as intermediaries between the report consumers and the report authors.

In the following sections, we shall present a reporting solution based on OLAP ontologies. The basic idea is to allow more seamless communication between different types of users of a reporting platform. We envisage a system where the report authors' time is saved using a software assisted tool for power users and reporting administrators. With the tool, reporting administrators can design the template of the report, whereas power users can decide what information will populate the template. The principle of making data available for reporting is based on ontologies, discussed in Section 5. In Section 6, we present a methodology where the report authors participate in the first two steps of a four-step process, namely: 1) building an ontology, 2) defining the data sources and how to access them, 3) defining a report and 4) generating a report. A web-based user interface has been developed for the first steps.

5   OLAP Ontology as the Framework for Data and Reports

OLAP (On-Line Analytic Processing) as introduced by Codd, Codd and Salley [10] emphasises the "multidimensional conceptual view" of data, forming a so-called OLAP cube (for formal definitions, see e.g. [20]). The OLAP cube can be seen as a set of coordinates that determine a measure value. The coordinates, or dimensions, can have a hierarchical structure making it possible to analyse data at different levels of statistical aggregation. This will also form the basis for the design of the final reports.

Since the reports consist of a phenomenon and its measurement for a given entity at a given time (like the population of a country in 2010), it is natural to model our domain as dimensions and measures. Dimensions like a geographical area can be hierarchical phenomenon and that these measures are identified by a set of attributes, called dimension keys. The dimension keys can be classified based on additional data. These data can come from different data sources, assuming they are based on "similar enough" ontologies. By similar enough, we mean that it must be possible to build a mapping between the data sources.

Our OLAP model is presented in Figure 1. This model, which includes logical information relevant to the design of the OLAP cube, forms the basis of issuing queries against the OLAP cube.

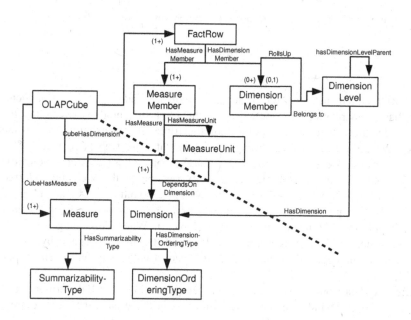

Fig. 1. An ontology model of OLAP cube

The dotted line in Figure 1 divides the structural side (below) from the data side (above). The structural side states that an OLAP cube must have at least one measure and at least one dimension (for summarizability type and temporality type, see [19]). On the data side, we find FactRows that have a MeasureMember and a DimensionMember. DimensionMembers belong to a DimensionLevels element, and there can be a RollUp-relation between two DimensionMembers. Sri Lanka and Asia are DimensionMembers of Dimension Geography. They belong to DimensionLevels Country and Continent, respectively. Moreover, Sri Lanka RollsUp to Asia.

An RDF (Resource Description Framework) ontology corresponding to the model is available at http://www.cern.ch/hiptek/olapcore3.rdf. A model is populated using data sources such that imported data is converted into an RDF format that corresponds with the ontology. An example of such data is shown in Figure 2.

RDF was developed for describing resources on the Web. This is done by making statements about Web resources (pages) and entities that can be identified on the Web, like products in on-line shops [1]. RDF is based on the idea of identifying entities using Web identifiers (called Uniform Resource Identifiers, or URIs), and describing resources by giving statements in terms of simple properties and property values.

```
<FactRow rdf:about="#FactRow_SriLankaPopul">
      <rdfs:label>FactRow_SriLankaPopul</rdfs:label>
      <hasMeasureMember rdf:resource="#20303000"/>
      <hasDimensionMember rdf:resource="#Sri Lanka"/> </FactRow>
<MeasureMember rdf:about="#20303000">
      <rdfs:label>29800000</rdfs:label>
      <hasMeasureUnit rdf:resource="#num_people"/> </MeasureMember>
<DimensionMember rdf:about="#Sri Lanka">
      <rdfs:label>Sri Lanka</rdfs:label>
      <BelongsTo rdf:resource="#COUNTRY"/>
      <RollsUp rdf:resource="#Asia"/>   </DimensionMember>
```

Fig. 2. RDF data of countries

An RDF statement is a triple of subject, predicate, and object. The statement asserts that some relationship, indicated by the predicate, holds between the things denoted by the subject and the object of the triple. As an example of a resource on the Web, we can have the following statement. The web page whose URI is "http://www.example.org/xyz.html" (subject) has a creator (predicate) that is N.N. (object). As an example of an entity outside of the Web, but referred to it by an URI, we can consider the following: A country, Sri Lanka referred to by the URI "http://www.cern.ch/hiptek/Countries.rdf#LK" (subject) has a population (predicate) of 20303000 (object). When describing types of resources, structures like classes are typically needed. This is possible by using the RDF schema language RDFS that enables us to construct classes with their properties (see [2]).

After the data from the sources has been converted into the RDF format, we shall need a method by which we can select from it only those parts that are required for the reports. For that we use an RDF query language shown in Figure 3. The language is a simplified version of RDQL [24]. The SELECT clause contains dimensions and measures to be included into the resulting OLAP cube while the WHERE clause gives restrictions on how these should be tied together. Other restrictions (at the end of the query) define that only some subsets of values are to be included into the result.

```
SELECT ?MeasureValue WHERE
  (?FactRow <olapcore3.rdf#hasDimensionMember> ?Country)
  (?FactRow <olapcore3.rdf#hasDimensionMember> ?Year)
  (?FactRow <olapcore3.rdf#hasDimensionMember> ?Indicator)
  (?FactRow <olapcore3.rdf#hasMeasureMember> ?MeasureValue)
and (?Year eq "2008") and (?Country eq "Sri Lanka") and (?Indicator eq "measles")
```

Fig. 3. RDF query language

Using RDF gives some clear benefits. Since each measure value has an ID, it possible to trace its origin. We can, for example, use the combination of the data source, query, and time as an identifier for each measure value. This also makes it possible to store the measure unit with each measure value and convert the values into the same unit just before aggregation operations or generating reports.

6 Methodology and Implementation

Our method consists of the following steps: 1) building an ontology, 2) defining the data sources and how to access them, 3) defining a report by using the ontology and RDF queries, and 4) sending the queries to data sources and filling in the report with query results.

In the first step the domain of application is modelled by using the RDFS language. The visual form of the ontology (in Figure 4, left) serves as a communication tool between the project participants. The visualisation illustrates that the ontology contains indicators (either generic or illness related), that are focused in time and geographical location. We omit here the details that geographical locations can have levels like country and continent and that the time is recorded in years. A combination of an indicator, geographical location and a year are mapped with a measure value, that has a value and a unit, as shown on the right of Figure 4.

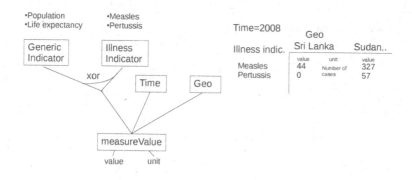

Fig. 4. Schema (left) and instance (right) of health ontology

For the second step, the ontology editor (in Figure 5) demonstrates how data sources are connected to the concepts. This is done by a data source definition tool (Figure 6) where for each indicator, an URL pointing to data and a suitable query is stored. The format of the data source definition file is discussed below in Step 3.

As an example we use the ontology shown in Figure 4. The user wants to find data on 'measles' in Sri Lanka in 2008:

Geo: 'Country = Sri Lanka'; Time: 'Year = 2008'; Indicator: 'Illness = measles'.

By using these parameters we can automatically form the query of Figure 3. The select clause of the query contains the wanted measure value of the measure dimension. The WHERE clause contains two parts: 1) the standard part binding the dimensions to the measure in a fact row, and 2) the part limiting the values taken into the result set. The result of the query will be the number of measles cases in Sri Lanka in 2008.

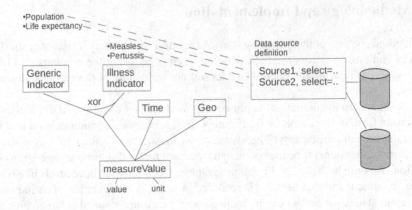

Fig. 5. The ontology and its mapping with data sources

Fig. 6. Data source editor

Table 1. Data sources

Geo	Time	Indicator	Data source
All	All	Population in urban areas (percent)	undata-api.appspot.com/data/query/Populati...
All	All	Life expectancy at birth (years), male	data.un.org/Handlers/DownloadHandler.ashx?...

The third step is to form requests retrieving data from data sources. This is defined by using a tool shown in Figure 7. The data sources can be detected by comparing the given query against the data source definitions. In our example the Indicator dimension alone determines a data source (see Table 1).

A query to the data source can return data in different forms. For the purposes of this project, we have assumed the output format to be XML. We can transform this XML data into RDF form by using a method presented in our earlier work [22]. As data

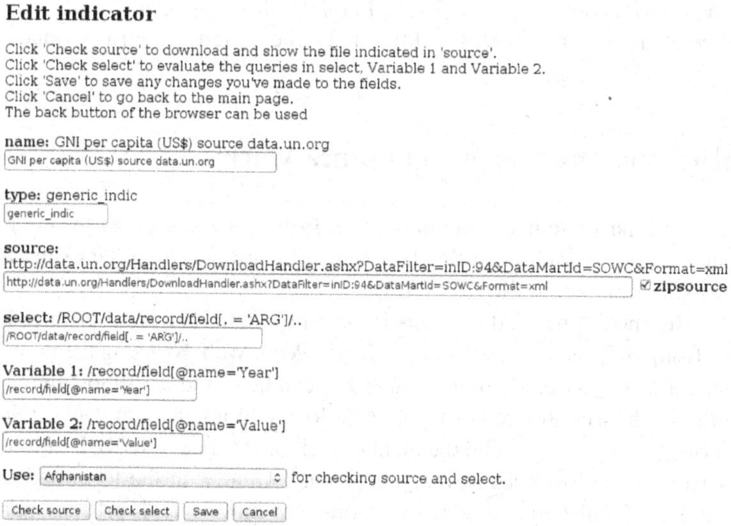

Edit indicator

Click 'Check source' to download and show the file indicated in 'source'.
Click 'Check select' to evaluate the queries in select, Variable 1 and Variable 2.
Click 'Save' to save any changes you've made to the fields.
Click 'Cancel' to go back to the main page.
The back button of the browser can be used

name: GNI per capita (US$) source data.un.org

    GNI per capita (US$) source data.un.org

type: generic_indic

    generic_indic

source:
http://data.un.org/Handlers/DownloadHandler.ashx?DataFilter=inID:94&DataMartId=SOWC&Format=xml

    http://data.un.org/Handlers/DownloadHandler.ashx?DataFilter=inID:94&DataMartId=SOWC&Format=xml   ☑ **zipsource**

select: /ROOT/data/record/field[. = 'ARG']/..

    /ROOT/data/record/field[. = 'ARG']/..

Variable 1: /record/field[@name='Year']

    /record/field[@name='Year']

Variable 2: /record/field[@name='Value']

    /record/field[@name='Value']

Use: Afghanistan   ⌄ for checking source and select.

    [Check source] [Check select] [Save] [Cancel]

Fig. 7. Indicator editor

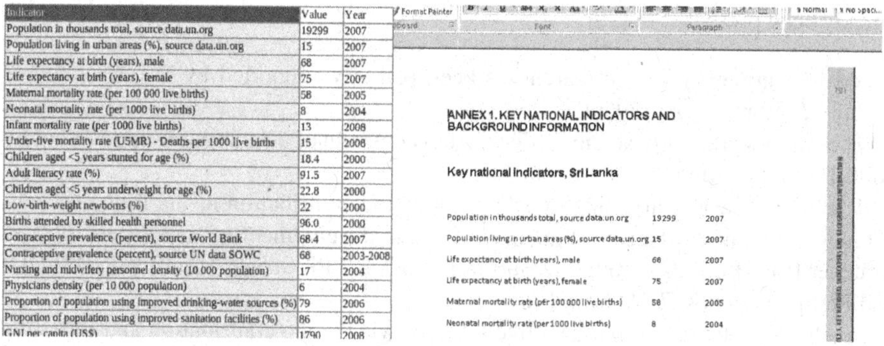

Indicator	Value	Year
Population in thousands total, source data.un.org	19299	2007
Population living in urban areas (%), source data.un.org	15	2007
Life expectancy at birth (years), male	68	2007
Life expectancy at birth (years), female	75	2007
Maternal mortality rate (per 100 000 live births)	58	2005
Neonatal mortality rate (per 1000 live births)	8	2004
Infant mortality rate (per 1000 live births)	13	2008
Under-five mortality rate (U5MR) - Deaths per 1000 live births	15	2008
Children aged <5 years stunted for age (%)	18.4	2000
Adult literacy rate (%)	91.5	2007
Children aged <5 years underweight for age (%)	22.8	2000
Low-birth-weight newborns (%)	22	2000
Births attended by skilled health personnel	96.0	2000
Contraceptive prevalence (percent), source World Bank	68.4	2007
Contraceptive prevalence (percent), source UN data SOWC	68	2003-2008
Nursing and midwifery personnel density (10 000 population)	17	2004
Physicians density (per 10 000 population)	6	2004
Proportion of population using improved drinking-water sources (%)	79	2006
Proportion of population using improved sanitation facilities (%)	86	2006
GNI per capita (US$)	1790	2008

ANNEX 1. KEY NATIONAL INDICATORS AND
BACKGROUND INFORMATION

Key national indicators, Sri Lanka

Population in thousands total, source data.un.org	19299	2007
Population living in urban areas (%), source data.un.org	15	2007
Life expectancy at birth (years), male	68	2007
Life expectancy at birth (years), female	75	2007
Maternal mortality rate (per 100 000 live births)	58	2005
Neonatal mortality rate (per 1000 live births)	8	2004

Fig. 8. An example report

sources, we have used the UNDATA API project (`http://www.undata-api.org`) and the World Bank data API (`http://api.worldbank.org`). Once they have been retrieved, the RDF data is initially stored in our local RDF database. Usually the data set is larger than that required to answer the given query. Therefore, the query that was formatted earlier is posed against the data stored in the local database. In our method, all the indicators related to a given country are retrieved.

Finally, we have query results available but they must be formatted according to the given report definition. For this, we have utilised XML import of the standard Microsoft Office software package, that is used at WHO to prepare the reports. The report, formatted as HTML is shown on the left of Figure 8. The same data, imported into Microsoft Word is shown on the right. Additionally, the system can also produce reports directly in the PDF format.

7   Conclusions, Discussion and Future Work

In this paper, we have studied combining data from diverse sources in order to produce on-line reports. Our case for the data collection are reporting the Communicable Disease Epidemiological Profiles for WHO.

We have presented a method for assisting the production of these profiles by combining data from multiple sources from the World Wide Web. By using the new method, the annexes for a country epidemiological report can be produced almost in real time.

The sources can be configured using an "ontology editor", the template for the report by another on-line application, and the meta model for the data is an RDF ontology. The data extracted from the sources is also presented, similarly, in the form of RDF. This brings us several benefits compared with a more conventional ETL process, namely: 1) the validity of the data can be checked against the ontology, and 2) standard RDF query languages can be used with the data. Technical details of the project can be found at https://twiki.cern.ch/twiki/bin/view/Main/ExHaDa.

For future research we are investigating a data storage technique that would enable us to create an efficient OLAP cube from RDF data. First results of this research have already been presented in [25].

Acknowledgments. This research has been partially supported by the Academy of Finland grant number 1139590.

The authors gratefully acknowledge the development of a data source editing tool by Antti Heikkilä during the summer 2011.

The authors would also like to acknowledge the contribution of the following colleagues at the World Health Organization in the development of this paper: Phillipe Boucher IER/HSE/HCT, Anthony Burton FCH/IVB/EPI, Steven Moore IER/HSI/HCI and Philippe Veltsos ITT/AME/HTS.

Finally, the authors would also like to acknowledge the contribution and reporting insight of Prof. Zheying Zhang and Mr. Maikel Perez Gort of the University of Tampere.

References

1. RDF Primer, W3C Recommendation. Tech. rep., W3C (February 10, 2004)
2. RDF Vocabulary Description Language 1.0: RDF Schema. Tech. rep., W3C (2004)
3. RDF/XML Syntax Specification. Tech. rep., W3C (2004)
4. Abiteboul, S., Buneman, P., Suciu, D.: Data on the Web – from Relations to Semistructured Data and XML. Morgan Kaufmann, New York (2000)
5. Abiteboul, S.: Querying Semi-Structured Data. In: Proceedings of the 6th International Conference on Database Theory, pp. 1–18. Springer, London (1997)
6. Axson, D.A.J.: Best Practices in Planning and Management Reporting. Wiley, New York (2003)

7. Bass, L.: A Graphical Interface for Report Specification. In: ACM 1982 Conference, New York (1982)
8. Bray, T.: RDF and Metadata. xml.com (1998)
9. Chawathe, S., et al.: The TSIMMIS Project: Integration of Heterogeneous Information Sources. In: Proc. of the 16th Meeting of the Information Processing Society of Japan (1994)
10. Codd, E., Codd, S., Salley, C.: Providing OLAP to User-Analysts: An IT Mandate. Tech. rep., Hyperion (1993)
11. Correndo, G., Salvadores, M., Millard, I., Glaser, H., Shadbolt, N.: SPARQL Query Rewriting for Implementing Data Integration over Linked Data. In: Proceedings of the 2010 EDBT/ICDT Workshops, EDBT 2010, pp. 4:1–4:11. ACM, New York (2010)
12. Hull, R.: Managing Semantic Heterogeneity in Databases: a Theoretical Prospective. In: Proc. ACM Symposium on Principles of Databases (1997)
13. Jepsen, B.: Microsoft SQL Server 2005 Reporting Services (2005),
    http://download.microsoft.com/a/a1a34973-9fb6-40c4-b8bb-786a14
    1aa559/SQL_Server_2005_Reporting_Services.ppt
14. Malinowski, E., Zimanyi, E.: Advanced Data Warehouse Design: from Conventional to Spatial and Temporal Applications. Springer, London (2009)
15. Mohania, M., Bhide, M.: New Trends in Information Integration. In: The 2nd International Conference on Ubiquitous Information Management and Communication, ICUIMC 2008, pp. 74–81. ACM, New York (2008)
16. Mori, M., Tanaka, T., Hirokawa, S.: A Document Authoring System for Credible Enterprise Reporting with Data Analysis from Data Warehouse. In: The 4th International Conference on Advances in Semantic Processing, Florence, Italy (2010)
17. Motro, A.: Superviews: Virtual Integration of Multiple Databases. IEEE Trans. Softw. Eng. 13, 785–798 (1987)
18. Näppilä, T., Järvelin, K., Niemi, T.: A Tool for Data Cube Construction from Structurally Heterogeneous XML Documents. J. Am. Soc. Inf. Sci. Technol. 59(3), 435–449 (2008)
19. Niemi, T., Niinimaki, M.: Ontologies and Summarizability in OLAP. In: Proc. SAC 2010, Sierre, Switzerland (2010)
20. Niemi, T., Nummenmaa, J., Thanisch, P.: Normalising OLAP Cubes for Controlling Sparsity. Data and Knowledge Engineering 46(1), 317–343 (2003)
21. Niemi, T., Toivonen, S., Niinimäki, M., Nummenmaa, J.: Ontologies with Semantic Web/grid in Data Integration for OLAP. International Journal on Semantic Web and Information Systems, Special Issue on Semantic Web and Data Warehousing 3(4) (2007)
22. Niinimäki, M., Niemi, T.: An ETL process for OLAP using RDF/OWL ontologies. In: Spaccapietra, S., Zimányi, E., Song, I.-Y. (eds.) Journal on Data Semantics XIII. LNCS, vol. 5530, pp. 97–119. Springer, Heidelberg (2009)
23. Reddy, M.P., Prasad, B.E., Reddy, P.G.: A Methodology for Integration of Heterogeneous Databases. IEEE Trans. on Knowl. and Data Eng. 6, 920–933 (1994)
24. Seaborne, A.: RDQL - A Query Language for RDF. Tech. rep., W3C Member Submission (2004), http://www.w3c.org/Submission/RDQL/
25. Thanisch, P., Niemi, T., Niinimaki, M., Nummenmaa, J.: Using the Entity-Attribute-Value Model for OLAP Cube Construction. In: Grabis, J., Kirikova, M. (eds.) BIR 2011. LNBIP, vol. 90, pp. 59–72. Springer, Heidelberg (2011)
26. Thanisch, P., Nummenmaa, J.: On Selecting a Suitable Set of Reporting Platforms. In: Proc. Business Informatics Research BIR 2006, Kaunas, Lithuania (2006)
27. The World Wide Web Consortium: XSL Transformations XSLT, Version 1.0, W3C Recommendation (November 16, 1999), http://www.w3.org/TR/xslt
28. Witkowski, A., Bellamkonda, S., Bozkaya, T., Naimat, A., Sheng, L., Subramanian, S., Waingold, A.: Query by Excel. In: 31st Intl. Conf. of Very Large Data Bases, Trondheim, Norway, pp. 1204–1215 (2005)

An Ontology-Based Quality Framework
for Data Integration

Jianing Wang, Nigel Martin, and Alexandra Poulovassilis

Department of Computer Science and Information Systems,
Birkbeck College, University of London, London WC1E 7HX
{jianing,nigel,ap}@dcs.bbk.ac.uk

Abstract. The data integration (DI) process involves multiple users
with roles such as administrators, integrators and end-users, each of
whom may have requirements which have an impact on the overall quality of an integrated resource. Users' requirements may conflict with each
other, and so a quality framework for the DI context has to be capable
of representing the variety of such requirements and provide mechanisms
to detect and resolve the possible inconsistencies between them. This paper presents a framework for the specification of DI quality criteria and
associated user requirements. This is underpinned by a Description Language formalisation with associated reasoning capabilities which enables
a DI setting to be tested to identify those elements that are inconsistent
with users' requirements. The application of the framework is illustrated
with an example showing how it can be used to improve the quality of
an integrated resource.

Keywords: Data Integration, Quality Assessment, Quality Metrics.

1 Introduction

Historically and currently, data conforming to different formats are gathered
and organised by different parties. Different users may need to access such data
sources according to their specific requirements. This may require redefining
data into different formats, combining relevant data from different sources, and
combining incomplete data sources in order to form a more complete view. Combining and transforming data from different data sources is a complex problem
and is the aim of *Data Integration (DI)*. In the DI context, data conforming to
different data models can be transformed and accessed through a *global schema*
using *mappings* between this schema and the data sources. A typical DI setting
can therefore be represented as a triple $\langle GS, LSs, M \rangle$, where GS is the global
schema, $LSs = \{LS_1, \ldots, LS_n\}$ is the set of local (i.e. data source) schemas and
M is the set of mappings between GS and the LSs.

Assessing the quality of a DI setting is a complex task. The data integration
process may involve multiple users with different roles, and their quality requirements may not be consistent, in the sense that the same integrated resource
cannot satisfy all requirements and, therefore, either the integrated resource or
the users' requirements need to be modified.

L. Niedrite, R. Strazdina, B. Wangler (Eds.): BIR 2011 Workshops, LNBIP 106, pp. 196–208, 2012.
© Springer-Verlag Berlin Heidelberg 2012

For example, in the Higher Education (HE) domain, an integrated resource with information about staff and programmes may be derived from information held at both institution and departmental level, and be intended for use by both administrative and academic staff each with their own requirements. While an administrator in the Human Resources (HR) department may want to ensure that complete staff information is retained from the original data sources, a user at the academic department level may only want to ensure that complete information is held for recent years about a programme's director and the performance of students on the programme, so enabling analysis of student data in those years. Also, it may be important to an HR administrator that staff information in the integrated resource remains consistent with just those constraints defined in the schemas of the original sources, while this might not be of significance to users at the academic department level more concerned to ensure that the resource supports the widest possible analysis of programme and student information.

A quality framework for the DI context needs to be capable of representing the varieties of user quality requirements and to provide mechanisms to detect and resolve the possible inconsistencies between them. With the need for these capabilities in mind, we have developed a formal quality framework supporting quality criteria such as completeness and consistency, metrics for measuring the extent to which an integrated resource satisfies the desired quality criteria, and the capability of representing the quality requirements of different users. Our quality framework is underpinned by a Description Logic (DL) formalisation, and users' quality requirements are formalised as logic statements in DL. This enables formal reasoning to be applied to detect inconsistencies between different users' requirements and to validate individual quality requirements with respect to the integrated resource.

The paper is organised as follows. Section 2 briefly reviews research relating to quality assessment in the DI context. In Section 3, we describe our quality framework for DI and its implementation. We discuss the completeness and consistency quality criteria in Section 4: these are examples of what is possible within our quality framework, which is extensible with new quality criteria. There follows in Section 5 an example relating to the Higher Education domain showing how our quality framework can be used to improve the quality of an integrated resource. Conclusions and further work are discussed in Section 6.

2   Related Work

Previous research [1,2] has indicated that users with different roles are important in the DI context. Such roles include database administrators, integrators and end-users. Different users may have different quality requirements in respect of an integrated data resource, from their different perspectives. Therefore such requirements need to be considered individually and also as a whole in assessing the quality of an integrated resource. Although existing DI tools are designed to assist in many integration tasks, DI is still a complex problem due to the heterogeneity of the data sources and the variety of the users' quality requirements. None of the current DI tools supports quality management functionality within the integration workflow, whereas in recent work we propose such a DI architecture and methodology [3,4].

In data integration, there are two common integration approaches, termed GAV and LAV. In GAV, each *GS* construct is defined by a conjunctive query over the *LSs*, or a union of such queries [5]. These are termed *GAV mappings*. In LAV, each local schema construct is defined by a conjunctive query over the *GS* [5]. These are termed *LAV mappings*. GAV and LAV mappings can be used to reformulate a query expressed on the *GS* into a query expressed on the *LSs* using query unfolding or query rewriting [6] techniques, respectively.

Recent research has proposed methods for determining the quality of a DI setting directly or indirectly. The work in [7] defines several quality measurement methods in the DI context, relating to the schema completeness, schema consistency and schema minimality quality criteria. These methods are based on information extracted from the schema metadata level, such as the proportion of the concepts in the application domain that are represented by the schemas. Other work [8] has presented an approach for mapping selection based on the comparison of instances between the source schema and target schema extracted via different mappings. The approach in [9] determines the quality of collaborative tasks, such as data integration, with respect to the users' quality requirements through users' feedback; this is in contrast to users' quality requirements expressed as logic statements over a quality hierarchy in our approach. While not motivated explicitly from a quality perspective, other techniques can also be adopted for measuring the quality of integrated resources. Such work includes instance checking methods which may be used to validate and refine mappings such as [10,11], constraint validation such as [12,13], and mapping cores to generate the minimum set of mappings with respect to the reformulation of users' queries in a data exchange context [14].

3   Our Quality Framework for Data Integration

We propose a *Quality Framework for Data Integration (QFDI)* that is composed of four major parts: *ITEM*, *METRIC*, *QUALITY CRITERIA* and *USER*, as illustrated in Figure 1.

ITEM contains representations of the elements comprising a DI setting. By 'elements' we mean the fundamental constituents of an integrated resource, including *Data Item*, *Schema Construct*, *Mapping* and *Assertion*. All of these are represented as sub-concepts of the *Item* concept. Links exist between these sub-concepts, represented by the *link* property, to represent how the extent of one concept relates to that of another. Schema Constructs are instances of the modelling constructs of the modelling language used to specify a given local or global schema (including constraints). Assertions express users' knowledge about the application domain. Assertions may be expressed with respect to a domain ontology, if one is available or is created during the integration process, or with respect to ontology representations of the local and global schemas.

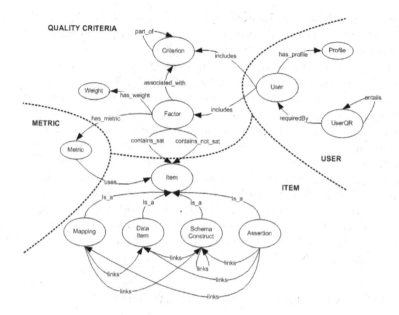

Fig. 1. The Quality Framework for Data Integration (QFDI)

In the METRIC part, different quality measurement methods (metrics) are represented by the *Metric* concept. Each metric is defined over instances of the Item concept in the ITEM part. The measurement results are stored as the extent of the Metric concept.

QUALITY CRITERIA contains the representation of the quality hierarchy as defined by the data integrator for a particular integrated resource. This hierarchy is built from two concepts, *Criterion* and *Factor*, and the relationships between them, namely *part_of* and *associated_with*. In order to interpret quality criteria from different perspectives, we allow different quality factors to be associated with each quality criterion. Each quality criterion can have several sub-criteria, linked by the *part_of* property. Each quality factor is associated with one (sub-) criterion, using the *associated_with* property. Each quality factor is associated with a quality metric in the METRIC part using the *has_metric* property. The *Weight* concept is associated with the *Factor* concept and indicates the weighting of each quality factor as defined by the users.

The *contains_sat* and *contains_not_sat* properties link the *Factor* concept and the *Item* concept. These properties represent the DI elements that satisfy and that do not satisfy a quality factor, respectively, and are disjoint.

USER contains the *User* concept. Users with different roles may have different quality requirements, as discussed in Section 1. Different user requirements are represented by the *UserQR* (User Quality Requirement) concept. Users' requirements are expressed as logical statements referencing the QUALITY CRITERIA concepts of the QFDI. Domain ontology concepts can also be referenced in these statements in order to define quality requirements that are domain-specific. User quality requirements can be related by the *entail* property, meaning that if the integrated resource satisfies one user requirement, the integrated resource also satisfies another user requirement that is entailed by the first one. The *Profile* concept represents the overall quality of the integrated resource with respect to a specific user, calculated as $w_1 \times r_1 + \ldots + w_n \times r_n$, where r_i and w_i are the measurement of a quality factor i and its user-specified weighting, respectively.

We have implemented our QFDI using the OWL-DL ontology language [15]. We use the FaCT++ reasoner [16] to undertake inferencing over the QFDI, which is able to discover inconsistencies between different users quality requirements and also inconsistencies of each individual requirement with respect to the DI elements in the integrated resource. We illustrate both of these aspects of our approach in Section 5. We have implemented the quality factors and associated metrics using the AutoMed DI system [17]. We refer the reader to [4] for full implementation details.

4   Quality Criteria, Factors and Metrics

In our research, we have investigated four quality criteria in the context of DI: *completeness, consistency, accuracy* and *minimality*. In this paper we focus on the completeness and consistency criteria, which we discuss next. We refer to [4] for full descriptions of these and the other quality criteria.

4.1   Quality Criteria

The *completeness* quality criterion comprises three sub-criteria: *schema completeness, mapping completeness* and *query completeness*. *Schema completeness* relates to the degree of coverage of the *GS* or the *LSs* with respect to the real-world concepts of the application domain. *Mapping completeness* relates to the degree of coverage of the schema constructs appearing in the mapping definitions with respect to the real-world concepts of the application domain. *Query completeness* represents the degree of coverage of the information extractable by a set of user-defined queries on the *GS* by reformulating these queries using the mappings into queries that can be evaluated on the data sources.

The *consistency* quality criterion considers the degree to which the integrated resource satisfies its semantics. Such semantics are expressed as constraints within the *LSs* and the *GS*, and also by additional constraints relating to the application domain. The consistency quality criterion comprises three sub-criteria: *schema consistency, mapping consistency* and *query consistency*. *Schema consistency* captures the degree of conformance of the *LSs* and the *GS* to the domain-related constraints. *Mapping consistency* captures the degree to which the mappings conform to the semantics of the *LSs* and the *GS* and to the domain-related constraints. *Query consistency* captures the degree to which results returned from a set of user-defined queries satisfy user-defined relationships between such result sets (for example, equivalence and subsumption relationships).

4.2 Quality Factors and Metrics

In [4] we develop eight quality factors, $f_1 - f_8$, relating to the completeness and consistency quality criteria. We define each quality factor separately for the GAV and LAV mapping approaches, and also for a combined GAV and LAV mapping approach (as supported by the AutoMed DI system, for example [17]). Here, due to space limitations, we discuss two of these quality factors only, f_2 and f_7, and only the definition relating to the GAV mapping approach in each case. We refer the reader to [4] for a complete discussion of the full set.

FACTOR 2, Related to the Schema Completeness Quality Criterion. The extents of the local schema constructs from different data sources may provide overlapping information. By 'overlapping information', we mean local schema constructs that represent the same real-world concept. The information contained in the data sources may be partially complete, and one of the purposes of data integration is to reduce incompleteness by combining information from different data sources. In the context of this factor, we consider that information represented by the *GS* is given by the extensional schema constructs in the *GS* (i.e. by those constructs that have a data extent associated with them). We denote by *concepts*(S, O) the set of real-world concepts in the domain ontology O represented by the extensional constructs of a schema S. We denote by *reduce*(C, O) the set of unique real-world concepts in a group of concepts, C, obtained by removing concepts that are equivalent to or subsumed by other concepts in the ontology O (ignoring the 'top' and 'bottom' concepts).

If the GAV mapping approach is used, this quality factor can be defined as the average level of coverage of the extensional local schema constructs that relate to the same real-world concept. The measurement of this quality factor is illustrated in Formula 1, where *extensional*(LSs, c) is the set of extensional local schema constructs representing the real-world concept c, and *sources*(LSs, M_{GAV}, c) is the set of extensional local schema constructs representing the real-world concept c that are also referenced in the set of GAV mappings, M_{GAV}:

$$\lambda_{2,GAV} = \frac{\displaystyle\sum_{c \in \cup_{j=1}^{n} reduce(concepts(LS_j, O), O)} \frac{|sources(LSs, M_{GAV}, c)|}{|extensional(LSs, c)|}}{|\bigcup_{i=1}^{n} reduce(concepts(LS_i, O), O)|} \tag{1}$$

FACTOR 7, Related to the Mapping Consistency Quality Criterion. Constraints in the local schemas form restrictions on the extents of the extensional schema constructs. When such information is transformed in deriving the *GS*, there is a risk that the data extracted from the data sources no longer complies with the constraints in the *GS*. For example, new constraints may be added via the mappings, explicitly or implicitly. In the former case, new constraints can be added to schemas using schema transformation primitives supported by the integration system (such as the *addConstraint* primitive in AutoMed [18]). In the latter case, new constraints may be expressed via the mapping queries, restricting the data extracted from the data sources.

For the GAV mapping approach, this quality factor can be measured as the degree to which local schema constructs satisfy both the queries representing the constraints on the *LSs* and also the new constraints introduced in the mappings. This can be calculated using Formula 2, where $constraints(LSs)$ is the set of local schema constraints, q_o is the query corresponding to the local schema constraint o, and $q_{s,o}$ is the set of queries introducing new constraints in the mappings relating to extensional schema constructs referenced in q_o. $evaluate(q_o, q_{s,o})$ is assigned 1 if both q_o and each member of $q_{s,o}$ evaluate to true, in the sense that all extents which satisfy q_o also satisfy all members of $q_{s,o}$. Otherwise, $evaluate(q_o, q_{s,o})$ is assigned 0.

$$\lambda_{7,GAV} = \sum_{o \in constraints(LSs)} \frac{evaluate(q_o, q_{s,o})}{|constraints(LSs)|} \tag{2}$$

5   Demonstration

To illustrate use of the QFDI, we use a simple case study (see Figure 2) composed of two data sources and a global schema. Database 1 (with schema LS1) contains detailed descriptions of the degree programmes (identifier PID) and the staff (identifier SID) of a university. Database 2 (with schema LS2) contains detailed information about the undergraduate and postgraduate programmes taken by students as well as their lecturers (identifier LID). A set of constraints are also defined over LS1 and LS2 including primary key, foreign key and value range constraints. The value range constraints are defined on the "Year" attributes in the "ug_prog" and "pg_prog" tables indicating that both programmes are recorded after year 1989. The 6 primary key constraints are represented as the underlined attributes of the entities in schemas LS1 and LS2 in Figure 2. Table 1 lists the 4 foreign key and the 2 value range constraints in the local schemas. We use the notation LS_{x_y} and $LS_{x\_z_y}$ in which x, y and z indicate the local schema number, table name and attribute name, respectively. A version of the global schema (GS) is created representing the programme directors of all programmes.

As described previously, users can state various quality requirements on an integrated resource based on their different perspectives, which are expressed as Description Logic statements over the quality factors and domain ontology concepts. Description Logic (DL) is a family of formal knowledge representation languages based on the notions of *concepts* and *roles*. DL is characterised by constructors that allow complex concepts and roles to be built from atomic ones [15].

Table 1. Constraints in the Local Schemas

Constraints	Description
Foreign Key	$LS_1\_Prog\_Dir_{programme}$ references $LS_1\_SID_{staff}$
	$LS_1\_SID_{ft\_faculty\_member}$ references $LS_1\_SID_{staff}$
	$LS_2\_Prog\_Dir_{ug\_prog}$ references $LS_2\_LID_{lecturer}$
	$LS_2\_Prog\_Dir_{pg\_prog}$ references $LS_2\_LID_{lecturer}$
Value Range	$LS_2\_Year_{ug\_prog} > 1989$
	$LS_2\_Year_{pg\_prog} > 1989$

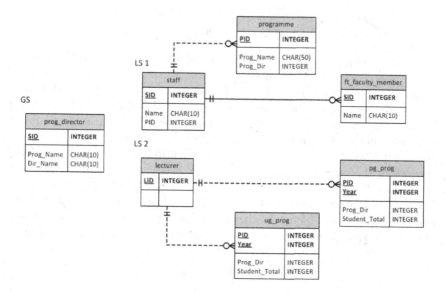

Fig. 2. Example Schemas

In our approach, users' quality requirements are expressed using *terminology axioms*. The terminology axioms that we consider are *inclusion*, $C \sqsubseteq D$, and *equality*, $C \equiv D$, where C and D are concepts expressed in the syntax of the $\mathcal{SI}$ DL [19]. More complex assertions can be created from these two basic ones plus negation.

The QFDI is also represented in the $\mathcal{SI}$ DL: each oval in Figure 1 (except the USER part of the diagram) is represented as a DL concept named by the text in the oval and each link is represented as a role named by the name of the link. The DI elements are represented as individuals of the *Data Item (Di)*, *Schema Construct (Sc)*, *Mapping (Ma)* and *Assertion (As)* concepts and are associated with quality factors via the *contains_sat* and *contains_not_sat* roles.

To illustrate, consider the case study introduced earlier and the following GAV mappings m_1 and m_2 that define the prog_director table in the global schema GS as the union of two conjunctive queries over the source schemas LS1 and LS2.

It can be seen that while m_1 maintains the programme director relationship between prog_director and ug_prog using variable s, m_2 does not do this for pg_prog given the distinct variables s_1 and s_2. This is representative of mapping deficiencies which arise in practice in complex DI settings.

$$m_1 = \forall s, pn, n.GS : prog\_director(s, pn, n) \leftarrow$$
$$\exists sp, pr, p, y, t. \; LS_1 : staff(s, n, sp) \land LS_1 : programme(pr, pn, s)$$
$$\land LS_2 : ug\_prog(p, y, s, t)$$
$$m_2 = \forall s_1, pn, n.GS : prog\_director(s_1, pn, n) \leftarrow$$
$$\exists sp, pr, p, y, s_2, t. \; LS_1 : staff(s_1, n, sp) \land LS_1 : programme(pr, pn, s_1)$$
$$\land LS_2 : pg\_prog(p, y, s_2, t) \land y > 2000$$

For quality factor f_2, consider the real-world concept "Lecturer". There are three schema constructs representing this concept: "staff", "ft_faculty_member" and "lecturer". However, only the "staff" schema construct from LS1 is referenced in the mappings. Therefore, the "staff" construct from LS1 satisfies f_2 and "ft_faculty_member" and "lecturer" do not satisfy this quality factor for the real-world concept "Lecturer". The same method is applied to all 7 real-world concepts represented by the local schemas to identify related schema constructs referenced in the mappings, as listed in Table 2. Given Formula 1, this quality factor can be calculated as $f_2 = \frac{0.33 + 0.71 + 0.66 + 1.00 + 1.00 + 1.00 + 1.00}{7} = 0.82$.

In the local schemas, there exist 6 primary key, 4 foreign key and 2 value range constraints. For quality factor f_7, the new value range constraint, $y > 2000$, introduced in mapping m_2 is not consistent with a value range constraint in the

Table 2. Concept Coverage

Concept	Referenced	Not referenced	Coverage
Lecturer	LS_1_staff	$LS_1\_ft\_faculty\_member$ $LS_2\_lecturer$	$\frac{1}{3} = 0.33$
ID	$LS_1\_SID_{staff}$ $LS_1\_PID_{staff}$ $LS_2\_PID_{ug\_prog}$ $LS_2\_PID_{pg\_prog}$ $LS_1\_PID_{programme}$	$LS_1\_SID_{ft\_faculty\_member}$ $LS_2\_LID_{lecturer}$	$\frac{5}{7} = 0.71$
Name	$LS_1\_Name_{staff}$ $LS_1\_Prog\_Name_{programme}$	$LS_1\_Name_{ft\_faculty\_member}$	$\frac{2}{3} = 0.66$
Programme	$LS_2\_ug\_prog$ $LS_2\_pg\_prog$ $LS_1\_programme$		$\frac{3}{3} = 1.00$
Programme_Director	$LS_2\_Prog\_Dir_{ug\_prog}$ $LS_2\_Prog\_Dir_{pg\_prog}$ $LS_1\_Prog\_Dir_{programme}$		$\frac{3}{3} = 1.00$
Year	$LS_2\_Year_{ug\_prog}$ $LS_2\_Year_{pg\_prog}$		$\frac{2}{2} = 1.00$
Student_Total	$LS_2\_Student\_Total_{ug\_prog}$ $LS_2\_Student\_Total_{pg\_prog}$		$\frac{2}{2} = 1.00$

data sources since this constraint introduces additional restrictions on the information extractable from the data sources. In addition, one of the foreign key constraints representing the programme leadership information is also not maintained by the mapping. Given formula 2, this quality factor can be calculated as $f_7 = \frac{6+3+1}{6+4+2} = 0.83$.

Assuming that equal weights have been assigned to each quality factor, the overall quality of this integrated resource is calculated as $0.50 \times 0.82 + 0.50 \times 0.83 = 0.825$. Table 3 summarises the DI elements that satisfy and do not satisfy quality factors f_2 and f_7.

Table 3. Quality Factor Satisfaction

	Satisfying Elements		not-Satisfying Elements
f_2	$\{LS_1\_staff,$ $LS_1\_SID_{staff},$ $LS_1\_Name_{staff},$ $LS_2\_ug\_prog,$ $LS_2\_pg\_prog,$ $LS_1\_programme,$ $LS_1\_PID_{staff},$ $LS_2\_PID_{ug\_prog},$ $LS_2\_PID_{pg\_prog},$ $LS_1\_PID_{programme},$	$LS_2\_Year_{ug\_prog},$ $LS_2\_Year_{pg\_prog},$ $LS_2\_Prog\_Dir_{ug\_prog},$ $LS_2\_Prog\_Dir_{pg\_prog},$ $LS_1\_Prog\_Dir_{programme},$ $LS_2\_Student\_Total_{ug\_prog},$ $LS_2\_Student\_Total_{pg\_prog},$ $LS_1\_Prog\_Name_{programme},$ $m_1, m_2\}$	$\{LS_1\_ft\_faculty\_member,$ $LS_1\_SID_{ft\_faculty\_member},$ $LS_1\_Name_{ft\_faculty\_member},$ $LS_2\_lecturer,$ $LS_2\_LID_{lecturer}\}$
f_7	$\{LS_2\_ug\_prog,$ $LS_2\_PID_{ug\_prog},$ $LS_2\_Year_{ug\_prog},$ $LS_2\_Prog\_Dir_{ug\_prog},$ $LS_2\_Student\_Total_{ug\_prog},$ $m_1\}$		$\{LS_2\_pg\_prog,$ $LS_2\_PID_{pg\_prog},$ $LS_2\_Year_{pg\_prog},$ $LS_2\_Prog\_Dir_{pg\_prog},$ $LS_2\_Student\_Total_{pg\_prog},$ $m_2\}$

Suppose now that there are three quality requirements issued by three users, A, B and C as listed in in Table 4. It is important for user A that the integrated resource is still consistent with the constraints defined in the original data sources. In particular, user A requires that the schema constructs which satisfy the schema completeness factor should also satisfy the mapping consistency factor ($A.1$). User B does not require that schema constructs satisfy both the schema completeness and mapping consistency factors, but there should not be any which satisfy neither ($B.1$). User C, while in general requiring that constructs which satisfy the schema completeness factor should also satisfy mapping consistency, is more concerned in the case of programme director information that as much data from the data sources as possible is retained in the integrated resource, and so in that specific case schema completeness without mapping consistency is permissible. Hence, user C requires that any schema construct which satisfies schema completeness but not mapping consistency must be related to the Programme Director concept ($C.1$). We discuss next the reasoning capability of our approach and how this can be used to determine the consistency of these requirements and the DI elements that violate any of them.

Given a quality hierarchy and logic statements representing different users' quality requirements, there are two validation steps in QFDI where reasoning can be applied. First, reasoning can be applied in order to validate different users' requirements, as specified from their different quality perspectives. Second, reasoning can be applied in order to validate individual quality requirements with respect to the integrated resource. In the former case, inconsistent logic statements can be identified. In the latter case, the DI elements that do not satisfy individual logic statements can be discovered. When an inconsistency is discovered, the DI elements relating to quality factors referenced in the logic statements or the logic statements themselves may need to be modified in order to resolve such inconsistencies.

Table 4. Users' Requirements Example

No.	Requirement	Logic Statement in DL
$A.1$	Schema constructs that satisfy f_2 should also satisfy f_7.	$(Sc \sqcap \forall contains\_sat^-.\{f_2\})$ $\sqsubseteq$ $(Sc \sqcap \forall contains\_sat^-.\{f_7\})$
$B.1$	There should be no schema constructs that satisfy neither f_2 nor f_7.	$((Sc \sqcap \forall contains\_not\_sat^-.\{f_2\})$ $\sqcap$ $(Sc \sqcap \forall contains\_not\_sat^-.\{f_7\}))$ $\equiv \emptyset$
$C.1$	A schema construct which satisfies f_2 but does not satisfy f_7 must be related to the Programme Director concept.	$(Sc \sqcap \forall contains\_sat^-.\{f_2\}$ $\sqcap \forall contains\_not\_sat^-.\{f_7\})$ $\sqsubseteq (Sc \sqcap Programme Director)$

The former case uses TBox reasoning and the latter case uses ABox reasoning [15]. In our example (see Tables 3 and 4), inferring from the users' logic statements first, without involving the DI elements (i.e., undertaking TBox reasoning), we can discover that $A.1$ and $C.1$ are not consistent since $A.1$ implies that the set of DI elements satisfying f_2 should be a subset of the DI elements satisfying f_7, whereas $C.1$ implies that there could exist some programme leadership-related DI elements that do satisfy f_2 and do not satisfy f_7. Therefore, either $A.1$ or $C.1$ has to be modified. Suppose the data integrator removes $A.1$ because $A.1$ is a general and overall requirement and loosening it enables the users to define more detailed and flexible quality requirements such as $C.1$. We then repeat the inference process. There is now no conflict between the remaining logic statements ($B.1$ and $C.1$).

Next, for each remaining user requirement, we undertake reasoning again, this time including the DI elements (i.e., undertaking ABox reasoning). We can discover that while $B.1$ is satisfied by the DI elements listed in Table 3, $C.1$ is not since there are schema constructs not related to the Programme Director concept which satisfy f_2 but do not satisfy f_7, for example $LS_2\_PID_{pg\text{-}prog}$ and $LS_2\_Year_{pg\text{-}prog}$. Hence, the reasoner throws an exception indicating there is a problem with the extent of $contains\_not\_sat^-.\{f_7\}$.

Once the data integrator has validated the users' requirements and identified the DI elements which are indicated by the reasoner as having a problem, the mappings referencing those DI elements can be re-examined. In our example, a problem has been identified with the attributes of $LS_2\_pg\_prog$ which do not satisfy f_7. These DI elements are referenced in mapping m_2. Suppose the data integrator modifies mapping m_2 by replacing the constraint $y > 2000$ with $y > 1989$, and also establishes the programme director constraint between the pg-prog and staff tables (a new mapping m_2' is generated):

$$m_2' = \forall s, pn, n.GS : prog\_director(s, pn, n) \leftarrow$$
$$\exists sp, pr, p, y, t.\ LS_1 : staff(s, n, sp) \wedge LS_1 : programme(pr, pn, s)$$
$$\wedge LS_2 : pg\_prog(p, y, s, t) \wedge y > 1989$$

This change does not affect the result of f_2 since no additional local schema constructs have been referenced in the mappings and no existing constructs have been de-referenced in the mappings. Therefore, the calculation of f_2 remains the same. However, this revised mapping does affect the result of f_7 since mapping m_2' now does not introduce a new constraint relating to the schema constructs referenced in the value range constraints on LS2 and also maintains the programme leadership constraint from the data sources. Hence, f_7 is calculated as $\frac{6+4+2}{6+4+2} = 1$. The change to mapping m_2 results in an empty set for $Sc \sqcap \forall contains\_not\_sat^-.\{f_7\}$. Both $B.1$ and $C.1$ are then satisfied. The overall quality of this updated integrated resource is calculated as $0.50 \times 0.82 + 0.50 \times 1.00 = 0.91$, which is greater than the previous overall quality 0.825.

6 Concluding Remarks

We have presented a quality framework that is able to capture users' quality requirements in respect of integrated data resources. Our quality framework is formally represented in Description Logic, and users' quality requirements are expressed as logic statements over a variety of quality factors as well as domain concepts. This allows reasoning to be applied in order to discover inconsistencies between different user requirements using TBox reasoning. It also allows reasoning to be applied to validate the requirements using ABox reasoning, so that DI elements that do not satisfy them can be discovered. When an inconsistency is discovered, the DI elements relating to quality factors referenced in the logic statements or the logic statements themselves may be modified. The reasoning capabilities may then be re-applied in order to iteratively improve the quality of the integrated resource. The novelty of our approach compared with previous work lies in its ability to formally capture and validate different users' quality requirements, and in its embedding of iterative quality assessment and improvement within the integration process.

Our quality framework forms part of the DI architecture and methodology described in [3,4]. Our future work entails completing the implementation of that architecture and evaluating our approach and metrics with real-world case studies and users.

References

1. Jarke, M., Vassiliou, Y.: Data warehouse quality: A review of the DWQ project. In: IQ, pp. 299–313 (1997)
2. Poslad, S., Zuo, L.: An adaptive semantic framework to support multiple user viewpoints over multiple databases. In: Advances in Semantic Media Adaptation and Personalization, pp. 261–284 (2008)
3. Wang, J.: A Quality Framework for Data Integration. Technical report, Department of Computer Science Information Systems, Birkbeck College (2010)
4. Wang, J.: A Framework and Architecture for Quality Assessment in Data Integration. PhD thesis, Department of Computer Science Information Systems, Birkbeck College, University of London (September 2011)
5. Lenzerini, M.: Data integration: A theoretical perspective. In: Proc. PODS, pp. 233–246 (2002)
6. Halevy, A.Y.: Answering queries using views: A survey. Journal VLDB 10, 270–294 (2001)
7. Da Conceiao, M.B., Salgado, A.C.: Information quality measurement in data integration schemas. In: Proc. QDB (2007)
8. Bonifati, A.: et al. Schema mapping verification: the SPICY way. In: Proc. EDBT, pp. 85–96 (2008)
9. Belhajjame, K., et al.: User feedback as a first class citizen in information integration systems. In: Proc. CIDR, pp. 175–183 (2011)
10. Yan, L.L., et al.: Data-driven understanding and refinement of schema mappings. SIGMOD Rec. 30, 485–496 (2001)
11. Chiticariu, L., Tan, W.: Debugging schema mappings with routes. In: Proc. VLDB, pp. 79–90 (2006)
12. Calì, A., et al.: Data integration under integrity constraints. Inf. Syst. 29, 147–163 (2004)
13. Cabibbo, L.: On keys, foreign keys and nullable attributes in relational mapping systems. In: Proc. EDBT, pp. 263–274 (2009)
14. Fagin, R., et al.: Data exchange: getting to the core. ACM Trans. Database Syst. 30, 174–210 (2005)
15. Baader, F., et al.: The Description Logic Handbook: Theory, Implementation, and Applications (2003)
16. Tsarkov, D., Horrocks, I.: Description logic reasoner: System description. In: IJCAR, pp. 292–297 (2006)
17. McBrien, P., Poulovassilis, A.: Data integration by bi-directional schema transformation rules. In: Proc. ICDE, pp. 227–238 (2003)
18. Brien, P.M., Poulovassilis, A.: A Uniform Approach to Inter-Model Transformations. In: Jarke, M., Oberweis, A. (eds.) CAiSE 1999. LNCS, vol. 1626, pp. 333–348. Springer, Heidelberg (1999)
19. Horrocks, I., Sattler, U., Tobies, S.: Practical Reasoning for Expressive Description Logics. In: Ganzinger, H., McAllester, D., Voronkov, A. (eds.) LPAR 1999. LNCS, vol. 1705, pp. 161–180. Springer, Heidelberg (1999)

Towards Introducing User Preferences
in OLAP Reporting Tool

Natalija Kozmina and Darja Solodovnikova

Faculty of Computing, University of Latvia,
19 Raina blvd., Riga LV-1586, Latvia
{natalija.kozmina,darja.solodovnikova}@lu.lv

Abstract. This paper presents an OLAP reporting tool and an approach for determining and processing user OLAP preferences, which are useful for generating recommendations on potentially interesting reports. We discuss the metadata layers of the reporting tool including our proposed OLAP preferences metamodel, which supports various scenarios of formulating preferences of two different types: schema-specific and report-specific. The process of semantic metadata usage at the stage of formulating user preferences is also considered. The methods for processing schema-specific and report-specific OLAP preferences are outlined.

Keywords: Data warehouse, user preferences, business metadata, reports.

1   Introduction and Related Work

Sometimes, during sessions of work with a reporting tool, a user has no notion about what kind of data he/she is able to find there. Moreover, a user might be unaware of a potentially useful report, because, for instance, it has been created recently and the user hasn't examined it yet. In one of our works [1] we focused on acquiring user preferences implicitly either by analyzing his/her previous activities or by learning the structure of the browsed report in order to suggest him/her other reports that might be helpful, meanwhile saving user's time and effort. In this paper we concentrate on preferences explicitly formulated by users of the OLAP reporting tool.

Apart from employing the reporting tool as a means of creating, modifying and executing reports on data warehouse schema, we also consider this reporting tool as an experimental environment for introducing OLAP personalization. Users of the reporting tool may have different skill levels (e.g., expert, novice), that's why reports' recommendations based on user preferences are more valuable for novice users than for experts. The reporting tool is a part of the data warehouse framework [2] developed at the University of Latvia.

The ideas of introducing personalization into data warehouses came from the field of databases [3] and still remain a subject of interest. Data warehouse can be personalized at schema level, applying rules for the data warehouse personalization, thus, giving a user an opportunity to work with a personalized OLAP schema, which matches his/her needs [4]. Users may express their preferences on OLAP queries [5];

L. Niedrite, R. Strazdina, B. Wangler (Eds.): BIR 2011 Workshops, LNBIP 106, pp. 209–222, 2012.
© Springer-Verlag Berlin Heidelberg 2012

in such case, the problem of performing time-consuming OLAP operations to find the necessary data is significantly improved. The other method of personalizing OLAP systems is to provide query recommendations to data warehouse users via investigating former sessions of the same user [6], or via collecting user preferences into a profile and processing it, while generating query recommendations [7]. Another aspect of OLAP personalization is the visual representation of data [8]: multiple layouts and visualization techniques may be interactively used for various analysis tasks. The summary of the research made in the field of personalization in OLAP is found in one of our previous works [9].

There are some distinctive features in the approach proposed by the authors of this paper comparing to [6] and [7]. We may notice that in [6] authors analyze unexpected differences in data; however, in this paper we analyze logical structure of the reports. In [7] both data preferences and preferences on logical structure of the reports are taken into account, however, in [7] to get recommendations, user has to state his/her preferences in a user profile first. As opposed to that, in this paper no user profile is needed, because user preferences are defined automatically without asking the user to provide information directly.

In [10] a survey of the existing methods for computing data warehouse query recommendations is presented. Authors of this survey marked out four methods, which are employed to convert a certain user's query into another one that is likely to have an added value for the user: (i) methods exploiting a profile, (ii) methods based on expectations, (iii) methods exploiting query logs, and (iv) hybrid methods.

The rest of the paper is organized as follows: Section 2 introduces interrelated metadata layers of the reporting tool, i.e. logical, physical, reporting, semantic, and OLAP preferences metadata. Various user preference modeling scenarios illustrate the OLAP preference metamodel. Section 3 describes the 5-step process of user preference formulation in business language and its further transformation. Section 4 concludes the paper.

2   OLAP Reporting Tool

All operation of the data warehouse framework and the OLAP reporting tool as a part of it is based on metadata that consists of five interconnected layers (fig. 1).

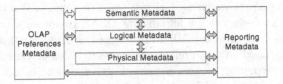

Fig. 1. Metadata connections

Logical metadata is used to describe data warehouse schemata. Physical metadata describes storage of a data warehouse in a relational database. Semantic metadata describes data stored in a data warehouse and data warehouse elements in a way that is understandable to users. Reporting metadata stores definitions of reports on data warehouse schemata. OLAP preferences metadata stores definitions of user preferences on reports' structure and data.

Particular classes of parts of metadata are connected by associations. Semantic metadata describes report's items from the reporting metadata and data warehouse schema elements from the logical metadata. Data warehouse schema elements from the logical metadata correspond to tables and table columns described in the physical metadata. Items of reports defined in the reporting metadata are obtained from table columns described in the physical metadata and correspond to data warehouse schema elements from the logical metadata. OLAP preferences metadata defines user preferences for data warehouse schema elements described in the logical metadata and for reports described in the reporting metadata. OLAP preferences are formally defined by concepts of semantic metadata. To be more precise, components of user preferences on reports' structure are OLAP schema elements from the logical metadata that correspond to concepts from the semantic metadata, and components of user preferences on reports' data are items of reports from the reporting metadata that are defined by concepts as well. Thereby, there is a latent connection between semantic metadata and OLAP preferences metadata.

Common Warehouse Metamodel (CWM) [11] was used as a basis for the semantic, logical and physical metadata.

2.1   Logical Metadata

Metadata at the logical level describes the multidimensional data warehouse schema (fig. 2.).

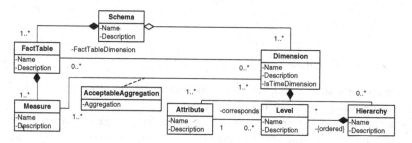

Fig. 2. Logical level metadata [12]

The logical level metadata is based on the OLAP package of Common Warehouse Metamodel (CWM) [11] and contains the main objects from this package such as dimensions with attributes and hierarchies, fact tables (cubes in CWM) with measures. Fact tables and dimensions are connected by FactTableDimension associations. OLAP package of CWM was extended by the class AcceptableAggregation, which stores information about aggregate functions (SUM, AVG, COUNT, MIN, MAX) acceptable for each measure and dimension. This metadata is essential for correct queries. The detailed description of all metadata levels of a data warehouse, including the description of the logical level, is found in the paper [12].

2.2   Reporting Metadata

Reporting metadata describes the structure of reports on data warehouse elements (fig. 3). Basically, reports are worksheets that contain data items defined by calculations, which specify computation formulas from parameters and table columns that usually correspond to schema elements (measures and attributes). Reports also consist of user-defined conditions and joins between tables.

Reports in the tool are defined by developers or experienced users themselves by choosing desired elements of a data warehouse schema and defining conditions, parameters, etc. According to the report definition, reporting metadata is created for each report. When a user runs a report in the OLAP reporting tool, an SQL query is built based on the report definition in reporting metadata [13], and its result is displayed to a user.

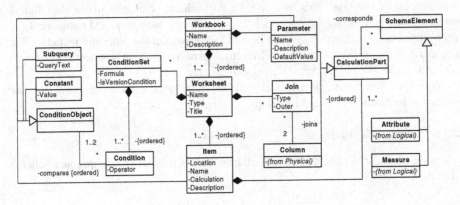

Fig. 3. Reporting metadata [13]

2.3   Semantic Metadata

It is essential for data warehouse users to understand the semantics of data that appears in reports from the business perspective.

There are multiple reasons why it is necessary to describe each element of the data warehouse model in business language. For instance, while working with the reporting tool, users also must be able to analyze this data using all necessary features, including OLAP operations drill-down and roll-up and using hierarchies. Besides, it is desirable that users can modify or construct reports themselves from elements, which are familiar to them, so that reports' creation becomes transparent. Moreover, users should be able to state their OLAP preferences, operating with business language terms, so that it would be possible to provide users of different skill levels (e.g., expert, novice) with recommendations on potentially interesting reports.

Data warehouse elements' description in business language is stored in the semantic metadata.

In CWM there is the package Business Nomenclature, which can be used to represent business metadata. This package was taken as a basis for semantic metadata depicted in fig. 4. The main classes that are used for description of data warehouse elements are Terms and Concepts, which are united in Glossaries and Taxonomies respectively. A concept is the semantic meaning or a notion of some data warehouse element or data stored in some element, but a term is a particular word or phrase employed by users to refer to a concept. In semantic metadata Concepts define elements of a data warehouse schema (class SchemaElement from the logical metadata) and items used in reports (class Item from the reporting metadata).

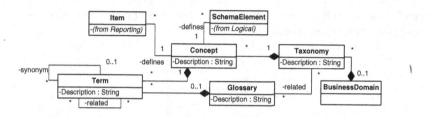

Fig. 4. Semantic metadata

2.4   OLAP Preferences Metadata

A metamodel describes OLAP schema preferences and is depicted in fig. 5. In this paper we present a revised version of the metamodel, previous versions of which are published in [14], [15].

A user may set the degree of interest (DegreeOfInterest, *DOI* [3]) for each OLAP preference. For instance, a user operates with values of the DOI attribute that may be the following: very low, low, medium, high, very high. Each DOI may have a defined real number equivalent that is assigned automatically. For example, if values of the DOI are in the interval [0; 1], then medium degree of interest corresponds to the numeric value 0.5, low degree of interest – to 0.2, etc.

In the reporting tool each workbook contains one on more worksheets, and each worksheet represents a single report. The scope of an OLAP preference may be either a specific set of reports (i.e. workbook), a single report (i.e. worksheet), or all reports defined in the reporting tool.

Each OLAP preference may be either simple (SimpleOlapPreference) or complex (ComplexOlapPreference). A complex OLAP preference consists of multiple equally important simple OLAP preferences. An advantage of a complex OLAP preference is that it allows a user to formulate sophisticated preferences assigning only one value of the degree of interest to a complex preference as a whole. For instance, *annual summary information about the average student grade in each course* is a complex OLAP preference that consists of five simple OLAP preferences (see Table 2), whereas *year=2011* is a simple OLAP preference. A simple OLAP preference may be of two types: (i) Schema-Specific preferences on OLAP schema, its elements and acceptable aggregate functions, and (ii) Report-Specific preferences on data in reports.

A PreferenceElement class describes the type of the element in user preference, which may be an OLAP schema, an OLAP schema element (e.g. dimension, fact table, attribute, measure, etc.) or a report's item. An acceptable aggregate function (AcceptableAggregation) may be applied to measures in order to get aggregated data w.r.t. one or many dimensions.

In report-specific preferences one or more preference elements (Items) may be included, and vice versa, a single preference element (Item) may be used in multiple user preferences of that type. Each item of the report is related to zero or one preferred term (Term) that a user selects as the most appropriate one to characterize the specific item of the report.

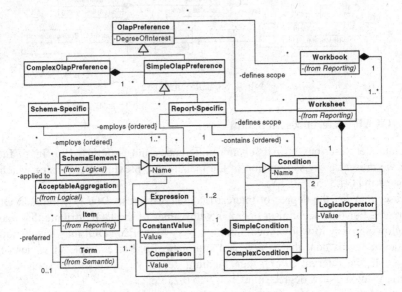

Fig. 5. OLAP preferences metadata

As report-specific preferences include restrictions on report's data, each report-specific preference may contain a set of conditions. A Condition class is divided into two subclasses: a SimpleCondition and a ComplexCondition. A complex condition consists of two or more simple conditions, joined with a logical operator (AND, OR). A simple condition consists of two expressions (Expression) and a comparison operator (Comparison). It is allowed to apply the following comparison operators: =, <>, >=, <=, >, <, *in/not in, is null/is not null, like/not like, exists/not exists.* Typically, one expression is a preference element and the other is a constant value (ConstantValue), which is either a string of symbols or a numeric value. There may be also just one expression, i.e. preference element, in case when the value of the comparison operator is *exists/not exists or null/is not null.*

We suggest several user preference modeling scenarios to motivate and illustrate the OLAP preference metamodel, demonstrated with preference examples. For more clearness, we suggest to display each example as a table with OLAP preference metamodel elements depicted as follows: (i) the simple or complex OLAP preference class is in the rightmost column, (ii) the subclasses or associated classes of either simple or complex OLAP preference are in all the rest columns, excluding the leftmost one (we intentionally did not include all classes of the metamodel in the description of examples due to the space limitations), and (iii) instances of the most specific classes of the OLAP preferences metamodel are in the leftmost column.

Scenario A

Description: A preference of a user contains solely an OLAP schema element or an aggregate function without any scope specified.
Type: Schema-Specific.
Scope: All worksheets in all workbooks.

In this case, a preference is schema-specific. We consider that such user preference refers to an OLAP schema element or an aggregate function, regardless of whether the given OLAP schema element or an aggregate function is used in any report or it doesn't appear in any report at all. A link to one or a set of either workbooks or worksheets is returned to the user, when user preferences are satisfied.

Example A. The user is interested in Program dimension, which contains descriptive attributes of study program. This statement could be formulated using our proposed OLAP preferences metamodel (Table 1).

Table 1. A formally described preference from the *Example A*

Instance	OLAP Preferences Metamodel Class			
Program	Dimension	Schema Element	Schema-Specific	Simple
<ALL>		Workbook		OLAP
<ALL>		Worksheet		Preference

The appearance of a certain dimension in one or several reports is not an indispensable condition. In other words, if currently there are no reports where Program dimension is involved, the preference is still retained and may be applied later, when at least one report that contains Program dimension is created.

Scenario B

Description: A preference of a user contains an OLAP schema element or an aggregate function in the context of a certain set of reports.
Type: Schema-Specific.
Scope: One or many certain workbooks.

Apart from an OLAP schema element or an aggregate function, user states in his/her preference a certain scope of the preference. Thus, the considered preference is schema-specific with a scope set to the workbook. A link to one or a set of workbooks is returned to the user, when user preferences are satisfied.

Example B. Student Grades workbook contains multiple worksheets with reports about student exam grades, grouped by faculties, courses, years and semesters. Besides, each report has a different level of data granularity.

Assume that there are two hierarchies available – Faculty hierarchy: *Faculty* → *Course*, and Time hierarchy: *Year* → *Semester*. The user is interested in reports that represent *annual summary information about the average student grade in each course*. This preference is complex and could be split into five different preferences such as: (i) *Acceptable aggregate function is average (AVG) applied to Grades*, (ii) *Hierarchy is Faculty*, (iii) *Hierarchy level is Course*, (iv) *Hierarchy is Time*, and (v) *Hierarchy level is Year*. These statements are formulated using our proposed OLAP preferences metamodel (Table 2).

Table 2. A formally described preference from the *Example B*

Instance	OLAP Preferences Metamodel Class				
AVG(Grade)	Acceptable Aggregation	Measure			
Faculty	Hierarchy		Schema Element	Schema-Specific	Complex OLAP Preference
Course	Hierarchy level				
Time	Hierarchy				
Year	Hierarchy level				
Student Grades	Workbook				
<ALL>	Worksheet				

Scenario C

Description: A preference of a user contains restrictions on data in several reports.
Type: Report-Specific.
Scope: One or many certain workbooks.

In this scenario we point out that a preference refers to multiple reports that contain a defined value of the given item of report. We emphasize that a preference of this kind is report-specific, because it contains restrictions on certain data values of reports' items with a scope set to the workbook. A link to one or a set of workbooks is returned to the user, when user preferences are satisfied.

Table 3. A formally described preference from the *Example C*

Instance	OLAP Preferences Metamodel Class				
Program	Item				
Semester	Item	Expression	Simple Condition	Report-Specific	Complex OLAP Preference
=	Comparison				
'2011-Spring'	Constant Value	Expression			
Registrations	Workbook				
<ALL>	Worksheet				

Example C. Let's consider that a user is interested in data on students' registrations to courses during the last semester, preferably, study programs are reflected in reports. The workbook that contains reports on students' registrations is titled Registrations. So, the complex preference that will be set for the Registrations workbook is the following: *Semester item value is equal to '2011-Spring' by Program* and apparently it consists of two simple OLAP preferences, which are: (i) *Semester item value is equal to '2011-Spring'*, and (ii) *Study Program should be present in the report*. These statements could be formulated using our proposed OLAP preferences metamodel (Table 3).

Scenario D

Description: A preference of a user contains restrictions on data in a single report.
Type: Report-Specific.
Scope: one or many certain worksheets.

In *Scenario C* a user specifies workbooks; in that way all worksheets of these workbooks are automatically included in the scope of preferences. Meanwhile, when the scope is set to worksheet (as in *Scenario D*), it signifies that a user may select arbitrary worksheets that do not necessarily belong to one and the same workbook. A link to one or a set of worksheets is returned to the user, when user preferences are satisfied. When a user runs a report of a recommended worksheet, the data in the report are already sorted in compliance with his/her preferences.

Table 4. A formally described preference from the *Example D*

Instance	OLAP Preferences Metamodel Class					
Program	Item					
Faculty	Item					
Program	Item	Expression	Simple Condition	Complex Condition	Report-Specific	Complex OLAP Preference
LIKE	Comparison					
'%Masters%'	Constant Value	Expression				
AND	Logical Operator					
Year	Item	Expression	Simple Condition			
=	Comparison					
'2010'	Constant Value	Expression				
Statistics	Workbook					
Graduated Students	Worksheet					

Example D. Assume that the worksheet titled Graduated Students of the Statistics workbook reflects yearly data on the total number of students that graduated in each study program. A user has stated the following complex OLAP preference that consists of three simple OLAP preferences on data of this worksheet: (i) *Study Program item should be 'Masters' of any Faculty, and Year item is set to '2010'*, (ii) *Reports with Faculties included are preferable*, and (iii) *Reports with Study Programs included are preferable*. These statements are formulated using our proposed OLAP preferences metamodel (Table 4).

Scenario E

Description: A preference of a user contains solely restrictions on data in reports without any scope specified.

Type: Report-Specific.

Scope: all worksheets in all workbooks.

In this scenario we consider the case, when a user probably is not very familiar with the contents of workbooks or worksheets in the reporting tool (for instance, a novice user). However, he/she has a certain vision of the data that he/she would like to explore. Thus, there is a possibility for a user to set report-specific preferences with restrictions on data without specifying any scope. A link to one or a set of either workbooks or worksheets is returned to the user, when user preferences are satisfied.

Example E. A user is looking for any reports that contain data about several courses. Say, a user states a simple OLAP preference on two courses as follows: *Course item is 'Data Warehousing' or 'IT Project Management'*. The statement is formulated using our proposed OLAP preferences metamodel (Table 5).

Table 5. A formally described preference from the *Example E*

Instance	OLAP Preferences Metamodel Class					
Course	Item	Expression				
=	Comparison		Simple Condition			
'Data Warehousing'	Constant Value	Expression		Complex Condition	Report-Specific	Simple OLAP Preference
OR	Logical Operator					
Course	Item	Expression				
=	Comparison		Simple Condition			
'IT Project Management'	Constant Value	Expression				
<ALL>	Workbook					
<ALL>	Worksheet					

3   Determining Preferences from Semantic Description

We consider semantic metadata as a means of formulating user preferences for data warehouse reports, applying pre-defined description of data warehouse elements.

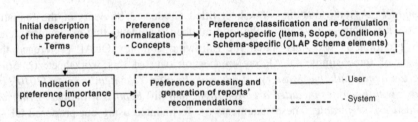

Fig. 6. Processing user preferences described with semantic metadata

The process of preference creation and transformation is briefly depicted in fig. 6, and is the following:

Step 1 – Initial Description of the Preferences. A user describes his/her preference, choosing one of the synonym terms from the glossary that seems to be the most suitable and understandable for him/her (fig. 4.). *Example*: terms "study program", "academic specialization", "branch", "field of study" are considered as synonyms, among which a user is free to select the most appropriate one. It is noteworthy that preferred terms, which the user picked out while formulating preferences, are also employed into reports to substitute the names of reports' items, thus, making the perception of the information clearer.

Step 2 – Preference Normalization. A set of terms corresponds to exactly one concept. Thus, we normalize user preferences, transforming terms into concepts. *Example*: terms mentioned in 3.1 are all related to one concept, which is "study program".

Step 3 – Preference Classification and Re-formulation. The type of the user preference is being detected. Bearing in mind that each concept defines either report items or OLAP schema elements, user preferences are later re-formulated, employing either items or OLAP schema elements instead of concepts (fig. 4.). If one concept corresponds to several OLAP schema elements or report items, then the number of preferences increases respectively. The scope (worksheet or workbook) of an OLAP preference may be indicated (optionally), if the user wants to set boundaries on the analyzed reports.

(i) *Concept → OLAP schema element.* If there is no data yet in a report's item or there is no report's item itself that would be linked to a concept, then a preference that contains the mentioned concept is classified as schema-specific. Such preference is reformulated so that a concept would be substituted with a corresponding OLAP schema element.

(ii) *Concept → Item.* If there is any data in a report's item of a linked concept, then a preference that contains the mentioned concept is classified as report-specific and is reformulated so that a concept is substituted with a corresponding item. If it is necessary, a set of conditions may be created, employing elements from the metamodel in fig. 5. *Example*: a condition is a restriction on data, for instance, "study program name = "Information Systems" ".

Step 4 – Indication of Preference Importance. In compliance with the metamodel in fig. 5, a degree of interest should be assigned by user to each OLAP preference. *Example*: a medium degree of interest is equal to 0.5 (if values of the degree of interest are normalized to the interval [0; 1]).

Step 5 – Preference Processing and Generation of Reports' Recommendations. When all OLAP preferences are formed, schema- and report-specific preferences are processed in order to provide user with recommendations on reports.

For explicitly defined schema-specific preferences, it is possible to apply the adapted hot-start method for providing recommendations on reports based on implicitly discovered schema-specific preferences described in [1]. The hot-start method is composed of two steps: firstly, user preferences for data warehouse schema elements are discovered from the history of user's interaction with the reporting tool; and secondly, we determine reports that are composed of data warehouse schema elements, which are potentially the most interesting to a user.

In case of explicitly defined preferences, the first step of the method is not applicable and must be adapted, since users specify preferences themselves. In the first step, the method should process user preferences for schema elements and propagate preferences to related schema elements. For example, if a user defines DOI for a hierarchy level, then this DOI should be propagated to the DOI of the hierarchy, which contains a level. This propagation should be proportional to the number of levels in the hierarchy.

The second step of the hot-start method should be performed, when the similarity score is calculated for each report defined in the reporting metadata and a user profile consisting of preferences..Using an adopted and adjusted formula that computes the user-item similarity score for items defined by a hierarchical ontology [16], we compute a coefficient of the hierarchical similarity between a report and a user history log. As a result, reports with the highest similarity score are recommended to a user.

However, if explicit and implicit preferences are considered together, there can be contradictory preferences, when a user explicitly defines a different DOI for a schema element then it is inferred implicitly. In such case, the explicit preference should be considered primary, so the explicitly defined DOI for a schema element should be used in the method for recommending reports.

According to the categorization of methods for computing data warehouse query recommendations presented in [10] (already mentioned in introduction and related work section of our paper), the hot-start method falls into the category of methods exploiting query logs. This method can be adapted and applied for explicitly defined schema-specific preferences.

The method for generating recommendations based on report-specific preferences is a subject of future research. However, general guidelines for such method can be specified. Firstly, reports recommended by the method based on report-specific preferences should contain items that have the highest DOI in a user profile. Secondly, recommended reports should satisfy as many conditions included into user preferences as possible.

4   Conclusions and Future Work

In this paper we paid attention to a reporting tool, developed and currently being used at the University of Latvia. We exposed five different layers of metadata that intersect each other: logical metadata that describes data warehouse schemata, physical metadata that describes storage of a data warehouse in relational database, semantic metadata that describes data stored in a data warehouse and data warehouse elements in a way that is understandable to users, reporting metadata that stores definitions of reports on data warehouse schemata, and OLAP preferences metadata that stores definitions of user preferences on reports' structure and data. We introduced various scenarios of formulating OLAP preferences as well.

We considered a possibility for a user to create OLAP preferences, using description in business language, operating with synonym terms and choosing the most appropriate among them. We briefly set forth a concept of the algorithm of OLAP preference creation, transformation and processing.

There are several directions of our future work; we would like to extend and supplement our algorithm of OLAP preference creation, transformation and processing, thus, leading it to the level, which is closer to implementation.

Also, we would like to review the existing approach for generation of reports' recommendations [1]. This approach is based on implicitly discovered schema-specific user preferences; however, it is worthwhile to adapt it to explicitly set user preferences. Along with that a method for handling report-specific user preferences should be developed. The evaluation of processing both types of explicitly set user preferences (schema- and report-specific) will follow.

Acknowledgments. This work has been supported by ESF project No. 2009/0216/1DP/1.1.1.2.0/09/APIA/VIAA/044.

References

1. Solodovnikova, D., Kozmina, N.: On Implicitly Discovered OLAP Schema-Specific Preferences in Reporting Tool. In: Niedrite, L., Strazdina, R., Wangler, B. (eds.) BIR 2011 Workshops. LNBIP, vol. 106, Springer, Heidelberg (2012)
2. Solodovnikova, D.: Data Warehouse Evolution Framework. In: Proceedings of the Spring Young Researcher's Colloquium On Database and Information Systems (SYRCoDIS 2007), Moscow, Russia (2007), http://ceur-ws.org/Vol-256/submission_4.pdf
3. Koutrika, G., Ioannidis, Y.E.: Personalization of queries in database systems. In: Proceedings of 20th Int. Conf. on Data Engineering (ICDE 2004), Boston, MA, USA, pp. 597–608 (2004)
4. Garrigós, I., Pardillo, J., Mazón, J.-N., Trujillo, J.: A Conceptual Modeling Approach for OLAP Personalization. In: Laender, A.H.F., Castano, S., Dayal, U., Casati, F., de Oliveira, J.P.M. (eds.) ER 2009. LNCS, vol. 5829, pp. 401–414. Springer, Heidelberg (2009)
5. Biondi, P., Golfarelli, M., Rizzi, S.: Preference-Based Datacube Analysis with MyOLAP. In: Proceedings of the 27th Int. Conf. on Data Engineering (ICDE 2011), Hannover, Germany, pp. 1328–1331 (2011)
6. Giacometti, A., Marcel, P., Negre, E., Soulet, A.: Query Recommendations for OLAP Discovery Driven Analysis. In: Proceedings of 12th ACM Int. Workshop on Data Warehousing and OLAP (DOLAP 2009), Hong Kong, pp. 81–88 (2009)
7. Jerbi, H., Ravat, F., Teste, O., Zurfluh, G.: Preference-Based Recommendations for OLAP Analysis. In: Pedersen, T.B., Mohania, M.K., Tjoa, A.M. (eds.) DaWaK 2009. LNCS, vol. 5691, pp. 467–478. Springer, Heidelberg (2009)
8. Mansmann, S., Scholl, M.H.: Visual OLAP: A New Paradigm for Exploring Multidimensonal Aggregates. In: Proceedings of IADIS Int. Conf. on Computer Graphics and Visualization (MCCSIS 2008), Amsterdam, The Netherlands, pp. 59–66 (2008)
9. Kozmina, N., Niedrite, L.: Research Directions of OLAP Personalization. In: Proceedings of the 19th Int. Conf. on Information Systems Development (ISD 2010), Prague, Czech Republic (2010)
10. Marcel, P., Negre, E.: A Survey of Query Recommendation Techniques for Data Warehouse Exploration. In: 7èmes Journées Francophones sur les Entrepôts de Données et l'Analyse en ligne (EDA 2011), Clermont-Ferrand, France, vol. B-7, pp. 119–134 (June 2011)

11. Object Management Group: Common Warehouse Metamodel Specification, v1.1, http://www.omg.org/cgi-bin/doc?formal/03-03-02
12. Solodovnikova, D.: Metadata to Support Data Warehouse Evolution. In: Proceedings of the 17th Int. Conf. on Information Systems Development (ISD 2008), Paphos, Cyprus, pp. 627–635 (2008)
13. Solodovnikova, D.: Building Queries on Multiple Versions of Data Warehouse. In: Haav, H.-M., Kalja, A. (eds.) Databases and Information Systems V - Selected Papers from the 8th Int. Baltic Conference, DBIS 2008, pp. 75–86. IOS Press (2008)
14. Kozmina, N., Niedrite, L.: OLAP Personalization with User-Describing Profiles. In: Forbrig, P., Günther, H. (eds.) BIR 2010. LNBIP, vol. 64, pp. 188–202. Springer, Heidelberg (2010)
15. Solodovnikova, D., Kozmina, N.: Determining Preferences from Semantic Metadata in OLAP Reporting Tool. In: Local Proceedings of the 10th Int. Conf. on Perspectives in Business Informatics Research (BIR 2011), Associated Workshops and Doctoral Consortium, Riga, Latvia, pp. 363–370 (2011)
16. Maidel, V., Shoval, P., Shapira, B., Taieb-Maimon, M.: Ontological Content-based Filtering for Personalised Newspapers: A Method and its Evaluation. Online Information Review 34(5), 729–756 (2010)

A Multimodal Approach
for Determination of Vehicle Position

Artis Mednis

Digital Signal Processing Laboratory,
Institute of Electronics and Computer Science,
14 Dzerbenes Str., Riga, LV 1006, Latvia
artis.mednis@edi.lv

Abstract. One of the most important tasks during development of
hardware/software systems for assisted and automatic driving is determination of vehicle position with sufficient accuracy in real time. Most
of experimental systems developed yet are based on relatively expensive Real Time Kinematic technique which primary usage is land and
hydrographical surveys with centimetre level accuracy.

The paper is describing technique for determination of vehicle position, based on multimodal data sources with subsequent data integration.
Data acquisition is performed using several GNSS receivers with SBAS
capability as well as stationary reference stations. Data acquisition and
integration methods are discussed as well as their performance analyzed
using data from real world experiments.

Keywords: Vehicle position, multimodal, data integration, GNSS,
SBAS, RTK over IP.

1 Introduction

Vehicle driving process is one of the human's activities characterized by large
amount of individual decisions. Decisions in this case should be taken especially
carefully because they affect not only own vehicle and passengers' safety but also
safety of surrounding vehicles and humans'.

Due evolution of various transportation types the optimization of traffic flow
becomes more and more important. This task can be solved in both ways - due
more advanced traffic flow management as well as more advanced dissemination
of traffic information for each individual driver and/or vehicle. Solutions developed for solving of this task include also appropriate hardware/software systems.
These systems could be divided in two main groups - systems for assisted driving
and systems for automatic driving. Systems from first group perform a part of
activities of driving process and give already pre-processed information to driver
and/or vehicle. Systems from second group act independently and perform vehicle driving process without human interaction.

Depending on their architecture and functionality systems for assisted or automatic driving are intended to perform several specific tasks. One of them is

L. Niedrite, R. Strazdina, B. Wangler (Eds.): BIR 2011 Workshops, LNBIP 106, pp. 223–235, 2012.
© Springer-Verlag Berlin Heidelberg 2012

determination of vehicle position with accuracy acceptable for successful operation of whole system. In the case of standalone automatic driving this information is used as input data for motion planning but in case of cooperative assisted driving this information is shared among several vehicles. Common approach for determination of position of an outdoor object is usage of generic GNSS ([1], p.2) receiver. Unfortunately accuracy of this approach is affected by several factors such as buildings in the urban area, trees in the forest, weather etc. Therefore this common approach is suitable for navigation of a person or a vehicle in the case when a human uses acquired data but is not suitable for assisted or automatic driving when a computer uses acquired data.

This paper is describing technique for determination of vehicle position with accuracy, suitable for particular assisted driving solution. This technique is based on data acquisition using several GNSS receivers with SBAS ([2], p.157) capability. Correction data from stationary reference stations received through wireless Internet connection is used as additional input.

Related work is described in Section 2. Approach is discussed in Section 3. The evaluation of proposed approach includes a series of real world experiments, analyzed in Section 4. The final section presents the conclusion that proposed approach is suitable for assisted driving system developed for GCDC competition vehicle.

2   Related Work

Systems which primary functionality is determination of exact vehicle position are components of almost all more advanced systems developed for automatic or assisted driving competitions. Typical examples of automatic driving competitions are events organized by Defense Advanced Research Projects Agency (DARPA) such as Grand Challenges in 2004 and 2005 [3] as well as Urban Challenge in 2007 [4,5]. A typical example of assisted driving competition is Grand Cooperative Driving Challenge (GCDC) in 2011 [6]. Different competition types are characterized by different scenarios and therefore different requirements for system parameters including accuracy of vehicle position. Two most successful position determination approaches from before mentioned competitions are described in this Section.

Team Tartan Racing [7], which represents Carnegie Mellon University in cooperation with General Motors, Caterpillar and Continental AG, won DARPA Urban Challenge. Their vehicle position determination solution was based on Applanix POS-LV [8] device consisting of GNSS receiver and inertial measurement unit. Additional sensors such as lidars, radars and cameras were used to ensure acceptable level of safety in mocked urban area.

Team AnnieWAY [9], which represents Karlsruhe Institute of Technology, won Grand Cooperative Driving Challenge. Their vehicle position determination solution, which was similar to previously mentioned, was based on OXTS RT 3003 [10] device consisting of GNSS receiver and inertial measurement unit. Additional sensors such as high definition laser scanner and multiple cameras were used to ensure safe distance to vehicle driving in front.

3   Approach

There exist several sources of data errors that affect position determination using GNSS signals. These sources include signal propagation in Earth's ionosphere and troposphere, reflected multipath signals, parameters of satellite orbits as well as clock drift both on transmitters' and receivers' side. All mentioned error sources could be divided in two main groups - local sources and global sources. Sources from first group are characterized by similar influence on the determined position in restricted geographical area. Sources from second group are characterized by similar influence on the determined position in wide geographical area ([11], p.144-198).

A simple approach to minimize data errors from local sources is making of several consecutive position measurements and subsequent calculation of average position values. This method is suitable only if calculation of the position is performed for stationary object therefore not suitable for calculation of the position for vehicle in motion. Proposed approach assumes quasi-simultaneous position measurements using several generic SBAS receivers instead of several consecutive measurements using one generic SBAS receiver. Calculation of average position data is performed immediate after data acquisition.

A simple approach to minimize data errors from global sources is usage of stationary placed dedicated local reference station in known position nearby as well as advanced multi-frequency (L1/L2) receiver. This method assumes usage of specific and therefore relatively expensive RTK ([12], p.15) hardware. The need for deployment of such specific and expensive hardware in wide area makes this method not applicable for real-world assisted and automatic driving experiments. Proposed approach assumes usage of public available RTK base stations and receiving of correction data using wireless Internet connection (Fig. 1).

4   Evaluation

After studies of literature about several types of vehicle positioning systems it was decided to build GCDC competition vehicle positioning system using multimodal approach. In this case data for position calculation should be acquired from several SBAS receivers as well as from inertial measurement unit (IMU). Such approach looked potentially attractive due relative low costs and in the same time accuracy sufficient in the context of published competition specification [13]. Selected SBAS receivers were tested using real world data in several modes including static data acquisition mode, dynamic data acquisition mode as well as correction data usage mode.

First experiment was carried out to estimate typical position deviation of single SBAS receiver in static data acquisition mode. During this experiment Magellan eXplorist XL receiver [14] was placed in fixed position on the roof of a stationary parked vehicle. Session of position data acquiring was 1 hour long and position data was recorded 1x per second. During this session SBAS receiver was

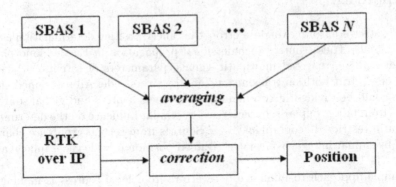

Fig. 1. Architecture of proposed vehicle position determination approach. First step includes data acquisition from several SBAS capable GNSS receivers and their averaging, second step includes position correction using data from public reference stations received over wireless Internet connection.

in the DGPS mode 100% of all time and every position was calculated using data from at least 9 satellites. Statistical analysis of recorded position data showed that maximal receiver position deviation in the west-east direction (lon) is 1.51 m and in the north-south direction (lat) 1.81 m (Fig. 2 - on the left). According to 2DRMS corresponding range of 98.2% ([15], p.153) receiver position deviation in the west-east direction (lon) is 1.51 m and in the north-south direction (lat) 1.48 m. Graphical analysis of recorded position coordinates and their distribution through deviation area showed that there are at least two main areas with high recorded positions concentration located in opposite deviation area corners (Fig. 2 - on the right). Such distribution does not correspond with Gaussian distribution and allows making of an assumption about influence of global data error sources what could be mitigated using additional correction data.

Next experiment was carried out to estimate typical position deviation of two SBAS receiver system in static data acquisition mode. There was an assumption about potential decreasing of system position deviation area due usage of two independent measurement devices and combination of simultaneously acquired position data. Setup of this experiment was similar to previous performed single SBAS receiver test except an additional SBAS receiver Magellan eXplorist 210 [16] placed on the roof of the same stationary parked vehicle but in opposite corner. During this session both SBAS receivers were in the DGPS mode 100% (XL) and 99.97% (210) of all time and every position was calculated using data from at least 7 (XL) and 8 (210) satellites.

Statistical analysis of recorded position data showed that maximal receiver position deviation in the west-east direction (lon) is 1.31 m (XL) and 2.31 m (210) and in the north-south direction (lat) 1.67 m (both XL and 210) (Fig. 3 - on the left). According to 2DRMS corresponding range of 98.2% receiver position deviation in the west-east direction (lon) is 1.21 m (XL) and 1.91 m (210) and in

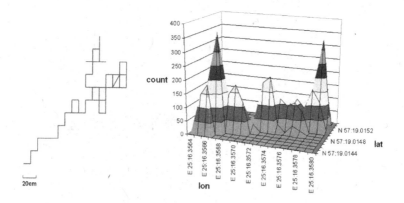

Fig. 2. Static data acquisition mode test using single SBAS receiver. On the left - position deviation track, on the right - position deviation distribution.

the north-south direction (lat) 1.67 m (XL) and 1.48 m (210). Graphical analysis of recorded position coordinates and their distribution through deviation area showed that there is one main area with high recorded positions concentration for each receiver used but these areas are located in opposite deviation area corners (Fig. 3 - on the right).

Combination of simultaneously acquired position data pairs was performed, calculating average latitude and longitude values. Statistical analysis of calculated position data showed that maximal system position deviation in the west-east direction (lon) is 1.31 m and in the north-south direction (lat) 0.74 m (Fig. 4 - on the left). According to 2DRMS corresponding range of 98.2% system position deviation in the west-east direction (lon) is 1.11 m and in the north-south direction (lat) 0.55 m. Graphical analysis of calculated position coordinates and their distribution through deviation area showed that there is one main area with high recorded positions concentration what corresponds with Gaussian distribution. Decreasing of the position deviation area allows making of a conclusion about improvement of position determination accuracy against usage of single SBAS receiver.

Next experiment was carried out to estimate typical position deviation of two SBAS receiver system in dynamic data acquisition mode as well as perform data capture from inertial measurement unit. Before this experiment two Magellan eXplorist receivers - XL and 210 were placed in fixed position on the dashboard of the vehicle. During this experiment vehicle carried out 67 km long route within 1 hour. Route selected for this experiment consisted of 58 km of highway with maximal permitted speed 90 km/h as well as 9 km of city streets with maximal permitted speed 50 km/h (on several fragments - 70 km/h) (Fig. 5). Maximal real speed of vehicle during this experiment was 63 km/h on a city street as well as 103 km/h on the highway. Position data was recorded 1x per second but data from inertial measurement unit (3D accelerometer and 2D gyroscope) 10x per second. During this session both SBAS receivers were in the DGPS mode 54.47%

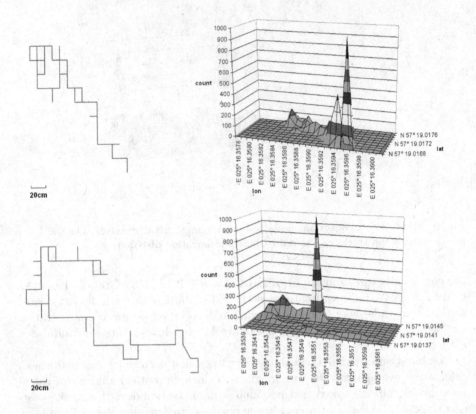

Fig. 3. Static data acquisition mode test using two SBAS receivers. On the left - position deviation tracks, on the right - position deviation distributions. At the top - data from Magellan eXplorist XL, at the bottom - data from Magellan eXplorist 210.

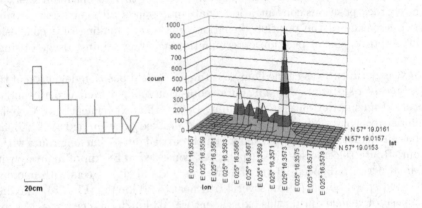

Fig. 4. Static data acquisition mode test using two SBAS receiver system. On the left - position deviation track, on the right - position deviation distribution.

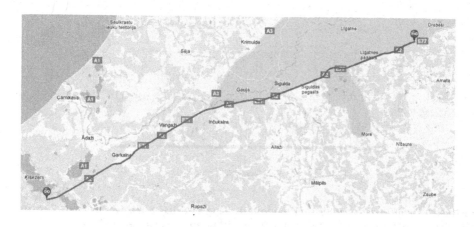

Fig. 5. 67 km long route selected for dynamic data acquisition mode experiment

(XL) and 88.57% (210) of all time and every position was calculated using data from at least 6 (XL) and 5 (210) satellites. Comparison of DGPS mode time and available satellites count with according parameters from static data acquisition mode experiments lets make a conclusion about more severe data acquisition conditions.

First combination of the position data from both SBAS receivers was performed using granularity identical to the data acquisition rate - 1 second. Statistical analysis of calculated position data showed that maximal system position deviation in the west-east direction (lon) is 9.79 m and in the north-south direction (lat) 6.50 m (Fig. 6). According to 2DRMS corresponding range of 98.2% system position deviation in the west-east direction (lon) is 9.08 m and in the north-south direction (lat) 5.01 m. Average deviation distances in the west-east direction (lon) is 4.71 m and in the north-south direction (lat) 2.16 m. Distribution function of deviation distances is shown in Fig. 7. Position deviation during dynamic data acquisition mode is affected not only by receivers' position calculation errors but also by speed of the moving vehicle. In this case vehicle speed during test could be responsible for position deviation up to 25 meters. Real position deviation values were less then 10 meters.

GCDC competition specification includes the requirement that prescribes vehicle position data actualization 10x per second. To comply with this requirement other data combination approach using granularity of 1/10 seconds range was performed. To reach this granularity, position data from one receiver was used unaltered, but position data from other receiver was transformed with the aim to obtain vehicle position data for the same moment of time (Fig. 8).

Statistical analysis of calculated position data using granularity 1/10 second showed that maximal system position deviation in the west-east direction (lon) is 2.42 m and in the north-south direction (lat) 3.71 m (Fig. 9). According to 2DRMS corresponding range of 98.2% system position deviation in the west-east direction (lon) is 1.90 m and in the north-south direction (lat) 2.86 m.

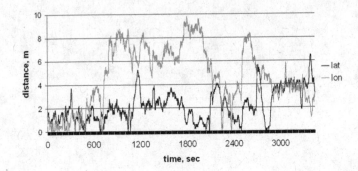

Fig. 6. Dynamic data acquisition mode test using two SBAS receiver system. System position deviations using data combination with granularity 1 second.

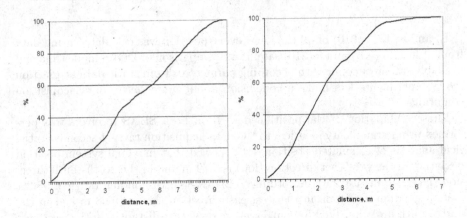

Fig. 7. Dynamic data acquisition mode test using two SBAS receiver system. Distribution functions of system position deviations using data combination with granularity 1 second - on the left west-east direction (lon), on the right north-south direction (lat).

Average deviation distances in the west-east direction (lon) is 0.90 m and in the north-south direction (lat) 1.26 m. Distribution function of deviation distances is shown in Fig. 10. Maximum increasing of the position deviation due moving vehicle speed in this case could be up to 2.5 meters. 94% of real measurements were under this value.

Additional improvements of two-receiver system performance in dynamic data acquisition mode could be achieved after next step that includes usage of acceleration data acquired using inertial measurement unit.

During GCDC Technology Workshop (19-21.01.2011, Helmond, Netherlands), author's colleague got an information about specific methodology - RTK over IP, potentially useful for positioning accuracy improvement. This methodology is based on usage of additional correction data received in real time through

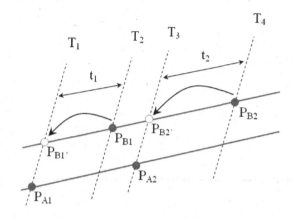

Fig. 8. Vehicle position data combination with the granularity of 1/10 seconds range. Positions from SBAS receiver B recalculated according timestamps from SBAS receiver A.

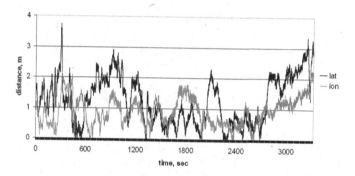

Fig. 9. Dynamic data acquisition mode test using two SBAS receiver system. System position deviations using data combination with granularity 1/10 second.

wireless Internet connection. To verify this methodology as potential improvement of developed GCDC competition vehicle equipment, several base stations such as TORA0 (Tartu, Estonia) and TITZ1 (Titz, Germany) for real world experiments were identified. To ensure access to resources of these base stations accounts in corresponding data distribution networks - www.euref-ip.net [17] and www.igs-ip.net [18] were created.

Next experiment was carried out to estimate how the usage of correction data from one or several RTK base stations improves position accuracy if the local position measurements are performed using generic single-frequency (L1) receiver instead of a dedicated multi-frequency (L1/L2) receiver. Local position measurements in Cesis were performed using Magellan XL SBAS receiver. Correction data were obtained from two LatPos system [19] base stations located in

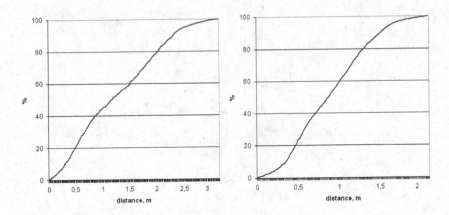

Fig. 10. Dynamic data acquisition mode test using two SBAS receiver system. Distribution functions of system position deviations using data combination with granularity 1/10 second - on the left west-east direction (lon), on the right north-south direction (lat).

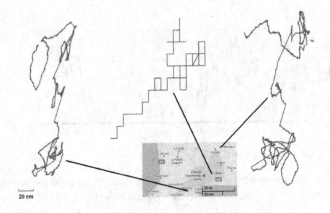

Fig. 11. Correction data from RTK base stations. On the left - data from station in Sigulda, on the right - data from station in Valmiera. In the middle - local position measurements from stationary placed SBAS receiver in Cesis.

Sigulda and Valmiera. Both of them were about 30 km from stationary placed SBAS receiver (Fig. 11).

First, combination of locally acquired position data and correction data from each one RTK base station was performed. Statistical analysis of corrected position data showed that maximal corrected position deviation in the west-east direction (lon) is in the range 1.53 - 1.65 m and in the north-south direction (lat) in the range 1.59 - 1.72 m. According to 2DRMS corresponding range of 98.2% corrected position deviation in the west-east direction (lon) is in the range 1.31 -

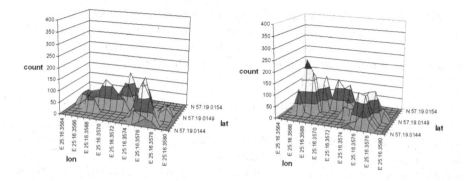

Fig. 12. Corrected position deviation distribution. On the left - correction data from RTK station in Valmiera used, on the right - correction data from RTK station in Sigulda used.

1.41 m and in the north-south direction (lat) in the range 1.48 - 1.67 m. Graphical analysis of corrected position coordinates and their distribution through deviation area (Fig. 12) showed that there is a tendency towards one main area with high recorded positions concentration in the middle of deviation area what could be appreciated as improvement against distribution in the case of uncorrected position data (Fig. 2 - on the right).

Next, combination of locally acquired position data and correction data from both RTK base stations was performed. Statistical analysis of corrected position data showed that maximal corrected position deviation in the west-east direction (lon) is 1.46 m and in the north-south direction (lat) 1.52 m. According to 2DRMS corresponding range of 98.2% corrected position deviation in the west-east direction (lon) is 1.31 m and in the north-south direction (lat) 1.30 m. Graphical analysis of corrected position coordinates and their distribution through deviation area (Fig. 13) showed that there is a strong tendency

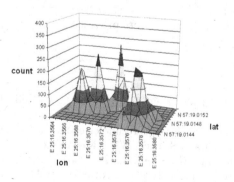

Fig. 13. Corrected position deviation distribution using correction data from two RTK stations located in Valmiera and Sigulda

towards one main area with high recorded positions concentration in the middle of deviation area. Decreasing of the position deviation area allows making of a conclusion about improvement of position determination accuracy against usage of single SBAS receiver without external correction data.

5   Conclusion and Future Work

Author proposed vehicle position determination approach that includes usage of several SBAS receivers as well as data from local reference stations. This approach was evaluated on particular application - developing GCDC competition vehicle positioning system. Vehicle position determination was performed using multimodal data sources and combination of their data. Author performed several real world experiments using selected position data acquisition devices. The experimental results were evaluated by statistical and graphical analysis of position deviation distribution area. The results show, that proposed vehicle position determination approach decreases range of position deviation in the north-south direction (lat) from 1.48 m to 0.55 m 2DRMS due usage of two SBAS receivers as well as from 1.48 m to 1.30 m 2DRMS due usage of correction data from RTK base stations. Changes of position deviation in the west-east direction (lon) is less notable - from 1.21 m to 1.11 m 2DRMS due usage of two SBAS receivers as well as from 1.51 m to 1.31 m 2DRMS due usage of correction data from RTK base stations. Therefore proposed approach is potentially suitable for GCDC competition vehicle [20] which position accuracy should be 1 meter 2DRMS or better.

The future work includes experiments with increased number of SBAS receivers and evaluation of their influence on position determination accuracy as well as improvement of position calculation process using data from the inertial measurement unit.

Acknowledgments. This work was supported by European Social Fund grant Nr. 2009/0219/1DP/1.1.1.2.0/APIA/VIAA/020 "R&D Center for Smart Sensors and Networked Embedded Systems." Author thanks to Reinholds Zviedris and Ojars Krumins for SBAS receivers provided for testing purposes.

References

1. Gleason, S., Gebre-Egziabher, D.: GNSS Applications and Methods. GNSS Technology and Applications. Artech House (2009)
2. Samama, N.: Global Positioning: Technologies and Performance. Wiley Survival Guides in Engineering and Science. Wiley Interscience (2008)
3. Buehler, M., Iagnemma, K., Singh, S.: The 2005 DARPA Grand Challenge: The Great Robot Race. Springer Tracts in Advanced Robotics. Springer, Heidelberg (2007)
4. Defense Advanced Research Projects Agency: DARPA Urban Challenge, http://archive.darpa.mil/grandchallenge/index.asp

5. Buehler, M., Iagnemma, K., Singh, S.: The DARPA Urban Challenge: Autonomous Vehicles in City Traffic. Springer Tracts in Advanced Robotics. Springer, Heidelberg (2010)
6. GCDC Organization: Grand Cooperative Driving Challenge, http://www.gcdc.net/
7. Urmson, C., Anhalt, J., et al.: Tartan Racing: A Multi-Modal Approach to the DARPA Urban Challenge, http://archive.darpa.mil/grandchallenge/TechPapers/Tartan_Racing.pdf
8. Applanix Corp.: POS LV Specifications (January 2011)
9. Geiger, A., Moosmann, F., et al.: Team AnnieWAY's Entry to GCDC (2011), http://www.gcdc.net/mainmenu/Home/news/News_-_current/GCDC_Final%3A_teams_videos_and_final_papers/Annieway
10. Oxford Technical Solutions: RT Inertial and GPS Measurement Systems. User Manual (December 2010)
11. Grewal, M.S., Weill, L.R., Andrews, A.P.: Global Positioning Systems, Inertial Navigation, and Integration. Wiley Interscience (2007)
12. LaMarca, A., Lara, E.: Location Systems: An Introduction to the Technology Behind Location Awareness. Synthesis Lectures on Mobile and Pervasive Computing. Morgan Kaufmann (2008)
13. GCDC Organization: GCDC 2011 Rules & Technology Document Final Version (April 2011)
14. Thales Navigation, Inc.: Magellan eXplorist XL Reference Manual (September 2005)
15. Farrell, J.: Aided Navigation: GPS with High Rate Sensors. McGraw-Hill Professional Engineering: Electronic Engineering. McGraw-Hill (2008)
16. Thales Navigation, Inc.: Magellan eXplorist 210 Reference Manual (June 2005)
17. Federal Agency for Cartography and Geodesy: EUREF-IP Ntrip Broadcaster, http://www.euref-ip.net/home
18. Federal Agency for Cartography and Geodesy: IGS-IP Ntrip Broadcaster, http://www.igs-ip.net/home
19. Latvian Geospatial Information Agency: LatPos, http://map.lgia.gov.lv/index.php?lang=2&cPath=2&txt_id=13
20. Strazdins, G., Gordjusins, A., et al.: Team "Latvia" GCDC 2011 Technical Paper, http://www.gcdc.net/mainmenu/Home/news/News_-_current/GCDC_Final%3A_teams_videos_and_final_papers/Latvia

Augmenting Multicriteria Decision Aid Methods by Graphical and Analytical Reporting Tools

Askoldas Podviezko

Vilnius Gediminas Technical University
LT-10223, Vilnius, Sauletekio ave. 11
askoldas@gmail.com

Abstract. Evaluation of the level of soundness and stability of commercial banks is an idiosyncratic task, since banks have a complicated internal business structure, intertwined cash flows and strong influence of market conditions on their soundness levels. Using several methods of multicriteria decision aid (MCDA) SAW, PROMETHEE II, TOPSIS and COPRAS in this paper to make the evaluation provided clear and intelligible evaluation in the form of rankings. Te result made in this format is designed to make rough comparisons of commercial banks. Nevertheless, more detailed evaluation must employ additional proprietary tools promptly exposing numerous specific data in a clear form. Reporting tools, simplifying thorough analysis of financial data, which exposes bank performance, are proposed in this paper. They help a decision-maker (depositor, bank management or a comptroller) to instantly observe both strength and weakness of commercial banks by categories of its performance criteria (capital, assets, management, earnings and liquidity) and dynamics of performance of a bank.

Keywords: Commercial banks, soundness and stability, evaluation, reporting, SAW, PROMETHEE, TOPSIS, COPRAS.

1 Introduction

The problem of evaluation of commercial banks is persistently popular among scientists since the beginning of the 20th century. One of the first analysis exploring causes of bank crises was attempted by Oliver M.W. Sprague in 1910. It was induced by financial panics in the U.S.A. in 1873, 1884, 1890, 1893, and 1907 in, which caused banking crises in that country. The book "History of Crises under the National Banking System" by Sprague suggests a few remedial tools based on his research findings [1]. That time computers were not yet invented and only simple arithmetical tools could be used for making the analysis. The most comprehensive contemporary survey on evaluating bank stability made almost after the whole century [2] reveals that there is no yet single fully reliable or most popular worldwide solution or framework, which assesses levels of soundness and stability of commercial banks, indicates causes of their strength or weakness. Nevertheless, the subject of evaluation

L. Niedrite, R. Strazdina, B. Wangler (Eds.): BIR 2011 Workshops, LNBIP 106, pp. 236–251, 2012.
© Springer-Verlag Berlin Heidelberg 2012

of soundness and stability has made a huge progress, new methods were invented and vast statistical data have been gathered and analysed in last decades.

Process of evaluation can be facilitated by the MCDA (multicriteria decision aid) approach, the most suitable for evaluation of commercial banks, since criteria used for the evaluation are conflicting [3]. MCDA methods provide clear and intelligible evaluation in the form of rankings, which are designed to make comparisons of banks. The approach allows setting a structured framework into the process of evaluation. The author of this paper suggests, first, to disaggregate criteria to a few categories. This boils down the task of choosing the whole set of criteria to smaller tasks of choosing criteria within each category, where choice of a smaller number of the most essential and mutually non-correlating criteria is more efficiently conceived. Second, the MCDA approach allows developing a preferential structure in terms of the weights of the criteria set by decision-makers. By setting uniform criteria and weights to all analysed objects, namely commercial banks in our case, an unequivocal and uniform framework of evaluation is developed. This ensures transparency of the evaluation. The MCDA methods allow obtaining results promptly, thus reflecting the reality within the time permitted for the decision-making.

History of operational research (OR) methods in finance spans a half-century after introduction of Markowitz' portfolio theory. In two decades after introduction of these methods to finance, they gained popularity and exposed advantages over already having been used statistical methods and the methods used by credit agencies. In addition, starting from the 80s, the subset of operational research methods, MCDA methods, were introduced to finance, and are being used wherever there is complexity involved in creating an objective. Evaluation of a financial firm or a bank encompasses more complex considerations and goals and is not narrowing to solely the risk-return modelling [4]. The methods also extend to the field of management science providing prompt support systems for decision-makers and managers.

As Fethi and Pasiouras pointed out in their survey of literature of OR techniques used to evaluate bank performance [5], currently two types of presentation of data obtained by OR methods in the field of evaluation of banks can be distinguished. One uses classification of banks between many categories in a way similar to lists of ratings used by credit agencies. Another approach classifies banks into broader groups, mostly between 'good' or 'bad' groups. Both approaches provide classification in broad terms, not providing any tool for more thorough examination of soundness and stability state of the bank and their causes.

The purpose of this paper is to enhance the framework of evaluation of soundness and stability of commercial banks by multicriteria methods described in [6]. Obtaining relative levels of soundness and stability of commercial banks by using multicriteria methods is not sufficient for exposing the particular causes of strength and weakness of a bank. A framework of more thorough examination of different aspects of financial performance of banks is proposed in this paper. The enhancement proposed here is based on additional reporting tools of values of aggregated into categories performance criteria of banks. In the paper evaluation results are presented for the commercial banks registered in Lithuania both in analytical and graphical form, which helps a decision-maker (depositor, bank management or a comptroller) to instantly observe both strength and weakness of commercial banks by categories of its performance criteria (capital, assets, management, earnings and liquidity) and dynamics of performance of a bank in terms of mentioned categories of its performance criteria.

2   Evaluation of Lithuanian Commercial Banks by MCDA Methods

2.1   Variables and Data

In accordance with the MCDA framework, categories of criteria representing soundness and stability of banks must be chosen. As Gonzalez-Hermosillo noted [7], there are two approaches in the literature covering evaluation of soundness and stability of commercial banks: one focuses on macroeconomic variables, while other focuses on bank-specific data. We attempt to evaluate aspects of performance of Lithuanian commercial banks in terms of soundness and stability, and choose banks, which are operating in the same macroeconomical environment, are governed by the same Law on Banks [8], and governed under the same deposit insurance scheme by the State Enterprise "Deposit and Investment Insurance". This predetermined our approach to be based on bank-specific data. We follow the CAMEL categorisation of bank-specific variables, which means that criteria representing soundness and stability are found in the following categories: Capital, Assets, Management Earnings and Liquidity [6, 9]. Criteria chosen within every mentioned category are described as follows.

Capital is represented by the variable CAPITAL, which is combined from Tier 1 and Tier 2 ratios, i.e. capital of mentioned type divided by risk-weighted assets (RWA). We use the weight of 0.666 for Tier 1 capital, and the weight of 0.334 for Tier 2 capital. Weights of different magnitude were applied due to the different riskiness of the two types of capital. The weights for this criterion as well as for the following ones were elicited from Lithuanian experts on commercial banks. It is a maximising criterion.

Assets category is represented by four criteria. NII (net interest income) stands for interest income, divided by RWA. This criterion more adequately accounts profitability of assets in terms of riskiness than in the case if interest income were divided by total assets, based on the two facts. First, riskiness of assets is accounted into RWA in accordance with Basel framework. Second, more risky assets normally are earning higher yields. It is a maximising criterion. The remaining ratios are as follows. TL (total loans) is the ratio between loans, the most risky assets, and total assets. DELINQ (delinquent loans) is the ratio of delinquent loans to total assets. In Lithuania loans are considered to be delinquent if they are overdue for 60 days or longer. And finally, LD (loan value decrease) is the last ratio within the category between the decrease of value of assets and total assets. The latter three criteria are minimising.

Management category is expressed by cost-efficiency of a bank ratio NIC (non-interest costs). It is a minimising criterion.

Earnings category is represented by two ratios, which gauge pre-provision profits and net income (PPP and NI respectively), comparing them to risk-weighted assets. The first ratio reveals the capability of a bank to generate cash, which could then serve as a remedy for various losses, while the second ratio expresses remaining profits after all deductions have been made. Both are maximising criteria.

The chosen ratios well agree with the findings of Wheelock and Wilson [10]: higher earnings, bigger capital ratios, cost-efficient management and better loan portfolio reduce a likelihood of failure.

Liquidity category is represented by two criteria. One is the ratio DEP between deposits and total loans. The second one is the regulatory liquidity ratio LIQ imposed by the central bank, i.e. the Bank of Lithuania. Both are maximising criteria.

2.2   Presentation of Relative Soundness and Stability Positions of Commercial Banks in the Form of the Ranking Table Obtained by Several MCDA Methods

Main ideas of the MCDA methods used in this paper are as follows. The ultimate goal of each method is to create a cumulative criterion for each alternative, reflecting the attractiveness of the alternative in quantitative terms. Thus, a more attractive alternative outranks a weaker alternative in case its cumulative criterion is larger. For making a quantitative evaluation of soundness and stability of commercial banks based on statistical data a set of essential criteria is formed by researchers as it was described in the previous section. The criteria are normalized in accordance with the following formula, so that the sum by all the alternatives of normalized values of every criterion i is equal to one (1):

$$\tilde{r}_{ij} = \frac{r_{ij}}{\sum\limits_{j=1}^{n} r_{ij}} \tag{1}$$

The SAW Method. The fact of simplicity of one of the methods used is reflected in its name: SAW (Simple Additive Weighing) [11]. Normalized values of criteria are multiplied by weights of significance of each criterion and are summed to the cumulative criterion of the method S_j:

$$S_j = \sum\limits_{i=1}^{m} \omega_i \tilde{r}_{ij} \tag{2}$$

The larger is the cumulative criterion S_j of the SAW method, the better is the alternative. It then outranks all other alternatives with smaller values of S_j. Minimizing criteria are transformed to maximizing ones by any chosen method, e.g. by taking their inverse values.

The COPRAS Method. The COPRAS method (Complex Proportional Assessment) [12, 13] uses similar idea with the difference that it accounts minimising criteria in a different way. The cumulative criterion of the method is calculated by the formula (3):

$$Z_j = S_{+j} + \frac{\sum_{j=1}^{n} S_{-j}}{S_{-j} \sum_{j=1}^{n} \frac{1}{S_{-j}}} \tag{3}$$

where $S_{+j} = \sum_{i=1}^{m} \omega_{+i} \tilde{r}_{+ij}$ is the sum of normalised values of maximising criteria multiplied by weights, similarly to the SAW method, and $S_{-j} = \sum_{i=1}^{m} \omega_{-i} \tilde{r}_{-ij}$ the sum of normalised values of minimising criteria multiplied by weights, $\tilde{r}_{+ij}$, $j=1,2,...,n$ (n is the number of alternatives) are normalised values of the maximising criteria; $\tilde{r}_{-ij}$, $j=1,2,...,n$; are normalised values of the minimising criteria.

The PROMETHEE II Method. The PROMETHEE II method (Preference Ranking Organisation Method for Enrichment Evaluation) [14, 15, 16] is descending from its simpler predecessor SAW method, nevertheless it discerns from other MCDA methods. By adding preference functions of chosen shapes $p_t(d_i(A_j, A_k))$ (the shape is represented by the index t) and by choosing boundary parameters q and s of the functions the method enhances the evaluation by providing more possibilities of eliciting knowledge of experts, who must choose both the shape of the function and its parameters. Preference functions eliminate the need of normalisation of values of criteria: they take values between 0 and 1. Another difference with the SAW is in the way the cumulative criterion is calculated. The calculation is now carried out in two steps. First, for every alternative A_j and all remaining alternatives A_k two inward and backward aggregated preference indices $\pi(A_j, A_k)$ and $\pi(A_k, A_j)$ are calculated in accordance with the following formula (4):

$$\pi(A_j, A_k) = \sum_{i=1}^{m} \omega_i p_t(d_i(A_j, A_k)) \tag{4}$$

by multiplication of values of preference function with weights in a similar way as in the SAW method. $\pi(A_j, A_k)$ shows the level of preference of the alternative A_j over A_k; conversely, $\pi(A_k, A_j)$ shows the level of preference of the alternative A_k over A_j. Now, for every alternative positive and negative outranking flows are calculated by summing inward and backward aggregated preference indices over all alternatives:

$$F_j^+ = \sum_{k=1}^{n} \pi(A_j, A_k)\,(j=1,2,\ ...,\ n) \qquad (5)$$

$$F_j^- = \sum_{k=1}^{n} \pi(A_k, A_j)\,(j=1,2,\ ...,\ n) \qquad (6)$$

The positive flow shows the magnitude of outranking of a chosen alternative relative to all other alternatives, while the negative flow shows the magnitude of outranking of other alternatives over the chosen alternative A_j. In other words, the larger is F_j^+ and the smaller is F_j^-, the better is the alternative. Finally, the cumulative criterion is very obvious:

$$F_j = F_j^+ - F_j^- \qquad (7)$$

Based on the cumulative criterion the final ranking of alternatives in the form of a sequence is obtained.

Preference function $p_0(x)$ used in the method by the author is of the following analytical expression and shape (Fig. 1):

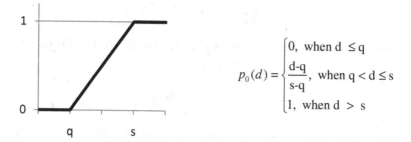

$$p_0(d) = \begin{cases} 0, & \text{when } d \leq q \\ \dfrac{d-q}{s-q}, & \text{when } q < d \leq s \\ 1, & \text{when } d > s \end{cases}$$

Fig. 1. The analytical expression and the shape of the preference function $p_0(x)$

The function proportionally accounts differences in values of criteria and also makes the method sightless on possible distortions of data due to accounting imperfections in the banking sector: it assigns the same preference levels whenever differences between values of criteria are smaller than q, and larger than s.

The TOPSIS Method. Finally, the idea of the TOPSIS method (Technique for Order Preference by Similarity to an Ideal Solution) [11, 17, 18] is considerably different to the above-mentioned methods. It is one of the most interesting and popular methods, used in many different fields. The idea of the method is that the alternative is considered to be better in case if its Euclidean distance from the best hypothetical solution is smaller and the distance to the worst hypothetical solution is larger than of other worse alternatives. The method requires already described normalisation of values of criteria by formula (1).

The best hypothetical solution V^* is found in accordance with the following formula (8):

$$V* = \{V_1^*, \ V_2^*, \ ...,V_m^*\} \ = \ \{(\max_{j} \omega_i \tilde{r}_{ij} \ / \ i \in I_1), \ (\min_{j} \omega_i \tilde{r}_{ij} \ / \ i \in I_2)\}, \tag{8}$$

where I_1 is the set of indices of the maximizing criteria, I_2 is the set of indices of the minimizing criteria.

Similarly, the worst hypothetical solution V^- is found in accordance with the following formula (9):

$$V^- = \{V_1^-, \ V_2^-, \ ...,V_m^-\} \ = \ \{(\min_{j} \omega_i \tilde{r}_{ij} \ / \ i \in I_1), \ (\max_{j} \omega_i \tilde{r}_{ij} \ / \ i \in I_2)\}, \tag{9}$$

The Euclidean distance to the best and the worst hypothetical solutions is calculated as follows:

$$D_j^* = \sqrt{\sum_{i=1}^{m} (\omega_i \tilde{r}_{ij} - V_i^*)^2} \tag{10}$$

$$D_j^- = \sqrt{\sum_{i=1}^{m} (\omega_i \tilde{r}_{ij} - V_i^-)^2} \tag{11}$$

And the cumulative criterion of the method C_j^* for each alternative j is calculated as follows:

$$C_j^* = \frac{D_j^-}{D_j^* + D_j^-} \ \ (j = 1, \ 2, \ ..., \ n) \ , \ (0 \leq C_j^* \leq 1). \tag{12}$$

The latter formula (12) reflects the idea that the alternative is the better the distance to the best hypothetical solution is the smaller and the distance to the worst hypothetical solution is the smaller.

2.3   Presentation of Relative Soundness and Stability Positions of Commercial Banks in the Form of the Ranking Table

Evaluation of commercial banks registered in Lithuania was carried out by several MCDA methods: SAW, TOPSIS, COPRAS and PROMETHEE [19-22] based on annual financial statements of 2007, 2008 and 2009 [23-38]. The way the evaluation was carried out has been described in the paper, which is currently in press and therefore is not presented here in detail. Obtained cumulative criteria of the methods shown good correspondence level with correlation coefficients between all pairs of cumulative criteria obtained by MCDA methods ranging from 0.98 to 0.80. For obtaining results of higher reliability, averages of rankings were taken. The final evaluation in the form of the ranking table is provided in Table 1.

Table 1. Average Relative Soundness and Stability Positions of Lithuanian Commercial Banks in 2007-2009

Years \ Alternatives	1	2	3	4	5	6	7	8
2007	6	7-8	7-8	3	2	4	1	5
2008	6	3	8	4	7	1	2	5
2009	5	1	8	7	4	2-3	2-3	6

Notes: Alternatives are: 1 - AB DnB NORD, 2 – UAB Medicinos Bankas, 3 - AB Parex bankas (now AB Citadele Bankas), 4 - AB SEB bankas, 5 - AB bankas SNORAS, 6 - AB Swedbank, 7 - AB Siauliu bankas, 8 - AB Ukio bankas. Author's calculations.

2.4   Reporting by Each Criterion in the Analytical Form

Information contained in Table 1 reveals relative soundness and stability positions of Lithuanian commercial banks in a standard ranking form used by most of MCDA researchers. It is outlined in the broad terms. Even if such reporting is unequivocal, the ranking table does not show causes of prominence or lagging of each bank.

For the purpose of more thorough analysis, the author suggests presentation of values of each criterion in percent. Values of criteria elicited from financial statements of the banks are transformed in such a way that 100% correspond to the best criterion value in the market, while 0% corresponds to the worst criterion value. We are suggesting the following formula (13) for transformation, where i is the index of criteria, and j the index of alternatives.

$$
\tilde{r}_{ij} = \begin{cases} \dfrac{r_{ij} - \min\limits_{j} r_{ij}}{\max\limits_{j} r_{ij} - \min\limits_{j} r_{ij}}, & \text{if } i \text{ is a maximising criterion} \\[4mm] \dfrac{\max\limits_{j} r_{ij} - r_{ij}}{\max\limits_{j} r_{ij} - \min\limits_{j} r_{ij}}, & \text{if } i \text{ is a minimising criterion} \end{cases} \tag{13}
$$

Values of above-mentioned criteria describing soundness and stability transformed in accordance with formula 13 are presented in Table 2. Information presented in this format, with relative positions of a bank in the market expressed in percent, broken down by each criterion, allows a decision-maker to identify strong and weak performance aspects of each particular bank. The percentage scale is more precise than the ranking table and is revealing bank performance in a more thorough way.

2.5   Reporting by Criteria Categories in the Graphical Form

Still, even a very experienced decision-maker observing the data presented in Table 2.

Table 2. Relative Positions of Commercial Banks in the Market, %

Ratios \ Alternatives		1	2	3	4	5	6	7	8
CAPITAL	2007	4	1	47	0	37	16	100	33
	2008	3	100	36	3	0	78	99	38
	2009	0	80	77	19	1	100	59	34
NII	2007	54	68	0	52	50	100	41	67
	2008	12	68	1	7	0	100	5	13
	2009	81	87	68	65	0	100	47	23
TL	2007	0	51	12	32	100	33	18	21
	2008	0	81	74	32	100	37	15	15
	2009	2	62	0	47	100	31	21	45
DELINQ	2007	81	0	100	76	38	66	68	78
	2008	90	0	100	89	66	90	95	87
	2009	64	69	31	70	0	18	100	32
LD	2007	53	28	46	60	100	63	43	0
	2008	74	0	38	65	56	100	88	51
	2009	33	90	42	0	100	18	86	86
NIC	2007	73	15	0	100	58	59	77	30
	2008	88	35	0	100	44	67	83	33
	2009	93	71	0	76	82	82	100	67
PPP	2007	51	57	100	6	36	6	36	0
	2008	57	41	100	37	58	0	58	32
	2009	18	30	100	49	31	0	61	79
NI	2007	50	35	0	100	84	95	69	98
	2008	50	55	0	69	48	100	58	71
	2009	62	99	26	0	100	14	83	79
DEP	2007	0	46	5	12	100	40	29	39
	2008	5	87	0	25	100	51	54	70
	2009	0	70	7	20	100	44	52	68
LIQ	2007	19	71	0	56	100	53	63	93
	2008	17	100	0	23	13	26	22	36
	2009	12*	81	24	100	26	42	0	63

Notes: Alternatives are: 1 - AB DnB NORD, 2 – UAB Medicinos Bankas, 3 - AB Parex bankas, 4 - AB SEB bankas, 5 - AB bankas SNORAS, 6 - AB Swedbank, 7 - AB Siauliu bankas, 8 - AB Ukio bankas. Sources: annual financial statements. Author's calculations. Sources: [23-38]. Description of variables is presented in Section 2.1.

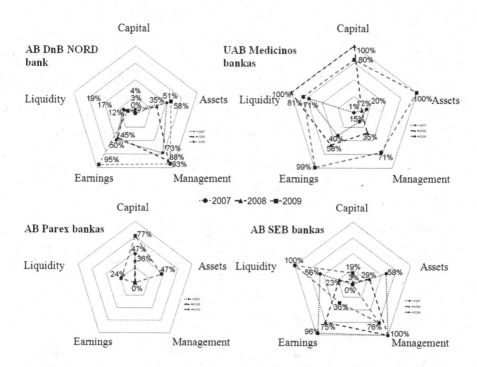

Fig. 2. Relative Soundness and Stability Positions of Lithuanian Commercial Banks by the CAMEL Criteria Comparing to the Best Value in the Market, 2007-2009

will not usually be able to view dynamics, improvement or worsening of performance of a bank in broader terms: capital, assets, cost-efficiency management, profitability, liquidity. For the purposes of simultaneous capturing of the composite of the components of soundness and stability of commercial banks and their dynamics, the author suggests presentation of relative position of soundness and stability of banks in charts broken down by the CAMEL categories (Fig. 2 and 3).

Values presented in the chart of such categories, which consist of composite criteria were calculated using the following formula (14).

$$C_j^t = \sum_{i \in K_t} \omega_i \tilde{r}_{ij}$$

(14)

where t denotes a category: Capital, Assets, Management, Earnings, and Liquidity; j – the alternative; ω_i – weights of criteria; $\tilde{r}_{ij}$ – transformed values of the i-th criteria for the j-th alternative; K_t. – the set of indices of the t-th CAMEL category.

In other words, the transformed values are multiplied by corresponding weights and summed within each CAMEL category. Again, the transformation by the formula 13 is applied. The weights were obtained by taking averages of weights elicited from seven experts in Lithuanian commercial banking using a proprietary questionnaire form.

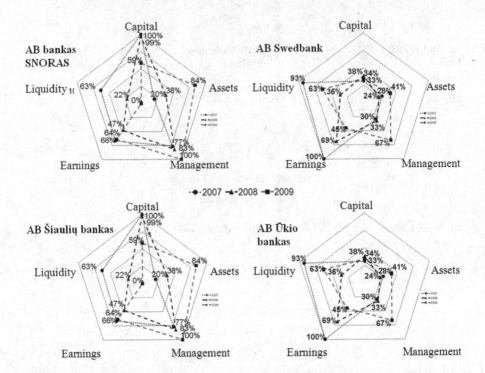

Fig. 3. Relative Soundness and Stability Positions of Lithuanian Commercial Banks by the CAMEL Criteria Comparing to the Best Value in the Market, 2007-2009

2.6   Framework of Data Analysis

After the data have been presented in three different formats, we hereby suggest a three-step framework of analysis of soundness and stability performance of commercial banks.

Step 1. Table 1 provides the rankings by overall soundness and stability strength of commercial banks in the market and serves as the initial tool of the evaluation.

Step 2. On the second step, evaluation in terms of CAMEL categories of soundness and stability of commercial banks is made using the graphs presented in Fig. 1 and 2. Strong and weak performance aspects of a bank by categories and their dynamics are therefore explicitly revealed on the graphs. By observation of the graphs a decision-maker captures a more detailed view of the strength of influence of CAMEL components to soundness and stability of a particular bank.

Step 3. On the third step, the table with relative values of categories outlined in the percent scale is analysed, identifying which criteria has influenced the relative position of a bank observed on the step 1.

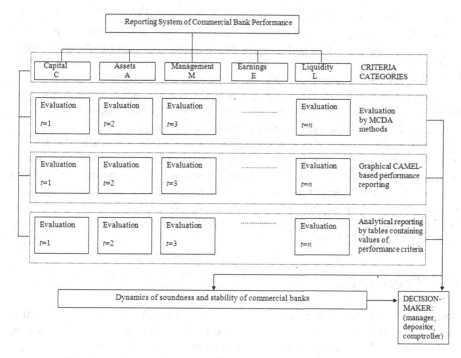

Fig. 4. Framework of Analysis of Commercial Bank Performance Data

A scheme of the evaluation procedure is presented on Fig. 4. Since the evaluation is being carried out using performance data from different periods, the decision-maker can observe dynamics of both overall performance of a bank and its particular performance criteria in terms of CAMEL categories by observing the charts or even in the more detailed form provided in the analytical table.

Observe dynamics of UAB 'Medicinos Bankas' as an example. In Table 1 it is found in the last position in the local market by soundness and stability criteria in 2007. Position of the bank gradually increased: to the 3-rd in 2008, and to the 1-st in 2009. The chart representing UAB 'Medicinos Bankas' in Fig.2 shows that the bank has improved its position in the market by all CAMEL criteria and became the leader in Assets and Earnings categories over the period. In particular, it is observed from Table 2, that in 2009 its loan value decrease (LD, a minimising variable) is second smallest in the market, net income (NI, a maximising variable) is second-highest in the market. Combination of good performance results in 2009 assured the first place in terms of soundness and stability for the mentioned bank in the local Lithuanian market.

3   Benefits of Data Analysis for Bank Management, Depositors, and Regulatory Institutions

Disaster myopia, risky behaviour of bank management [39] could lead to a failure of a bank under certain powerful macroeconomic circumstances (shifts of real-estate prices, interest rates, etc.). Constant monitoring of financial strength of a bank by all aspects of its soundness and stability is therefore vitally important for bank management. The proposed framework of data reporting provides timely and accurate map of the financial state of a bank in a detailed format. The same framework could be used by regulatory institutions of commercial banks in a country.

It is a rather obvious fact that even if financial statements of commercial banks are being published in a timely manner and are readily available to depositors, information on soundness and stability of banks is highly asymmetric. Depositors are unable to perceive financial data in annual reports and are prone to believe to lagging and inaccurate ratings of rating agencies or emotional and often destructive information published in the mass media. In cases of bank panics, information asymmetry induces dangerous deposit withdrawals [40]. This paper proposes reporting tools, which expose levels of soundness and stability of commercial banks in a clear and understandable format, accessible by depositors, as well as bank managers and comptrollers.

4   Conclusions

Methods of multicriteria decision aid provide clear and intelligible prompt evaluation in the form of rankings, which are designed to make comparisons of commercial banks. Nevertheless, more detailed information aimed for a decision-maker is provided by using additional proprietary tools promptly exposing numerous specific data in a clear form. Reporting tools, simplifying thorough analysis of financial data, which represent bank performance, are proposed in this paper. Such tools provide both detailed information on soundness and stability state of commercial banks in the market by presenting it in the analytical form by its performance criteria, and more general information in a graphic form allowing to instantly capture bank soundness and stability state by CAMEL categories of its performance (Capital, Assets, Cost-Management, Earnings, and Liquidity). The way the data is presented helps a decision-maker (depositor, bank management or a comptroller) to instantly observe causes of strength and weakness of commercial banks and dynamics of performance of a bank.

The evaluation tools proposed in this paper do not prevent from the cases when bank management requires false financial statements of a bank to be produced. Such a case has been recently disclosed by Lithuanian comptroller institution the Bank of Lithuania. A large gap of around 3.5 billion euros has been found in reported assets of AB bankas SNORAS upon inspection carried out after the bank's licence was withheld.

For further research other MCDA methods such as UTA, DEA ELECTRE III, IV, MUSA, MULTIMOORA, etc. could be applied and correspondence of results obtained by each MCDA method could be verified similarly as it was described in this paper using four different MCDA methods: SAW, TOPSIS, COPRAS and PROMETHEE.

References

1. Sprague, O.M.W.: History of crises under the national banking system. Government Printing Office, Washington (1910)
2. Houben, A., Kakes, J., Schinasi, G.: Toward a Framework for Safeguarding Financial Stability. IMF Working Paper No. 04/101, 1–47 (2004)
3. Zavadskas, E.K., Turskis, Z.: Multiple Criteria Decision Making (MCDM) Methods in Economics: An Overview. Technological and Economic Development of Economy 17, 397–427 (2011)
4. Spronk, J., Steuer, R.E., Zopounidis, C.: Multicriteria Decision Aid/Analysis in Finance. In: Figueira, J., Greco, S., Ehrgott, M. (eds.) Multiple Criteria Decision Analysis: State of the Art Surveys, pp. 799–857. Springer, New York (2005)
5. Fethi, D.F., Pasiouras, F.: Assessing Bank Efficiency and Performance with Operational Research and Artificial Intelligence Techniques: A Survey. European Journal of Operational Research 204, 189–198 (2010)
6. Ginevicius, R., Podviezko, A.: A framework of evaluation of commercial banks. Intellectual Economics 1(9), 37–53 (2011)
7. Gonzalez-Hermosillo, B.: Determinants of Ex-Ante Banking System Distress: A Macro-Micro Empirical Exploration of Some Recent Episodes. IMF Working Paper No. 99/33, 1–144 (1999)
8. Seimas of the Republic of Lithuania,
   http://www3.lrs.lt/pls/inter3/dokpaieska.showdoc_l?p_id=230458&p_query=&p_tr2=
9. Podviezko, A., Ginevičius, R.: Economic Criteria Characterising Bank Soundness and Stability. In: The 6th International Scientific Conference Business and Management 2010. Selected papers, Technika, Vilnius, Lithuania, pp. 1072–1079 (2010)
10. Wheelock, D.C., Wilson, P.W.: Why Do Banks Disappear? The Determinants of U.S. Bank Failures and Acquisitions. The Review of Economics and Statistics 82, 127–138 (2000)
11. Hwang, C.L., Yoon, K.: Multiple Attribute Decision Making-Methods and Applications: A State of the Art Survey. Springer, Heidelberg (1981)
12. Podvezko, V.: The Comparative Analysis of MCDA Methods SAW and COPRAS. Inzinerine Ekonomika-Engineering Economics 22, 134–146 (2011)
13. Tupenaite, L., Zavadskas, E.K., Kaklauskas, A., et al.: Multiple Criteria Assessment of Alternatives for Built and Human Environment Renovation. Journal of Civil Engineering and Management 16, 257–266 (2010)
14. Brans, J., Mareschal, B.: Promethee Methods. In: Figueira, J., Greco, S., Ehrogott, M., et al. (eds.) Multiple Criteria Decision Analysis: State of the Art Surveys, pp. 163–186. Springer, New York (2005)
15. Podvezko, V., Podviezko, A.: Dependence of Multicriteria Evaluation Result on Choice of Preference Functions and their Parameters. Technological and Economic Development of Economy 16, 143–158 (2010)
16. Podvezko, V., Podviezko, A.: Use and Choice of Preference Functions for Evaluation of Characteristics of Socio-Economical Processes. In: The 6th International Scientific Conference Business and Management 2010, Selected papers, Technika, Vilnius, Lithuania, pp. 1066–1071 (2010)
17. Zavadskas, E.K., Zakarevicius, A., Antucheviciene, J.: Evaluation of Ranking Accuracy in Multi-Criteria Decisions. Informatica 17, 601–618 (2006)

18. Antucheviciene, J., Zavadskas, E.K., Zakarevicius, A.: Multiple Criteria Construction Management Decisions Considering Relations between Criteria. Technological and Economic Development of Economy 16, 109–125 (2010)
19. Ginevicius, R., Podvezko, V., Bruzge, Š.: Evaluating the Effect of State Aid to Business by Multicriteria Methods. Journal of Business Economics and Management 9(3), 167–180 (2008)
20. Zavadskas, E.K., Kaklauskas, A., Banaitis, A., Kvederyte, N.: Housing Credit Access Model: The Case for Lithuania. European Journal of Operational Research 155, 335–352 (2006)
21. Ginevicius, R., Podvezko, V.: Housing in the Context of Economic and Social Development of Lithuanian Regions. Int. J. Environment and Pollution 35(2/3/4), 309–330 (2008)
22. Opricovic, S., Tzeng, G.-H.: Compromise Solution by MCDM Methods: A Comparative Analysis of VIKOR and TOPSIS. European Journal of Operational Research 156, 445–455 (2004)
23. AB DnB NORD bankas Annual Report (2008),
    `http://www.dnbnord.lt/files/Ataskaitos/metine%20ataskaita%202008.pdf`
24. AB DnB NORD bankas Annual Report (2009),
    `http://www.dnbnord.lt/Dokumentai/konsoliduotas_metinis_pranesimas_2010_03_19.pdf`
25. AB Parex bankas Annual Report (2008),
    `http://www.citadele.lt/files/PB_FS_2008_LT_final2.pdf`
26. AB Parex bankas Annual Report (2009),
    `http://www.citadele.lt/files/finansine-atskaitomybe-2010-01-01.pdf`
27. AB SEB bankas Annual Report (2008),
    `http://www.seb.lt/pow/content/seb_lt/pdf/lt/SEB_bankas_2008.pdf`
28. AB SEB bankas Annual Report (2009),
    `http://www.seb.lt/pow/content/seb_lt/pdf/lt/20091231_TFAS_LT.pdf`
29. AB Siauliubankas Annual Report (2008),
    `http://www.sb.lt/filemanager/download/696/2008%20metine%20lt%20new.pdf`
30. AB Siauliubankas Annual Report (2009),
    `http://www.sb.lt/filemanager/download/696/2008%20metine%20lt%20new.pdf`
31. AB bankas SNORAS Annual Report (2008),
    `http://www.snoras.com/files/SNORAS_2008_Finansine_ataskaita.pdf`
32. AB bankas SNORAS Annual Report (2009),
    `http://www.snoras.com/files/Snoras2009LT-Audituota.pdf`
33. AB Swedbank Annual Report (2008),
    `http://www.swedbank.lt/files/ataskaitos/2008f.pdf`
34. AB Swedbank Annual Report (2009),
    `http://www.swedbank.lt/files/ataskaitos/2009f.pdf`
35. AB Ukiobankas Annual Report (2008),
    `http://www.ub.lt/forms/070327_1%20priedas_UB_IFRS_2008%20_lt.pdf`
36. AB Ukio bankas Annual Report (2009),
    `http://www.ub.lt/forms/UB_IFRS_2009_LT.pdf`

37. UAB Medicinos bankas Annual Report (2008),
    http://www.medbank.lt/images/stories/Ataskaitos/metine_
    ataskaita_2008.pdf
38. UAB Medicinos bankas Annual Report (2009),
    http://www.medbank.lt/images/stories/file/MB%20LT%202009%
    20Ataskaita.pdf
39. Herring, R.J., Wachter, S.: Bubbles in Real Estate Markets. University of Pennsylvania
    Wharton School Zell/Lùrie Real Estate Center Working Paper no. 402, 1–15 (2002)
40. Calomiris, C.W., Gorton, G.: The Origins of Banking Panics: Models, Facts, and Bank
    Regulation. In: Hubbard, R.G. (ed.) Financial Markets and Financial Crises, pp. 109–173.
    University of Chicago Press, Chicago (1991)

Towards Automated Education Demand-Offer Information Monitoring: The System's Architecture

Peteris Rudzajs

Department of Systems Theory and Design, Riga Technical University,
Kalku iela 1, LV-1658, Riga, Latvia
Peteris.Rudzajs@rtu.lv

Abstract. Rapid economic changes in the knowledge requirements for labor cause a necessity to monitor education demand and offer. In this paper education demand and offer information monitoring (EduMON) system is proposed. The system can obtain the monitoring information from unstructured or semistructured textual information sources. The use of the monitoring system in educational institutions can foster study course compliance with knowledge required in job market. In enterprises it can help to evaluate knowledge potential of educational institutions for selecting employees or providing continious education possibilities. Human Resource management systems, job seeking portals, educational institution information systems and other systems could also use the analysis services provided by the EduMON system. Vacancy descriptions and university course descriptions are the main information sources wherefrom the education information in terms of skills, knowledge, and/or competences is retrieved. EduMON architecture accommodates the scope of services starting from the information retrieval to information analysis and presentation. Brief overview of the services is given by describing their basic functionality and implementation considerations.

Keywords: Education, information, monitoring system, systems architecture, services.

1 Introduction

Rapid economic changes foster changes in knowledge requirements for labor. Therefore it becomes more and more important to be constantly aware of what education is currently demanded and what education is currently offered. Education demand can be described in terms of competencies, knowledge, and skills of professionals being demanded by the work environment (further in the text - Industry). Education offer can be defined as competences, knowledge and skills obtainable in educational institutions, e.g., in universities (further in the text the educational institutions are referred as University). For simplicity in this paper the terms "education information" and "skills" are used interchangeably, they are used to denote competences, knowledge and skills [1]. Currently the research is conducted in the area of Information and Communication Technology (ICT) education information.

L. Niedrite, R. Strazdina, B. Wangler (Eds.): BIR 2011 Workshops, LNBIP 106, pp. 252–265, 2012.
© Springer-Verlag Berlin Heidelberg 2012

Maintaining the correspondence between the education demand and offer becomes possible only with continuous monitoring of both – the demand and the offer (further in text d/o) of knowledge, skills, or competences. Education d/o monitoring both for University and Industry can provide an insight in knowledge, skills, or competences currently demanded/offered in educational and industrial environment. Based on the analysis of the monitoring results University can adjust curricula to continuously correspond to industrial demand for education. The analysis of the results of the education d/o information monitoring could help to raise the quality of curricula and establish closer connection between University and Industry in the context of educational information exchange and Industry participation in study course content design and teaching. It is worth mentioning that University should not concentrate on Industry needs only, but has to comply with advances in science and innovation, too [2].

Currently the above-described benefits of education d/o monitoring are achievable only by investing a lot of manual work in overviewing, extracting, and analyzing the information from various information sources. Education d/o usually is reflected in such information sources as University course descriptions and certification course descriptions (in the educational institutions) and vacancy descriptions (in Industry). Additionally, various competence frameworks [3, 4] and national occupational standards [5] can extend the list of relevant information sources. In order to obtain current information, e.g., about University graduates, social network profiles such as *LinkedIn.com* and *Facebook.com* can also be considered as sources of information. The education information in each information source is encoded in different ways and therefore needs specific handling mechanisms.

Large amount of manual work and the diversity of information sources are features that let to draw a hypothesis that the IT solution can be helpful to process various information sources, extract education information, and provide the analysis mechanisms in automated manner. In the author's previous paper [6], education d/o analysis was already discussed in the context of using mediated educational information comparison method. In this paper the description of the proposed solution is structured as follows. In Section 2, related work is discussed. Further, in Section 3, overview of proposed monitoring system's architecture is provided. In Section 4, basic functionality and implementation considerations of services are provided. Conclusions and further research are outlined in Section 5.

2   Related Works

Related works are selected from areas relevant for the education d/o information monitoring and include the architectures of monitoring systems, information retrieval and information extraction, and classification structures fostering the information extraction.

2.1   Monitoring Systems' Architectures

Monitoring systems are designed for various purposes but mainly for: 1) Mechanical systems monitoring (e.g. in aerospace [7]); 2) Earth's condition monitoring [8]; 3) Surveillance [9]; 4) Grid systems monitoring [10], [11]; 5) IT infrastructure monitoring [12]; 6) Quality of Service (QoS) monitoring [13]; 7) Social network monitoring [14]; and 8) Key Performance Indicators (KPI) monitoring in business environment [15]. Basic functionality of monitoring systems include gathering of source data (mainly quantitative data), data processing, and analysis in order to provide decision support information to the users of the system. In most cases the architectures of monitoring systems are represented in layers (e.g., data collector, data analyzer, data presentation facilities), where each layer is designed for a specific purpose and for providing of services to other layers. In most cases the service oriented architecture (SOA) is adopted for the design of the monitoring systems [16]. SOA is a system design concept that builds an information system by connecting loosely coupled services. This architecture type is well suitable for designing the architecture of monitoring systems as it supports connections of distributed services available in monitoring system. The monitoring system proposed in this paper differs from other above-mentioned monitoring systems with its ability to obtain the monitoring source information from unstructured and semistructured textual information sources. These sources can not be handled in the same way as sensors where information is quantitatively measurable.

2.2   Information Retrieval and Extraction

For the education d/o monitoring purposes, the unstructured information should be retrieved from various sources and then transformed into the structured form in order to enable information analysis in automated manner. Thus the information retrieval is intended here for finding relevant documents representing education information and information extraction is used for obtaining information from retrieved documents. Semantic annotation of source documents is considered as an approach for information extraction. In a document the semantic annotation is an additional information that identifies or defines a concept in a semantic model that helps to describe a particular part of the document [17].

For semantic annotation Kiryakov et al. [18] suggest in the most of the cases to apply light-weight ontologies for the following reasons: (1) they are easier to understand (the same applies to metadata based these ontologies); (2) they are easier to build, verify, and maintain; and (3) they are easier to get consensus upon. Kiyavitskaya et al. [19] have developed *Cerno*, a framework for semi-automatic semantic annotation of textual documents according to a domain-specific semantic model which uses code analysis methods instead of Natural Language Processing techniques. *Cerno* document text analysis process includes four steps: (1) document parsing, (2) recognition of basic facts, (3) their interpretation with respect to a domain semantic model, and (4) mapping of the information identified to an external database [19].

For course information extraction, Biletskiy, Y et al. [20] demonstrate the CODE (Course Outline Description Extraction) approach which suggests that the inputs to the application are a semi-structured course outline in the form of an HTML file, a predefined XML template, and several libraries of patterns and key terms. The CODE approach is oriented only to simple HTML documents and does not deal with documents containing PHP, XHTML, JavaScript, etc.

Janev et al. [21] discusses the process of building expert profiles in a form of ontology database by integrating competences from structured and unstructured sources. Success so far is automatic identification and extraction of skills from available structured and unstructured sources and semi-automatic population of the ontology database.

Indirectly education d/o information monitoring system could be also considered in the context of expert search, where basic aim is to retrieve experts' information (in terms of skills, knowledge, or competencies) based on the required characteristics of the expert for particular task or topic. This is also task of information retrieval and extraction. Many works aim at retrieving expert information based on various approaches, e.g., semantic-enabled expert search [22], document ranking [23], etc.. Monitoring system presented in this paper differs from expert search approaches. It provides continuous monitoring of education information and provides the change detection and management, which are not present in the "one time" expert retrieval.

2.3   Classification Structures

Skills are concepts that can be encoded in many different ways and are hard to identify [24], therefore skills information extraction is a challenging task. Frameworks (classification structures) can be used to solve this task. In the context of skills information extraction valuable classification structures include 1) European Dictionary of Skills and Competencies (DISCO) [25]; 2) European Taxonomy of Skills, Competencies, and Occupations (ESCO) [26]; 3) EURES Taxonomy [27]; 4) European e-Competence framework (e-CF) [4]; 5) Skills Framework for Information Age (SFIA) [28]; 6) Association for Computing Machinery (ACM) taxonomy [29]; and 7) WordNet lexical database [30].

3   Overview of EduMON System's Architecture

Author refers to *Edu*cation demand/offer information *mon*itoring system as "EduMON system". The acronym has also a figurative explanation where *Edu* stays for "education" and *MON* means - "above mountains" [31]. It is understood as "education above mountains". "Mountains" - as real-life problems and difficulties that need to be overcome. "Education" - as a tool to overcome mountains. Education information monitoring system is one of the supplementing tools toward overcoming the "mountains".

When developing the architecture of EduMON system, we make the following assumptions:

- We do not focus on all details of the system; instead we identify and describe high-level design elements and relations between the elements.
- By design elements we mean modules, components, databases, and external systems. As SOA approach is used, modules and components in this paper are denoted as services.

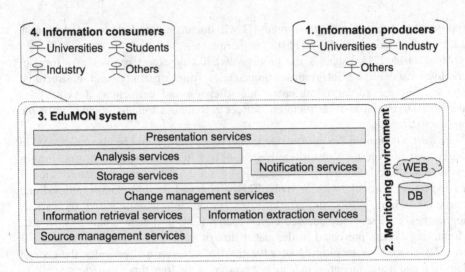

Fig. 1. EduMON system's overview

Scope of service types of EduMON system's architecture is similar to architectures proposed in [10] and [14]. EduMON differs from them with the presence of information source change management services. As discussed in Section 2.1, basic functionality of the monitoring systems includes gathering of source information, and information processing and analysis in order to provide decision support information to users of the system. EduMON system (see Fig. 1) gathers source information prepared by Information producers (see 1 in Fig. 1) from the Monitoring environment (see 2 in Fig. 1). Information producers are Universities (providing course descriptions), Industry (providing vacancy descriptions) and other institutions (e.g., ones providing occupational standards, social network profiles, etc.). Monitoring environment is the medium where information is stored, namely, World Wide Web (further denoted simply as Web) available publicly and various databases available locally in organizations. After gathering source information, EduMON system processes and analyses this information and via internal services provides it to Information consumers for decision support (see 4 in Fig. 1). Information consumers are University, Industry, or other users interested in information provided by the EduMON system.

EduMON system's architecture is designed as a set of extendable services of the following classes:

- *Source management services* for preparation and management of information sources
- *Information retrieval services* for information gathering from various information sources
- *Information extraction services* for information extraction based on information source models and for annotation (the assignment of metadata) of information source documents

- *Change management services* for management of information source changes
- *Storage services* for storing information source descriptions and extracted information
- *Notification services* for notification of interested parties in case of the changes in the information sources
- *Analysis services* for any kind of analysis based on gathered information, e.g., most demanded skills in Industry, differences between skills provided by University courses and skills included in other information sources such as vacancy descriptions, occupational standards, and certification standards that represent actual demand of competencies in Industry
- *Presentation services* are intended to be a web-based graphical user interface that offers concise (in the form of tables, charts, figures etc.) monitoring information. It is designed according to a role-based strategy to offer different views depending on the type of Information consumer.

4   Details of EduMON System's Architecture

EduMON system provides various services organized in classes forming the service inventory. Each service in the service inventory should be designed based on SOA principles to ensure loose coupling, reusability, autonomy, and interoperability that fosters the connection of the services from various service classes in EduMON system. Fig. 2 represents detailed architecture of EduMON system indicating the possible services as rounded boxes inside service classes. The number of services in each service class is not restricted. Thus providing new services, e.g., for information retrieval and analysis purposes could extend the scope of services and EduMON system's functionality.

Each service of the class 2, 3, 4, and 5 of EduMON system's architecture is dedicated for dealing with the different information source, e.g., services for processing vacancy descriptions, University courses, occupational standards, etc. (see Fig. 2; e.g., for *Information retrieval services* class variety of services indicated as IRS1, IRS2,..., IRSn). Because of the diversity of functionality necessary for the different information source processing, services for dealing with each information source can also have multiple implementations. For example, information retrieval service (see class 2 and service IRS1 in Fig. 2) for the retrieval of the University course descriptions can be implemented in two ways (boxes inside IRS1): one service for the course description retrieval from databases and another one - from University's Web sites. Example of information flow and description is given in Section 4.5. In the remainder of this section, the brief overview of service classes is presented describing basic functionality and implementation considerations of the services of particular classes.

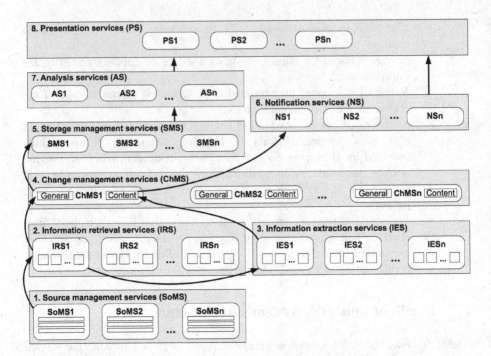

Fig. 2. EduMON system's architecture indicating the possible services as rounded boxes inside service classes. Connecting arrows between services SoMS1, IRS1, IES1, ChMS1 and SMS1 in classes 1, 2, 3, 4, and 5 illustrate the adjusted information processing for one information source, e.g., for University course description processing.

4.1   Source Management Services

Services of the *Source management services* class (see class 1 in Fig. 2) are responsible for the management of information sources. As the EduMON system is not a general-purpose information retrieval system, specific information sources should be added to the EduMON system thus limiting the scope of information retrieval. As indicated in Fig. 2, architecture provides different source management services (SoMS1, SoMS2, ..., SoMSn), such as services for dealing with databases, web pages, and structured information sources (based on XML, such as RDF, OWL, and other). Each source management service provides mechanisms for adding/updating/removing databases, web pages, and structured information sources. New information sources usually are added on demand from Universities and companies willing to use the services provided by EduMON system.

4.2   Information Retrieval Services

As mentioned at the beginning of Section 3.2, each service of the class 2, 3, 4, and 5 of EduMON system's architecture is dedicated for dealing with the different information source, e.g., services for processing vacancy descriptions, services for processing University courses, services for processing occupational standards, etc. Services for dealing with each information source can also have multiple implementations. Variety of information source processing services and their implementations is necessary because of the diversity of information sources since each information source requires a specific approach of information processing.

Services of the *Information retrieval services* class (see class 2 in Fig. 2) are responsible for gathering the information from information sources provided by the services of the *Source management services* class. Information gathering from Web pages can be implemented as focused Web crawlers (different crawlers for retrieval of University course descriptions, Vacancy descriptions, and other information sources; in Fig. 2 indicated as IRS1, IRS2, ..., IRSn). Author has developed and conducted experiments [32] with focused crawler for the retrieval of vacancy descriptions from specified web pages. In order to include this crawler in EduMON system as one of the services, it should be improved by incorporating the use of the classification structures to provide more correct information retrieval.

4.3   Information Extraction Services

Services of the *Information extraction services* class (see class 3 in Fig. 2) are responsible for information extraction based on information source models and for annotation (the assignment of metadata) of information source documents by using classification structures. Education information (knowledge, skills, competences) extraction from source documents is one of the main parts of EduMON system. Extracted structured information could be used as basis for the services of *Analysis services* class.

Information extraction from retrieved information sources is a document analysis task including the structural and semantic analysis of the document. Before semantic analysis structural analysis of the document should be conducted. Structural analysis includes the identification of paragraphs, sentences, words and terms. The output of structural analysis can be used as input for semantic analysis of the document. Semantic analysis of a document is a semantic annotation process where necessary concepts (e.g., skills) are identified based on available classification structures (see Section 2.3).

Information extraction services can be implemented based on existing unstructured text analysis platforms, such as Unstructured Information Management Architecture (UIMA) [33] and General Architecture for Text Engineering (GATE) [34]. In both platforms text analysis tasks can be pipelined. It means that the results of one task could serve as input to some other tasks. For example, after identification of structural parts of a document, e.g., paragraphs, the document can be further processed to identify concepts (e.g. title of course, skills, knowledge, etc.) in particular structural parts.

4.4   Storage Services

Access to internal databases and repositories for each EduMON system's service is provided by services of the *Storage services* class (see class 5 in Fig. 2). Two types of storage services can be identified:

1) Storage of source documents. For the storage of source documents and annotated documents version control systems, such as Subversion (SVN) [35], Concurrent Versions System (CVS) [36], or Fast version control system GIT [37] could be used.

2) Storage of extracted information. For this kind of storage database management systems could be used.

Data structures for extracted information storage are designed based on information source models. Conceptual model of University course description is given in Fig. 3a). In Fig. 3b) data structure for structured course description storage is provided as an example. Each course can include many skills and topics (see corresponding tables in Fig. 3b). For each skill in the course description, status information is maintained in the table *Course_skill_status*. This table is intended for storage of changes of skills information by using such attributes as *current* (values 1 or 0, indicating if the skill is currently available in course description), *date_added* (indicates the date when the skill for a particular course had been added), *date_removed* (indicates the date when the skill for a particular course had been removed).

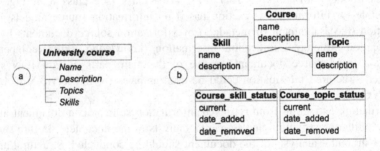

Fig. 3. Conceptual model of University course description (a) and example of the data structure for storage of structured course descriptions (including information about skills and topics) (b)

4.5   Change Management Services and Example of Change Detection

EduMON system provides continuous monitoring of information sources; one of the significant service classes is the *Change management services* class (see class 4 in Fig. 2). The services are responsible mainly for change detection in information sources thus enabling accurate identification and notification of detected changes.

In EduMON system two types of change detection are introduced: general change detection and content change detection. *General change detection* includes the renewal of existing document version in repository and the identification of any changes (in the case of no changes in the source document, further source processing is not useful because we already know that nothing has changed). *Content change detection* includes the identification of changes (e.g., new skills, removed skills) and extracted skills information storage. Both types of change detection services are related to *Storage services* thus enabling the storage of changes in EduMON system.

In order to demonstrate basic information flow and change detection in EduMON system, simple example is provided (represented in Fig. 4):

1) University web site is provided as information source.
2) Based on classification structures available in EduMON system, Web pages containing course descriptions are retrieved (access to classification structures are provided by *Storage services*).
3) Retrieved pages are checked against existing page versions in the repository. If any changes are detected, then new version of unstructured course description is stored in the repository. After storage of new version proceed to next task. If no changes are detected, then proceed with next retrieved course description.
4) Based on classification structures available in EduMON system, information about skills is extracted from the course descriptions.
5) Extracted skills are processed by *Content change detection service* and annotated course description is stored in course description repository. Annotated description is necessary for further reference to original course description to enable manual rechecking of extracted skills.
6) If any changes in the content of the course description (e.g. new skills) are detected, then changed items are updated in database (basic algorithm for change management of skills is described in the reminder of this section). All updated information of particular course are gathered and passed to *Notification service,* which sends notification that requests manual rechecking of changed items.

In the context of course descriptions the basic algorithm for change management of skills uses data structures described in Section 4.2 (see Fig. 3). It consists of the following steps:

1) Obtain existing skills (with attribute *current*=1) for particular course from the database.
2) Compare existing skills with extracted skills.
3) If there are new skills, then they are added to database with attributes: *current=1* and *date_added=current date.*
4) If some of existing skills are not available in the set of extracted skills, then the status information of the skills are updated: *current=0* and *dated_removed=current date.*
5) If some new skills are extracted, but in the database they exist with status *current=0*, then new record is added in *Course_skill_status* table.

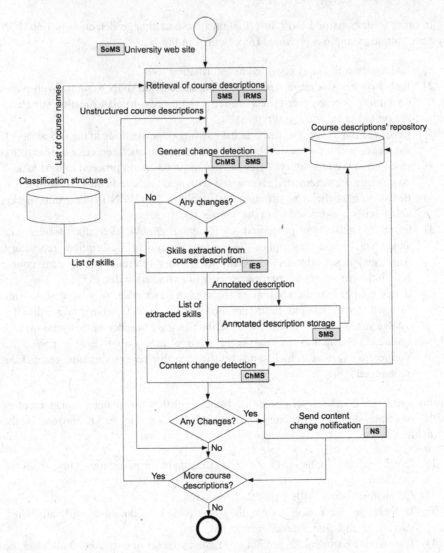

Fig. 4. Example of basic information flow including course description retrieval, extraction of skills, and change detection. Small grey boxes identify the process linkage to the particular service class.

4.6   Analysis Services and Presentation Services

Services of the *Analysis services* class are responsible for any kind of analysis based on gathered and extracted education information. Analysis services in EduMON system can be used internally or externally. In order to enable the external use of analysis services, Web Service interfaces should be provided. This means that the results of analysis services can be used, e.g., in job seeking portals where the service can provide information about University courses that give an opportunity to obtain skills that correspond to the skills required in particular vacancy. In similar way Human Resource management systems can use analysis services for identification of University courses where necessary skills can be obtained.

Analysis services can provide analysis based on the single information source and integrated analysis of information retrieved from several sources. Examples for single information sources include, e.g., most demanded skills in Industry, most popular vacancies, the set of skills obtainable in particular University curriculum, etc. Examples of integrated analysis of information retrieved from several information sources include analysis of the differences between skills provided in University courses and skills included in other information sources such as vacancy descriptions and occupational standards that represent actual demand of skills in Industry.

Services of the *Presentation services* class in EduMON system are responsible for maintaining access to analysis services, visualization of analysis results, and providing dashboard of EduMON system's notifications (e.g. reflecting changes in information sources, see Section 4.5).

5   Conclusions and Future Work

In this paper the approach of application of the monitoring system in education domain had been proposed. The approach is new and can provide benefits both for University and Industry, e.g., help to get an insight into current education d/o in industrial and education environment and provide information for decision support regarding curriculum management and continuous education. In this paper the architecture of the education d/o information monitoring (EduMON system) had been proposed. Basic functionality and implementation considerations of the services of each service class had been discussed. Education d/o information monitoring involves the process from retrieving and extracting information from relevant sources to finding correspondence between education information (knowledge, competence, or skills) in various sources.

Main advantages for EduMON system over typical monitoring systems are the following: 1) extendibility of service classes by adding new services, 2) provision of analysis services for external use, 3) obtaining monitoring information from various unstructured and semistructured textual sources of education information, 4) available mechanisms for change management, and 5) integrated analysis of information retrieved from conceptually diverse information sources.

For service of the *Information retrieval services* class some experiments had been conducted with developed web crawler. For one service of *Analysis services* class the application of interactive inductive learning for study course comparison [38] had been investigated, since the services of the *Information extraction services* class can provide necessary functionality for the extraction of course attributes (e.g. topics, skills).

Currently the limitation of EduMON system includes the limited number of identified and analyzed education information sources, such as University course descriptions, vacancy descriptions, certification course descriptions, competence frameworks, national occupational standards, and social network profiles. Further work will include the identification and analysis of additional information sources and application of different techniques to retrieve and extract education information. Further work also includes the incremental implementation of EduMON system.

Acknowledgments. The author acknowledges scientific adviser of the doctoral thesis Dr.sc.ing. prof. Marite Kirikova for valuable comments and suggestions on the draft of the paper. This work has been supported by the European Social Fund within the project "Support for the implementation of doctoral studies at Riga Technical University".

References

1. Winterton, J., Delamare-Le Deist, F., Stringfellow, E.: Typology of knowledge, skills and competences: Clarification of the concept and prototype (2005)
2. Kirikova, M., Strazdina, R., Andersone, I., Sukovskis, U.: Quality of Study Programs: An Ecosystems Perspective. In: Grundspenkis, J., Kirikova, M., Manolopoulos, Y., Novickis, L. (eds.) ADBIS 2009. LNCS, vol. 5968, pp. 39–46. Springer, Heidelberg (2010)
3. SFIA Foundation, Framework reference SFIA version 5, http://www.sfia.org.uk/v5/en/
4. European Committee For Standardization, European e-Competence Framework 2.0, http://ecompetences.eu/
5. Latvian Nacional Occupation Standard Registry, http://visc.gov.lv/saturs/profizgl/stand_registrs.shtml
6. Rudzajs, P.: Education offer/demand monitoring approach. In: 10th International Conference on Perspectives in Business Informatics Research, BIR 2011, Doctoral Consortium, pp. 427–436 (2011)
7. Phillips, P., Diston, D.: A knowledge driven approach to aerospace condition monitoring. Knowledge-Based Systems 24, 915–927 (2011)
8. Wang, X., Gao, W., Slusser, J.R., Davis, J., Olson, B., Janssen, S., Janson, G., Durham, B., Tree, R., Deike, R.: USDA UV-B monitoring system: An application of centralized architecture. Computers and Electronics in Agriculture 64, 326–332 (2008)
9. Vallejo, D., Albusac, J., Castro-Schez, J.J., Glez-Morcillo, C., Jiménez, L.: A multi-agent architecture for supporting distributed normality-based intelligent surveillance. Engineering Applications of Artificial Intelligence 24, 325–340 (2011)
10. Andreozzi, S., De Bortoli, N., Fantinel, S., Ghiselli, A., Rubini, G.L., Tortone, G., Vistoli, M.C.: GridICE: a monitoring service for Grid systems. Future Generation Computer Systems 21, 559–571 (2005)
11. Pop, F., Dobre, C., Stratan, C., Costan, A., Cristea, V.: Dynamic meta-scheduling architecture based on monitoring in distributed systems. Int. J. Autonomic Comput. 1, 328–349 (2010)
12. Hsieh, Y.-M., Hung, Y.-C.: A scalable IT infrastructure for automated monitoring systems based on the distributed computing technique using simple object access protocol Web-services. Automation in Construction 18, 424–433 (2009)
13. Mehaoua, A., Ahmed, T., Asgari, H., Sidibe, M., Nafaa, A., Kormentzas, G., Kourtis, T., Skianis, C.: Service-driven inter-domain QoS monitoring system for large-scale IP and DVB networks. Computer Communications 29, 1687–1695 (2006)
14. Semenov, A., Veijalainen, J., Boukhanovsky, A.: A Generic Architecture for a Social Network Monitoring and Analysis System. In: Proceedings of the 2011 14th International Conference on Network-Based Information Systems, pp. 178–185. IEEE Computer Society Press (2011)

15. Wetzstein, B., Danylevych, O., Leymann, F., Bitsaki, M., Nikolaou, C., Heuvel, W.-J.V.D., Papazoglou, M.P.: Towards Monitoring of Key Performance Indicators Across Partners in Service Networks. In: 1st Workshop on Monitoring Adaptation and Beyond (MONA 2009), pp. 7–17. Springer, Heidelberg (2009)
16. Erl, T.: SOA Principles of Service Design. The Prentice Hall Service-Oriented Computing Series from Thomas Erl. Prentice Hall PTR (2007)
17. W3C, Semantic Annotations for WSDL and XML Schema,
    http://www.w3.org/TR/sawsdl/
18. Kiryakov, A., Popov, B., Terziev, I., Manov, D., Ognyanoff, D.: Semantic annotation, indexing, and retrieval. Web Semantics: Science, Services and Agents on the World Wide Web 2, 49–79 (2004)
19. Kiyavitskaya, N., Zeni, N., Cordy, J.R., Mich, L., Mylopoulos, J.: Cerno: Light-weight tool support for semantic annotation of textual documents. Data & Knowledge Engineering 68, 1470–1492 (2009)
20. Biletskiy, Y., Brown, J.A., Ranganathan, G.: Information extraction from syllabi for academic e-Advising. Expert Systems with Applications 36, 4508–4516 (2009)
21. Janev, V., Mijović, V., Vraneš, S.: Automatic Extraction of ICT Competences from Unstructured Sources. In: Quintela Varajão, J.E., Cruz-Cunha, M.M., Putnik, G.D., Trigo, A. (eds.) CENTERIS 2010. CCIS, vol. 110, pp. 391–400. Springer, Heidelberg (2010)
22. Abramowicz, W., Bukowska, E., Kaczmarek, M., Starzecka, M.: Semantic-enabled Efficient and Scalable Retrieval of Experts. In: eKNOW 2011: The Third International Conference on Information, Process, and Knowledge Management, IARIA 2011, pp. 30–35 (2011)
23. Macdonald, C., Ounis, I.: The influence of the document ranking in expert search. Information Processing & Management 47, 376–390 (2011)
24. Maynard, D., Yankova, M., Aswani, N., Cunningham, H.: Automatic Creation and Monitoring of Semantic Metadata in a Dynamic Knowledge Portal. In: Bussler, C.J., Fensel, D. (eds.) AIMSA 2004. LNCS (LNAI), vol. 3192, pp. 65–74. Springer, Heidelberg (2004)
25. European Dictionary of Skills and Competencies,
    http://www.skills-translator.net
26. European Taxonomy of Skills Competencies and Occupations,
    http://www.destree.be/esco/
27. EURES Taxonomy,
    https://joinup.ec.europa.eu/asset/eures_taxonomy/description
28. SFIA Foundation: Framework reference SFIA version 4. (2008)
29. Association for Computing Machinery (ACM) taxonomy,
    http://computer.org/portal/web/publications/acmtaxonomy
30. Princeton University, About WordNet, http://wordnet.princeton.edu
31. EuroTermBank, http://www.eurotermbank.com/
32. Rudzajs, P.: Development of knowledge renewal service for the maintanace of employers' database. B.S. Riga Technical University, Riga (2008)
33. UIMA, http://uima.apache.org/
34. GATE, http://gate.ac.uk/
35. Subversion (SVN), http://subversion.tigris.org/
36. Concurrent Versions System (CVS), http://www.nongnu.org/cvs/
37. Fast version control system GIT, http://git-scm.com/
38. Birzniece,I., Rudzajs, P.: Machine Learning Based Study Course Comparison. In: IADIS Conference on Intelligent Systems and Agents (ISA 2011), pp. 107–111 (2011)

Author Index

Bassano, Clara   38
Blümel, Eberhard   90
Borchardt, Ulrike   26

Charoy, François   51

Etalle, Sandro   64

Fredrich, Helge   90

Gaaloul, Khaled   51
Giorgini, Paolo   77
Goethals, Frank   130
Grundspenkis, Janis   143

Herrmann, Andrea   64
Hochmeister, Martin   171

Kirikova, Marite   38
Kozmina, Natalija   209

Makna, Janis   38
Martin, Nigel   196
Martin, Stephen   184
Mednis, Artis   223
Meister, Sven   1
Meland, Per Håkon   77
Merkuryev, Yuri   158
Mitasiunas, Antanas   102
Morali, Ayse   64

Niedrite, Laila   117
Niemi, Tapio   184
Niinimaki, Marko   184
Novickis, Leonids   102, 158
Nummenmaa, Jyrki   184

Paja, Elda   77
Paul, Stéphane   77
Piciocchi, Paolo   38
Podviezko, Askoldas   236
Poulovassilis, Alexandra   196
Proper, Erik   51

Romanovs, Andrejs   158
Rudzajs, Peteris   252

Sandkuhl, Kurt   14
Shilov, Nikolay   14
Smirnov, Alexander   14
Solodovnikova, Darja   209
Soshko, Oksana   158
Stecjuka, Julija   38

Thanisch, Peter   184

Vagale, Vija   117

Wang, Jianing   196
Wieringa, Roel   64
Winge, Andre   90